JOHN OKADA

THE LIFE & REDISCOVERED WORK
OF THE AUTHOR OF *NO-NO BOY*

EDITED BY

**FRANK ABE, GREG ROBINSON,
AND FLOYD CHEUNG**

UNIVERSITY OF WASHINGTON PRESS

Seattle

John Okada was supported by a grant from the Scott and Laurie Oki Endowed Fund for publications in Asian American Studies.

UNIVERSITY OF WASHINGTON PRESS
www.washington.edu/uwpress

LIBRARY OF CONGRESS CATALOGING-IN-PUBLICATION DATA

Names: Abe, Frank editor. | Robinson, Greg, 1966– editor. | Cheung, Floyd, 1969– editor. | Okada, John. Works. Selections.
Title: John Okada : the life and rediscovered work of the author of No-no boy / edited by Frank Abe, Greg Robinson, and Floyd Cheung.
Description: Seattle : University of Washington Press, 2018. | Includes bibliographical references and index. |
Identifiers: LCCN 2018003963 (print) | LCCN 2018011915 (ebook) | ISBN 9780295743530 (ebook) | ISBN 9780295743523 (hardcover : alk. paper) | ISBN 9780295743516 (pbk. : alk. paper)
Subjects: LCSH: Okada, John—Criticism and interpretation.
Classification: LCC PS3565.K33 (ebook) | LCC PS3565.K33 Z69 2018 (print) | DDC 813/.54—dc23
LC record available at https://lccn.loc.gov/2018003963

THE SCOTT AND LAURIE OKI SERIES
IN ASIAN AMERICAN STUDIES

For Dorothea and Matthew

America is a country which has made mistakes and will make more but, at the same time, it is a country which is striving constantly to rectify the conditions which breed those mistakes.

JOHN OKADA
letter to Meredith Weatherby
FEBRUARY 14, 1956

CONTENTS

ESSAYS ON JOHN OKADA AND HIS WRITINGS

JOHN OKADA

Introduction

Saying "No! No!" to the Community Narrative

FRANK ABE

THIS BOOK SEEKS TO RECOVER THE LITERARY VISION OF JOHN Okada, a pioneering American novelist whose unpublished work was lost to an early death and a widow's grief. Okada was a Nisei, second-generation Japanese American—the child of immigrants—and two passages of writing bookend his pursuit of what he and his peers envisioned as "the Great Nisei Novel."[1] The first he composed as a college freshman in Seattle the night after the attack on Pearl Harbor. Okada was hearing frantic reports of the FBI yanking community leaders from distraught wives and crying children on suspicion of collusion with the enemy, and his immediate instinct was to write about it: "On the evening of December 7, 1941, after there was no doubt as to the significance of the dastardly move taken by the Japanese nation, I sat in my room and thought of the situation in which I, as well as others like me, had been placed by this unforeseen attack on the United States. I attempted to put down my thoughts on paper for a home theme, but my mind was in such a state of confusion and entanglement that I was unable to produce an organized and well-unified paper."[2]

He tried his hand instead with poetry. The result, "still unorganized and disunified," is the first surviving piece of creative writing we have by John Okada (reprinted here as "I Must Be Strong"). In it, he confronts the shock of others suddenly seeing him only for his race, and he vows, "I know they will, and I must be strong."[3]

Fast-forward to 1957. Now in Detroit with a family of his own, the thirty-four-year-old Okada wrote with the authority of experience. "DECEMBER THE SEVENTH of the year 1941 was the day when the Japanese bombs fell on Pearl Harbor. As of that moment, the Japanese in the United States became, by virtue of their ineradicable brownness and the slant eyes which, upon close inspection, will seldom appear slanty, animals of a different breed. The moment the impact of the words solemnly being transmitted over the several million radios of the nation struck home, everything Japanese and everyone Japanese became despicable."[4]

By then, Okada had seen how guilt by association led to betrayal by the federal government, the eviction of 110,000 Americans of Japanese ancestry from their homes on the West Coast, and their four-year incarceration in American concentration camps—a mass violation of civil protections under the Constitution. Okada himself stayed strong: he left camp early for college, then joined the Military Intelligence Service and flew twenty-four reconnaissance missions in a B-24 over the Japanese coastline. Immediately after the war he earned degrees in English and librarianship, and wrote some short fiction.

From these experiences, John Okada created the voice of *No-No Boy*. Brought out in a tiny edition by a small-scale publisher of works on Asia, it received little attention at the time. Yet *No-No Boy* emerged after its author's premature death to become a much-studied and celebrated work of American literature.

THE WRITER AS RESISTER

The power of *No-No Boy* derives from its portrait of the unexpressed rage of the Nisei at their unjust imprisonment, which collectively disinherited them as a generation through the combined losses of homes, farms, and businesses. After having been "gone four years, two in camp and two in prison," draft resister Ichiro Yamada returns to Seattle to find his community fragmented and its people divided against one another by the nation's wartime demand for proof of loyalty. Parents mourn sons lost in battle; veterans return maimed and succumb to their wounds; a woman abandoned by her soldier husband finds comfort in Ichiro's arms; his mother goes mad when forced to admit that Japan lost the war.

When published in 1957, everything about this story challenged the overall amnesia about the camps and the prevailing values of Okada's own community, which mostly wanted to forget and fit in. The Nisei adopted the guise of "Quiet Americans," a public face codified by the Japanese American Citizens League (JACL), a social and political federation of Nisei professionals led just before the war by president Saburo Kido and national secretary Mike Masaoka. After Pearl Harbor, the JACL fingered Issei leaders for arrest, waived the Nisei right to protest eviction, and cooperated in the community's removal and incarceration—all as proof of loyalty to the government.[5] The organization did support select legal challenges, but the overriding JACL response to mass incarceration could be captured in two phrases: *shikataganai,* Japanese for "it can't be helped"— passive resignation in the face of injustice; and *go for broke,* Hawaiian pidgin for "shoot the works, give 110 percent"—patriotic self-sacrifice and the spilling of one's blood to prove one's loyalty. And when several hundred incarcerees defined as loyal by the government contested their incarceration in 1944 by refusing to be drafted from camp, the JACL collaborated with the government to crack down on dissent.

Okada never mentions the JACL by name, the word *resistance* never appears in his text, and there's no evidence he consciously saw his work as an act of rebellion—yet he wrote a novel that accurately captures the bitter divisions within his community triggered by the JACL's collaboration with the government. He subverted the JACL's jingoistic ideal of "Better Americans in a Greater America" by featuring a pariah as his protagonist, a draft resister who served two years in prison.

Two definitions are essential here. "No-no boys" were the twelve thousand young men who answered "no" to two questions on an otherwise procedural 1943 government questionnaire administered in the camps. Question 27 asked, "Are you willing to serve in the armed forces of the United States on combat duty, wherever ordered?" Answering "yes" could be taken as an offer to volunteer. Number 28 asked a compound question: "Will you swear unqualified allegiance to the United States of America and faithfully defend the United States from any and all attack by foreign or domestic forces, and forswear any form of allegiance or obedience to the Japanese Emperor, or any other foreign government, power, or organization?" For the Issei, barred by racial laws from naturalized US citizenship, to answer "yes" to the question as a whole would mean renouncing the only citizenship they had and render them stateless persons; for a Nisei to answer "yes," to renounce an allegiance one never had, could be taken as an admission of having at one time or another actually harbored a loyalty to Japan. Both were viewed as trick questions by most. No one, not even the camp administrators, fully understood the consequences of a "yes" or "no" answer to what became known as the loyalty oath. The government removed those who answered "no" and sent them to the Tule Lake Segregation Center on the California-Oregon border, a move backed by JACL.

"Draft resisters" were the roughly 315 young men who in general answered "yes" or a qualified "yes" to the questionnaire but who, a year later in 1944, were drafted from inside camp. They refused to report for their pre-induction physical exams until their rights were first restored and their families freed to return home. At the camp at Heart Mountain, Wyoming, this resistance became organized as the Fair Play Committee, whose members broke the law to bring a test case into federal court in a last-ditch attempt to challenge the constitutionality of the eviction and their continued confinement. In every case, except ironically at Tule Lake, the courts refused to hear their constitutional argument and convicted them. This group served an average of two years in federal prison, and this group included Ichiro.

The title of Okada's novel, the way Ichiro is addressed, and Ichiro's own statements all foster the misperception that Ichiro was part of the "no-no" group. The author himself, whether as an artistic choice or in error, twice conflates "no-no boys" and draft resisters in his text. Nowhere in the novel, however, does Okada mention the questionnaire, nor say how Ichiro answered it; he also never suggests that Ichiro was segregated to Tule Lake. Moreover, one's answers to the questionnaire had no effect on one's initial eligibility for the draft; the two processes were legally distinct.[6]

Okada clearly presents Ichiro's story as that of a draft resister, one who says "no" to many things—the draft, a federal judge, his country, his ancestry, his mother—but not explicitly to the questionnaire.[7]

It is within this context that John Okada inserts his own persona into the preface of his novel as the "good Japanese-American," an army enlisted man sitting in the belly of a B-24 and thinking "about his friend who didn't volunteer for the army because his father had been picked up in the second screening" after Pearl Harbor. This fictional friend refused the draft because a judge would not release his father from a Justice Department internment camp for enemy aliens to rejoin his mother and sisters in a civilian detention camp. As revealed in my new biography, Okada was drawing here from his own pain and that of his friend Hajime Jim Akutsu, a draft resister. Both their fathers were arrested on February 21, 1942, in the second round of FBI arrests in Seattle, and both were interned at the Justice Department camp at Fort Missoula, Montana. Okada petitioned for help to get the US attorney general to release his father from "that other camp" so he could rejoin his family at the Puyallup detention center because his mother was "an old woman but misses [the father] enough to want to sleep with him." In the cinematic dissolve from the preface to chapter 1, as the point-of-view shifts from the soldier in the B-24 to that of his friend in prison, the author who was a soldier imagined himself in the shoes of his friend Akutsu who was a resister, and *No-No Boy* can be read as the author acting out the script from there.[8]

But writing in 1957, Okada could take the story only so far. He was unable to provide his protagonist with "a range of viable scripts"[9] because those narratives—whether redress for the constitutional violations of camp or history's validation of the resisters—would not be written until several years after the author's death in 1971. The first "Day of Remembrance" for the camps would not be mounted in Seattle until 1978, and the campaign it sparked for congressional action on redress would not work its way into law until 1988. There is no evidence that Okada knew of the organized resistance at Heart Mountain, and it would not be until the new millennium that books and films (among them my PBS film *Conscience and the Constitution*) would expose the false constructions of loyalty and disloyalty created by the government and enforced by the JACL, and frame the principled protest of draft resisters, even loners like Ichiro, as a classic example of civil disobedience in the American twentieth century.

THE SEARCH FOR JOHN OKADA

Tragically, John Okada died at the age of forty-seven and never saw his work find an audience. Worse yet, his distraught widow tossed or burned his work on his unfinished second novel about the Issei. In a now familiar story, a group of young writers—Frank Chin, Shawn Wong, Lawson Inada, and Jeffery Chan—found the first edition of Okada's novel in a used bookshop in Berkeley just weeks after his death. Three of them flew to Pasadena to interview his widow, Dorothy. As the Combined Asian-American Resources Project, or CARP, they introduced *No-No Boy* to the just-emerging field of Asian American studies by including chapter 5 of the novel in *Aiiieeeee!,* their groundbreaking 1974 anthology of Asian American literature. CARP then republished *No-No Boy* itself in 1976.

This book descends from that effort. As an original member of Chin's Asian American Theater Workshop in San Francisco, I had the privilege of transcribing the two audio cassettes of interviews with Dorothy Okada for the Bancroft Library Regional Oral History Office. I was intrigued by Dorothy's description of the first novel's development and as shocked as anyone by the loss of the second. I adapted Ichiro's interior monologues as audition pieces, even as artist Bob Onodera based his cover art for the CARP paperback on a photo of me from the theater workshop. Interest in the novel was part of the appeal for me in moving to Seattle, where David Ishii Bookseller proudly displayed the photo that appears on the cover of this book in his shop in Pioneer Square, mere steps from Okada's birthplace, and where poet Garrett Hongo introduced me to Okada's geography: the clock tower of King Street Station, the Wah Mee Club on Maynard Alley, the neon sign over Wonder Bread at 18th and Jackson, and Okada's signature scrawled backstage at the Nipponkan Theater. I also interviewed Okada's family and friends in the making of a short film.

The search took a new direction when historian Greg Robinson came to me with material by Okada he had uncovered while scrolling through microfilm of a postwar Seattle newspaper: five short stories and a one-act play. These pieces, most likely started as class exercises, were long rumored to exist but had disappeared from view. We teamed with literary scholar Floyd Cheung and uncovered three more works: the youthful poem "I Must Be Strong," which escaped notice because it was published anonymously, and two long-buried trade journal articles, one appearing under a pseudonym, in which Okada could not resist inventing fictional characters to satirize wasteful practices in the aerospace industry.

Accompanying these primary materials are the first full-length biography of Okada and original essays interpreting his work. The biography reveals new information about the sources of Okada's inspiration for his novel and corrects several long-standing errors. Floyd Cheung investigates the circumstances and influences behind the creation of Okada's rediscovered works, and shows the young writer experimenting with genre a decade before *No-No Boy.* Greg Robinson's historical analysis places *No-No Boy* within the evolution of writing in the Japanese American community. Stephen H. Sumida advances a theory of how the novel's protagonist could have been both a draft resister *and* a no-no boy, in the course of decoding the twisted logic of incarceration and the author's intentionally unreliable-narrative point of view. Journalist and researcher Martha Nakagawa speaks for readers long confounded by Ichiro's interior monologues, which, by making him appear confused and remorseful, generated resentment among the real resisters. Jeffrey T. Yamashita reviews two generations of critical literature on *No-No Boy,* reflecting shifts in approaches by the academic community. Finally, Shawn Wong shares an insider's account of the republication of *No-No Boy* and offers techniques he's developed for teaching the novel in class.

No-No Boy has sold more than 200,000 copies over twenty-one printings by Charles Tuttle, CARP, and the University of Washington Press.[10] It remains the most-read and most-analyzed novel by a Nisei who spent time in camp, and a foundational work in Asian American studies. With the benefit of rediscovered works and fresh insights, we hope to open new avenues for study and place John Okada in context for a new generation.

A Note on the Texts

Texts for the rediscovered work of John Okada reside in microfilms and bound volumes of the original publications, held at the Suzzallo and Allen Libraries of the University of Washington. Typographical and other errors have been emended. Each text is introduced with a headnote by Floyd Cheung.

THE LIFE OF
JOHN OKADA

"An Urgency to Write"

FRANK ABE

BY HIS OWN DESCRIPTION, JOHN OKADA WAS "ENDOWED WITH a larger capacity for normalcy than most people," and outwardly he appeared to be the kind of Nisei Everyman who adhered to a familiar ethic: study hard, work hard, raise a family. But Okada had the added desire to write, and immediately after the defining events of World War II, after publishing five short stories and staging a one-act play, he developed ideas for a more ambitious work, a novel to capture the "hopes and fears and joys and sorrows" of the Nisei generation.[1]

For his subject, he might have drawn upon his dramatic wartime service as a voice interceptor for the Military Intelligence Service (MIS)—but his operations were classified, and MIS veterans upon discharge were sworn to secrecy. Okada instead created a character with the opposite experience: His protagonist would be a draft resister, not a returning veteran. He would be estranged from his family, not close like Okada was to his own.

Until now, the few facts known of Okada's life were those movingly recounted in Frank Chin's 1976 essay for the *Seattle Weekly*, "In Search of John Okada," which was appended as an afterword to the CARP paperback of *No-No Boy* and all subsequent editions. For four decades those facts were endlessly cited and recycled, supplemented only in 2015 with new research by German scholar Thomas Girst. The destruction of Okada's manuscripts and letters after this death complicated the task of documenting his story, but through interviews with family and friends and fresh research into the written record we can reconstruct enough to appreciate how John Okada transformed the events of his life into the imaginative world of *No-No Boy*.

BEFORE THE WAR: "EVERY CHILD IS BORN TO SEE SOME STRUGGLE"

Just as heartbreak followed John Okada's death, tragedy preceded his birth. Three months before he was born, one of his two brothers died of pneumonia.

The infant, Joseph Masaharu Okada, developed whooping cough in the spring of 1923. When he later contracted measles, his parents took him to a doctor in downtown Seattle, but the child died on June 29, two weeks shy of his first birthday.[2] His parents held a community funeral, and the ashes were interred in Japan. The loss was still fresh when, with the help of a Japanese midwife, John Kozo Okada was born on September 22, 1923, in the family's quarters at the Merchants Hotel.[3]

Joseph's death brought misfortune to Yoshito and Takayo Okada just as they were starting a family in America. In Japan, the two grew up on adjoining farms in Hiroshima-ken, Asa-gun, Nakahara-mura.[4] Yoshito was the eldest of five sons; Takayo Ota was a younger cousin.[5] Labor agents active in Hiroshima recruited young men for work in America,[6] and Yoshito's uncle got hired by the Great Northern Railroad as a foreman, his father as a cook. When the youngster turned fourteen in 1908, he was sent to join them in Montana as a water boy. The gang of forty workers lived out of boxcars as they crossed the Rocky Mountains and laid three hundred miles of track.[7]

At eighteen, Yoshito was brought back to Hiroshima to see his family and "incidentally to get married" to fourteen-year-old Takayo, but he didn't feel he earned enough to take care of her in the United States, so when he returned to Montana for work at a railroad roundhouse, he left his new bride behind.[8]

From 1914 to 1917, Yoshito wore a suit and tie as a salesman for the M. Furuya Company at Second and Main in Seattle's Pioneer Square. Business tycoon Masajiro Furuya had capitalized on Seattle's nexus as a seaport to prosper from the Klondike Gold Rush, the Sino-Japanese War, and the growing Japanese immigrant community.[9] Yoshito enjoyed music, and in the city he took lessons from Mr. Kashiwagi, a teacher of classical violin.[10] But the railroads proved more lucrative, and he returned to Montana for a job as a section foreman. An alien land law prevented Yoshito from buying land in Washington state, but no such prohibition then existed in Montana and he saved enough to invest in two lots in rural Loma.[11]

By 1919 Yoshito's father had returned to Japan, and Yoshito went back to Seattle, for work as an auto mechanic and other odd jobs. He boarded at the Merchants Hotel, a rooming house operated by Keichi and Sueko Takemura. The hotel business in Seattle provided an entry for the early Issei entrepreneurs, and in 1920 Yoshito went into business for himself by taking over the lease on the Merchants from the Takemuras.[12] With a stable home and earnings from the hotel averaging $125 a month, Yoshito was finally able to send for the wife he had not seen for seven years. Nine months after Takayo's arrival in the US, their first son was born, Yoshitaka Robert Okada, followed by Joseph, the infant who died, and John. The *ko* in John's middle name, Kozo, means happy or happiness, and *zo* means three or the third, indelibly marking the absence of the second child who had been lost.[13] A fourth boy, Roy Hiroo Okada, was born in 1927. As was customary at the time under Japanese law, all their births were registered with the Japanese consul in Seattle.[14]

Pioneer Square: "The Japanese landlord"

The Merchants Hotel sat on Yesler Way between First and Occidental— a few steps from Smith Tower, then the tallest building west of the Mississippi, and at the foot of "Skid Road," down which freshly cut logs were once greased and skidded from First Hill to a sawmill on Elliott Bay. Yesler was historically Seattle's "Deadline," dividing downtown businesses from the "bawdyhouses and low theaters" to the south,[15] and the color line between the early white settlers and the immigrant families of Chinatown. The Great Seattle Fire of 1889 destroyed all the wood-frame buildings of Pioneer Square, and the Merchants Hotel was rebuilt entirely of brick, with sixty rooms on two floors above the Merchants Exchange

Saloon. Yukon miners could trade gold dust for cash in the saloon, and drink, before heading upstairs to a brothel on the third floor.[16]

By the time the Okadas took over, the brothel was gone and the saloon had been renamed the Merchants Cafe.[17] The proprietors worked around the clock, answering whenever the night bell rang in their bedroom ("Rooms by Day and Week"). To his boarders and the public, Yoshito was known as "Fred."

ROY OKADA

As you go up the stairs you find an office, and we were living right off the office area. We lived close to the water, so when we had time to play we would go down to fish off the docks and catch little fish and bring them home for dinner. Most of our activity was roaming the streets and going fishing.[18]

Yoshito Okada joined 127 Issei who operated hotels and apartments in Seattle, nearly all close by railroad hubs like King Street Station,[19] and through the Seattle Japanese Hotel and Apartment Operators Association he mixed with the likes of Ritoji Nishimura, one of three Issei "hotel kings." Nishimura owned ten properties, including the Puget Sound Hotel, the largest in Chinatown with five stories and 444 rooms.[20] Like other Issei, Yoshito did his civic duty on committees for the Japanese Chamber of Commerce and the Hiroshima Kenjinkai, a fraternal society of those from Hiroshima. On Sundays, the family attended the Seattle Buddhist Church at Sixth and Main, passing the sign-painting shop of noted artists Kamekichi Tokita and Kenjiro Nomura, and the Okada boys would play with the Nishimura boys at community picnics at Jefferson Park on Beacon Hill. Yoshito continued practicing the violin along with the flute and Japanese oboe.[21] With friends, he unwound with a good drink at home or at one of the many taverns and beer halls on Jackson Street, where the men could polish off bottles of wine and fifths of whiskey at a sitting.

Kazuko Itoi lived a block south, at the Carrollton Hotel on Occidental and Main. Writing as Monica Sone in her memoir, *Nisei Daughter,* she

The family of Yoshito and Takayo Okada wore their Sunday best for a portrait in 1937. (From left: Takayo, Roy, Frank, Robert, Arlene, John, Yoshito.) *(Yoshito Okada family)*

recorded the small world she shared with the Okadas: a mission hall, a barbershop, a hot dog stand, the Rialto burlesque house, a cigar shop, and sidewalks populated with labor agitators and a Salvation Army band. Like the Okada boys, she made the "long and fascinating journey" from First Avenue to Bailey Gatzert School on 12th Avenue,[22] a journey Robert remembered for the sight of prostitutes in the red-light district tapping on windows in daytime to draw trade.

When John was six, his father moved the family to a larger hotel at 811 Maynard Avenue, just south of Dearborn Street. "I took over Yakima Hotel February 1, 1930," he wrote, "but the stock market crashed and Depression attacked us along with everyone else, and we had a hard time because of running in the red."[23] With 154 rooms and shops at street level, the Yakima Hotel was three times the size of the Merchants. The family partitioned 1,000 square feet in one storefront into a kitchen, dining room, and bedrooms, and the three boys were put to work in hotel management.[24]

ROY OKADA

Yosh was old enough to be able to manage the office, John would be doing things that required a little more skill, like painting the rooms and cleaning toilets and fixing things, and I would help wherever I could, mopping and sweeping. My mother would be working all day making beds, and my dad would be working managing the whole operation. They had ladies come in to help them make the beds, and my father had a night manager that would take care of the office between midnight and seven in the morning. On weekends we would take turns working on Sunday and managing the office.[25]

YOSHITAKA ROBERT OKADA

Yeah, washing windows. That really put me off the idea of being a hotel manager.[26]

At the Yakima, Yoshito enjoyed having a big office that adjoined a lobby spacious enough for a half-dozen boarders to lounge with the newspaper or play cards. He put up Christmas trees in December and on New Year's laid out tables with fruits, candies, and cigars. If a boarder became inebriated, Yoshito "picked him off the sidewalk and deposited him in his bed," as his son would later write about a fictional Japanese landlord.[27] Another son, Frank Sumio Okada, was born in 1931, and the family's first daughter, Arlene Yukiko, arrived in 1936. John and the older boys, being in school, were each given a bedroom upstairs, where John could keep his stamp collection and comic books and listen to jazz records.

YOSHITAKA ROBERT OKADA

John's room was not what you'd call neat. He had a lot of books and things piled up on his desk. Large desk. And a bureau, and a radio. Room was real small, enough for a bed and desk and a chest of drawers. There was a sink in each room. No spring on the faucet; it didn't turn off when you wanted.[28]

John saw his name in print on his eighth birthday by enrolling in the *Seattle Daily Times* "Trojan Club" for kids.[29] From the time he was eleven,

The Yakima Hotel at 811 Maynard near Dearborn was home for the Okada family from 1930 until their eviction by the government in 1942. The three oldest boys, including John, each got a room of his own on an upper floor. *(1937 photo from Washington State Archives)*

he earned "anywhere from 25 cents to a dollar a day hoeing weeds or picking peas and various kinds of berries."[30] When not helping their parents, the older boys were looked after by some of the long-term boarders, whom they came to regard as "second parents."[31] One in particular, a shipyard watchman they knew as Mr. Collins, would take them to the Western Washington State Fair at the Puyallup Fairgrounds, horse races at Longacres Racetrack, and Civic Field, where they could watch Seattle Indians baseball games through gaps in the wooden fence.

Bailey Gatzert: "The Good American Citizenship Club"

The move to the Yakima cut the length of John's walk to Bailey Gatzert School by half. Located at the time where Beacon Hill meets Chinatown on 12th Avenue S. and Weller Street, the K–8 school was run by Principal Ada Mahon. "Miss Mahon" was known to be "'Irish tough' and proud," and taught her charges to embrace their heritage even as she schooled them in what it meant to be American.[32] She started a "Good American Citizenship Club," which met on Wednesday mornings before class and opened with the Pledge of Allegiance and a singing of "America."[33] After school, she lined up the students and marched them out single-file to the strains of patriotic music played on a 78 rpm record.[34]

Okada's class photo was filled with Japanese and Chinese faces. Each child wore a white top, and each boy a necktie—all except thirteen-year-old John Okada, who wore a wide smile and a dark shirt with bolo tie. Two classmates, Frank Ashida and Roy Kumasaka, would become lifelong friends. They knew John as "a real nice fellow. Not loud or brash, but not quiet either. Just ordinary." And smart.[35]

FRANK ASHIDA

John was an intellectual. But on the other hand, he was a lot of fun. He liked to play poker, go fishing—and we did a lot of that, especially stream fishing for trout. He liked to talk. His conversations were not just about sports or anything like that; he would get more into the whys.[36]

ROY KUMASAKA

John was a real nice fellow. Not loud or brash, but not quiet either. Everyone liked him because John listened well. He wasn't one to tell people what to do. He expressed his opinion but not in a pushy way. He thought before he spoke.[37]

Their homeroom teacher, Millie Bethke, taught them how to diagram a sentence in English and learn the structure of a language that they'd picked up by listening to the radio.[38] Once school ended at 3 P.M., the Nisei students would troop one long block east on Weller Street to continue their schooling from 4 to 5:30 at Kokugo Gakko, the Japanese Language School on Rainier Avenue. Yoshito Okada served as one of seventy councilmen for the school. He wanted his children to learn Japanese "because (my) wife does not understand English. She had no time to learn because she was working in the home all the time."[39] Instruction at Kokugo Gakko was far more rigorous than at Gatzert. Monica Sone wrote that her teacher would ring a bell at her desk for students to stand at attention. "Another 'ping!' We all bowed to her in unison while she returned the bow solemnly. With the third 'ping!' we sat down together."[40]

At Bailey Gatzert, John was the only child in a dark shirt in his eighth-grade graduation photo in June 1937. (Top row, far left: Principal Ada Mahon; third from left,
homeroom teacher Millie Bethke; center, Roy Kumasaka.) *(Roy Kumasaka)*

John Okada excelled within the discipline and was placed in an
advanced class. As his father hoped, learning the language helped the
youngster have deeper conversations with his mother. Takayo Okada
had "a good sense of humor and sweet disposition."[41] She battled chronic
high blood pressure, but still made guest beds during the day and Japanese food for the family at night. After supper, she would take the kids
for long walks, past the three-story US Immigration Detention Center
behind their hotel.[42]

Besides Ashida and Kumasaka, Okada's friends had names like Pete
Fujino, Masao Frank Shigemura, Joe Owaki, and Spud Tsuji. Older brother
Robert was known alternately as "Charlie" or "Horse." On Halloween 1936,

the boys were hanging around the Gatzert schoolyard when they saw an intoxicated woman in a black overcoat trying to jump off the 12th Avenue South Bridge. As the boys gawked, a passerby struggled to keep the shrieking woman from falling to sure death onto Dearborn Street one hundred feet below. Police arrived to take the woman away, and one of the boys wrote up the dramatic vignette for a Nisei newspaper: "William Hasegawa, Troop 59 boy scout member, chirped up and said, ''Tis no laughing matter' while little John Okada, who seems to be quite popular with the other lads, probably dreamed of himself being the gallant Sir Galahad, instead of just another bystander."[43]

The youngster made the newspaper again the next year through the *Seattle Times*–Park Board Old Woodenface Contest, a citywide competition to aim baseballs through a wooden frame dubbed "Old Woody." Little John Okada made the semifinal, but lost to another Nisei boy, whose prize was a silver watch fob.[44] The same year, Okada won a coveted pair of tickets to a first-run, downtown movie theater by writing a clever caption for a cartoon extolling the benefits of advertising in the *Seattle Times* want ads—a warm-up for one of his future careers.[45]

Broadway High: "Shy, retiring, but industrious"

Students who graduated from Bailey Gatzert in the summer of 1937 moved on to one of three Seattle high schools: Franklin, Garfield, or Broadway. Okada was sent to Broadway, which meant a nearly two-mile walk north to Capitol Hill. Named for the arterial on which it stood, the school's grandiose stone architecture was modeled after that of the Petit Palais in France. The student body was fully one-quarter Nisei, "by far the most Japanese-American students of any high school in the city," among them future journalist James Omura and memoirist Monica Sone. While Okada was enrolled, Nisei students were named both valedictorian and salutatorian four years in a row.[46]

YOSHITAKA ROBERT OKADA

John was considered an ideal son. He was very studious; he didn't horse around like most of us did.[47]

At Broadway, Okada excelled in his college prep classes. He was elected a first-semester officer his sophomore year, and made Honor Society his sophomore and junior years.[48] He was "said to have an excellent mind and to know how to use it. In high school he was permitted to do a semester's work on his own, reporting to the teacher at intervals, and he did it perfectly." His Latin teacher, Jessie Lichtenberger, characterized John as "shy, retiring, but industrious" and reported that she "very much approves of his mental ability."[49] He and his friends walked home together after school, on occasion stopping at the Wonder Bread factory on 18th and Jackson, "where a nickel used to buy a bagful of day-old stuff" from the thrift store.[50]

Although slight of build—his adult height was 5'3", his weight 125 pounds—Okada turned out for several sports, including basketball, tennis, and swimming. He would ride the Seattle Transit Route 7 bus south to Mount Baker Beach, where he reputedly swam the one and a half miles across Lake Washington to Mercer Island. Family friend Keichi Takemura provided an empty lot in Chinatown for the kids to play ball games.[51] James Sakamoto, a former professional boxer, a founder of the national Japanese American Citizens League (JACL), and local publisher of the *Japanese-American Courier*, organized the Courier League for Nisei sports teams. Okada's Class C basketball team was called the "Hi-Shots," and with teammates George Mamiya, William Hasegawa, and Kazuo Watanabe he played at the Cleveland High School gym on Beacon Hill against his pals Ashida and Kumasaka on the rival "Lotus Ashuras."[52]

The Atlas Theater in Chinatown showed second-run films, and when the boys didn't have enough money, one would buy a ticket and hold open the back door on Maynard Alley for the others to sneak in. Their parents preferred the plays and movies in Japanese at the Nipponkan, the former Astor Hotel, a grand brick community center on a hill above the Japanese shops on Main Street. On a backstage wall, John Okada scrawled his name in black ink, a prewar "Kilroy was here."[53] The Tokyo Cafe on Jackson was the place for a late-night snack. Okada made it a point to go hear top jazz musicians like Louis Armstrong when they came to town to play at small venues like Washington Hall.[54]

In the summers of 1940 and 1941, Okada worked as a warehouseman and a slimer at Kadiak Fisheries, a salmon cannery in Kodiak, Alaska. (*Roy Okada*)

Like other Nisei teenagers, John worked in the summer at a salmon cannery in Alaska, starting in 1940 as a warehouseman for Kadiak Fisheries in Kodiak and making $80 a month that he could save for college.[55] He lived in the bunkhouse, ate salmon and rice at every meal, and put in ten hours a day of hard labor, six days a week.[56] He would later recall it wistfully as an exciting time of his life.[57] He probably learned how to gamble there. His companions all smoked cigarettes and it could be there he picked up the habit that would stick with him for his lifetime.[58]

As Germany went to war in 1939, a fifth son of sorts joined the household. Eiichi Fred Haita had been born in 1915 in Havre, Montana, taken to Japan when he was two for his education, then brought with his family to Seattle in 1931 when he was fifteen.[59] Fred, as he was known, was working at a lumber mill in Snoqualmie, east of Seattle, when his father decided to take him and his brother back to Japan before global hostilities worsened. Fred didn't want to leave, so the Okadas took him in as their ward. Fred called the elder Okadas Mom and Dad, and became like a brother to John and the others. The arrangement lasted two years until October 1941, when Fred turned twenty-six and was drafted into the US Army.[60] His brother in Japan, meanwhile, was drafted into the Japanese Army.[61]

Yoshito followed the unfolding news of world tensions through the Japanese-language press, including a magazine called *Sokoku*, a copy of which he purchased only after a friend and solicitor named Teshirogi begged him to. The title translates as "Fatherland," or less ominously as "Native Country." Yoshito had little interest in politics and merely glanced at the headlines and pictures; his civic involvement with all things Japanese was purely business-related and fraternal. His father in Hiroshima was close to eighty by now, and Yoshito sent him $100 a year from the hotel's earnings. He had younger step-brothers in Japan but did not know whether they had been conscripted into the army there. He contributed $5 a few times for humanitarian war relief in Japan, bought a few hundred dollars' worth of Japanese government bonds to earn a little interest, and deposited several thousand yen in Japanese banks to save for a trip to see his father. He obtained a visa in 1941 for that trip, but decided it was too risky to leave the United States without assurance he would be allowed back in. He also put the hotel business in the name of his eldest son when Yoshitaka Robert turned twenty-one.[62]

John graduated from Broadway High in June 1941. For the third year in a row he was named a member of the Honor Society,[63] and with his strong academic record he was accepted at the University of Washington (UW). He departed for a second summer at Kadiak Fisheries as a slimer, gutting freshly caught Alaskan salmon for $115 a month. Upon his return in September, Okada entered college. From Jackson Street, the young freshman boarded the electric trolley that ran north on Route 7 through downtown and across Portage Bay to the UW.[64] Leaving behind the constant clatter of streetcars and trains near Chinatown, he arrived at a bucolic campus where one could hear birds chirping in the trees between the Gothic-style buildings. He took freshman composition and declared a major in pre-law, telling his brothers he was thinking of becoming a lawyer and opening a law office.[65]

But the law was not a career John Okada would be able to pursue. He'd completed only three months of study when the United States went to war.

In his last days as a student before the mass incarceration, Okada posed for a portrait at Takano Studio in Chinatown. (*Roy Kumasaka*)

THE WAR: "A PREJUDICE HATEFUL AND MIGHTY ENOUGH TO UPROOT A THOUSAND SEEMINGLY AMERICAN HOMES"

Hajime Jim Akutsu knew John Okada as just another kid around town. He and his brother Gene had also attended Broadway High School, where Jim was three years ahead of Okada. Jim Akutsu was compact and feisty. He held a black belt in *kendo* and lettered in baseball, basketball, football, and hockey, breaking his nose a half-dozen times. He was not a violent person, but he could give as good as he got, never one to back down from a fight.[66] Nor did he tolerate what he called "monkey business," such as the color line at the popular Spanish Castle Ballroom, midway between Seattle and Tacoma on old Highway 99.

JIM AKUTSU

At that time, Japanese Americans weren't going to dance halls that were public. They were turned away. Well, the person that I am, I said, "We're gonna see about that." With the guys at Mount Baker

Cafe, we went out to the Spanish Ballroom to break it and a bunch of other places.[67]

Jim and Gene's father, Kiyonosuke, was a shoemaker, owner of the New Golden Shoe Repair Shop at Sixth and King in Chinatown. Their mother, Nao, had been a high school math teacher in Japan and was proud to be descended from the samurai class. In 1941, Jim was studying civil engineering at the UW. He had twice tried to volunteer for military service, for ROTC and the National Guard, but his flat feet kept him out. On the morning of Sunday, December 7, he was with friends at the Civic Ice Arena.

JIM AKUTSU

We were playing ice hockey when an announcement came over the PA that the guys who were in the National Guard were being called up right now. "You got to all report." And the guys that I had tried to get into the National Guard with, they came over and said, "Okay Jim, don't worry. We'll take care of the Japs. You take care of the girls." And they left.[68]

That night, John Okada started a poem. The FBI had arrested fifty-one Issei—or "Japs," as the headlines proclaimed—community leaders whose names were already known to authorities. Fears of aerial attack swept the West Coast, and the mayor put the city on a "fast war-time footing," ordering the first nighttime blackouts and issuing directives to protect the water supply and electrical grid, establish a phone hotline for reporting of sabotage, and mobilize five thousand air raid wardens. The mayor urged tolerance for the resident Japanese, but he warned that they "must not congregate or make any utterance that could be used as grounds for reprisals."[69] *Courier* publisher James Sakamoto immediately proclaimed his community's loyalty to the United States.[70] Plate glass windows and neon signs at downtown buildings were shattered—not by enemy planes, but by rioters upset at businesses that neglected to switch off their lights at the 11 P.M. blackout deadline.[71] Jim Akutsu went to the Seattle Armory to try again to enlist; they gave him a physical, but he was again rejected. Okada huddled with Roy Kumasaka to talk about what it all meant.

Okada's finished poem, titled "I Must Be Strong," appeared anonymously December 11 on the front page of the *University of Washington Daily*, under the heading, "Behind the Headlines." He introduced it by sharing his immediate reaction to what he called the "dastardly" attack: "I am a Japanese-American descendant from Japanese parents and sworn to the allegiance of the United States. In thought, background, history, culture, language, and religion I am fully American and proud to be so. I owe my all to this land of my birth, and I will gladly uphold the laws, traditions, and policies of this nation."

The poem attracted the attention of the city's evening daily, the *Seattle Star*, which reprinted it on December 16 as "Student Tells Dilemma of U.S.-Loyal Japanese."[72] Okada's desire for anonymity may have had less to do with modesty than with personal safety. During the citywide blackout on the night of December 11, a gang had confronted an Asian man at Fifth and Main, forced him to kneel, tied his hands behind him, and struck him with an ax so hard he was nearly decapitated. The *Star* at first headlined it as a "Murder Mystery in Chinatown,"[73] but police soon came to believe that Choy Get Ming, a popular young tutor at the Chong Wa Benevolent Association, was executed in the mistaken belief he was Japanese.[74] With the Issei leadership stripped away overnight, James Sakamoto saw the urgent need to organize an Emergency Defense Council of the JACL to act as an intermediary between his community and the authorities, with Garfield High School graduate Bill Hosokawa as executive secretary.[75] The Buddhist church the Okadas attended had just finished building a new temple two months before Pearl Harbor; on December 22, Sakamoto packed the church and its adjoining gym for a JACL "Americanism Rally." Fifteen hundred people, a quarter of the city's entire Japanese American population, saluted the Stars and Stripes as the flag was paraded through the crowd. Sakamoto urged young and old to "repudiate" any in their midst who were disloyal to the United States, and announced formation of "an intelligence service of our own" to report "any un-American activity" to the FBI.[76] In successive weeks, the government widened its net as it investigated membership lists of Japanese community organizations and collected tips from informants inside the Japanese American community.

Arrest: "The security screen was sifted once more"

One government action in particular alarmed and angered the Nisei. Early in 1942, the Selective Service System changed the status of Nisei registrants from the draft-eligible I-A to IV-C, the category for "aliens not acceptable to the armed forces."[77] Jim Akutsu and Roy Kumasaka shared the same reaction: "That's not right!"[78] They took it as a sign that the government meant to revoke their US citizenship, their birthright under the Constitution. In quick succession, President Roosevelt signed Executive Order 9066 on February 19 authorizing the exclusion of all persons of Japanese ancestry from the West Coast; US attorneys on February 20 signed warrants for the arrest of more alien Issei; and on Saturday, February 21, more than one hundred FBI agents, backed up by state and local police, launched a fast-moving, coordinated second wave of arrests across the Pacific Coast states and Arizona. At 10 A.M. on a cold, frosty morning, as Takayo Okada prepared breakfast in the family storefront at the Yakima Hotel, two King County Sheriff's deputies came to the door, led by FBI agent Hugh McMenamin, who brandished a warrant for the arrest of Yoshito Okada.[79]

ROY OKADA

I was awakened by two men in suits who came into my bedroom to search through my belongings. They took my small radio and a crystal set that I was building. . . . I quickly put on my clothes and went downstairs to the family area; I found out my father had been taken away.[80]

Agent McMenamin seized $150 cash from the hotel safe and confiscated letters and address books for later translation.[81] At the Akutsu household at 311 Tenth Avenue near First Hill, Nao Akutsu was knitting afghan squares for the Red Cross to make into sweaters and blankets for US soldiers when the FBI came for her shoemaker husband.

JIM AKUTSU

When I got home, the FBI was already there. I came in and my parents and brother were sitting up against the wall in the living room. They picked up a hunting knife, for use up in the hills, binoculars, radio, and I had collected pennies, Indian heads in a gallon jug. They even took that. They didn't talk much. When they left, they took my father with them. Dragged him to the immigration building. They didn't take my mother. She was the head of the house now.[82]

The *Seattle Times* breathlessly called it "the greatest mass raid on fifth-columnists and suspected spies since the United States entered the war." The elder Okada and Akutsu were two of 103 Issei arrested in Seattle that day on suspicion of belonging to "organizations having pro-Japanese sympathies."[83] In all, five hundred Japanese, German, and Italian aliens were arrested that day in simultaneous raids across four states.[84] Once in custody, the Issei men were stripped naked and thoroughly inspected for contraband.

The Okadas spent frantic days trying to locate Yoshito. They were relieved to learn he was being held with Mr. Akutsu at the Immigration Detention Center, just a block from the Yakima Hotel. The family was permitted to bring him food once a week, which he shared with fellow inmates.[85] Through the barred windows, Yoshito could see the backside of his hotel.

That left Robert to run the hotel, but the Okada boys faced their own dilemmas. On the radio, Lt. General John DeWitt of the Western Defense Command made his first pronouncement. Under Public Proclamation No. 1, issued March 2, he drew a line down the center of Washington, Oregon, California, and half of Arizona, and designated the coastal half as Military Area No. 1. Both the immigrant Issei and the Nisei, who were American citizens, would have to leave this prohibited zone.[86] At the UW, where more than four hundred Nisei students had begun the school year, this was the signal for the nearly two hundred still enrolled to withdraw from class and help their families start packing and dispose of years of investment in businesses, homes, machinery and vehicles. John finished winter quarter and did not bother registering for spring.[87]

The FBI interrogated Yoshito Okada at the immigration building on March 18, and in the predawn darkness of the next day he and Kiyonosuke Akutsu were among the 150 Issei transferred from King Street Station to the Department of Justice internment camp at Fort Missoula, Montana, not far from where Mr. Okada had worked on the railroad three decades earlier. The Okada family, living so close by the train station, and the Akutsus were without doubt among the throng pressed against a tall iron fence along the train tracks, reaching through the bars and their own tears to scream out well-wishes and goodbyes in Japanese to husbands and fathers.[88] The government confiscated the suitcases of the men and replaced them with paper sacks for their towels, toothbrushes, and tobacco.[89] Formally dressed in suits, ties, and hats, the men boarded three barred railway cars. Masao Takahashi, a cannery foreman arrested the same day as Mr. Okada, recalled that they were allowed a few minutes to walk to the fence to say goodbye. "Boarding the train, I heard my daughters crying out, 'Papa, papa.' I cannot describe how I felt at the time. I can still hear the ring of their crying in my ears today. This was the first time it occurred to me that I might not see them again."[90]

The Western Defense Command next divided Military Area No. 1 into 108 smaller exclusion zones, six of which targeted the 6,247 Japanese American residents of Seattle. Civilian Exclusion Order No. 18 designated a line along Jackson Street from the waterfront east to Fifth Avenue, then south to Dearborn and zigzagging east to Lake Washington. The Yakima Hotel lay just south of this line. On April 24, a Friday, soldiers nailed posters to walls and telephone poles throughout Chinatown proclaiming INSTRUCTIONS TO ALL PERSONS OF JAPANESE ANCESTRY, with the word JAPANESE emblazoned three times as large as the surrounding text. The fine print below gave such persons less than one week, until noon on Friday, May 1, to pack up homes and businesses, admonishing them that "the size and number of packages is limited to that which can be carried by the individual or group." On the weekend of April 25, one of the Okada brothers registered the family at the Civil Control Station hastily set up at 1319 Rainier Avenue S.[91] Takayo Okada and her five children were given the family number of 11583.

In one week, Miss Mahon's Bailey Gatzert School lost 45 percent of its student body.[92] At the Buddhist church, scene of the Americanism rally, the government seized the temple, removed the shrine, and installed offices for the US Maritime Commission. Fellow Buddhists Jim and Gene Akutsu were in the eviction group from First Hill.

JIM AKUTSU

We used to get what we call these carpetbaggers who used to come around with a big truck. Boy, they almost knocked the door down. And we tell 'em, we got nothing to sell. They knew we didn't have any money. Oh, it made me mad. And we'd tell them to get out, and there were two or three men who just pushed their way in, saying, here, I'll give you a dollar for this, fifty cents. And we didn't sell anything, no, no. Well anyway, people had to get money, so they did sell. My father's store was unlocked and we started to sell the boots to generate some money quickly. We were selling them mostly to Nisei for five, six dollars.[93]

The Akutsus also owned rental properties that Jim had bought in tax foreclosure sales, but lost those too. The Okadas had spent a decade to successfully build up the Yakima Hotel business, but with the eviction all they could get was twenty cents on the dollar.

YOSHITAKA ROBERT OKADA

When the lease was up and the future uncertain, our father asked if we should sell it and return to Japan. John and I said we preferred staying in the United States. We got about a fifth of the value of the hotel.[94]

Puyallup: "Let my father out of that other camp
and come back to my mother"

On April 30, the Okadas gathered as ordered with thousands of their neighbors on South Lane Street between 8th and 10th Streets in Chinatown. US soldiers brandishing bayonets on their rifles kept sightseers away from the dozen or so Greyhound buses. Mr. Collins from the hotel came to see them off. Monica Sone saw Miss Mahon standing in front of the quiet crowd and weeping openly.[95] Families waited anxiously, with suitcases and duffel bags packed on the sidewalks. Jim was approached by a schoolmate's father, John Wesley Dolby, the honorary vice-consul for Spain in Washington State, who acted on behalf of the Japanese.

JIM AKUTSU

I knew this was wrong and Dolby told me that day, "You being an American citizen, them taking you away like this, you better do something. It's unconstitutional. Contest it."[96]

As the buses were filled and pulled away, the families took one last look at the clock tower of King Street Station, the spire of Smith Tower, King County Hospital on the hill overlooking downtown, and the Veterans Hospital atop Beacon Hill. From his bus headed south on old Highway 99, Jim Akutsu saw more armed soldiers guarding workers in the fields of the Green River Valley.[97] After noon, Monica Sone's bus pulled alongside the state fairgrounds in Puyallup, southeast of Tacoma, where to the left she saw a block filled with rows of low shacks resembling chicken houses. To her dismay, the bus made a left turn and she was "inside the over-sized chicken farm."[98]

JIM AKUTSU

They drove us in, dumped us out, and gave us each a mattress tick by a huge pile of straw and said, "You fill it in. That's your bedding." They sent us in 100-foot-long barracks where they had cots and one blanket, and it was cold.[99]

The buses had arrived at Area A, a fenced-in community of three thousand, slapped together in just two weeks on top of a parking lot next to the grounds where Mr. Collins once brought the boys to enjoy the

Western Washington State Fair. A soldier with a 30 caliber Thompson sub-machine gun now stood in a guard tower at the main gate of Area A.[100] The land around the fairgrounds was divided into four areas, one inside the grandstand. The Okadas were also dumped off at Area A and assigned to Barrack 4.

ROY OKADA

The only one of our friends who came to visit us was Mr. Collins. He came to see the most hated people on earth.[101]

❨The design used for the flimsy, shiplap barracks was intended for temporary army shelters, not long-term housing for families with children.❩ Each narrow barrack had to be divided into cubicles just long enough for a window, a few army cots, and a wastebasket–sized heating stove.[102] The cubicles were separated by eight-foot-high low-grade plywood partitions that extended short of the ten-foot ceiling, allowing the noise of crying babies, family fights, and lovemaking to ricochet the length of the building. Rain seeped through the tarpaper roof onto blankets and faces.[103] The Okadas were housed in cubicle 4-76, with Frank Ashida and family on the other side of the plywood wall in 4-77.

Whatever feelings John harbored about the injustice of it all, he did not share. Ashida would have been a natural confidant, but "we didn't get into any deep discussion like that," he said.[104] All around them, resentment against James Sakamoto's anointment to lead the self-government in camp, and a feeling by the Issei that he had betrayed them with his rabid Americanism and informant operation, boiled over into a plot to kill the JACL leader and publicly surrender with honor.[105] Jim and Gene Akutsu beat up a mess hall cook they caught stealing food to sell on the black market.[106] But for the Okadas, their personal focus was to reunite the family. In Puyallup, they received a box of rocks their father had picked up from a dry lakebed in Montana and spent his idle hours polishing.[107]

At the Fort Missoula internment camp, two separate compounds held Japanese and Italian internees, surrounded by a high chain link fence topped with barbed wire and surveilled with floodlights. Yoshito Okada's barrack was weathertight, with central steam heating.[108] On April 28, the weekend of his family's eviction from Seattle, Yoshito was interrogated by an Alien Enemy Hearing Board consisting of just two officials, one of them a local judge. Yoshito Okada had never lifted a finger against the country where he had chosen to buy land, run a business, and raise his family, but the board referred to him throughout the proceedings as "this alien" and scrutinized his face and his record for any hint of disloyalty to the United States. Like other Issei with little stake in Japan's military ambitions, Yoshito had told the FBI "he would hate to see either one side or the other lose." All his previous associations were now viewed with suspicion: his committee work with the Japanese Language School, the Japanese Chamber of Commerce, the Hiroshima Prefectural Society, the hotel association, even his attendance at Seattle Buddhist Church. The panel zeroed in on his contributions to Japanese war relief; the money he sent to his father in Japan, his visa application, and the money he saved in Japanese banks for the trip to see his father; and the unknown military status of his stepbrothers in Japan.

Yoshito impressed the Board as "honest and frank, but not thoroughly Americanized, retaining considerable interest in, if not loyalty to, Japan." In the end, the board seized upon his possession of the *Sokoku* magazine; he had bought one copy at the pleading of Teshirogi, who then put the elder Okada on a subscription list that was confiscated by the FBI. As Tetsuden Kashima observes, the magazine's name was similar to that of the Sokoku Kai, or "Fatherland Society," classified by the Justice Department as a category A suspect organization.[109] Based on a magazine subscription, the board jumped to the mistaken conclusion that Yoshito Okada "was a member of SOKOKU KAI for two years," denied his release, and recommended he remain interned at Fort Missoula.

At Puyallup, the Okadas saw other fathers being released from Missoula. As the writer in the family, John was given the task of appealing for help. Somewhere he gained access to a typewriter, and in June 1942 he wrote to William Collins asking for a letter vouching for their father. Okada opened by expressing concern for their former boarder.

A-4-76
Camp Harmony

Dear Mr. Collins:

We haven't heard from you in such a long time that we are getting worried about you. The last we heard was that you were not feeling very well. I hope your condition has not taken a turn for the worse. If you are unable to write, I wish you would ask one of the other fellows to write us regarding your health. All in all, Mother, Sumi, Yuki, Roy and Charlie and I all are hoping and praying that you are in the pink of health.

A few days ago we received a letter from my father saying that he had received the pen and pencil set. He sounded very pleased and also asked that we give you his best regards. We will never be able to thank you enough for even just that one favor. In connection with father, we would like to ask of you something which would mean to us more than anything else in the world, now or ever. To come right to the point, we would like very much for you to write to Attorney General Biddle in Washington D. C. about our father. Give your honest opinion about him, whether he isn't as good an American as anyone else even though he hasn't been naturalized. Several men have been allowed to return to their families in this manner. It may be that your letter will result in the happiest moment of our lives. If you are unable to write it now, please do so when you are. Kindly send it via air mail to

> *Attorney General Biddle*
> *Department of Justice*
> *Washington D. C.*

Gratefully yours,
John Okada[110]

Collins responded with a July 4 letter to the attorney general signed by himself and six other residents of the Yakima Hotel. While acknowledging he knew nothing about any charges, he wrote, "I do believe that

Mr. Okada—during the twelve years that I have known him—has been an honest, sincere man, and loyal to this country, though an alien." He added, "I'm sure that Mr. and Mrs. Okada have always taught their children to be good Americans, and to adhere to the American way of living."

Both letters helped. Edward Ennis, director of the Alien Enemy Control Unit, wrote Mr. Collins that his letter would be made part of the review of the case. An unsigned reviewer noted that no specific charge had been lodged against Yoshito Okada and that there was nothing in his record to identify him as a menace of any kind to the security of the United States. The elder Okada was recommended for parole, and on July 21, 1942, US Attorney General Francis Biddle overturned the recommendation of the Alien Enemy Hearing Board and signed an order paroling Yoshito Okada to the custody of a "reputable United States citizen, not related to the alien." On August 4, Yoshito was released from Fort Missoula and sent back to the Puyallup detention center. What John Okada predicted would be "the happiest moment of our lives" ended five and a half months of separation from his father.[111]

The return of his father freed Okada to plan his escape from his parking-lot prison and return to school. By this time, fifty-eight of his Nisei classmates had transferred to colleges outside the exclusion zone, but four hundred more like himself remained in camps along the West Coast. The War Department and the War Relocation Authority asked agencies assisting the Nisei to create an administrative means of determining the loyalty of students so the public would accept their transfer to colleges and universities in the East and Midwest. The resulting National Japanese American Student Relocation Council set up a process for students to submit letters attesting to their loyalty; prove their financial ability to pay for tuition, room, and board; and secure admission to a college that was not worried about opposition from local residents.[112]

Okada named two references: his Latin teacher at Broadway High School, Jessie Lichtenberger; and Pat Halstrom, another Yakima Hotel boarder. Robert Okada furnished a letter showing a deposit of $3,000 he had made in John's name at Seattle-First National Bank at Fifth and Jackson. A suggestion for the choice of college came from a friend of Frank

Ashida's brother: Shogi Sakurada recommended that Frank and John try a school in his hometown in Nebraska, Scottsbluff Junior College.

FRANK ASHIDA

My brother had researched quite a few different colleges and because of his friendship with Sakurada, [Sakurada] told him about Scottsbluff. And that just fit our pocketbook, budget-wise: small college, low tuition, a job, a place to stay. So we wrote Scottsbluff.[113]

The austere campus of Scottsbluff Junior College could not compare to the elegant gothic buildings on the University of Washington quad, but it met Okada's needs: it was not in the exclusion zone, and it would accept him. Other Nisei who were admitted to Ohio University had been threatened with rumors of lynching,[114] compelling Scottsbluff dean Wayne Johnson to assure relocation officials, "We believe the attitude of this community is such that American citizens of Japanese ancestry, fully accepted for admission at this college, may reside here without being molested." Johnson admitted Okada, Ashida, and Roy Kumasaka with letters that offered part-time work with "some of the Japanese people here."[115]

The final requirement for each student was to pass background checks by the army, navy, and FBI. Because of John's father's FBI arrest, the relocation council questioned Miss Lichtenberger about the son. "She very much approves of his mental ability," its report noted, "but cautions us to watch his loyalty as he is young and the parental influence is strong." The piece Okada composed for the *UW Daily*, however, met with the reviewer's approval: "Soon after Pearl Harbor he wrote a poem indicative of his loyalty entitled, 'I Must Be Strong' which was published anonymously in the *Seattle Star*." The student relocation council cleared Okada to leave camp for college.[116]

As the government completed construction of ten permanent concentration camps, it began transferring families from the temporary ones. Okada, Ashida, and Jim Akutsu volunteered to stay back at Puyallup to help clear out the bedding and other furnishings left behind, while their families boarded a train for the Minidoka War Relocation Center, arriving in Hunt, Idaho on September 2, 1942.

Minidoka, Idaho: "Places which even Hollywood scorned for backgrounds"

JIM AKUTSU

They loaded us up on these old train coaches, something they took out of mothballs. We didn't know where we were going. They drew the blinds down. And they had armed guards, two of them at both ends. When we got there, whatever time, and raised the blinds: sagebrush. That's all we saw in every direction. A guard points out to the horizon and says, "See where that dust cloud is? That's where you're going."[117] I was appalled at my first sight of the desolate camp. The first thought that came to my mind was CONCENTRATION CAMP. As I entered the camp over the guarded bridge a sinister feeling overcame me—CONCENTRATION CAMP.[118]

With 7,300 incarcerees at its peak, Minidoka became the third-largest city in the state of Idaho, a place in the high desert of sagebrush, ticks, and rattlesnakes. The camp was surrounded by five miles of barbed wire fencing. Eight guard towers were staffed by military police armed with machine guns that pointed in at the thirty-six blocks of tarpaper barracks.[119] Okada arrived to find his family roughly in the center of camp, in Block 28, Barrack 4, Room E—the largest room in the barrack due to the size of their family. He found a job as a waiter in the Block 28 mess hall along with Frank Yamasaki, a student interested in the fine arts whose parents also ran a hotel.

FRANK YAMASAKI

In between washing dishes, we would play poker and there was the regulars like John and Pete and Mutt, all these interesting names. We had regular poker sessions. [John was] quiet. He looked very studious with his glasses and playing poker, he was very analytical. . . . He was generally quiet, not as outgoing as most of the people. He loved poker. He was a chain smoker.[120]

Okada worked less than a week in the mess hall before learning on September 23, a day after his nineteenth birthday, that he and Ashida were among the first students cleared to leave for college.[121] Okada spent just three weeks at Minidoka. A joke Roy Kumasaka made in a questionnaire held up his clearance for several weeks: as one of the periodicals he read he listed the *Daily Worker,* the newspaper of the American Communist Party.[122]

Scottsbluff: "A blond giant from Nebraska"

Set squarely in the western Nebraska Panhandle, Scottsbluff was home to a small Japanese American community of about 250, established by Issei like Okada's father who built the railroads. The sugar beet industry kept them there. The town held a Japanese social hall and several Japanese-owned cafes and boardinghouses on Broadway, the main street through town.[123] The three students from Minidoka got jobs at the Eagle Cafe, working for an Issei owner and cook, Shigemori Hangui ("unusual name for a Japanese," mused Ashida).[124] They called him Sam, and cleared tables and washed dishes for him; Okada took over scrubbing the heavy pots when Ashida could not.

FRANK ASHIDA

I had to quit because my fingers were getting raw, so I took odd jobs, like painting the barn or something. But John stuck it out, he worked at the restaurant because we got our meals there. He wasn't a complainer. I hated it, but a job was a job for him, and he did a good job.[125]

Twice during the war the Eagle Cafe was busted up by rowdy servicemen on leave.[126] A cross was burned at the Japanese Americanization Society hall in the nearby town of Mitchell, and the building was later scorched by arson, but the people of Scottsbluff continued to patronize the Eagle.[127] For lodging, Okada and Ashida shared a bedroom, with a bathroom down the hall, in a boardinghouse adjacent to the restaurant.

FRANK ASHIDA

We took our showers at the restaurant. Then when Roy came, he didn't have any place to stay so we offered him a space, so the three of us slept in the same bed. Three in a bed. When you turn, the one in the middle gets all the cold air because Nebraska, the winters are cold. We had a space heater in the window, which was not very warm. John got the middle. He was the lightest I think, he was on the slim side, so he was a better fit in the middle. That lasted about two months.[128]

At Scottsbluff, Okada took the general courses offered in English, math, social science, and continued his studies of German and Latin. Getting good grades was no problem, and he earned nearly straight A's.[129]

The students soon befriended their history professor, Gordon Wilson, who taught the avid poker players the more refined game of contract bridge. Wilson would come to their boarding house to play, when they weren't at the pool hall playing snooker, and got their help correcting the test papers of other students.

In the middle of the school year, the government, at the urging of JACL, created a segregated army regiment for Nisei volunteers from camp. At Minidoka, Yoshitaka Robert Okada asked his father for permission to enlist and join Fred Haita in the 442nd Regimental Combat Team (RCT). The elder Okada told him, "This is your country, you ought to volunteer."[130] Despite misgivings about leaving his mother, who required frequent hospitalization in camp for her high blood pressure, Robert left camp on June 11, 1943, with three hundred other young men.

School ended for John that same month: he ranked seventh out of a class of 439.[131] For a while, Okada, Ashida, and Kumasaka stayed on at the home of a Wilson friend in Denton, but the students didn't have the resources to remain indefinitely in Nebraska. Once again, Ashida's brother suggested colleges to which the young men might transfer. When they couldn't decide, he then suggested the three could stay together by enlisting in the army's Military Intelligence Service (MIS), which was actively recruiting Nisei linguists from the camps for secret work in the Pacific as interpreters and translators.

The three met MIS qualifications: a fair degree of fluency in oral Japanese and ability to read Japanese newspapers.[132] "We didn't want to shirk our duty," said Ashida, but their decision was as much practical as patriotic. "All our classmates were going in, so we said, 'Why not?'"[133]

Gordie Wilson drove the three in his Lincoln Continental from Nebraska to Cheyenne, Wyoming, where on September 6 the Nisei enlisted at Fort Warren and were sent to Colorado to be fitted for uniforms. Once again, Roy Kumasaka was held back two months by the crack he'd made earlier about the *Daily Worker*.

Camp Savage, Minnesota: "A good Japanese-American who had volunteered for the Army"

The Japanese military thought their documents to be secure because they believed Americans could never learn their language, especially the specialized military terminology known as *heigo*. They were nearly right—the army found only a few whites qualified in Japanese, and when they turned to the Nisei, they found what any Issei parent could have told them: overall, the Nisei's Japanese was terrible. A prewar survey of 3,700 enlisted Nisei showed only 3 percent to be fluent in Japanese,[134] but army officers bargained that Nisei who had at least some exposure to Japanese language and culture could learn faster than Caucasians.

By mid-1942, the MIS was operating a secret Japanese language school at Camp Savage, a former Civilian Conservation Corps camp in an isolated area southwest of Minneapolis–Saint Paul. On seeing the old CCC barracks, a recruit exclaimed it looked "just like another concentration camp."[135] Okada and Ashida arrived to join the third cohort of 733 enlisted students already under way, the class of July 1943. Thanks to his abilities gained from Kokugo Gakko, Okada was again placed in the upper division for advanced students. He was assigned to academic section 36, Frank to section 35, and Roy, when he finally arrived, to section 34.

FRANK ASHIDA

We were all in different classes because John was in the more select class, the honor class, because he was smarter. [laughs] We had to learn so many *kanji* per day, and in the short period they really crammed it into us.[136]

Reveille was at 6 A.M., breakfast at 7, and students marched to class in the morning and marched back in the afternoon. The language immersion

In 1943, after a year at Scottsbluff Junior College, John Okada, Frank Ashida, and Roy Kumasaka (left to right) all enlisted for the MIS so they could stick together for Japanese language immersion training at Camp Savage, Minnesota. Weekend passes were granted for Saturday nights in Minneapolis–St. Paul. (*Roy Kumasaka*)

training meant seven hours in class during the day and two more hours of mandatory study at night. Students memorized up to sixty *kanji* (Chinese ideograms) per day, and were tested every Saturday. "Lights out" was at 11 P.M., and the more serious recruits crammed by the light from the latrine or from flashlights under their sheets—but not Kumasaka: "I hated the army!"[137] Ashida's bunk was next to a fellow with the last name of Eto, whom they called "the stinky guy" after he wet his bed.[138] For physical conditioning, students were marched five to ten miles across the Minnesota countryside, where winter temperatures could drop to forty degrees below zero. There were regular poker games in the barracks and weekend passes into the Twin Cities for movies and dinners at Chinese restaurants.[139]

John's language training with the MIS, however, combined with Robert's service in the 442nd, caused trouble for their family back at Minidoka, where the atmosphere had grown toxic. After more than a year of imprisonment with no end in sight, incarcerees in all ten camps seethed with anger at JACL's continual exhortations for the Nisei to prove their loyalty by spilling their blood for America. In some blocks at some camps, volunteers for the army were threatened or beaten, and some who enlisted were disowned by Issei parents who did not want them fighting the only country that granted citizenship to the parents. Army recruiters were forced to conduct interviews at night, and "rumors spread that the War Department was using Japanese-speaking Nisei as spies inside the camps."[140] A draft resistance would later emerge in 1944 when the War Department, again at the urging of JACL, reinstituted Selective Service for the Nisei in camp. The Okadas at Minidoka suffered what Robert called "a backlash of hatred directed towards families of the volunteers."

YOSHITAKA ROBERT OKADA

The animosity got so intolerable that our family had to leave camp on work release. It must have been quite a terrible ordeal living side by side in such close quarters, eating in the same mess hall three times a day, using the same laundry facilities and rest rooms— all the while being shunned. The people in camp, I feel, should have been more supportive.[141]

Yoshito Okada was released alone from Minidoka on January 20, 1944, with plans to send for his family later. He left to work for Tokuichi Teraoka, a distant cousin who owned a steam laundry in Ione, a town in the northeastern corner of Washington State that lay outside the exclusion zone.[142] By coincidence, Okada and Ashida were permitted a furlough to visit their families back in camp on January 23. It was the first time in sixteen months for Okada to see his family, and he had the unnerving experience shared by all visiting Nisei servicemen of seeing parents and siblings guarded by armed soldiers wearing the same uniform as them. If Okada missed seeing his father, he could at least check on the condition of his mother and meet his baby sister, nine-month-old Constance Tokiye, who was born after their father rejoined their mother at Puyallup. Recently promoted to corporal, Okada and Ashida were feted as "honored guests" at a Sunday-night social in his old Block 28, and Okada joined friends at the camp newspaper, the *Minidoka Irrigator,* for a "rousing get together" in Block 22 with games and refreshments.[143]

Roy was the oldest son remaining with the family, and it fell to the eighteen-year-old to organize their packing and a series of bus rides to get his mother, younger brother, and two sisters away from the hostility in camp and join their father in Ione, where Yoshito had found an abandoned house with peeling wallpaper in which to squat.[144] Frank and Arlene were sent to the Ione grammar school, where they were the only Asian students. The family was put to work at Teraoka's Ione Steam Laundry, which washed the clothes of the loggers and miners of rural Pend Oreille County. Yoshito shoveled coal into two big boilers in back, and with the heat they generated he operated a steam presser. Roy and the local boys earned money by chopping wood from buckskin tamarack trees to feed the boilers, and the scalding water filled two giant wooden tubs for the clothes washing. In the humidity a huge fuchsia plant thrived that was the talk of the town.[145]

John Okada and Frank Ashida graduated from the MIS Language School after six months, and the army sent them for basic training to the infantry replacement training center at Camp Blanding near Jacksonville, Florida, where they negotiated obstacle courses and endured twenty-mile forced marches. Okada qualified on two semi-automatic weapons, the M-1 rifle and the lighter M-1 carbine.[146] After three months, the two returned to Minnesota, where the army had closed Camp Savage and moved the language school to nearby Fort Snelling. Ashida and Kumasaka continued their schooling there, while Okada was put on a train in June back to Florida. By now promoted to sergeant, he was assigned to voice-intercept training with the radio intelligence unit of the 4th Radio Squadron Mobile at MacDill Field near Tampa.

Okada's deployment orders came in August 1944: he and others from Camp Savage were attached to the 8th Army Air Forces Radio Squadron Mobile (RSM), which was finishing its field training at Camp Pinedale, near Fresno, California. The Nisei linguists were believed to be the first large group of Japanese Americans to be allowed back on the west coast since the mass exclusion.[147] Two years earlier, Camp Pinedale had been the site of the Pinedale Assembly Center, a temporary detention center for 4,800 exiled Japanese Americans, and John Okada had to be keenly aware that some of his former neighbors from Seattle had been imprisoned there.[148]

Guam: "The Flying Nisei"

By the time Sgt. Okada arrived on August 22, 1944, the 8th RSM had been stationed for months at Camp Pinedale. Okada trained for another five weeks with the unit's direction finders, translators, and intelligence evaluators, learning how to pluck enemy radio signals out of the air and mine them for valuable intelligence. On September 29, the squadron prepared for overseas movement, and Okada enjoyed the traditional "last supper" of a steak dinner before the unit fell out in full uniform—helmets, rifles, and backpacks—to march to the train that took them to their port of embarkation at Fort Lawton in Seattle.[149]

Okada had last seen Seattle from the windows of the bus taking him to Puyallup. Passes to the city were permitted, but by this time Okada's family was across the state in Ione, and everyone else he knew in the Japanese American community was still imprisoned at Minidoka. The unit shipped out in the dark of October 10, 1944, aboard the SS *Frederick Lykes*, a cargo steamship used for troop transport. The women of the Red Cross served coffee and donuts, and a military band played as their ship slipped away from the pier. Okada had sailed the open sea before on his trips to Alaska, but many first-timers got badly seasick.

It didn't take us very long to discover that we were much better soldiers than sailors, and the majority of us spent the first few days leaning over the rails, or moaning in our bunks, or watching the ocean from
the port-holes of the "head" . . . All available space was jam-packed
with men or equipment. We were served two meals a day in a mess
hall that was hot enough to serve as the steam room of a Turkish Bath.
The chow line twisted round and round the decks like an endless
snake. It took three to four hours to feed all the troops. There was very
little fresh water aboard for washing purposes, and saltwater showers left you feeling no cleaner than before you took them.[150]

After eight days of discomfort, the ship arrived at the Territory of Hawaii
and tied up next to the Aloha Tower, where the clock remained frozen at
the exact hour of the Pearl Harbor attack. The men slept in tents in the Aiea
staging area above the harbor and were awakened by the takeoff of planes
at all hours. During the day they could trek into Honolulu, which was
jammed with servicemen gawking at the sight of the Royal Hawaiian Hotel
and swimming at Waikiki.[151] After a week, the men resumed their journey,
and after three more weeks at sea, their destination was revealed to be
Guam, a strategic location in the Central Pacific from which the United
States could eavesdrop on radio signals from the Japanese mainland.

Guam had been an American territory until its capture by the Japanese
days after Pearl Harbor. It was retaken by the US in July 1944, and the
XXI Bomber Command arrived on Saipan to begin raids against the
Japanese home islands in late November. Around fifty Nisei were part of
the 8th RSM that landed on the beach of Sumay on November 10, and for
two weeks the entire squadron of 470 men labored to unload their equipment. Japanese stragglers on the shore surrendered when confronted by
the landing force, but one GI standing guard was shot and killed in a
skirmish.[152] The squadron established a secure joint communications
activity (JCA) compound consisting of corrugated-metal, semi-circular
Quonset huts on the northern tip of the island.

The Nisei in the voice intercept unit quickly found themselves marginal-
ized by interservice rivalry and racial stereotyping. The mission of the

Army-Navy Radio Analysis Group (Forward), known as RAGFOR, was to locate enemy targets for bombing by the B-29s of the XXI Bomber Command. Okada's Army Air Forces squadron was on loan to the navy, but the navy did not trust the army, and it did not trust the Japanese Americans. On top of this, the War Department wanted white officers to lead the Nisei teams;[153] with none available, a Korean American from Honolulu was put in charge of the voice intercept unit. Lt. Samuel S. K. Hong graduated from Camp Savage in the same cohort with Okada. Hong told military historian Larry Tart that the Nisei were viewed as "gofers" and "second-class citizens" and kept busy with garbage detail. They were also denied top-secret clearances, which meant only white officers could work as cryptanalysts, limiting the Nisei to work as translators.[154]

SAMUEL HONG

At the intelligence compound, the Navy had a tall fence around the compound, and we could not enter. They built a little hut for us outside the compound and put another fence around our hut. We were fighting not only the Japanese but the US Navy.[155]

The Nisei experience on Guam was the reverse of that in the mainland camps: instead of being fenced in, the Nisei were fenced *out* of the JCA compound, which was secured by a twelve-foot-high enclosure and guarded around the clock.

MAMORU ISHII

We Japanese boys did the voice intercepts in a little bungalow outside the fence. Everyone else in the 8th RSM—the Morse intercept operators, communicators, DF [direction finder] operators and others—worked inside the compound. That upset me somewhat— kinda griped me then.[156]

The Nisei inside their segregated shack at first simply listened to and translated tapes of Japanese radio transmissions recorded by B-29s during bombing raids.[157] Lt. Hong argued for clearance to enter the JCA compound, and once inside he learned that modified B-24s were being flown

"The Flying Nisei," as featured in 1945 in the unpublished squadron history, *The Story behind the Flying Eight-Ball.* Sgt. John Okada kneels (second from right), while standing are Lt. Samuel Hong (center) and Mamoru Ishii (second from right). *(Dorothea Okada)*

off the coast of Japan on ferret missions to pick up Japanese radar signals tracking the B-29s. Hong argued that his Nisei operators could get better intelligence and save lives by intercepting Japanese voice communications in real time from a position in the air, and in the spring of 1945 he got them on board flights from Harmon Field in the center of the island with the XXI Bomber Command's 3rd Reconnaissance Squadron.

At least two B-24 Liberator bombers were modified for their new missions. On each, the nose gun turret was removed and replaced with "an enclosure that was barely large enough for two receivers and two Nisei operators," who had to crawl in past the pilots. A fifty-yard-long wire trailed behind each aircraft for an antenna.[158] Only ten operators were needed, for rotation on missions on which they might be captured or killed. All the Nisei volunteered to go. Of the ten selected, half had learned their Japanese in Hawaii: Mamoru Ishii and Herbert Kawashima of Oahu, and Yoshio Kimoto, Yoshio Hoshide, and James Yoshioka from Honolulu.

Three volunteered for the MIS directly from an incarceration camp: George Hanafusa and Ted Ishisaka from Heart Mountain in Wyoming, and Mike Deguchi from Rohwer in southeastern Arkansas. John Okada and Hiroshi Tanouye enlisted from the free zones of Nebraska and Denver, respectively.[159] The ten were dubbed "The Flying Nisei," and the 8th RSM quickly became known as the "The Flying Eight-Ball." Okada's comrades called him "Johnny," and as he described it later in fiction, his job "was to listen through his earphones, which were attached to a high-frequency set, and jot down air-ground messages spoken by Japanese-Japanese in Japanese planes and in Japanese radio shacks."[160] With no devices for recording the radio chatter, each operator wrote down the messages in shorthand.

MAMORU ISHII

Our missions had to be in place along the Japanese coast during bombing raids. We were there when the first B-29 went in on its raid, and we stayed until the last B-29 made its raid. Missions were flown under radio silence. We copied mostly ground communications; by that time the Japanese air force was depleted. I never felt threatened. On one flight, our pilot said that a picket ship near the Bonin Islands fired on us, but we were not hit.[161]

After each raid, the Nisei joined the flight crew for a steak dinner, then typed up their intercepted messages to be analyzed for patterns to learn how the Japanese were defending themselves.[162] The men "flew about two missions each per month and were happy to be flying because they were paid flight pay amounting to about half of their regular enlisted pay," and the ten "Flying Nisei" made the 8th RSM "the most highly visible airborne voice intercept program of all the RSM's during WWII."[163]

EDWARD BRADFIELD

Although most of the group had been trained for Combat Intelligence, they quickly adapted themselves to the intricacies of our type of work, and performed their duties remarkably well. The Nisei boys proved themselves praiseworthy time and again, and we who worked with them, will always respect their loyalty and devotion to duty.[164]

Okada wrote a message to his brother Roy on the back of this photo with his B-24. It may have been taken the same day he posed with his "Flying Nisei" comrades. (*Roy Okada*)

Okada logged one hundred hours of flight time over twenty-four missions, aboard planes adorned with such nose art as "Hellcat Belle," "Tipsy Gypsy," and "The Laden Maiden," flying so low at times that he could see people in their outhouses waving up at them.[165] He posed proudly for a photo next to his plane, dwarfed by the size of the heavy bomber described by poet and fellow Seattleite Richard Hugo as a "flying pregnant water buffalo."[166] Okada sent a copy to his brother Roy with a message on the back: "Myself in Guam with plane I made missions on. B-24's look clumsy and ugly; but my respect for them will never die out. At least this one brought us all back safely every time. From the plane I saw Mt. Fujii in July 1945, and the clustering of bombs on Tokyo during night raids."[167]

By July 1945, language officers used Japanese prisoners of war to develop propaganda leaflets warning civilians that "your city has been listed for destruction by our powerful air force."[168] Ashida believed Okada's plane accompanied B-29s that scattered millions of the airborne leaflets: "He dropped messages on Tokyo to surrender, but you know in

Yoshitaka Robert Okada (left) and Fred Haita (right) both served with I Company, 3rd Battalion, 442nd RCT, which fought campaigns in France and Italy in 1944. A year later Haita was hit by an artillery shell in Italy, just two weeks before the German surrender. *(Yoshito Okada family)*

Japan at that time, surrender was the last thing in their mind."[169] Meanwhile, Nisei linguists on the ground in frontline areas had white bodyguards for protection, as they were "constantly at risk of being shot at, not only by the enemy, but out of mistaken identity by their own men."[170] That's what Okada reportedly told his brother Robert.[171] His brother Frank understood it differently, believing that "if they ever got into a fight, with the enemy Japanese, the guard was supposed to shoot John first. So he wouldn't be taken prisoner, you see. He was Intelligence."[172]

During this time, Okada received tragic news from Europe, where Robert and foster brother Fred Haita were serving together in the 442nd RCT. Robert was an infantryman and Fred was the radioman in I Company, 3rd Battalion, which fought in three major campaigns: Rome-Arno in 1944; the rescue of the "Lost Battalion" in the fall of 1944 at Vosges, France; and the Po Valley Campaign, the final Allied offensive in Italy.[173] Along the way, Robert was hit by shrapnel in his knee, a "million-dollar wound" that could have removed him from combat, but he insisted on staying with his buddies even if only as a cook in the field kitchen.[174] By April 1945, the Fifth Army had broken through the well-fortified Gothic Line, and the Germans were in retreat. I Company set up a command post in an abandoned mine shaft near Foce il Pulica in Fosdovino.[175] On the night of April 21, Cpl. Haita was at the mine entrance; Sgts. Robert Okada and Junwo "Jimmy" Yamashita were nearby.

JIMMY YAMASHITA

Haita carried the 300 MHz radio in his backpack. It was the most powerful radio in our company. The Germans must have zeroed in on the radio signal, and lobbed an artillery shell that exploded in the mine shaft. It blew up our own ordnance shells, causing a massive explosion. I was assigned to take charge of the bodies' removal. It made me sick to see the mutilated bodies of people who I had seen sitting on the bank in front of the mine shaft opening just a few hours before.[176]

Haita and four others were killed. Robert could only watch in horror as Fred's body was removed from the tunnel.[177] Yamashita had the dirty job of carting the remains to the US military cemetery at Castelfiorentino for burial. Two weeks later, the Germans surrendered.

Okada's reconnaissance flights continued until early August. On August 5, intercept operators on Guam noticed a sharp decline in Japanese radio traffic, followed by a message in Morse code alerting all listeners that the United States had dropped an atomic bomb on Hiroshima, the birthplace of Okada's parents and the home of his extended family.[178] The B-29 that delivered the bomb, the *Enola Gay*, had taken off from the nearby island of Tinian. After the detonation of a second A-bomb above Nagasaki, Japan surrendered on August 15, and by October the soldiers on Guam were packing up to go home. Army brass commended the 8th RSM for producing "intelligence of immediate tactical value to the Air Forces," thanks to their "keen analysis and thorough knowledge of Japanese communications."[179]

It is a measure of the dislocation felt by Nisei servicemen from the West Coast that when asked by the unit historian for their mailing address, "in case your buddies owe you money," Okada was at a loss. He no longer had an address in Seattle, and his family had already left Block 28 at Minidoka. The only home he could claim was the Teraokas' remote, rural stream laundry where his family had moved: "J. Okada, Box 239, Ione, Washington."[180]

Occupation Forces, Tokyo: "When in Japan . . . "

As the 8th RSM was being deactivated, their comrades teased the Nisei that they would have to stay in Japan for the Occupation while everyone else got to go home. Many Nisei regarded it as racial prejudice that they had not received promotions during the war, so to retain their valuable services as interpreters the Army quickly awarded them commendations.[181] Okada was already a sergeant, but his specialty was changed from voice interceptor to that of a face-to-face interpreter. He volunteered to interpret for the US Strategic Bombing Survey in Tokyo and was assigned to Major General Grandison Gardner, deputy to the survey chairman and an expert in weapons systems who worked on early development of bomb sights.[182] The mission of the Strategic Bombing Survey included an assessment of the effects of dropping explosives on civilian populations, including studying the firebombing of Tokyo and the atomic bombing of Hiroshima and Nagasaki.[183] Okada was quartered at the New Kaijo Building, across from the emperor's palace and near General MacArthur's occupation headquarters.

Amid the devastation of Tokyo, the Meiji Building in Marunouchi survived, and it was conscripted by the survey for training interviewers in research techniques perfected before the war by pollsters George Gallup and Elmo Roper. A cross-section of 3,700 air raid survivors was selected, and interviewers were briefed using terms that Sgt. Okada would echo in his own writing: "We are dealing with the thoughts, the attitudes, the ideas, the fears, the hopes that exist in people's minds. We are after opinions and attitudes. That's the raw material that we deal with."[184] Sgt. Okada interrogated public officials in Japanese about the effects of the 160,800 tons of bombs dropped on the home islands, and joined survey teams to inspect bomb damage.[185] He located a cousin in Tokyo from whom he likely learned that his own extended family in

Sgt. Okada volunteered for service in Occupation Japan, interviewing survivors on behalf of the US Strategic Bombing Survey. At Kyobashi Station in Tokyo, Okada walked amid the rubble of the city he had witnessed being bombed from the air. (*Yoshito Okada family*)

Hiroshima was safe.[186] Ground zero was eleven miles from the family home in Asakita Ward, far enough removed for them to have survived the blast and fallout.

The eventual report of the Strategic Bombing Survey not surprisingly concluded that the bombing was a decisive factor in the Allied victory, but it also conceded, based on the testimony of surviving Japanese military leaders, that "Japan would have surrendered even if the atomic bombs had not been dropped, even if Russia had not entered the war, and even if no invasion had been planned or contemplated"[187]—a conclusion that likely weighed heavily on the American soldiers of Japanese ancestry.

John Okada's war was soon over. He spent Christmas Day 1945 at the New Kaijo around a decorated tree with comrades named Bennett, Meyers, Thompson, and Belk. He departed the Occupation Forces on February 22, 1946, and by March 10 he was back at Fort Lewis, fifty miles south of Seattle. He was honorably discharged with an American Campaign Medal, an Asiatic-Pacific Service Medal, a Good Conduct Medal, and a Victory Medal. Throughout their service, the MIS'ers were told to "keep your mouths shut" about their classified operations, and John Okada would keep his word.[188]

AFTER THE WAR: "IT WAS A DIRTY CITY"

With the end of war and closing of the camps, many families had no homes to return to. In Seattle, the Japanese Language School where Okada once studied was converted into a hostel for twenty-seven homeless families and dubbed "Hunt Hotel." Two Issei, broken financially and emotionally, took their own lives there.[189] Artist Kamekichi Tokita lived there for two years with his family of eight, taking the bus to South Lake Union where he worked as a sign painter at St. Vincent de Paul.[190] Nao and Kiyonosuke Akutsu took refuge at the Nichiren Buddhist Church at 12th and Weller—without their sons.[191] Jim and Gene Akutsu were among those who had refused to be drafted from the camp at Minidoka and were serving sentences at the McNeil Island federal penitentiary west of Tacoma; Nao Akutsu would take the ferry from Steilacoom once a month to visit her sons in prison, alternating her visits between the two.

Yoshito Okada was finally released from his parole as an alien enemy. "Apparently not deportable," grumbled his district parole officer in a scrawled note closing the file.[192] The elder Okada brought his family from Ione back to Seattle on August 3, 1945, three days before the bombing of

Hiroshima, with little to show from his twenty-one years of hotel management except the knowledge in his head and hands.

ROY OKADA

He was looking forward to having a business and not pushing coals in a laundry. So he found a friend that was doing fairly well, and got a hotel that he could run, the Pacific Hotel.[193]

That good friend was Keichi Takemura, the same owner who transferred management of the Merchants Hotel to the Okadas back in 1920. Their families had remained close throughout the incarceration. Takemura was among those fortunate to have had a white friend to manage his properties during the war, and he now hired the Okadas to run the Pacific Hotel at the corner of Sixth and Weller in Chinatown.[194] With sixty-four rooms on two upper floors and storefronts at street level, the brick building was close in size to the Merchants Hotel, it was centrally located, and it provided a home for the family, including the two sons returning from war.

Yoshitaka Robert was back from Italy, but not Fred Haita. Roy was drafted and went to serve in the Occupation after John came back. John Okada, like the character he would later create, had been gone four years—in John's case, five months in camp, one year in college, and two and a half years in the service. Also like his character, he returned home by taking a half-hour bus ride north—not from prison, but from Fort Lewis, on March 15, 1946. He was twenty-two years old. He arrived at the Pacific Hotel to find that his father's black hair had turned white.[195] William Collins, their boarder at the Yakima, had moved to the Pacific to rejoin them.[196]

The clock tower of King Street Station was the same, but not the racial mix on Jackson Street. Defense work at the Boeing aircraft factory had drawn African Americans from the South, where they had never known Japanese Americans as neighbors, and some enjoyed seeing the returning incarcerees occupy a lower rung in the racial pecking order.[197] Okada helped out at the hotel as night clerk, and when he got off work he mixed easily with the vibrant jazz scene outside, at cabarets with doormen and floor shows and names like the Black and Tan, the Black Elks Club, Club

Maynard, and New Chinatown. One could walk up Jackson from First Avenue to Fourteenth after midnight and pass thirty-four nightclubs, and "buy a newspaper at the corner of 14th and Yesler from a man called Neversleep—at three in the morning."[198] Frank Okada attended Garfield High School and got to know a teenaged Quincy Jones, who impressed him by playing in nightclubs until four in the morning and still showing up for school.[199]

John used his GI Bill to reenroll at the University of Washington, taking the same Route 7 to campus as before. His subjects were English, history, and sociology, with a solid block of creative writing courses: Introduction to Fiction, Dramatic Composition, and Narrative Writing. His creative writing instructor was Prof. Grant Redford, a published writer who encouraged his students to create meaningful narratives from the "stuff of their lives." He was from Montana, "a very good short story writing teacher and a sad man who was to commit suicide twenty years later," according to Richard Hugo, another GI returning to the UW for creative writing classes.[200]

Okada quickly got involved with the university's first attempt at staging an original, all-school musical comedy. Called "They Can't Do This," it was an awkward mix of dance revue and comic farce shoehorned into a story of intolerance faced by a returning soldier, "with scenes of race conflict, bar-room killing, and lynching."[201] Okada and another Asian student were cast in small parts as drum majors leading a marching band onstage. The *UW Daily* noted "Chinese Thomas Locke and Nisei John Okada doing interesting roles considering both have never before been on the boards."[202] The show played to near-capacity crowds at Meany Hall May 2 to 4, 1946.

That same month, Okada finished writing his own play. The restriction on talking about his wartime intelligence work did not extend to his peacetime duty in the Occupation, which provided the basis for a one-act called "When in Japan." Whether he modeled the captain in the piece on General Gardner or another officer is not known, but Okada's drama instructor saw its potential and selected it for production.

Playwright and teacher George Milton Savage was a proponent of workshopping new plays to further their development; he also had an eye for the royalties to be earned from the production of new plays on Broadway or at regional theaters and schools. To advance both goals, he founded the off-campus Tryout Theatre, which he billed as the "only theatre of its kind in America—where aspiring playwrights whose plays are worthy of production can have them produced before offering for sale."[203] The semi-professional group worked out of a fifty-five-seat playhouse at 1316 East 42nd Street, just off University Way, in a narrow building with a tiny stage and only enough floor space to seat eight people across.[204] "When in Japan" was regarded as among "the semester's outstanding contributions" written for Professor Redford's spring English 76 class, and Savage scheduled it and three other student works for a June 6 debut under the umbrella title *4-by-Four*. "These four plays offer a fresh, vigorous look at timely themes," Professor Redford declared in the *UW Daily*, "and should give anyone who sees them an exciting evening in the theater. We hope to make the production of student-written plays an annual event and in this way provide an outlet for beginning playwrights comparable to 'Month's Best' in the creative writing division."[205]

The three other pieces in *4-by-Four* were decidedly downbeat: an allegorical fantasy from a "Seattle house wife" about "an old woman about to lose her last worldly possession—her home"; a drama by a returning air force gunner about "an air crew in Italy waiting to start off on a mission, knowing it will be their last"; and one by an ex-newspaperman who survived D-Day about "a veteran trying to readjust himself to civilian life." Okada's play, described as "a comedy of American occupation," was slotted second in the program.[206] With only a few weeks for rehearsal, all four playwrights helped provide costumes and props. Just three months after returning from the Occupation, Okada saw his Occupation satire played before a live audience.

Okada appeared on stage once again, this time in his own play. His brother Roy remembered the venue as half full, with about thirty in the audience, and that John played "one of the parts with a lot of lines,"[207] possibly Mr. Ko, the "dignified" president of the documentary film company. "'When in Japan,' by John Okada," wrote the *UW Daily*, "relates the efforts of an American officer of the occupying forces to indoctrinate the Japanese with democracy. Okada was himself in the army of occupation and only recently was a featured player in the all-University musical show, 'They Can't Do This.' The cast, directed by Dan Thompson, includes Okada, Kenneth Connelly, Kathleen Brix, Lyle Jones, William Hagerman, Jim Ikoma and Paul Locke."[208] The *Seattle Times* reported the new works received "bouquets from first-night audiences."[209]

4-by-Four ran for four weekends. At one performance, Roy was enlisted by his brother as a last-minute replacement.

ROY OKADA

He asked me to take one of the very small parts of one of the envoys. The three of us wearing a suit and a hat would come into the office of one of the officers that we were visiting, and by some stupid action on my part I sat on the hat that was given to me. That created a little comedy that wasn't intended but it was embarrassing for me.[210]

Professor Savage pitched several Tryout Theatre scripts to the American Educational Theater Association's Manuscript Play Project in Chicago. "When in Japan" was among eight accepted "for production consideration on a royalty basis"; two were optioned for Broadway, but Okada's Occupation satire was not among them.[211]

With school out for summer, Okada bought a black Oldsmobile—the same make and color he would later assign to the fictional Kenji—and drove Roy and an army buddy to Los Angeles to check out opportunities and see the sights, taking photos at Grauman's Chinese Theatre and other tourist spots. In July, he helped his friend Chessie Tsubota open a war surplus store, the North American Trading Company at 420 Fourth Avenue, where they sold clothing, hardware, and hotel supplies at both retail and wholesale.[212] When school resumed in the fall of 1946, Okada turned to the study of short stories, developing several for a class with Professor Redford and making the UW honor roll that fall.[213]

John's creative output helped launch publisher and editor Budd Fukei's new vernacular newspaper, the *Northwest Times*. Whether offered or solicited, "When in Japan" appeared in the second and third issues of the newspaper in January 1947, on page 2 with an editor's note describing the contributor as "an English major at the University of Washington." Five short stories followed in quick succession from March through April. An unpublished short story title recalled by Okada's family was either "Shanghai Girl" or "Hong Kong Girl."[214] Another told of a confrontation between a US soldier and "a Japanese soldier that was captured or met the enemy on Guam or something like that, where they had to fight (and it) ended up with kind of a man-to-man, hand-to-hand type of (combat)."[215] The stories were exercises in style and form. Okada had not yet found his true subject matter—but that changed when Jim and Gene Akutsu, Frank Yamasaki, and other Nisei draft resisters from Seattle were released from federal prison.

Return of the Resisters: "I got reasons"

When Frank Yamasaki received his draft notice in Minidoka, his retort was the same as the Akutsu's: "If you will restore our lifestyle like before this evacuation, yes, I would be more than willing to serve in the armed forces. If not, I will not."[216] He, Jim, and Gene were among the thirty-three who refused induction from Minidoka and were convicted and sentenced to three years and three months of hard time. The resisters served nineteen months and were discharged from McNeil Island on April 30, 1946. Their homecomings were much like that of the fictional Ichiro Yamada.

FRANK YAMASAKI

I walked a few blocks down to James Street, where my parents were. And when I went into the house, my mother was there. And she greeted me. And we weren't the kissing kind or anything. We just shook hands. We weren't even the embracing kind, so first thing she would say is she got fried chicken for me. [laughs] That was one of my favorite food. So while she was cooking, we talked, and I noticed how small the room was, and it just . . . We'd lost everything, and now we had to start all over again. I think the pain of coming out of the concentration camp was even greater than the pain of being in there.[217]

JIM AKUTSU

Steilacoom was a half-hour bus ride to Seattle. I wore a thin pin-striped blue suit. Got off at 2nd and Main Street. That's where John

Okada's book starts. Looking around to see changes, I saw none. Crossed Jackson on the south side, walked and turned right. I went to the store and just walked in, and they were very happy to see me. My mother was almost dead. She wanted to get out of here, go back to Japan. She was physically shot.[218]

Jim and Gene found their parents living in a hovel behind the storefront where they had reestablished the New Golden Shoe Repair Shop at 619 S. Weller Street, side by side with the Okadas' Pacific Hotel. Chinatown had grown dirtier in Gene's eyes, with paper bingo slips fluttering on the sidewalks. The people had also changed. The expulsion order, the demands to show loyalty, and the drafting of soldiers out of camp all merged to create two classes of Nisei: those who complied with the government, and those who resisted the injustice. Entering cafes and nightclubs, the resisters saw the icy stares and heard the whispers from the patriots and the fence-sitters.

JIM AKUTSU

Only thing is: the silent treatment. Like, somebody that I know be coming down the street, they walk across. I say hi to 'em, they just . . . You know which one's are going to evade you, would walk on the other side of the street . . . And the people that would have spit on me, they knew I used to handle myself pretty good.[219]

GENE AKUTSU

It was no sooner [Jim] came up from the penitentiary than he was confronted with a number of people, and they threatened to beat him up, and all that, and he would stand up and argue his point. The vets were very bitter towards us, and from what we heard while we were in the prison, the vets are going to confront us, and there's going to be a showdown. But fortunately, nothing like that happened.[220]

Out in Chinatown late one night, Frank Yamasaki was challenged by a group of Nisei veterans, and saw among them former classmates and people he once considered friends.

FRANK YAMASAKI

I was drunk. They were drunk. Everybody was drinking at late hours. I didn't get struck or anything. It was intimidation, name-calling, and things like that . . . But most people just kept quiet. And that silence is even more painful than being called some names.[221]

One of the few people in town who would talk to the resisters was John Okada. Jim remembered him from Broadway High when he saw Okada working at the surplus store.

JIM AKUTSU

John would be sitting there just looking down. He might have ten people there, he just doesn't care. So anyway, the person I am, after I finish my dinner, I'd go and talk to John. . . . We got to talking and he'd say, "Hey, let's go to Wah Mee," or "Let's go to Wah Chang," or whatever, and I'd go with him.[222]

Everyone on the street knew the notorious Wah Mee Club on Maynard Alley, a onetime speakeasy with dancing and drinking in the back bar.[223] One could "walk up to the door, and there was a little eight-by-eight-inch window, and a man with a grey beard, just like in a movie, would look out. And if you were Asian, he would let you in. As soon as you opened the door, you were flooded with smoke and really loud music."[224] There were "tables upstairs for the gambling. Bar downstairs. More Caucasians than Oriental people in the bar. Fight[s] in the alley."[225] John Okada was the first to take Jim Akutsu there, and Jim said it's where "John taught me how to drink."[226]

Unlike other dissidents, who would clam up when questioned, Jim Akutsu liked to talk. He spoke emphatically, in bursts of thought that at times could be hard to follow. Over drinks at the Wah Mee, Akutsu filled in Okada on all he had missed by leaving camp early. He told of his own father being interned for nearly two years, far beyond the time Okada's father was held, because of the same magazine subscription to *Sokoku* but also because of unnamed informants who cast doubt on his loyalties. He told of the botched loyalty questionnaire to which Jim had answered "yes-no" but for which he was never shipped to Tule Lake. He told of how

Hajime Jim Akutsu was released in April 1946 from his sentence for draft resistance and worked for a time at his father's New Golden Shoe Repair Shop at 619 Weller Street, next to the Okadas' Pacific Hotel. Okada saw Jim's mother get the "news from Brazil" here. *(Akutsu family)*

his mother was forced to kneel and apologize for trouble Jim had made in camp. He told of the "monkey business" of his being sent a draft notice in June 1944 that impossibly called for him to report for a physical in May. He told of refusing the draft in camp, being convicted of failure to report for induction, and serving time at McNeil.[227] He told of his mother's mental and physical breakdown upon getting her husband back in an emaciated condition and then losing both her sons to prison. He told of acquiring skills in prison as an ironworker that helped him land a job back in Seattle at the Olympic Foundry on Airport Way, which hired a number of Nisei draft resisters despite their felony records because they "were good at making the molds for the iron."[228] He told of being warned about Nisei veterans on the job who were out to kill him, and of his response to "Let them try." He told of befriending an African American coworker whose job he saved during a round of layoffs by sacrificing himself and leaving to work at his father's shoe shop: "I left one opening for a black," he said.[229] Finally, Jim told of taking the streetcar to the UW engineering building, taking the stairs to the third floor, and visiting Professor Jim Chittenden, who remembered him from before and was happy to discuss Jim's possible return to study civil engineering.[230]

Jim's story was a long and rambling one and it tumbled out all at once, some of it possibly becoming confused as Okada took notes. The two also talked on benches at the Akutsu shoe shop, which Jim called "the only place where a no-no boy got a friendly welcome."

JIM AKUTSU

There used to be a half dozen people there, including John's father. They all talk back and forth about their old times and so on, and this one guy keeps bringing up this about Japan didn't lose the war, and he gets his news from Brazil or someplace and he'll come and talk about it. Anyway, my mother's listening to all of that. And for what happened to us here in United States from '41 on, she wants to go back to Japan. And I told her, "Japan lost the war and I don't want to go back." Because listening to people coming back . . . we had to send old clothes to Japan because their house burned, or food to them, so I knew, and she knew, because she was making these CARE package. But she kept listening to this one guy saying that Japan didn't lose.[231]

The "news from Brazil" came over shortwave radio from a South American cult known as Shindo Renmei (League of the Way of Emperor's Subjects). Shindo Renmei claimed more than one hundred thousand adherents of *kachigumi* (victory faction), who refused to believe in Japan's surrender, and admonished skeptics that "only the true Japanese with Japanese spirit can hear the correct messages from Japan."[232] Okada tucked all of Jim's stories into his notes, along with one more from his uncle Tetsuo: that of Tetsuo's brother-in-law in California, who protested incarceration at Tule Lake by renouncing his US citizenship along with 5,500 others and expatriating to Japan.[233]

At the shoe shop, Okada witnessed for himself how Mrs. Akutsu no longer felt she had a place in the United States. In her experience, this was a country that had stripped her family of their home, livelihood, and real estate and repeatedly imprisoned her, her husband, and her sons in a succession of detention centers, internment camps, incarceration camps, and penitentiaries. She had not one ex-convict for a son, but two. The final straw came when she was cast out by members of the Nichiren church, where she had been cleaning sinks and scrubbing toilets every Saturday before going to service on Sunday.

JIM AKUTSU

It was the Issei who constantly (said), "Hey, your son's a draft evader, coward, chickenshit," and kept pressing, and cut her off, cut her off, cut her off. Just isolated her. . . . And the parents of the people who lost a son (in the war) took an even stronger attitude.[234]

GENE AKUTSU

The people asked her, "Don't come to church anymore." It was a disgrace to the church. "We don't want anybody that has kids that refuse to go to the service, that's being disloyal to the country. We don't want you here. Don't come anymore." . . . So one Sunday, Jim and I were at the church, Jim was called, and he went home, and found out that mother had tried to commit suicide.[235]

Their mother, a daughter of the samurai, had attempted hara-kiri by slashing her abdomen with a razor. She was rushed to the King County hospital at Harborview, where for her protection she was temporarily restrained. Four days later, however, on September 25, 1947, Nao Akutsu managed to tie one end of the cord of her hospital gown to the foot of her bed, wrapped the other end around her neck, "then crouched down and waited for death."[236]

GENE AKUTSU

I guess her determination in dying just got the best of her and she took her life, once again. I guess that must be part of being a samurai's

In Kokura, Japan, an Army Signal Corps photographer was present when Fred Haita's remains were returned to his parents on March 22, 1948. *(Henry U. Milne Collection, Army Heritage and Education Center)*

daughter, that committing suicide is something of an honor, and that's the way she went.[237]

Nao Akutsu's service was held where she had been ostracized, at the Nichiren Buddhist Church.[238] Okada joined Jim and Gene in the front pew. When a white cat tiptoed out from under the casket, Jim imagined it was his mother's spirit and muttered to Okada, "Good thing I became a Buddhist."[239]

Jim fought to get the job he wanted, as a civil engineer with the city of Seattle. Okada graduated from the UW in the summer of 1947 with a bachelor's degree in English, and he stayed on full-time with the surplus store as general manager to earn money to attend graduate school.

In 1948, the parents of Fred Haita petitioned the Eighth Army to return his body to them in Japan so that "our declining years would be made much happier."[240] In the spirit of postwar reconciliation, the army transported Haita's remains from Italy.[241] At the 24th Infantry Division headquarters in Kokura, the army presented Mr. and Mrs. Haita with their son's service medals and a $150 death benefit.[242] The story was carried nationwide and made the front page of the *Seattle Times*, where Okada could not have missed the irony of seeing his Kibei foster brother, born in Montana but educated in Japan, incorrectly described as being "buried in the soil of Japan which he never saw."[243]

Teachers College, New York City: "To be a student in America was a wonderful thing"

For one year, John Okada bided his time, managing Tsubota's war surplus store and helping out at the Pacific Hotel. He'd work until midnight, then get together with friends to eat at Tai Tung, see a late-night movie at the Florence Theater, or play poker with Hiromi Nishimura at his Puget Sound Hotel. The State Liquor Control Board stored its confiscated barroom equipment in a warehouse that was next to the store, and at a sidewalk auction Okada bid $20 for two dozen cases of mixers, coasters, cherries, and a half-filled bottle of "Zombie mix"—a rum-based cocktail. He expanded the store to a chain of three, with a fourth "in the planning stage."[244] But life as a business entrepreneur was not for Okada. He made plans to qualify as a high school English teacher, and by fall 1948 he was accepted for the master's program in English at Teachers College in New York City.

Teachers College sits on the Upper West Side of Manhattan close to Harlem, on Broadway and W. 120th Street. Although affiliated with Columbia University, Teachers College was and still is a separate institution. Okada took a small eighth-floor apartment near campus. Living on the ground floor of the same building was Dorothy Arakawa, an interpreter who had recently returned from Japan and was studying English at Columbia. Okada majored in Teaching English, earning As and Bs in courses such as "Social Ideals in the Contemporary Novel," all of which continued the development of his voice on the page as a writer.[245] According to classmate Will Alpern, "Some of the scenes in *No-No Boy* were sketched out at Columbia Teachers College where John got his master's back in 1949"—the first evidence of work by Okada on a novel.[246]

Okada enrolled at Teachers College in New York City to get a master's degree to teach English. It was there he reportedly sketched the first scenes for *No-No Boy* in early 1949. (*Yoshito Okada family*)

Close to the end of the school year in spring 1949, Dorothy met John at a party where, for the first and only time in Dorothy's experience, John was red-faced drunk. She didn't know what she found attractive in him—"He wasn't rich, he wasn't good-looking, he was about my height," she would later laugh[247]—but they shared the experience of interpreting in Occupied Japan, and neither felt a particular attachment to living in the Japanese community.

Dorothy was a fiercely independent woman. She was born in Hawaii, three years before John. Her father was a Methodist Episcopalian minister from Iwate prefecture who sent her as a child to be educated in Japan, defining her as a Kibei Nisei whose culture was different from that of American-educated Nisei or Japanese war brides. As John's sister Arlene recalled, she was "more of an individual than most Nisei. She had her own ideas on life and everything else."[248] By her own account, Dorothy did not fit in with the Japanese in Japan, whom she dismissed as "big liars,"[249] and after the war she looked for a way to get back to the United

Okada appeared happy to shovel snow outside his apartment on the Upper West Side of Manhattan in February 1949. (*Yoshito Okada family*)

States. Through her job as an interpreter in the Occupation, she found a sponsor in an army sergeant who arranged for her to stay with his parents on a farm in Deposit, upstate New York, until she could get herself established.

Once in New York City, Dorothy studied English, took piano lessons, worked as a clerk for a small company, and planned a career. She never thought she wanted to get married. That, in fact, was one of her reasons for leaving Japan, and in New York she deflected bids by acquaintances to match her with Kibei men.[250] John Okada was different. They took walks through Central Park, "not speaking, just staring at the sky, enjoying ice cream and cantaloupe."[251] They attended a whirlwind of movies, plays, even a ballet, which Okada didn't like. Dorothy insisted they go Dutch. She learned that Okada was "just writing little things, short novels."[252]

Okada mugged for the camera in spring 1949, around the time he was ready to graduate and met Dorothy Arakawa. *(Yoshito Okada family)*

DOROTHY OKADA

He wasn't like the average Japanese people around there.[253] He was very gentle. He did not have a single rough word in his conversation. I thought he was very serious, but studious. He was very considerate of everybody and anybody. He was very soft. He was a very delicate person.[254]

Very quickly, an unspoken agreement was reached.

DOROTHY OKADA

We met and a few weeks later he was gonna go back to Seattle, so in other words within the two weeks we already decided we were going to get married. So, he didn't propose and I didn't propose, but we just kept saying, "When we get to Seattle, when we get to Seattle." [laughs][255]

Back in Seattle in 1949, John Okada took his mother and sisters shopping downtown at Fourth and Pike past Sanders Fountain Lunch. A year later they lost their mother at the age of fifty-one. (From left: Arlene, Takayo, Connie, John.) *(Yoshito Okada family)*

The two agreed that Okada would pick up his master's degree in English, return home as scheduled, and send for Dorothy later. But once back in Seattle, Okada found no demand for his services as a high school English teacher; the only job he could find was as a typist at the Mt. Rainier Ordnance Depot in Tacoma. Typing six copies of everything for eight hours a day, he doubled his touch-typing speed from thirty-eight words per minute to an admirable seventy-five.[256]

Then his mother died.

Takayo Okada was only fifty-one, but her high blood pressure had been exacerbated by incarceration at Puyallup and Minidoka, and it finally claimed her life on January 4, 1950. Her service was held at the Seattle Buddhist Church. Okada would later describe in fiction the head priest, Rev. Tatsuya Ichikawa, as having a "shiny, bald head" that "bulged at the temples, the pink skin stretched tight as if ready to burst," with a voice "pitched too high."[257] A bereft Yoshito Okada wrote, "I worked day and night in order to rear our six children alone."[258]

Seattle: "Just a minister with a prayer"

As Okada would later joke, "Dorothy was broke and so was I, so we got married."[259] John was twenty-six, Dorothy was twenty-nine. She quit her job in New York and came to Seattle. They were wed on June 24, 1950, at the upscale Beacon Hill home of Sueko Takemura, whose husband Keichi had passed away. Yoshitaka Robert was best man, his new wife, Jane, was matron of honor, and the service was officiated by Rev. Andrew Otani of St. Peter's Episcopal Mission.[260] For the *Northwest Times*, it was society-page news: "A white slipper satin gown was worn by the bride. The gown had a net yoke edged in lace, long, tapering sleeves and a full skirt which made a beautiful picture with overskirts of illusion and net."[261]

DOROTHY OKADA

We had [the wedding] at John's father's best friend's house. Just a simple, just a nothing, just a minister with a prayer. John's father had *his* friends over, you know, the way the Isseis go through all that ritual.[262]

The wedding party celebrated with a reception at Gyokko-Ken Cafe, a popular chop suey house at Fifth and Main. The couple lived for a month at the Pacific Hotel before moving to a housing project, possibly near Boeing Field south of downtown. If he couldn't get a job as a teacher, Dorothy said John "really wanted to go into advertising," perhaps after

John and Dorothy waited a year after meeting in New
York before reuniting in Seattle and getting married
in June 1950. (*Roy Okada*)

exposure to Madison Avenue while he was in New York. But, she said,
"Japanese, Orientals were just out, y'know, so he couldn't find a job" as
an ad man, so for the fifth time in his life John went back to college,
enrolling at the University of Washington for a second bachelor's degree,
one in Librarianship.[263] This time around he studied the more mundane
sciences of the Dewey Decimal System, reference work, book selection,
and the history of printing.[264] At night he worked part-time alongside
Roy Kumasaka at the DeLamar Bed Spring Company on Airport Way,
making box spring mattresses by laboriously hand-tying spring coils to
the steel grid frame.[265]

Exactly nine months and a day after their wedding, in March 1951, a daughter was born. They named her Dorothea, a name Dorothy told her was from the Bible. That spring Okada interned for one month as a "practice student" in the Business Department at the Seattle Public Library. He "took hold of the work exceedingly well," according to department head Doris Mitchell, and when he graduated in June 1951 with his library degree, Mitchell quickly hired him full-time as her assistant.[266]

The Seattle central library had been built in 1906 in the neoclassical Beaux Arts style with funds from philanthropist Andrew Carnegie, but by the time Okada arrived the once-luxurious building with its lavish reading rooms was nearing the end of its useful life.[267] Mitchell had led the Business Department, a busy resource for investors looking for financial reports and business data, since its inception in 1946. Okada was paid $2,760 a year to answer questions on the floor and over the phone, cut articles from the newspapers for clip files, index pamphlets, give tours of the department's holdings, and run the department in Mitchell's absence.[268] She felt he "did a splendid piece of work" preparing a UW Extension course on "library literature for business men."[269] He also performed such tasks as helping Miss Mitchell plan a display for an open house[270] and representing the business department on a KING-TV program called *Community Workshop*.[271] Mitchell liked his "bright shining eyes."[272] "Mr. Okada had an excellent professional spirit, a keen mind and sense of responsibility," she wrote. "His respect for and interest in the customers and their requests won him an enviable standing with them and the Staff."[273]

In July 1951, Hiromi Nishimura came to Okada with a business proposition. His family had just acquired the Prince of Wales Apartments, a three-story brick building with forty rental units in the area between Capitol Hill and the Central Area, and he needed help.

HIROMI NISHIMURA

We had bought this apartment building and I didn't want to run it. I was running around with John and I asked him and his wife to manage it, and he agreed to stay on for a while.[274]

From working in his family's hotels, Okada was an experienced caretaker and handy with tools, and "with the assistance of my wife, I handled the collection of rents, maintained the building and lawn, made minor electrical, plumbing, and mechanical repairs, and carried a 5th-grade engineer's license to operate the heating plant."[275]

John and Dorothy wanted their children to be close enough in age to be friends growing up, as John was with his brothers, and tried to space them eighteen months apart. Matthew, named after the first book of the New Testament, was born in September 1952. The new father was working three jobs: days at the library, part-time at the bed spring company during busy periods, and managing the apartments with Dorothy. With the family growing, Okada worried about his ability to support them all. Dorothy talked of having a third child, "but John said we weren't making enough money, so he thought it would be very unfair."[276] Meanwhile, he kept his eyes open for something that might pay more. Just as workers flocked to the Boeing aircraft plant in Seattle during the war, in postwar Detroit he saw that the Ford and Chrysler factories were churning out cars—and the city's growing workforce needed libraries.

Detroit: "Thirty years of living and two years of hard work"

With the likely help of Doris Mitchell, Okada secured a job at the Detroit Public Library, which paid half as much more—$4,311 in the prosperous Motor City, compared to his $3,000 final salary in Seattle.[277] In August 1953, Okada gave his notice at the Seattle library and the bed spring company, handed back the keys to the Prince of Wales, and he and Dorothy packed Dorothea and Matthew into the black Oldsmobile for the drive east.

In Detroit, Okada worked in the Business and Commerce Division alongside another reference librarian with a degree, Mary Klanian, who recalled, "There was a shortage of librarians in the country, and the Detroit Public Library had a high reputation, paying one of the highest salaries in the library world at the time."[278] Mary lived nearby, and she and John would drive together to work at the library's old Technology

Building in the Midtown area. Their main duties were to answer patron questions "on a vast range of subjects ranging from accounting to personnel management to automotive mechanics to nuclear physics to differential equations," a job he said required "a thorough familiarity with the numerous reference and bibliographic tools including encyclopaedias, handbooks, yearbooks, almanacs, directories, and abstracts."[279]

MARY KLANIAN

We were in the main library, in the little red brick building on one corner of the lawn facing the Wayne State University student union building. The technology department of the library was on three floors. The first and second held the reference part. The top floor had the automotive history collection, and was well regarded by the auto industry.[280]

Around nine hundred Nisei had moved to Detroit during and after the war, making it the fifth-largest center of resettlement after Chicago, Denver, New York City, and Cleveland.[281] The Okadas settled in a modest two-story, wood-frame bungalow at 15787 Belden Street, off Puritan Avenue, a few blocks from the University of Detroit and a few miles north of downtown. It was just a ten-minute drive from Highland Park, where many Nisei had resettled, but there's no evidence the family socialized much with those in the Detroit Bowling League, the Motor City Golf Club, or the Detroit Buddhist Church.[282] Okada sent the first of several letters back to Doris Mitchell at the Seattle library, and she relayed through the staff newsletter that Okada "has bought a home in the University district and he and his family are very happy to have a place of their own."[283] But Okada also wrote to Miss Mitchell of an unpleasant incident that occurred when the family went in search of a Christian place of worship.[284]

DOROTHEA OKADA

They took us to a church, with the idea of finding a church that might look after us if something happened to them. I think it was a Baptist church. I was about to start kindergarten and Matthew was four.

After the service, some people came back and told us not to come back. This was shortly after the war. They didn't like Japanese people, and some pretty nasty words were said. After that incident, Dad never went to church again.[285]

Dorothy wanted their children to learn music, as she had, and living across the street she met Marian Stickels, a piano teacher with a fourteen-year-old daughter, Betsy.

BETSY STICKELS PERRY

In the area where we lived, racial tensions were very evident. I grew up afraid. Our neighborhood was still primarily white into the middle 1950s, at that time when black families started to move in. It was peculiar. Block by block they seemed to move, then they moved into our block. White families at that time, they didn't like it.

Matthew started getting violin lessons, like his grandfather, and Dorothy hired Marian Stickels to teach piano to him and Dorothea. Stickels welcomed Dorothy and the children into the Puritan Avenue Baptist Church, on Puritan and Inverness, where Stickels directed four choirs. She invited Dorothy to accompany them on piano, and the two would also play "beautiful duets."

BETSY STICKELS PERRY

My mother took her under her wing. My mother just loved her so much. They were soul mates through their music. Both were highly intelligent, it was like a mutual admiration society. Dorothy was sweet and kind and gentle and nurturing as a mother. If I saw John in passing, he was busy, and Dorothy had her music and she would be at our house. My mother told me he was opposed himself to attending church, but he didn't prevent them from attending.[286]

To keep in touch with his family in Seattle, Okada sent newspaper clippings about Dorothea and Matthew's music recitals, and Kodacolor prints of the two in the laps of department store Santas. Now established in place—a wife and children, a home, a good-paying job in a career for which he trained—and holding fast to the directive from Grant Redford to create a meaningful narrative from "the stuff of his life," John Okada purchased a big Remington Standard office typewriter and buckled down to work nights and weekends on the novel growing in his mind. The distance from Seattle provided the artistic freedom to draw from memory and reimagine the city of his birth on the page.

FRANK OKADA

He wrote probably most of it in Detroit . . . He loved living in this town [Seattle]. He loved his friends . . . But he would never write that book, because when I was in Detroit, he did mention a couple of times how he enjoyed going fishing with his friends on the weekends and things. So I think he felt that if he's going to write the book [he needed] to isolate himself, simply on a social level, because I think he enjoyed that camaraderie.[287]

At first Okada named his protagonist Hajime, after his friend Jim Akutsu, then switched it to Ichiro, possibly after Ichiro Morita, a Heart Mountain resister nicknamed "Itch" from Mountain View, California, with whom Akutsu had served time at McNeil.[288] The surname Yamada was in his family through his sister Arlene's marriage to accountant John Yamada. He gave the names of Ashida and Kumasaka to the two families that Ichiro's mother drags him to see on his first day home, and the story told by Jun at the Kumasaka house is in essence that of Fred Haita's death in Italy two weeks before the German surrender. Taro was the name of the Takemuras' son, with whom Okada played as a child.

Okada's geography of Seattle in the novel is precise. Ichiro steps off the bus at Second and Main in Pioneer Square, directly in front of the Furuya Building, where Okada's father once worked. He walks south past the clock tower of King Street Station, east on Jackson past the pool halls, turns right on Sixth Avenue, then goes four blocks south to Dearborn. There he opens the door to the Yamada grocery at Sixth and Dearborn, "just as he had done a thousand times when they had lived farther down the block."[289] The Yakima Hotel where Okada grew up indeed sat farther down that block, across Dearborn. The Yamada grocery is within sight of a hotel emblazoned with a floodlit sign for "444 Rooms"[290]—the same sign that was painted on the Nishimuras' Puget Sound Hotel at Sixth and Dearborn, the only hotel in Chinatown with that many rooms. A Japanese-owned storefront grocery did exist on the northwest corner of Sixth and Dearborn; it was, as Ichiro calculates it, fourteen blocks from there to the actual Wonder Bread factory at Nineteenth and Jackson to which "Mama walks." The bakery is thirteen and a half blocks uphill from the grocery, and another half block to Washington School, Ichiro's old grade school, which in reality Roy Okada attended: "Easily an hour to make the trip up and back" on foot.[291] The "neighborhood Safeway" to which Kenji's father walks to buy a roasting chicken was located on the corner of 8th and Jackson.[292]

With her husband typing at all hours, Dorothy took care not to ask for help around the house or with the children. At times Okada could exhibit flashes of temper. Once, in frustration, he struck a sink and cracked it. That cost him $60. When Dorothy and Matthew quarreled over him not practicing his music, Okada grabbed the violin and threatened to bust it up, but Dorothy intervened. "Well, the violin is about $600," she recalled.[293] Dorothy left her husband alone when he was writing, and never asked him what he was writing about. She kept busy with the children, until one day as she watched them splash in the backyard wading pool, his voice called down from his study.

DOROTHY OKADA

He said, "Ohhh! I finished!" I remember that very well. "Ohhh! I finished!" That's all he said.[294]

By mid- to late 1955, Okada had a 280-page manuscript. He also had a start on a second novel. But he had no literary agent, so he personally queried a half-dozen publishers or more. One kept the manuscript for half a year, and Dorothy said her annoyed husband "used to wonder, 'gee, what happened,' but it eventually came back with a rejection letter."[295] Some objected that the language was too strong, and Dorothy agreed: "Why, this is [1955], and if I said 'damn,' it would have been an awful shocking thing."[296] Facing rejection in the US, Okada tried a different approach. He wrote to a publisher in Japan, the Charles E. Tuttle Company, whose home office was in Rutland, Vermont, and whose editor-in-chief was Meredith Weatherby.

February 14, 1956

Dear Mr. Weatherby:

I recently submitted several chapters of my novel to your home office, inquiring at the same time as to the possibilities of having it published in Japan and Mr. Charles V. S. Borst suggested that I communicate with you. I enclose a copy of his letter.

While I am primarily interested in finding a market for my work in the United States, I feel that the subject matter with which I naturally concern myself would be of interest to the Japanese. This is my first novel and I am now at work on a second which will have for its protagonist an immigrant Issei rather than a Nisei. When completed, I hope that it will to some degree faithfully describe the experiences of the immigrant Japanese in the United States. This is a story which has never been told in fiction and only in fiction can the hopes and fears and joys and sorrows of people be adequately recorded. I feel an urgency to write of the Japanese in the United States for the Issei are rapidly vanishing and I should regret it if their chapter in American history should die with them. Providing my efforts are unsuccessful, I pray equally fervently that there is another like myself who is creating a similar work which will find its way into publication.

The novel, of which I send you a few pages, deals with Hajime, a Nisei who has gone to prison for having refused the draft and faces the problem of finding his way back into the American stream of life. His error, his act of treason if we might call it such, can never be fully rectified. The reasons for his refusal are many and varied. There is the bitterness of the evacuation, the unrelenting pressure of his fanatically pro-Japanese mother, the faith in his country which has been shattered and the ugliness of the knowledge of a prejudice hateful and mighty enough to uproot a thousand seemingly American homes. There is no final answer, of course. There never is for treason. Yet, America is the only home that he knows and there is some comfort in the thought that his own mistake was no more detestable than the mistake of the nation which doubted him in the moment of crisis.

He returns from prison to a home which has not changed in spite of the four years of global warfare. His mother is still the super patriot of Japan. But, where in the past the son was content to be molded by the mother, there is now a struggle of basic beliefs. Hajime realizes that his mother's views are a dream which she has nourished throughout the years of struggle in America into a sort of unreasoning madness. The mother, more and more alone in her fight to keep her sons for the glory of Japan, chooses suicide as an admittance of her defeat. There is also a second death, that of quiet, unobtrusive Take, a combat veteran whose stump of a leg is being gnawed away by an incurable gangrenous condition. While he lives, however, he impresses upon Hajime with the fact that having risked one's life for his country does not necessarily make him less oriental or less subject to discriminatory acts. Then there is Freddie, another No-No Boy who lashes back at the big world which persecuted him for being Japanese and the little world which shuns him for being a Japanese who did not fight in the army. There is no worthwhile end to his method that Hajime sees. The girl in the book is Emi who waits for a husband who chooses to remain with the army in Europe because shame over a brother who chose repatriation makes it impossible for him to face former friends. She helps Hajime as only a woman can, with love and tenderness and a fierce stubbornness that refuses to let Hajime yield to his doubts.

There are others, of course, who point up different aspects of the big problem of interracial existence. The conclusion, though indefinite, is unavoidable. Hajime chooses to continue his life in America. There is hope still of a good life notwithstanding the mistake that he has made. He sees that in many ways he has been a victim of circumstances. He sees also that America is a country which has made mistakes and will make more but, at the same time, it is a country which is striving constantly to rectify the conditions which breed those mistakes.

The novel, completed now, comprises some 280 pages. Should you feel that you would like to consider it in its entirety, I shall be glad to send it on to you. Or, in the event that you do not feel that it fits in with your own publishing program, I would appreciate your advising me as to the *marketability of this type of material in Japan. Any criticisms and suggestions which you have to offer will be gratefully and thoughtfully received.*

Very truly yours,
John Okada[297]

Charles Egbert Tuttle Jr. served in the Occupation, as did Okada, and not unlike the captain in Okada's play, Tuttle's mission was to help revive the newspaper and publishing industry in postwar Japan.[298] Tuttle's father was an early collector and dealer of African American literature in Vermont. Author James Michener described Tuttle Jr. as "a canny Vermonter who had the foresight to expand the family business from its rare-book New England background to include a very active Tokyo publishing operation."[299] Tuttle was also known as "a prodigious drinker, and was not infrequently tossed out of, and off, bars and restaurants, golf courses and tennis courts, on six continents—unabashedly, and not without some élan."[300] Tuttle pitched his titles as "books to span the East and West," and several introduced the Japanese martial arts of *karate* and *aikido* to the West. His associate Meredith Weatherby was another Japanophile, a "discerning Texas-born editor-in-chief" who had translated the works of Yukio Mishima into English.[301]

Tuttle and Weatherby liked what they saw in Okada's sample chapters and, in the correspondence that followed, became sold on the idea of publishing the first-time novelist. After about two months, Okada got the news he'd been longing to hear.

May 1, 1956

Dear Mr. Tuttle:

Your decision to publish my book comes at a time when I have been experiencing considerable difficulty prodding my second novel along its way. A full day's work, a precious hour or two with the children and a moment of relaxation with the newspaper leaves little time or energy for writing, but the gratifying news your letter brings means a great deal more to me than I can adequately express. While digesting the import of your words, I've sat out the urge to turn cartwheels, to shout the news to the world and to dash off a letter of resignation to the library where I am employed. I will, of course, do none of these things. There is too much to think about and, for the moment, I feel simply a need to thank all the people who have encouraged and made it possible for me to stick to my writing.

The terms which you describe are thoroughly acceptable to me. I shall be very happy to sign the contract. The only question in my mind is whether or not you plan to publish the book in both Japanese and English. It doesn't really matter except that my father could not appreciate it in English and it won't mean a great deal to me in Japanese.

Thank you, Mr. Tuttle.

Sincerely,
John Okada[302]

Okada typed his reply on the thin tissue paper of a US aerogram, a prestamped air letter that was folded and sealed to make for an inexpensive means of writing overseas in the midcentury. Tuttle made a photostat copy of it, and in the margin below he scrawled a note: "contract with option next book," a standard clause in book contracts. Okada's joy was not just for his first novel; he was thrilled at the interest in publishing his second. Within four months of his query letter, Okada and Tuttle struck a preliminary agreement on June 16, but it came with one condition.

DOROTHY OKADA

When he submitted it, I think it was minus two chapters. He ended there. Then they said [it] didn't sound comfortable, something like that, and [the publisher] asked him [to] give it a sort of a finishing feeling.[303]

As directed, Okada worked to bring his story's narrative to a more satisfying conclusion. He did not quit the library, as he might have liked; in fact, he was promoted to senior technical reference librarian in the Technology Department. His new duties included editing the *News Bulletin,* the quarterly newsletter of the Detroit Public Library Staff Association,[304] where he learned the skill of "assigning reporters to cover various departments and affairs, writing and rewriting copy, layout, editing, defining art work, reading proofs, and following a copy through reproduction."[305] Then, in September 1956, Okada was offered the chance for a new career in the burgeoning aerospace industry.

In Detroit, the Chrysler company wasn't just making cars. Engineers at Chrysler Missile Operations in suburban Sterling Township were busy developing the Redstone, America's first large, short-range ballistic missile—the first to carry a live nuclear warhead, the missile later used in high-altitude nuclear tests over the Pacific, and the precursor to the Mercury-Redstone Launch Vehicle that thrust the first American astronauts into space. John Okada was hired to write about development of this top-secret weapons program. As technical writer-editor, he was given a security clearance to examine designs on the board, observe engineering tests, and supervise five writers in compiling quarterly progress reports.[306] The job paid $6,600 a year, thirteen percent more than he was getting from the Detroit library. Mary Klanian followed him to Chrysler Missile, and the two again shared driving duties for the twenty-mile commute to the plant east of Detroit.

At home, Okada finished writing what would become chapters 10 and 11 of his novel, and on November 20, 1956, he signed a final contract for publication of a novel to be called *No-No Boy,* with an advance of ¥54,000, or $150.[307] Tuttle copyrighted the book in Japan but not in the United States, as most countries observed a Japanese copyright.[308] At a Detroit photography studio, Okada sat for a portrait for Tuttle to send out with the press release and review copies.[309] Okada was being treated like a real author. He kept Doris Mitchell up-to-date on everything but his book's provocative title and topic. In March 1957, the Seattle library staff newsletter reported, "OLD FRIENDS: John Okada—ex-Business Department—has written a book which is now in the hands of the printer. He is not sure yet of the publication date. Judging by the letters he has sent to Miss Mitchell the book will be well-written. The plot and subject matter has not yet been disclosed."[310]

With *No-No Boy* in production in Japan, Okada tried to focus on his novel on the Issei, but he was growing restless with the demands of his new job at Chrysler Missile. He reportedly complained to Doris Mitchell

In Detroit, Okada sat for an author's portrait, which he sent to Charles Tuttle for distribution to the press with review copies of *No-No Boy*. (*Roy Okada*)

that "the work was long hours, no growth and unrewarding . . . he had no time to write his new book and he felt Dorothy and the children were unhappy."[311] In April or May 1957, after only about seven months at Chrysler, Okada updated his resume and sent it out with a personal statement:

> At age 33, I am a married man who feels that he is uncommonly devoted to his wife and unusually fortunate in having two wonderful children, a son approaching five and a daughter who recently touched six. Normal feelings for a normal husband and father, one might say, but I choose to think that my family is quite special. Perhaps, I have been endowed with a larger capacity for normalcy than most people.
>
> Next to my family, and of somewhat lesser importance, is my personal writing. Reduced to an avocation, though a disciplined one, my writing finally seems to be making headway. A novel completed a year ago is scheduled for distribution this coming June or July. A second is in the works and progressing sporadically.

My health is good (two days lost because of illness in the past five years); I make an effort to be consistently punctual (both a four and a nine-inch snowfall combined with a 16-mile drive proved somewhat time consuming this past winter, however); and I do not mind working under pressure or digging my way out from under a mountain of material (no objections to overtime, homework, or disrupted vacation plans).

I enjoy writing in spite of the attendant labor pains whether the effort is being expended towards the composition of a letter or the construction of a technical report or operating manual. More creative forms of writing such as ads, brochures, scripts, and articles also interest me. While I cannot boast of proven skills in the latter media, I feel adequately equipped with intelligence and imagination to handle such assignments and, certainly, more than adequately endowed in the way of willingness and enthusiasm.

My present position as an editor-technical writer is one which I do not relish leaving. I am, moreover, under no compulsion to leave. I feel, however, that because of the advanced nature of the research and development project in which I find myself, my work will necessarily become increasingly less demanding and more routine. The time has come, obviously, when I would be wise to find another position which will permit me to work and learn and continue to grow.[312]

Even as he sought a better job, copies of Okada's novel were being printed by Kenkyusha in Tokyo: 1,500 in hardcover, with 1,500 softcover copies for sale only in Japan.[313] Tuttle "reversed the usual sequence of publishing" by printing his books in Japan for distribution in the United States.[314] The edition notice establishes the date of publication as May 1957, and the flyleaf on review copies sent from Tuttle's Tokyo office promised "a dynamic first novel" that held "an explosive, revealing story." When the author held an advance copy in his hands, he was struck by two things: the anguish of the character in the jacket art by M. Kuwata, and the dramatic typography designed by Weatherby. Kuwata was a prolific illustrator who provided dust jackets for Kodansha and other publishing houses in Japan, and his cover for No-No Boy depicted red strands of barbed wire crossing in an X over a sketch of a mop-haired Ichiro pressing his clenched fists into his face. Weatherby had an eye for fine art, and behind the title on the title page he introduced a single, half-tone "NO" in big block letters. On the half-title pages he placed a giant exclamation point behind the title, and he repeated the words "No! No! No! No!" as a graphic element around each chapter number, with an emphatic "No! No!" next to each page number. Okada was ecstatic with the book design by his Texas-born editor, and after a full year of collaboration felt comfortable enough to call him by a nickname.

7 May 1957

Dear Tex,

What can I say except that it is the most beautiful book that I have ever seen. It arrived yesterday and I would have written rapturously about the book right then and there had it not been for an unexpected guest. Dorothy fully expected me to take it to bed with me.

Emotions aside, the physical features are thoroughly gratifying. The paper, the typography, and the general makeup of the book (particularly the effective title and preliminary title pages) are all more than I expected. Were you to ask me just what it was that I had expected, I really couldn't say. It seems to me that I worried in a similar vein when the children were about to be born. I worried lest they be born without the proper number of arms or legs, that they might be born without life, that they might be denied their full mental capacity. They were both beautiful babies, perfect in every respect, and, now, I feel that a third, equally perfect, has joined them.

About the cover. I can sit for hours just looking at it. I only hope the book says as well what the cover says to me without words. I am sure it must be you to whom I am greatly indebted for the conception of a design which plucks the heart of the book and displays it for all to see and feel. Even if the book should not sell, I am sure the cover will. And, certainly, Mr. Kuwata who rendered the artwork has my undying respect and thanks. There is so much I want to say, to shout, even to scream out, but words seem not to suffice at the moment. Let me just say that Dorothy has heaped praise ungrudgingly as regards the cover and the dynamic use of black and red. The very same Dorothy, I might add, who shows little patience with my

rooster-ish delight over seeing and touching the book. To her, it is a project
already filed under 'Finished'; a thing to be sensibly accepted as done so
that I might devote my energies seriously to another, more important under-
taking. —book number two which feels at the moment like a bigger mouth-
ful than I can adequately chew.

She is right, of course. It is time that I went back into serious and disci-
plined concentration. For a while, however, she will have to put up with
my childishness. As one gets older, Christmas doesn't come around quite
so frequently.

Gratefully,
John[315]

John Okada's enthusiasm for *No-No Boy* was shared by Charles Tuttle, who felt it "seemed to cry out for special treatment." As a small publisher he had little money for advertising, but his marketing plan included sending "review copies very generously and to those places that we thought would take some notice," and his sales representative in Los Altos, California, reached out to the "American Japanese" community as well as to bookstores. Tuttle submitted *No-No Boy* to a competition for best book on race relations sponsored by Knopf publishing in New York, without success.[316]

Four early notices appeared in Japan's English-language press in May and June, and they were mixed. While the *Japan Times* felt this "first serious attempt at writing a novel by an American citizen of Japanese ancestry" could not be "classed side by side with the best in literature," it did presage "a bright, vast future in Nisei literary annals."[317] The *Yomiuri Japan News* looked patronizingly upon its "Japanese-American cousins" as a "'lost generation' looking for an identity," and assessed the work as "interesting" but "not a great book."[318]

With the shipment of books via ocean cargo requiring several weeks to cross the Pacific, *Publishers Weekly* announced US publication as "during the last week in June,"[319] and North American reviews did not appear until late summer and early fall. Okada prized his favorable notice in the prestigious *Saturday Review*, whose Earl Miner owned up to the tragedy that befell the "Americans of Japanese descent whom we herded into concentration camps" and who grasped Okada's goal of showing how America was "truly both the hero and the villain of the piece."[320] And where the JACL's Bill Hosokawa might have been expected to pan the book for its draft-resister protagonist, he praised it. Hosokawa was an opinion leader through his weekly "From the Frying Pan" column in the JACL's house organ, the *Pacific Citizen*, and he wrote, "The people who walk and talk and live through the novel are completely genuine." He commended Okada as "a writer of considerable promise" and concluded, "Perhaps here at last is the man who will write the Great Nisei Novel which so many have aspired to but none has accomplished."[321]

Okada dedicated the novel "To my wife Dorothy," and sent copies to each of his siblings back in Seattle. The copy for Roy was inscribed, "Fondly." The inscription for his neighbors on Belden Avenue was more expansive: "To Mr. and Mrs. Stickels / To a friendship which has given all of us much comfort and happiness, John Okada."

BETSY STICKELS PERRY

My mother treasured the book. He said he was almost embarrassed to have her read it because some of the language might offend her. She told him there was no need to worry.[322]

Dorothy said John himself never cursed much in person, but she was among many who were uncomfortable with the cuss words in his book, which jump at the reader from the very first pages. She understood the salty language was necessary, however, and never said anything to him about it: "It's all finished, and he's not going to change it."[323] The profanity may have framed the book's reception as much as its touchy subject. As reported by Girst, "when the book was published, [John's] father snatched it away from his younger sister Connie telling her not to read 'that kind of stuff!'"[324]

FRANK OKADA

When the book came out his generation were just starting to estab-lish themselves, and I guess we couldn't picture someone who went to jail as being heroic in nature, even thou~

to jail because of a matter of principl~

~~respect for those people who refused t~~

~~self wanted to go.~~

When I read it, I knew that many in the com~

the military in the US forces would not be very s~

can't see them really accepting the protagonist as bei~

tive of the community at that time. But I think my family's

that he could publish a book. At least for me personally, it's

a role model. I'm grateful for that.[325]

Roy Kumasaka's reaction upon learning of his friend's novel was,
didn't know he could write!" Kumasaka immediately recognized Jim
Akutsu as a model for the character of Ichiro, but was convinced there
were others.[326] Akutsu did not recall receiving a copy, but when he saw
one he recognized many elements—starting with Kenji, the veteran who
came back with only one leg, who he said was based on two mutual
friends: Kenji Ota, a platoon sergeant whose arm was shattered by
machine-gun fire the day before the 442nd rescued the Lost Battalion,
and who walked with a limp;[327] and a neighbor, Shiro Yamaguchi, who
stepped on a land mine in Italy and lost a leg to gangrene.[328]

JIM AKUTSU

Shiro was living across the street before evacuation. He played football, not in high school but in sandlot games. He used to play end,
and I could always count on him to take out the tackle. And he was
very good and we were real good friends. He was in the 442 and he
came back, but they had to cut his leg off, a part at a time. He used
to go down to Portland to the Veterans Hospital.

Wah Mee is the Club Oriental in the book. The billiard part in the
book that I used to go to was this pool hall, Main Pool Hall.[329]

Akutsu identified the roadhouse where Ichiro and Emi danced as the
Spanish Castle Ballroom, which he had helped desegregate. But Akutsu

ter and sure of himself, and he was not pleased with the charac-
n of Ichiro as someone who tormented himself with doubt.

A AKUTSU

,t no time did I tell, give authority or release to John to write about
me. He did it quietly because he used to follow me around, just follow me around. . . . But he writes of me not as a strong person but
as a weakling that I made a mistake of not going into the army. But
that I don't like . . . Yeah, so I am told that I am the "No-No Boy," Ichiro,
okay, so be it.[330]

Frank Yamasaki also took offense at the portrayal of draft resisters, and
turned on the author. Contrary to his earlier, more companionable view
of Okada, he later characterized him as "a bitter, unattractive little guy
lacking in self-esteem," and claimed that Robert Okada called him to
apologize on behalf of the family.[331] Dorothy was unaware of any reaction
from local Nisei in Detroit, and said John had no visible reaction to critical
letters.

DOROTHY OKADA

All the mail that came was from white people. One of them said,
"Well, what are you trying to do? Are you trying to become a John
Steinbeck?" . . . Somebody else wrote to say the words were too
vulgar or something, y'know.[332]

Only one published interview with John Okada is known to exist, conducted by Bebe Horiuchi for the Detroit JACL newsletter and reprinted
by National JACL's *Pacific Citizen*:

At first glance modest and unassuming, Detroiter John Okada does not
appear to be the possessor of two master's degrees as well as being the
author of "No-No Boy," a dynamic and controversial first novel recently
published by Charles E. Tuttle, Co. . . . Writing chiefly on weekends and
evenings, John states that his novel is the result of "thirty years of living

and two years of hard work." ... He is now working on a new novel which deals with the hopes, feelings, and problems of the Issei.[333]

Horiuchi was a personnel interviewer for the Detroit Civil Service Bureau, with a trained eye for behavioral characteristics, and in meeting Okada she was struck by his demeanor.

BEBE HORIUCHI RESCHKE

I thought, "Wow, he doesn't look like an author." He was a quiet person, not too large. I thought he was decent. Honest. Maybe a little rigid, kind of stiff, because he didn't move his body around. Kind of nerdy.[334]

At Chrysler, the *Supervisors Digest* newsletter for Missile Operations ("The *Forward* Look in Missiles") featured technical writer-editor Okada as a published author, with a photo taken in his office showing his ID badge for the Jet Engine Plant pinned to his white shirt and his pens clipped inside a pocket protector.[335] Mary Klanian threw him a little party. When Doris Mitchell in Seattle finally learned the subject of the novel, she was surprised to discover that her former assistant harbored some "inner conflicts which were not generally revealed in his daily work."[336]

Despite decent reviews for a first novel and Tuttle's marketing plan, the book was not selling. Okada complained to his brother Roy, and Roy got the feeling "it was an open wound" for John. Charles Tuttle felt he had given the book "a little more effort than we normally do," and was "quite disappointed that the book did not find a wider audience," possibly because it was "ahead of its time."[337] He lamented that "the very people whom we thought would be enthusiastic about it, mainly the Japanese American community in the United States, were not only disinterested but actually rejected the book. I think the time simply was not ripe."[338]

Dorothy, however, knew John didn't write the book for money: "Even if it didn't sell, even if it was put on the shelf, I think he was satisfied because it came out."[339]

At Chrysler Missile Operations in Sterling Township, Okada had a security clearance to study engineering reports and write the history of the Redstone missile program. September 17, 1957. *(Yoshito Okada family)*

Southern California: "No objections to overtime, homework, or disrupted vacation plans"

For a year after his book's publication, Okada spent his time at Chrysler writing a history of the research and development program for the Redstone missile. In the fall of 1958 the resume that he had sent around earlier finally landed him a new job: the Hughes Aircraft Company, a leading defense contractor founded by Howard Hughes, offered him a position at its brand-new Ground Systems Group in Fullerton, thirty miles east of Los Angeles. Okada had complained that his job at Chrysler took too much time away from his writing, but if there was a choice to be made between his second novel and support of his family, Okada chose his family. So in August 1958, the family once again packed up the car and drove back across the country. At least on the West Coast he wouldn't be shoveling snow off his vehicle to get to work.

In Fullerton, they bought a suburban tract house of the kind springing up throughout the Golden State: a four-bedroom, two-bath home at 530 West Baker Street with a big olive tree in the front yard. Each of the kids got a bedroom, and Okada took one as his study. He brought home professional magazines he shared with Matthew: *Printers' Ink*, a journal for advertisers, and defense industry periodicals like *Aviation Week*, *US Naval Institute Proceedings*, and one for which he would later write, *Armed Forces Management*.[340] The Russians had launched the Sputnik satellite the year that *No-No Boy* was published, and the Cold War was driving the space race and an arms race. At the Fullerton plant, nicknamed "Disneyland East,"[341] Okada required another security clearance to work with engineers on secret defense programs. As head of the writing services group, he supervised staff in preparing bids to capture lucrative government contracts for advanced electronics systems. To keep up in his new field, Okada attended night classes at Fullerton Junior College and Chapman College in computers, electronics, technical communications, and corporate public relations, and he took courses at Hughes on management principles and proposal writing.[342]

But in April 1961, after just two and a half years, John Okada left Hughes. Dorothy believed that he just decided to quit.[343] With a home in the suburbs and the children growing up, Okada may have felt secure enough to pursue his earlier dream of working as an ad man. He started in May with the firm of Compton Advertising as senior copywriter.[344] Compton was known for handling the big Proctor & Gamble account, and it's possible that the author of *No-No Boy* wrote ads pitching Gleem toothpaste, Comet cleanser, Crisco shortening, and Tide detergent. John Okada became a chain-smoking, 1960s Nisei "Mad Man."[345]

Unconstrained by working for Hughes, Okada took a parting shot at the industry he'd just left. President Eisenhower in 1961 warned against the growth of a military-industrial complex. Aerospace engineers were known for pushing performance and technology over considerations of cost,[346] and that competitive spirit extended to the extravagant packaging of defense bids costing hundreds of thousands of 1960s dollars. Okada personally found the practice "ridiculous," along with the industry's fondness for impenetrable acronyms.[347]

Around the time he left, Hughes was bidding on an advanced radar system for Japanese air defense called TAWCS, or Tactical Air Weapon Control System, with high-level briefings for the Japanese Air Force.[348] Okada published a satire for *Armed Forces Management* in December 1961 called "The High Cost of Proposals and Presentations," which he opened with "Mr. Blunt," an anxious supervisor eager to pamper a visiting general while overseeing pitches for such projects as MAD, for "Missile Advanced Defense," and JERK, for "Joint Equatorial Radar Kluge." Okada followed this caricature with a stinging essay directly addressed to his former colleagues: "To those in the Defense industry who have spent sleepless, pressure-filled nights, weekends, and holidays preparing ever bigger and fancier, but not necessarily better, proposal documents and presentations under impossible schedules, each word will probably irritate the ulcer further."[349]

MATTHEW OKADA

That got published. And it had some influence.[350] Mom said after the article came out the government issued some guidelines to defense companies about presenting their proposals with plain and simple bindings.[351]

Okada followed up in March 1962 with another satire for *Armed Forces Management,* "The Technocrats of Industry," in which he created the character of "Mr. S.V.," through whom he could poke fun at the exalted status afforded to aerospace engineers over others in the industry. This time, his byline appeared as "John Hillfield."[352] As observed by Girst, the name Okada roughly translates to English as "field of hills."[353] It was the second time in his life Okada disguised his authorship, either because of blowback to his first piece or perhaps to mask the thinly veiled bitterness he expresses over the industry's second-class treatment of technical writers like himself. Dorothea believed her father also used the pen name to fire off letters to the editor whenever he read something with which he disagreed.

Okada jumped from Compton Advertising in June 1962 to work as senior copywriter at West, Weir & Bartel, the thirty-third-largest shop in US advertising and one that produced ads for MGM movies as well as Squirt soft drinks and several brands of cigarettes.[354] In Seattle, his siblings were all advancing in their careers as well. Yoshitaka Robert designed magazine ads and commercial graphics; Roy managed a team at the Boeing Company testing systems for the Minuteman missile and B-52 bomber; Frank had emerged as an acclaimed painter and proponent of Northwest Abstract Expressionism; Arlene provided administrative support for National Park Service planners in Seattle; and Connie, like John, became a librarian, in her case the art librarian for the University of Washington. Their father retired from running the Pacific Hotel in 1962, and in 1964 word came that Mr. Collins, their "second father" at the hotels, had passed away at the age of eighty-two. After close to thirty years as their boarder, and with no next of kin, Yoshito arranged for William Arthur Collins to be buried adjacent to the Okada family plot at Evergreen Washelli Cemetery in Seattle.

By 1964, the drive from Fullerton to downtown LA felt longer, the kids were growing into adolescence, and Dorothy wanted a bigger backyard where she could keep chickens and plant fruit trees. With his income from advertising, the family moved that year to a larger house in South San Gabriel, then a semirural area. The new home at 8134 Celito Avenue was closer to work and offered nearly twice the square footage on a half-acre lot. "It was a little bit too much for us when we first bought it, but we tried hard," Dorothy said.[355] She grew peaches and kept rabbits, fifteen chickens for fresh eggs, a pair of turkeys, and a lamb. The lamb died one day when Dorothy went to Tijuana by herself and left John instructions on how to feed it, "and I guess he didn't do it right," she laughed.[356] Indoors she kept six cats and a dog, a brown German shepherd named Willie, and later a collie, Sandy, named after Dodgers pitcher Sandy Koufax, even though no one in the house was a great baseball fan. Dorothy later joked that John talked more to the dog than to her.

The 1940s-era house had only two bedrooms, which the parents gave to each of the kids, while Okada built a dividing wall in a big family area to create a TV room and a third, master bedroom for himself and Dorothy.[357] The living room was big enough for a grand piano, on which Dorothy played Beethoven's *Appassionata* and Dorothea could practice for her

After moving to Southern California, Okada sent his family in Seattle snapshots of Dorothy, Dorothea, and Matthew, like this one from a week's vacation in March 1959 to the Painted Desert and Grand Canyon in Arizona. *(Yoshito Okada family)*

lessons with influential teacher Robert Turner, while Matthew practiced in his room for his violin lessons with concertmaster Joachim Chassman, featured soloist on many film and TV scores.

DOROTHEA OKADA

The way my father treated my mother was very special, because he did not like animals, but he would build structures for them. He didn't like classical music, but he allowed her to take us to our lessons, and I haven't seen a lot of married men that would give that much to their wives, and he didn't do it with any kind of grudge.[358]

All the family space left no room for an office, so Okada improvi[ged]
a shack in the backyard next to a brick barbecue pit where he could get
away from the animals and the music and sneak in some time on his
work.

DOROTHEA OKADA

It was about the size of a trailer. It was pretty simple. It was just some
glass panels and then a door. It was glass; you could see through at
all angles—well, except on the back side it was concrete.[359]

MATTHEW OKADA

It just had a heater, a typewriter, and a lot of folders with his work,
his technical writing work. But it was kind of cool that he had an
office in the back that he had built, like a detached patio house in the
back. He ran some wires from the main house, to give him power for
the light and the heat.[360]

Matthew and Dorothea would get home from school around 3:30.
Their father would come home at 5:30, always carrying a briefcase full of
papers and looking relieved to be home.

MATTHEW OKADA

He was a very stressed-out individual. He always took his work
home with him. And he would go out to his little office in the back
to do his work. He'd be furiously typing all night doing his assignments, trying to meet his deadlines. And then he'd relax and watch
TV and get ready for the next day at work.[361]

The TV in the house was shared between teenaged Matthew, who on
nonhomework nights enjoyed 1960s spy shows like *The Man from
U.N.C.L.E.*, and Okada, who favored anthology series like *Kraft Suspense
Theater* or *Run for Your Life*, starring Ben Gazzara as a man with a terminal
illness determined to "squeeze 30 years of living into one, or two." When
U.N.C.L.E. moved from Friday nights to Mondays, Okada insisted on

In Fullerton, a friend took this picture around the time of John Okada's thirty-sixth birthday in February 1959—the last known photograph of the author to survive. (Yoshito Okada family)

watching *Gunsmoke* instead. He listened to the radio and enjoyed reading the newspaper comic strips, teasing Dorothy about not getting a lot of the jokes.[362] He collected hundreds of books, mostly classics of American and European literature, but he also "liked spy novels and James Bond, with a copy of Ian Fleming's *Moonraker* lying around with many more paperbacks in his study."[363]

When it came to politics, John was a Democrat. Dorothy was a Republican because she liked Ike, while John hated Eisenhower because he found him too mild and ineffective.[364] As for the war in Vietnam, he may have harbored doubts. One day he brought Matthew a flyer for a college antiwar protest and became upset when Matthew threw it in the trash without reading it. At the same time, he told Matthew that if he were drafted, it was his duty to go and serve.[365]

To his children, Okada was a quiet man who did not talk much, and like other Nisei fathers he did not burden his children with his camp stories. An exception came in 1965, when Okada gathered the family to watch an episode of *The Twentieth Century*, a CBS documentary series hosted by Walter Cronkite, titled "The Nisei: The Pride and the Shame." Okada told his children it was about "something he had lived through" and watched with intense interest. He had no discernible reaction to the appearance of JACL national executive Mike Masaoka, a figure revered by many Nisei for his silver tongue and reviled by others for his preaching of cooperation with the mass expulsion, opposition to test cases, and vilification of the draft resisters in camp.[366]

Okada remained a chain smoker of up to two packs a day, always Lucky Strikes, and not even the 1964 Surgeon General's report on the harm from smoking was enough to deter him. He told Matthew, "Until they can definitively say that smoking will take five years or ten years off your life, then I'm not gonna quit."[367] He no longer drank, but he enjoyed a good steak dinner and anything fried or salty.[368] Okada encouraged his children to always try to better themselves, no matter where they were in life. He also wanted to see them mix more with whites.

DOROTHEA OKADA

One thing our parents always told us was, "Don't think of yourself as Japanese, think of yourself as human beings." My first year in college I had invited some friends over for dinner and they were all Asians, and then many years later my mother told me my father was very disappointed that I had only brought Asian friends home. I think he was expecting more of a mixture.[369]

When it came time to teach about the birds and the bees, Dorothy took aside their daughter, and Okada spoke to their son.

MATTHEW OKADA

He told me once that if I really needed to know about that stuff, that he would take me to a cathouse in Las Vegas. At that time I wasn't really sure what he was talking about, or what Las Vegas cathouses were, [but] he never did that.[370]

In an interview, Dorothy freely disclosed that "because of the way I was brought up in Japan," she did not desire the same level of physical intimacy as her husband. She told him several times to go out with somebody else, "I won't get mad," but no one believes he ever did.[371]

The Issei Novel: "This is a story which has never been told in fiction"

Okada's complaint from 1957 that his second novel was "progressing sporadically" was prophetic. His brother Frank believed Okada wanted to take time away from writing to just "enjoy his family,"[372] but Okada told friends in Seattle that he had a plan.

HIROMI NISHIMURA

He said he was trying to write the Great American Novel. He said he's going to do it before he dies. He had it halfway written, not complete, but he started on it. And we were saying, "Oh, you're never going to finish that." [chuckles][373]

DOROTHY OKADA

He was wanting to write this book about the Isseis for so long, and he couldn't get started. And I used to nag about that, y'know, but then I thought I better quit.[374]

MATTHEW OKADA

He did start working on sketches for a second book. I remember seeing some notes that he had written on some yellow papers about a possible plot for a second book. Just some plot points of what the characters might do.[375]

In retirement, his father now had time to visit Okada at Celito Drive. The family didn't keep liquor in the house, so the old man brought his own bottle and winked at Dorothy as he poured himself a drink while the younger Okada pumped him for stories.

FRANK OKADA

I knew he was starting to gather information, and he was going to write about the first generation, my father's generation . . . Because about three years or two years before [John] passed away, he went to my father and asked him questions about the life, what was going on, and after the First World War, in the twenties, their experiences. He was gathering material for the book.[376]

To help her husband conduct research, Dorothy collected books and magazine articles about the Issei in America. From what she could see, the manuscript was, at best, unfinished.

DOROTHY OKADA

Well, it was a very, very rough draft. I think it was started out by Issei jumping overboard, and swimming, and then went to the shore, and then he walked and walked until he saw that, you know that soy sauce barrel? So that's the way you can identify that there was Japanese living, when you see the soy sauce. Have you ever seen that? He said they would always have that in the front with some kind of a plant or something in it. He said the Isseis would do that, they would just walk and walk and walk until they would come across to that. And then they would go in and ask for help. That's a true story. So he started out with that.[377]

Japanese immigrants to Seattle were often advised to look for the tallest building in town, Smith Tower, and walk in that direction to reach Seattle's Japanese community. Dorothy "read through the manuscript and found it to be 'very true,' especially remembering a scene where American customs inspectors would lift up Japanese women's kimonos to ascertain whether they were trying to enter the country while pregnant, as many of them did."[378] Dorothy believed her husband may have even had a trilogy in mind.

After the second book, he was gonna write a third book about the Sansei and then after the Sansei, he was gonna write about the Yonsei, and he said . . . oh, but the Yonseis are not Japanese anymore. Yonsei means fourth generation. It's no use writing about the Yonsei, they're all Americanized and there's no use. So he said he's going to stop it right there.[379]

In September 1965 Okada switched ad agencies again to take a job at Chalmers-Johnstone as chief copywriter. He served as account executive for General Film Corporation, a motion picture film processing house, and wrote copy to sell LPs for Dot Records, eight-track cartridge tape players for Lear Jet Industries, and health supplements for Jack LaLanne, the 1960s health and fitness guru. Okada also drew from his technical training to write aerospace and industrial ads for another defense contractor, Litton Industries, ads that possibly appeared in the same magazine that published his satires.[380]

Work on the Issei novel suffered a setback around 1966 when Okada "came home in a state of shock."[381] He had lost his job with Chalmers-Johnstone. Dorothy believed that the company went bankrupt, but at the same time she suggested he may have been forced out in a merger: "They said they don't want old people, they want young guys in the agency." Whatever the reason, Okada remained unemployed on and off for a year or more. Dorothy called it the toughest period of their marriage but, again, felt it was no use nagging: "If it's not there, it's not there."[382]

DOROTHEA OKADA

I don't think he ever really found the job that he wanted. He was never really satisfied, I think, with his jobs. I felt like he was never really doing what he wanted to do, and maybe that made him unhappy sometime and disappointed. And I think he experienced some prejudice too, [in] some of the jobs that he wanted and didn't get.[383]

To support his family, Okada fell back on his library experience. The head of the circulation department at UCLA's University Research

Library, James Cox, had been trying for nine months to find a deputy. On October 13, 1967, he sent an effusive two-page letter to all staff announcing that "a long search for the right person has led us to Mr. John Okada" as his chief assistant department head. Okada was given broad responsibility for budget, payroll, and personnel, as well as direct management for operation of the loan desk, the book stacks, and student billing services. Cox set up "an extensive orientation program" to bring Okada up to speed.[384]

Okada hoped UCLA would be a more stable employer. He was remembered by colleague Bill Osuga as a "clean desk" manager and "an unpretentious and amiable person,"[385] and Cox was preparing to recommend Okada for a raise. But Okada once again grew unhappy with his job. He complained to Dorothy that his conversations at work were about little more than what people watched on TV the night before.

MATTHEW OKADA

I think he was just completely bored with working in the library. He'd get defiance from students. He mentioned one argument with a student over late fees that he said was kind of tough and not a pleasant situation to be in.[386]

After just half a year, Okada left UCLA with a confessional letter that laid bare a soul in torment.

March 22, 1968
Mr. Robert Vosper
University Librarian

Dear Mr. Vosper:

In conversations with Jim Cox yesterday evening and with Miss Ackerman this afternoon, I informed them of my decision to resign at the close of April.
My decision to leave the library was made after long, constant and painful deliberation and a distressing failure entirely on my part to adjust to the pace, climate, attitude and style of library and campus life. In view of my brief

*stay here, the statement may smack of levity, but I assure you that I make
it with the utmost sincerity and an enormous sense of regret.*

*I cannot tell you exactly why I have come to this decision because, in
truth, I do not fully know myself what all the reasons are. I do know all
too desperately, however, that after five months of being a librarian, I still
find myself literally pacing the floor on evenings and weekends dogged by
a maddening sense of emptiness, of hanging hopelessly in limbo, of being
cut off from that world out there where things are changing, moving and
rushing forward. In the process, I have undergone changes which are obviously beginning to try the patience and affect the well being of my family.*

*I am sorry that things have not worked out and am genuinely embar-
rassed in view of the willing and gracious manner in which everyone has
accepted and assisted me. Jim Cox, in particular, has shown me every
possible consideration as supervisor, colleague, adviser and friend. I shall
always feel fortunate and grateful that what will quite likely be my final,
active participation in librarianship has meant a close and thoroughly
happy association with one who is as wholeheartedly and enthusiasti-
cally committed to the UCLA Library and the library profession in general as Jim.*

*I have no firm plans for the future other than to situate myself as rapidly
as possible in some area of writing outside of the advertising business. A small
consulting assignment and the promise of several possible freelance projects
will help me buy time beyond the first of May should I need it.*

*I shall always remain indebted to you for having been instrumental
in responding favorably and generously to my needs at a time when I was,
quite frankly, at as low a point psychologically as I ever hope to be. I trust
you will find it possible to view my failure to stay on with a like measure
of understanding and forgiveness.*

*Respectfully yours,
John Okada*[387]

Clearly, management was not for him. He did not mention it, but
underneath Okada's anguish may have been the frustration of wanting to

finish the Issei novel. He may also have missed the excitement of being part of the space race, as engineers at NASA were "rushing forward" to fulfill President Kennedy's pledge to put a man on the moon. In a letter to staff, Cox accepted the resignation "with a sense of very great regret," acknowledging that the hire had been "an experimental return" on Okada's part to library work. Cox added that Okada had "reached a difficult decision to pursue actively a writing career outside the field of professional librarianship" and wanted "to return to a career of writing in the business world."[388]

By this time Okada's novel was forgotten by most, but not by the JACL's Bill Hosokawa, who quoted a passage from *No-No Boy* as an epigraph to a chapter in his 1969 history *Nisei: The Quiet Americans*.[389]

Okada eventually found a home back in aerospace earning $19,000 a year as publications manager for a start-up in Pasadena. Analog Technology Corporation developed instruments for NASA's Apollo space program and the Surveyor "moon buggy" lunar rover. Its cofounder and president, Conrad Josias, fostered a creative environment. He played clarinet in the Pasadena Symphony and would later publish two novels.[390] Another published writer on staff was Angela Dunne, editor of 1965's *Mathematical Bafflers*. Okada took his son on a tour of the electronics labs and computers, and Matthew could see his father was pleased to be in a place where his talents were appreciated.

MATTHEW OKADA

One of the younger workers in the company went up to my Dad and asked him some questions about writing, about literature. So I guess some of the people there knew he was a writer and that he had some writing experience.[391]

Matthew did not believe his father was working regularly on his novel during this time, and that the furious typing he heard from the backyard hideaway was work from the office, a return to the kind of proposal packaging his father had parodied years before. Okada worked a lot at home at night, according to Milford Davis, an accountant at Analog and a self-professed "bean counter."

MILFORD DAVIS

He was a great guy, just sort of a tech writer who put the right things in order after he got the information. I was sorry for him that he had to work extra-long hours. One morning at 11 A.M. in June 1970, the president made four or five changes in reviewing a proposal and he asked John to stay on and rewrite it. It was going to take him 9 or 10 long hours and he would have to stay late. I felt sorry for him and took him to dinner at a lobster house in Pasadena. He talked about the 442 and how his brothers served in Italy. Then he said his son was graduating from high school that night. I was appalled, but he said, "My first responsibility is to get this proposal in." He was that devoted to his work.[392]

Okada had also missed Dorothea's high school graduation the year before, again working overtime. "Dad was working," she says. "I understood. He worked long hours."[393] Both children were studying music in college: Dorothea boarded at the University of Southern California, majoring in piano, and Matthew left for New York for advanced study in violin at the Eastman School of Music at the University of Rochester. With the kids out of the house, John talked of finally having time to finish the Issei novel and travel more with Dorothy. The two even talked of joining the Peace Corps once he retired. But the years of smoking and greasy foods had taken their toll. After feeling pains in his chest, in December 1970 Okada visited the doctor, who confirmed he was suffering from coronary heart disease.

DOROTHY OKADA

Sometimes I think that he had kind of an instinct that he was gonna die because he went to the doctor about a month before he passed away and he gets these angina pains. Chest pains. It blocked up his heart, and he would say things in the past tense like, "Didn't we have a nice marriage?"[394] He didn't say, "Aren't we having?" y'know.[395] I didn't know how to drive, and he would tell me, "Gee, I'm glad you're learning how to drive." And two or three days before he died he told me, "When I die, take out all the money and go on the trip to Europe."[396] . . . I think he knew that his time was near.[397]

The diagnosis finally made him quit smoking. One Saturday morning, John was helping Dorothy dig in her big garden when he announced he was going back inside to work on their tax return. After about five minutes, she followed him in.

DOROTHY OKADA

And when I came in, he was already dead. He was just lying flat on the floor. And the funny thing was, I did not get excited or anything. I just took it. I accepted that. Because I knew that someday he was gonna go anyway.[398]

In Dorothy's telling, all the clocks in the house stopped at the hour of his death, even his wristwatch. He was rushed to Garfield Hospital in Monterey Park, where he was pronounced dead just after noon on February 20, 1971. John Okada was just forty-seven years old. His death certificate incorrectly stated his birthdate as September 23, and gave the immediate cause of death as acute myocardial infarction due to coronary heart disease: a heart attack.[399] When he heard the news, Milford Davis shared the suspicion held by others, that overwork aggravated his condition—that Okada had more or less worked himself to death. Davis talked to Josias at Analog Technology and they successfully advocated for an award of $11,000 in state workers' compensation for Dorothy and the kids.[400]

DOROTHEA OKADA

When she was cleaning out his belongings she went through his wallet, and she had never gone through his wallet before and he had pictures of my brother and me but he didn't have pictures of her, and she was a little hurt by that.[401]

Okada's relatives flew down from Seattle two days later for a small memorial service at Rose Hills Mortuary in Whittier. Rev. Sherwood Eddy of Norwalk Methodist Church read the Twenty-Third Psalm. Okada was put in his army uniform for the open-casket ceremony. The next day, his remains were cremated, like those of the infant brother he never knew, and the family brought the urn back to Seattle for a local service on March 20 at Butterworth Funeral Home on Queen Anne Hill. In a black-bordered obituary in the Seattle library staff newsletter, his former colleagues remembered him as "a man of great ability, possessed of a subtle wit and a wry humor which endeared him to those who knew him well."[402]

In the novel, the character of Kenji breaks the tension of his imminent death by joking with his father, "I'll come back and haunt you if you stick me in Washelli with the rest of the Japs," but in the end that's just where the author was laid to rest, in the family plot in the Japanese American section of Evergreen Washelli Cemetery. The site adjoins Meridian Avenue N. across Interstate 5 from Northgate Mall. Okada's grave is marked by a bronze plate from the Department of Veterans Affairs set flush with the grass, engraved with the incorrect birthdate from his death certificate. Though he was raised a Buddhist and was never much of a churchgoer, the plate bears the emblem of the Latin cross, reflecting perhaps his widow's desire to remember him as a Christian. It was his father's idea for a military marker that identified Okada as a "SGT 8 RADIO SQ AAF WORLD WAR II." Dorothy didn't like it, and didn't make the trip to Seattle.[403]

What happened next was the final misfortune. To economize, Dorothy moved to an apartment in Pasadena and needed to clear out her husband's backyard hideaway. Seeing his unfinished work, and the research she'd collected for him, she felt overwhelmed. Part of her was also "mad he did not take me with him."[404]

DOROTHY OKADA

I threw everything that belonged to him . . . His father gave me all his childhood photos but I threw them all out . . . And I thought people would be asking, you know like you are, I thought of that too but I thought, well, I have him in my heart and I have him in my head, what more evidence would I need?[405]

All Dorothy kept was one photograph, plus her husband's book contract and army discharge record—"for practical use," she said. Just after the New Year of 1972, writers Frank Chin and Shawn Wong flew to Pasadena to interview the widow and ask to see the manuscript for his second novel.

WONG: How many pages had he written?

DOROTHY: Well, there was about like that . . . [indicates a space with thumb and index finger]

CHIN: Yeah, couple of hundred pages. You say you threw it out. Before you threw it out did you try to, I mean was anybody interested in . . . I mean, we would have been glad to collect it.

DOROTHY: I didn't try anything, I just threw it out.

CHIN: Ahh. Did you offer it to the university or anything?

DOROTHY: Well, I offered the material that we had collected about the Issei, y'know newspaper clippings and books, and books that the Isseis had written when they had landed in Hawaii. Oh, I had a . . . oh, must have been like that . . . [indicates]

CHIN: Hmm, pile of them.

OKADA: Um hum. And I wrote to UCLA, Dean of Japanese Language I think I wrote, and no answer, so when I had to move I just threw it out.

CHIN: How about, did you try Asian American Studies or, uh…

OKADA: Well, I didn't know there was such a thing.

CHIN: Ahh. [pause][406]

Her answer left unclear whether the Issei novel was included in the "newspaper clippings and books" that she offered to the "UCLA Dean of Japanese Language."[407] Two versions of the legend have grown around this moment. The first appears in the afterword of all editions of *No-No Boy* since the 1976 CARP reprint, where Frank Chin wrote: "After John died she offered all of John's manuscripts, notes and correspondence to the Japanese American Research Project at UCLA . . . but the Japanese American Research Project refused to so much as look at the Okada papers. These champions of Japanese American history encouraged Dorothy to destroy the papers. . . . I wanted to burn UCLA down."[408]

This story mutated in Chin's 2002 documentary novel on the Heart Mountain resisters, *Born in the USA,* in which he transformed Dorothy's letter to "the Dean of Japanese Language" into a telephone exchange between Dorothy and one of Mike Masaoka's brothers: "When Okada died in 1971, his wife called the UCLA Japanese American Research Project and offered them a manuscript of her husband's unfinished novel on the Issei generation and his papers. The JACL's Joe Grant Masaoka, running the UCLA program, told her to burn the papers, sight unseen. He thought Okada was a No-No boy."[409]

Both versions of the story are vivid, and the first has been repeated as fact for four decades. The first, however, is not borne out by the academic department Dorothy named in her interview, and the second scenario is impossible because Joe Grant Masaoka passed away in July 1970—seven months before John Okada's death and well before Dorothy ever wrote to UCLA.

FRANK OKADA

Frank Chin wrote something about how Dorothy tried to give this [material to UCLA]. Well, this outfit was designed just to take things written in Japanese. Frank doesn't say that. . . . At that point, it wasn't this Asian [American department].[410]

There is no evidence Okada kept a backup copy for safekeeping, or mailed a draft to a friend.

DOROTHEA OKADA

I understand why she did it. When my mother gets mad she just throws things out. Also, if no one was interested in it, she didn't want to keep it because it would remind her of my father and it would be easier for her to forget him without having all these reminders, physical things in front of you to constantly remind you that he's not there anymore. That's the part that I think she was trying to erase. And I know that sounds strange to people, and it did to me for a long time, but I do understand it now. Because that person is always inside of your head.[411]

One year after John's death, Frank Okada created a blue and red oil painting on canvas, titled it *Shiva II*, and donated it to the Seattle Public Library as a "Gift of the Artist in honor of his brother, John Okada."[412] Also in 1972, President Nixon signed Executive Order 11652 to downgrade and declassify most national security information more than thirty years old, formally lifting the veil of secrecy on MIS activities.[413] Had he lived a little longer, John Okada would have been free to write about his own wartime experience.

UNKNOWN WORKS BY JOHN OKADA

I Must Be Strong

JOHN OKADA

John Okada, then an eighteen-year-old student at the University of
Washington, authored the following poem right after he learned about
the bombing of Pearl Harbor. Published anonymously in the student
newspaper *University of Washington Daily* four days later, and reprinted
shortly thereafter in the mainstream daily *Seattle Star,* this poem reflects
an earnest consideration of the tensions that he knows will arise from
the fact that he is, as his introduction puts it, simultaneously "fully
American" and a "descendant from Japanese parents," and poignantly
meditates on the difficulties of any choice faced by someone of his
racialized identity. We know that Okada ultimately decided to join
the Military Intelligence Service, but this poem demonstrates, even at
such an early date, his awareness that Nisei might legitimately choose
dissent.

◆ — ◆ — ◆ — ◆

I AM A JAPANESE-AMERICAN DESCENDANT FROM JAPANESE
parents and sworn to the allegiance of the United States. In thought,

Published anonymously on December 11, 1941, in the *University of Washington Daily.*

background, history, culture, language, and religion I am fully American and proud to be so. I owe my all to this land of my birth, and I will gladly uphold the laws, traditions, and policies of this nation.

On the evening of December 7, 1941, after there was no doubt as to the significance of the dastardly move taken by the Japanese nation, I sat in my room and thought of the situation in which I, as well as others like me, had been placed by this unforeseen attack on the United States.

I attempted to put down my thoughts on paper for a home theme, but my mind was in such a state of confusion and entanglement that I was unable to produce an organized and well-unified paper. As a consequence I tried the same thing with poetry. The improvement was slight, but in poetry the reader can read a great deal between the lines. The result was the following poem, still unorganized and disunified, but most of my thoughts have been captured as they were that evening before I had little chance to discuss the matter with anyone.

I Must Be Strong

I know now for what war I was born.
Every child is born to see some struggle,
But this conflict is yet the worst.
For my dark features are those of the enemy,
And my heart is buried deep in occidental soil.
People will say things, and people will do things,
I know they will, and I must be strong.

I dread the thought of having to leave home each day,
The thought that I must continue as naught has happened,
For clouds will hang where the sun was bright.
Everyone will smile, but what of their thoughts
As they gaze on one whose eyes are so black?
People will say things, and people will do things,
I know they will, and I must be strong.

JOHN OKADA

When in Japan

The Captain Wasn't Too Sharp on Diplomacy

JOHN OKADA

After serving in the army during World War II and in the postwar occupation of Japan, John Okada returned to the University of Washington to study creative writing with help from the GI Bill. He found his first creative outlet in a playwriting class taught by Prof. George Milton Savage, for which he submitted a one-act play, "When in Japan." An advocate of staged production as part of his students' learning process, Savage then helped Okada to mount and direct a performance in the summer of 1946 at the Tryout Theatre, a workshop Savage organized to promote the development of new plays. Following the staging, the script was published in two parts in the fledgling all-English-language Japanese American newspaper *Northwest Times* on January 2 and 10, 1947, with the added subtitle "The Captain Wasn't Too Sharp on Diplomacy." In this work, Okada tested his comic voice as he considered the absurdity of the US occupying force trying to teach democratic ideals in a conquered Japan. The play satirizes a captain who leads a propagandistic communications office, a

---

Premiered June 6, 1946, at the Tryout Theatre; published on January 2 and 10, 1947, in the *Northwest Times*.

real-life counterpart of which—the Civilian Information and Educational Division—Okada may have encountered during his five-month stint in Japan as an interpreter.

◆　—　◆　—　◆　—　◆

(A COMEDY IN ONE ACT)

Characters

CPL. REEVES—a runner in the building.

SGT. BARR—secretary to captain. By no means fond of the old man, but humors him.

CAPTAIN HARRISON—past fifty, grey-haired, mustached, full around waist but not fat, likes to hear himself talk.

MR. KO—president of All New Japan Educational and Documentary Film and Cinema Corp., dignified, old, speaks perfect English.

MR. ICHI—scenario writer of corporation.

MR. NI—translator of corporation.

MR. SAN—artist.

MR. SHI—director.

All five men neatly dressed in suits which they have somehow managed to retain through the long years of war. The suits are of ancient vintage and fit too, brilliant cut, and pleasingly built.

Scene—An office in Tokyo occupied by the U.S. Army. The usual chairs, desks, coat rack, telephone, filing cabinet, maps, poster, and a huge sign on wall saying:

CAPTAIN HARRISON

EDUCATIONAL MOVIES SECTION

CIVILIAN INFORMATION AND EDUCATIONAL DIVISION
"OUR JOB IS TO TEACH DEMOCRACY"

SCENE 1

Office is empty except for Sgt. Barr who is industriously typing.
Cpl. Reeves walks in from right with a bulging folder under his arm.

CPL. – Mornin', Sgt., and how's the captain's boy today?

SGT. – *(looking up)* Don't say that. It's bad enough that I have to work for the old phoney.

CPL. – Hasn't he shown up yet?

SGT. – No, thank God.

CPL. – You talk as if you hated the boss.

SGT. – I wouldn't shed any tears if he choked on his damn whisky bottle some evening.

CPL. – Now, now, let's not be bitter. By the way, I'd better give you this stuff before I forget. *(reaches into folder, pulls out envelopes and sheets of paper and tosses them into In-box on desk)*

SGT. – Anything new?

CPL. – I don't know. I never read the stuff. I just deliver it.

SGT. – Give me a cigarette. *(takes envelopes and papers out of the box and starts to look through them)*

CPL. – Why don't you smoke your own sometimes?

SGT. – I never bring any to work. Can't stand the captain mooching off of me.

CPL. – I'm beginning to feel the same way about you. *(gives him cigarette)*

SGT. – *(picks out news-sheet and skims through it)* This damn rag's the same every day. Two lines of news and four pages of stuff on strikes. Why don't they bring some decent news sometimes?

CPL. – Maybe there's nothing else going on except strikes. If it gripes you, why read it?

SGT. – Somebody has to read it. The captain never does. Look at that, will you. *(points to stack of similar sheets on captain's desk)* Been piling up for months now. I don't know why the old man doesn't throw them away. *(tosses new sheet onto pile)*

CPL. – I hear he saves old beer bottles, too.

SGT. – I wouldn't put it past him, the old stinker.

CPL. – Lucky you, how does one go about getting a job with the old fellow?

SGT. – Go on, will you? Beat it.

CPL. – *(laughing)* O.K. O.K. *(heads for door, stops abruptly)* Oh, say, I noticed some jerks waiting out in the other room. They looked like movie people.

SGT. – Naturally, they're movie people. Can't you read? *(points to sign on wall as Cpl. walks out still laughing. Sgt. returns to his desk and resumes typing. Captain Harrison walks in looking quite unhappy. He takes off over-coat, cap and scarf and hangs them up. He walks to his desk and drops into chair.)*

SGT. – *(cheerfully)* Good morning, Captain.

CAPT. – *(gruffly)* Mornin'.

SGT. – Aren't you feeling well, sir?

CAPT. – Get on with your work, Sgt. Can't you see I'm thinking?

SGT. – *(noticeably crushed)* Yes, sir. *(Sgt. goes back to typing, deliberately keeping his eyes off the captain who sits moodily in chair. Captain looks up and studies Sgt. for a while.)*

CAPT. – What are you working on?

SGT. – Huh, I mean, yes, sir. That is, ah. I'm typing out this article on the history of the motion picture industry in Japan. In quadruplicate just like you told me, sir. *(proudly)* I've already completed forty-seven pages, sir.

CAPT. – History of motion picture industry, hunh? That's rather foolish, isn't it, Sgt., considering that we are no longer concerned with what is in the past? This is the New Japan that we are helping to create, and with capable men, sir . . . like myself at the helm to direct the policies of occupation. The future of Japan has never looked more brilliant.

SGT. – Yes, sir.

CAPT. – Tear up that rubbish, Sgt.

SGT. – But sir, I've already completed forty-seven pages in quadruplicate. I'll be finished in . . .

CAPT. – I said tear it up. Must I repeat myself?

SGT. – *(realizing argument is useless)* O.K.

CAPT. – What was that, Sgt.?

SGT. – Yes, sir. *(rips paper out of typewriter, crumples everything together and hurls it madly into waste basket)*

CAPT. – You're easily angered, aren't you? Well, that's a youngster for you. When you've passed the half century mark as I have, you'll understand a lot more. And you'll be more capable for it all. We officers of the occupation have been appointed to our special tasks because we are capable. Capable men, democratic men, that's what we are and that's what Japan needs today to guide it through its most vital period, the years during which it will learn the ways of democratic people. We have a job to do here, a big and important job; and educational movies will be one of the leading instruments in the process of democratizing Japan.

SGT. – Yes, sir.

CAPT. – Is that all you have to say about it?

SGT. – No, sir. I mean everything you say is right, absolutely right. I agree with you wholeheartedly, sir.

CAPT. – Fine. Fine. I was beginning to think you were no longer interested in our work.

SGT. – But I am, sir. I really am.

CAPT. – Good. You've been of wonderful help to me, Sgt. I have seriously been considering a promotion for you. How long have you been in grade?

SGT. – *(hopefully)* A long time, sir. Two whole years.

CAPT. – Hmmmmmm, two years, that's not too long. As you know, I've been a captain for five years. I've been turned down for a majority a dozen times, but I still do my work to the best of my ability. I am the most senior of all the senior captains in the whole of MacArthur's headquarters, but I'm not a bit ashamed. And why? Simply for the reason that I know why I have never been granted my rightful majority. Brass, that's what, big brass who are afraid to promote junior officers who have been proved themselves too capable. There's a lesson for you, Sgt. You mustn't ever be so capable that other men fear you. Be capable, but never too capable or you'll find yourself in my position some day.

SGT. – I'll remember, sir.

CAPT. – Excellent. Now to get down to business.

SGT. – Yes, sir.

CAPT. – What appointments do we have today?

SGT. – *(taking notebook out from his desk drawer)* The people from All New Japan Educational and Documentary Films and Cinema Corporation are bringing in a new script for approval this morning. They are now waiting in the other room. After lunch, the Grand Nippon Democracy School Film Co. is submitting a series of proposed slide films on Aesop's fables at two o'clock; the Red, White and Blue Motion Pictures Co. is bringing in Film No. 4 on the Daniel Boone series; and at four o'clock you are to address General MacArthur's Club of Free Japanese Laborers on the possibility of obtaining American films depicting labor activities in the United States. You were invited to a banquet this evening by the Glorious Daughters of Democratic Japan Club, but, in accordance with your policy not to attend any functions where food is offered, I declined the invitation.

CAPT. – Yes, yes, absolutely right, Sgt. Those people have hard enough a time trying to keep their own stomachs full. We cannot accept food from them. Did you say we had something this morning?

SGT. – Yes, the people from the All New Japan Educational and Document . . .

CAPT. – The AN . . . the AN . . . er, the ANJEDFCC, Sgt., the ANJED-FCC. No sense wasting time expounding the whole thing. So they're coming again this morning, huh? Wonder what brilliant idea they've cooked up this time. A big job trying to teach these people the meaning of democracy. I know that they try their hardest; but, somehow, they don't quite seem to grasp the main idea firmly enough. That's our task, to make them understand it, and it's going to be far from easy. But we'll do it if it takes a hundred years. We can do it and we will. Can't afford to leave a single stone unturned, no, by God, not one little pebble. We can't risk their starting another war. This one was bad enough. In the years to come our efforts will. . . .

SGT. – The ANJEDFCC people are waiting outside, sir.

CAPT. – What, uh, there you go interrupting me again. Now, I've forgotten what I was saying. *(stares thoughtfully at the ceiling, then turns back to Sgt.)* Any mail come in this morning?

SGT. – Yes, sir.

CAPT. – Did I have a letter from my wife?

SGT. – No, sir, no letter this morning.

CAPT. – Been a week since I last heard from her. Wonder what's wrong? Have you been writing to her for me like I told you to?

SGT. – Yes, sir, twice a week. Every Monday and Wednesday like you said.

CAPT. – Perhaps you aren't saying the right things. I'd better dictate one myself. Get your notebook out.

SGT. – Yes, sir, I'm ready.

CAPT. – Let's see now. *(stands up and starts to pace floor)* Dearest Dora, Having not heard from you for quite some time, I hardly know what to think, but I sincerely hope that you are not in poor health. If you were to . . . *(paces over to open door and sees men out there)* Sgt., don't I know those people out there?

SGT. – Yes, sir, they are from the ANJEDFCC.

CAPT. – Why doesn't someone let me know when people are waiting to see me? Hurry and bring them in here. You can finish the letter later. *(Sgt. rushes out and leads five men into the room. He gets chairs for them and lines them up in front of Captain's desk.)*

CAPT. – *(extending hand)* Good morning, Mr. Ko, I'm glad to see you again.

MR. KO – Good morning, Captain Harrison.

CAPT. – I'm terribly sorry I kept you waiting, but we're very busy you know.

MR. KO – I understand, Captain Harrison.

CAPT. – *(noticing other men standing around uncertainly)* Please sit down. Thoughtless of me to keep you standing, but we try not to be formal in this office. One big happy family, you know. We've all a big job to do and I'm anxious to help you people in every possible way. *(everyone sits down)* Now, what have we got this morning?

MR. KO – Before we start, Captain, I'd like to introduce you to these men.

CAPT. – Certainly, certainly. *(stands, and as he does, so do the others)*

MR. KO – This is Mr. Ichi, scenario writer of our company, the All New Japan Educational and Documentary Film and Cinema Corp.

CAPT. – Glad to have you, Mr. Ichi. *(Mr. Ichi beams and shakes hands)*

MR. KO – Mr. Ni, translator of our company, the All New Japan Educational and . . .

CAPT. – Yes, yes, Mr. Ko, the ANJJ . . . er, the ANJEDFCC. How are you, Mr. Ni?

MR. NI – Quite fine, I believe, Mr. Captain. *(they shake hands)*

MR. KO – And also of our company the All New Japan Educational and Documentary Film and Cinema Corp., Mr. San, the artist, and Mr. Shi, the director *(Capt. shakes hands with both men vigorously. He sits down and so do the men. They sit rigidly at attention, waiting for Capt. to speak.)*

CAPT. – I hope all you men speak English as fluently as Mr. Ko. Do you? *(all nod their heads affirmatively except Mr. Ichi who does not until he notices the others and imitates them)*

CAPT. – Wonderful. Wonderful. It always makes our work a great deal simpler when we all speak the same language. Ha, ha, ha.

MR. KO – Ha, ha, ha, very clever captain. *(everyone laughs but Mr. Ichi, who is again a little behind)*

CAPT. – Well, that's us Americans, always good natured. You have a new script don't you? *(Mr. Ichi continues to laugh loudly although everyone else has stopped. Mr. Ko nudges and glares at him. He stops laughing immediately.)*

CAPT. – *(giving Mr. Ichi a strange look)* Let's proceed with the business, please.

MR. KO. – Certainly, Captain Harrison.

CAPT. – Sgt., you will take notes on what is discussed here.

SGT. – Yes, sir. *(readies himself with pad and pencil. Mr. Ko mumbles to Mr. Ichi and Mr. Ni who both give him folded papers. Mr. Ko spreads them out and hands them to the captain.)*

MR. KO – This is the script of our new production entitled "Shojiki na Musuko," which, in English, is "The Honest Son." I think it's quite

good and I hope you will grant your approval so that we can start production right away.

CAPT. – *(glances at script on top, looks up sheepishly realizing that he cannot
read Japanese. Hurriedly switches the scripts around and skimming over
it says)* Your organization has been doing marvelous work, Mr. Ko, and
I have no doubts this new script will equal your previous standards.
(continues to look over script) Hmmmmm, hmmmm, hmmm. Sounds
pretty good. Ah, can you give me a general idea of the whole thing?

MR. KO. – Yes, absolutely. Mr. Ni, the translator, is best qualified to do
so, I believe. *(nods to Mr. Ni)*

MR. NI. – This story is about a farmer's son, a very honest boy. When he
is five years old, his father presents him with a brand new plow. It is
about the time of the year when the rice is almost ready for the harvest.
The son, being an ambitious lad—he is also very honest—takes his
little plow and plows up ten acres of rice while his father is away on
business for several days. Naturally, when the father returns home and
discovers the catastrophe that has befallen his rice field, he is very
angry. At this time, the son comes into the room where his father is
raving and confesses the whole thing, showing that he is most honest.
Naturally, the father is overwhelmed by his boy's honesty and, instead
of throwing him down the well, praises him. The son naturally grows
up to be a rich and respected man. He may some day even be president
of New Japan. *(Mr. Ni has finished. He grins modestly at the captain and
sits back proudly in his chair.)*

CAPT. – By God, that's a wonderful story. Has an important moral. *(leans
back in chair and remains thoughtful for a few seconds)* Strange, though,
are you sure it's an original? Seems to me I've heard that story before.

MR. KO. – To be perfectly honest, captain, the writer did pattern it after
one of your own country's stories, but only the basic idea has been
copied, I assure you. We felt that the most effective way to make democratic films was to get ideas from American stories.

CAPT. – Splendid, splendid, wish all the companies showed as much
initiative as you've shown, Mr. Ko. Was the story written by one of
your men?

MR. KO. – Yes, our writer Mr. Ichi wrote it. *(indicates Mr. Ichi)*

CAPT. – *(leaning over towards Mr. Ichi)* So you wrote this, did you? *(Mr. Ichi, as if frightened, nods negatively furiously. Mr. Ko whispers into his ear, and Mr. Ichi smiles and nods affirmatively.)*

CAPT. – *(still talking only to Mr. Ichi)* Well, Mr. Ichi, you've done a fine job, but it's not quite the sort of thing that is timely. This would make an excellent film for grade-school children, but considering the present economic situation of your country . . . *(Mr. Ichi looks thoroughly dumbfounded)*

MR. KO. – Er, pardon the interruption, Captain, but Mr. Ichi does not understand what you are saying.

CAPT. – Oh, I thought you all spoke English.

MR. KO. – We all do, in varying degrees, of course, but Mr. Ichi has not yet progressed beyond "good morning" and "good evening" as yet.

CAPT. – I see. *(to Mr. Ichi)* Good morning.

MR. ICHI – *(breaking into an enormous smile)* Good morning. Good evening.

CAPT. – Good evening. Hell, that is . . . Now what was I trying to tell you.

SGT. – You were speaking about timely subjects for films, sir.

CAPT. – Yes, yes, thank you, Sgt. Now, Mr. Ko, this script you've just submitted isn't bad at all, but under the present circumstances, I feel that the available film should be used for the production of timely pictures. Your country has suffered a great deal from the war, and the people should know about the existing conditions. In a democracy, nothing is kept from the people. There is no oppression of ideas or the deliberate suppression of information as has been the case in your country, unfortunately. Your main task always is to inform your people of the real, existing conditions—social, economic and political. You must give them topics which will make the people think and, more important, encourage them to do something to remedy the wrongs. Do you see what I mean?

MR. KO – *(as if inspired)* Yes, Captain, I do perfectly. I will produce a film on the terrible transportation system of my country. For five years now I have been unable to visit my ailing mother because the trains have been overcrowded.

CAPT. – We mustn't let personal feelings enter our decisions, Mr. Ko. You are right about the transportation system being poor, but I'm convinced that your most vital national problem is food. All these people starving, it's too cruel to even talk about it. You know, I never accept an invitation to dinner out here. Not that I mean to be rude but purely for the reason that I can't bear to eat your food when you haven't enough for yourselves. And where does this food come from? Why, from the farms of course. And farms mean agriculture. Your company should by all means produce a film on the agriculture of Japan. Nothing could be finer and more timely than that.

MR. KO – Yes, Captain, but for five long years now I have not seen my poor mother.

CAPT. – I sympathize with you, Mr. Ko, for I know just how you feel. I have not seen my dear wife, Dora, for six months and it has been two weeks since I last heard from her. Is that not so, Sgt.?

SGT. – Yes, sir, that's quite right.

MR. KO. – You are most understanding, Captain. However, I still feel quite strongly that transportation is as vital a problem as agriculture.

CAPT. – Now, now, Mr. Ko. I know what is best for you. I realize how deplorable a situation the transportation companies have allowed themselves to fall into, but how can people be concerned with traveling when their empty stomachs are gnawing for food? You must be both careful and sympathetic in your choice of subjects if you wish to make a success of your films in this new democracy that you are helping to build. Do I make myself clear?

MR. KO. – I cannot help but think of my poor ailing mother longing for a final meeting with her favorite son, but . . . yes, Captain, I understand.

CAPT. – I knew you would. Now, I'm not supposed to interfere with your activities. My capacity is that of an adviser; but, I think a great deal of your company and I want to help you as much as possible. I've spent twenty years in educational movies back home, and consequently, I can understand your difficulties better than anyone else. So, if you like, I'll make a few suggestions on how to make a movie on agriculture.

MR. KO. – Please do, Captain. We'd appreciate any suggestions which you have.

CAPT. – Good. Good. *(reaches into his drawer and pulls out a weighty volume)* This is a little thing I whipped up over the week-end on the agriculture of Japan. You may even be able to use it as it is. I think it's pretty good, myself. You just take that along with you. You should have some American newspapers, too. Gives you fresh ideas about how things are being done in America. *(notices pile of news-sheets on desk, grabs whole pile and hands it to Mr. Ko)* Here you are, just what the doctor ordered.

MR. KO. – Thank you, Captain. We will study these very thoroughly.

CAPT. – Fine. When can you have the script ready for this agriculture movie? *(Mr. Ko confers with the others. There is a great deal of nodding of heads, smiles, frowns and finally everyone beams in approval. Phone rings and everyone freezes in silence as Sgt. answers phone.)*

SGT. – Captain Harrison's office. Educational Movies Section. Civilian Information and Educational Division. Sgt. Barr speaking ... Who? ... Oh, yes ... just a moment, sir. I'll call him *(to Captain)* For you, sir.

CAPT. – Well, who is it?

SGT. – Col. Davis, sir.

CAPT. – I'm entirely capable of carrying on here, Sgt. Agriculture is the backbone of every nation. Your people are hungry and empty stomachs are never kind to new ideas. In a democracy everyone has plenty of food, no one is hungry, but nothing can be accomplished by merely talking about the problem. The people must be shown what's wrong with the present system and how it can be improved. That's where you come in. With a movie on the agriculture of your country, you can teach your people what democracy really means. Perhaps, all this may sound a bit vague to you as yet, but follow that *(holds up his volume)* and you won't have any trouble at all.

MR. KO – We will, Captain. We are prepared to do everything possible to show our people what democracy means. *(He looks to his associates for approval and they all nod vigorously except Mr. Ichi who has been prodded into doing so by Mr. Ni.)*

CAPT. – Fine, fine. You've got the right spirit, exactly. And one more thing. You cannot teach democracy without practicing it; no sir, you have to practice it also. See what I mean?

MR. KO – We do, captain. Even now we have been discussing a project which should show beyond a doubt that our organization is thoroughly of a democratic nature.

CAPT. – Oh, that sounds super. What do you have in mind?

MR. KO – We shall let you know as soon as our plans are complete.

CAPT. – I can hardly wait, Mr. Ko. I'm sure it'll be colossal. Give me just a little idea what it's all about, won't you?

MR. KO – (hesitantly) Well, Captain, we wanted to surprise you, but I'll ask the others. (He leans over and begins whispering with the others. Mr. Ichi pulls out a worn cigarette case, picks around in it and selects a fair-sized butt which he places in his mouth. Captain sees him and in alarm snatches butt out of Mr. Ichi's mouth.)

CAPT. – Oh, no, Mr. Ichi. Please let me offer you a cigarette. (He searches in his own pockets fruitlessly.) Sgt., do you have any cigarettes?

SGT. – I've given up cigarettes, sir. I've switched to a pipe. (pulls one out of shirt and displays it)

CAPT. – (noticeably flustered) God, I'm sure I had a pack somewhere. (resumes search. Cpl. Reeves walks in with a folder under arm.) Cpl., do you have any cigarettes?

CPL. – (surprised) Why, yes sir. (dumbfoundedly pulls out pack. Captain grabs whole thing and rushes back to his desk)

CAPT. – Here you are, gentlemen. Please help yourself. (All five men take cigarettes, mumbling thanks, and so does Capt. who pockets what's left. He takes a deep drag, looking up as he does.)

CAPT. – (as if just noticing Cpl. Reeves). Well, Cpl., if you have any business in here, get on with it.

CPL. – (stupefied) My cig . . . I mean . . . that is, sir, there's a lieutenant waiting outside to see you, sir.

CAPT. – Can't you see I'm in conference. Tell him to wait.

CPL. – She's not a him, sir. She's a her, a WAC lieutenant.

CAPT. – (eagerly) A WAC Lt.? Send her in. Excuse me, gentlemen. I'll only be a minute.

MR. KO – We'll be glad to wait outside for you, sir.

CAPT. – Good, good. Do that, will you? (*Men get up and leave the room. Capt. hastens to door to await Lt. brushing hand through his hair and patting mustache. Lt. struts in very businesslike.*)

LT. – Captain Harrison?

CAPT. – Yes, Lt., what can I do for you?

LT. – I'm Lt. Wink of the Women's Activities Section. (*shakes hands with Captain*)

CAPT. – Women's Activities Section?

LT. – Yes, Captain. The section has been formed only recently to meet the demands presented by the numerous women's organizations which have been springing up.

CAPT. – Ah, but certainly. You can do a world of good here.

LT. – That is the purpose, Captain, but, being new here, I shall require some assistance in getting started properly.

CAPT. – Of course, of course. I shall do everything I can do to aid you, Lt. Wink. (*takes seat out from under Sgt.*) We won't be needing you, Sgt. You can wait outside. (*Sgt. walks out looking malignantly at Capt.*) Please sit down, Lt. No reason why we shouldn't start right away. (*They take seats, Captain overdoing himself in making Lt. comfortable. Offers her a cigarette and lights it gallantly.*)

LT. – I really intended to speak to Major Brown first, but he was unable to see me till this afternoon.

CAPT. – (*with disgust*) Did you say Major Brown?

LT. – Yes, Major Brown of the newspaper section.

CAPT. – Well, I'm certainly glad you came here first.

LT. – (*surprised*) Why do you say that, Captain?

CAPT. – Forgive my saying so, Lt., but Major Brown is what we might justifiably term a . . . a . . . well, I just won't say what. You must have spoken to one of his own men. Apparently, you are not familiar with his reputation.

LT. – His reputation?

CAPT. – Yes, Lt., he's, well, he's . . .

LT. – (*in alarm*) Noooo.

CAPT. – Unfortunately, yes.

LT. – *(with relief)* Well, I am glad I came to you first.

CAPT. – I can be of more assistance to you than a dozen Major Browns, and I do not say that boastfully.

LT. – Oh, but to be sure.

CAPT. – And now, Lt., let's get down to work.

LT. – Of course, Captain.

CAPT. – Have you set any policies regarding your work yet?

LT. – No, as I've already said, I'm new here and I felt that I should study some of the other sections before I make any definite plans.

CAPT. – A very wise idea, Lt. I, myself, having been here since the birth of the occupation, can well understand your predicament. Teaching democracy is a strenuous task.

LT. – I understand, Captain.

CAPT. – I'm certain that the most effective way to insure the success of your new section is to adopt exactly the same methods which I utilized.

LT. – What would those be?

CAPT. – Movies, my dear Lt.

LT. – *(puzzled)* Did you say movies?

CAPT. – Yes, Lt., movies. Thru movies you not only tell them about democracy, but also show them how to act in a democratic manner.

LT. – That does sound possible.

CAPT. – It is and it always works. I've been in the movie business all my life and I should know. One must not only know what democracy means but he should know how to disseminate it in the most effective manner and that, I repeat, is through motion pictures.

LT. – But, won't that take a great deal of time?

CAPT. – Not at all, Lt. The army felt so too at first, but when I made them see how wrong they were, they sent me out here immediately to guide the motion picture industry in Japan. Naturally, like anyone else, I confess I had my difficulties, but not for long. In the few short months that I have been here, I've made the most wonderful progress with my children.

LT. – *(alarmed)* Children?

CAPT. – *(modestly)* Oh, that's just a term I use to refer to the people over here. Actually, they're grown men and women, but when I see them struggling to learn the meaning of democracy, I cannot help but feel as a teacher must toward her little pupils. And in the simple analogy, I find the inspiration and strength to carry on my work. My job—our job *(pointing to the sign on wall)* is to teach democracy. It's a huge task, Lt., but we can do it.

LT. – With your help, I'm sure we can.

CAPT. – And as proof of the things I say, you need only to glance at the movie people whom you just saw. Two months ago, they didn't know Buddhism from democracy, but now you couldn't possibly distinguish between them and some John Jones walking the streets back home.

LT. – Amazing, Captain, simply amazing.

CAPT. – We are merely doing our duty, Lt., not as members of any army, not as colonels, majors, or captains, but as citizens of all the democracy-loving nations of the world.

LT. – *(with excitement)* Oh, I must get some films immediately for my children too.

CAPT. – And you shall. I have some reels here that should fit right into your work. You can have them as soon as you wish. In the meantime, I will order some special films for you.

LT. – Thank you so much, Captain. You don't know how much hope you've give me already.

CAPT. – Think nothing of it my dear, er, Lt.

LT. – Oh, but I do.

CAPT. – Good of you to say so. Ha! ha! ha! *(pounds table and jumps up)* By God, why didn't I think of it before.

LT. – What, Captain?

CAPT. – Those men waiting out there. The men from the AN., ah, ANJ., er, ah, from a film company. They would make excellent films for you. Imagine this. Films with Japanese actors speaking their own language—I don't know how they ever learn it—moving around in their own surroundings and conforming to our ideas.

LT. – But can they do it?

CAPT. – Of course they can. You just tell them what you want and they'll handle it in exactly the same way you or I would. Their knowledge of American ways will astound you.

LT. – Oh, may I talk to them, Captain? I've already got some splendid ideas.

CAPT. – Certainly you may talk to them. *(goes over to door and calls out)* Sgt., call the men in here.

SGT. – *(from outside)* Yes, sir!

CAPT. – Now, Lt., if I may make a few suggestions as to the kind of films which will be most effective in your work . . .

LT. – But I have some wonderful ideas, Captain. Movies of women's clubs showing how they are organized, the manner in which the club constitutions are written up, the election of the club officers, and the procedure of discussions.

CAPT. – Yes, yes, true enough those are splendid ideas, Lt., but will they appeal to these people at the present time? These people are hungry, women as well as the men. Now, mind you, I'm only suggesting but I'm sure you could do much more good by emphasizing the food situation. Food means farms, and farms mean agriculture, and there you have the greatest stumbling block in our efforts. Agriculture in Japan today is the most vital problem—without a doubt.

LT. – Well-l-l-l

CAPT. – I knew you would agree. Now, here's what I propose.

SGT. – *(comes running in)* Captain, the men refuse to come in here.

CAPT. – Nonsense, bring them in here!

SGT. – But, Captain. I already told them that you . . .

CAPT. – Sgt., do as I say.

SGT. – *(helplessly)* Yes, sir. *(goes out)*

CAPT. – Fine boy the Sgt., but lately he's been inclined to shirk a little. Perhaps, a promotion will snap him out of it, eh, Lt.? All these people scrambling for rank can't understand it. At any rate, Lt., coming back to what we were discussing . . . er . . . ah . . . er . . . what were we talking about anyway, Lt.?

LT. – The organization of women's clubs, Captain.

CAPT. – Women's clubs?

LT. – Yes, Captain. Considering what you have said about the potency of educational films, I'm sure that I can use films most effectively to show the Japanese women how democratic clubs should be organized. First of all, they must be shown the method of electing their officers, how to write up their constitutions, and how the meetings should be conducted. They, like the men, have undergone terrible suffering during the war and . . .

CAPT. – Suffering. Now I remember. The people have suffered. Horribly, especially in regard to food, and food means farms and farms mean agriculture. Agriculture is most definitely our greatest problem.

LT. – I can see the importance of agriculture, Captain, but I'm concerned with the women.

CAPT. – Of course you are, and that is exactly why agriculture is of such vital importance. Women are human. They suffer from hunger too. These people whom I want you to meet have a splendid project in mind which will revolutionize the agricultural system of Japan.

LT. – But is it not more important that the women be shown how to organize properly before anything else is done?

CAPT. – Ahhh, it is natural for you to think so, my dear, but you are young yet. When you've had as much experience with people as I've had, you seldom make a mistake. Can't you see that?

LT. – Well-l-l-l

CAPT. – Fine. Now, the script I have in mind . . . er . . . that is . . . the script these gentlemen have in mind will expose the inadequacies of the feudal system of agriculture that has long been practiced in this country. Moreover, it will . . .

SGT. – *(tearing back into office)* Captain, they refuse to come in. They won't even listen to me.

CAPT. – Now, look here, Sgt., if you're incapable of carrying out a simple order, I'll find it necessary to take drastic steps.

SGT. – But, Captain, please sir. I tried my best to tell them . . .

CAPT. – Sgt., the Lt. is waiting. Bring the men in here.

SGT. – But sir, they're leaving.

CAPT. – (jumping up) Leaving?

SGT. – Yes sir, they're putting on their hats and coats and . . .

CAPT. – They can't do this. I'll be right back. (dashes out, heads for door, stops, looks back quickly at Lt.) Forgive me, Lt. (with Sgt. trailing behind him. Sound of voices heard in outer room. It builds up quickly to a roar. The captain's angry voice dominating the scene, the men speaking excitedly in Japanese. Lt. strains forward to hear what's being said. Suddenly, silence falls. Capt. comes back into room wiping brow with handkerchief. Mr. Ko and his four associates also file in and stand as if in formation.)

CAPT. – (attempting smile) Just a slight misunderstanding, Lt. Ha! ha! ha! Everything is fine now. (He stomps to his desk, sits down and looks grimly at men.) Gentlemen, this is Lt. Wink of the Women's Activities Section. She would like to talk with you. (men bow to Lt. She smiles at them, impressed.)

CAPT. – Sit down, gentlemen. (men remain standing) Gentlemen, I asked you to sit down. (nothing happens) (hardly able to control himself) What's wrong with you men today? We have work to do! (hollers) Now sit down. (points imperatively at chairs. Mr. Ichi, obviously frightened, steps forward hesitantly but one of the others grabs him and jerks him back into line.)

CAPT. – What's going on here? You men act as if you didn't want to work anymore.

(Mr. Ko confers excitedly with other men.)

CAPT. – What was that?

MR. KO – We are temporarily unable to do any more work.

CAPT. – Don't talk nonsense! There's nothing wrong with you men.

MR. KO – We are compelled to refuse work, Captain.

CAPT. – But why?

MR. KO – Captain, isn't all this perfectly natural?

CAPT. – Natural! What in hell are you talking about?

MR. KO – But everyone in America is doing it.

CAPT. – Doing it? Speak up man: make yourself clear.

MR. KO – Yes, Captain.

CAPT. – Well, go on. What is it?

MR. KO – *(looks at his associates and they all smile and nod excitedly)* The All New Japan Educational and Documentary Film and Cinema Corporation declared a state of strike. *(men nod and smile)*

CAPT. – STRIKE?

(men jump back in horror)

MR. KO – Yes you know what that means, don't you, Captain?

CAPT. – Of course, I know.

MR. KO – Then, may we be permitted to leave now?

CAPT. – Not until I get to the bottom of this damn affair. You can't strike, I tell you. I won't permit it.

MR. KO – But why, Captain? Is it not our right as democratic men?

CAPT. – Er...er...ah, certainly, certainly, but you must have a reason. What grounds can you possibly have for striking?

MR. KO – My poor mother whom I have not seen for five years simply because the transportation system...

CAPT. – Good God, my dear fellow. Must we go back to that?

MR. KO – My mother is ninety-one years old. For five long years she has been waiting to see her long absent son. She has not long to live and were it not for the people who run the trains in so inefficient a manner...

CAPT. – Mr. Ko. Gentlemen. Now, you all listen to me. I'm a reasonable man, wouldn't you say? Have I not done my best for you always?

MR. KO – Of course, Captain, but...

CAPT. – But what are you implying? Do you mean to stand there and tell me that you think me unreasonable?

MR. KO – Please, Captain. There is no necessity for us to lose our tempers over this matter.

CAPT. – Who's losing his temper? You can't talk to me like this. I'll ... I'll ... *(starts to count slowly to ten)*

MR. KO – I think we should leave, gentlemen. Good day, Captain.

CAPT. – Stop! I forbid you to leave! I forbid you to strike! You don't know what you're doing! Come back here! *(Mr. Ichi suddenly runs back, thrusts news-sheets into Captain's hands and departs hurriedly with a cheerful "good morning." Captain, waving paper in air, runs after them, hollering at the top of his voice.)* Wait a minute, you damn fools! Get back in here or I'll lose my temper! In the name of General MacArthur, I command you to come back. Gentlemen! Gentlemen!

LT. – Sgt., what is the number?

SGT. – Room 205, Lt., 205.

LT. – Thank you, Sgt. *(she goes out, snubbing Captain who is returning to the room. He drags himself wearily to his desk, sees Sgt. watching him, glares angrily at him and says)*

Get on with your work.

CURTAIN

What Can I Do?

JOHN OKADA

This short story and the four that follow were probably written initially
to fulfill an assignment for Prof. Grant H. Redford, the writing professor with whom John Okada worked most often and most closely.
"What Can I Do?" features a wounded, hungry Japanese American
vagrant named Jiro as he jumps off a moving freight train and attempts
to find food and work at a local café. In this story Okada demonstrates
his early mastery of a psychologically realistic style, as well as a noir
voice. "What Can I Do?" is the only published short story by Okada
to include a Japanese American character, and while issues of race and
identity are not on the surface of the narrative, they certainly can be
read in the subtext. Additionally, Jiro can be read as foreshadowing the
two main characters of *No-No Boy*. His emotional desperation anticipates that of Ichiro, and his physical disability prefigures Kenji's war
injury. The cause of Jiro's wound is unnamed, but it is entirely possible
that he is a Nisei veteran whose limp stems from a war injury. If he is a
veteran and has been riding the box cars for three years, then the setting
could be in the mid to late 1940s, when the story was published.

Published on March 25, 1947, in the *Northwest Times*.

◆ — ◆ — ◆ — ◆

THE CLICKING OF THE HEAVY WHEELS RESOUNDED THROUGH the freight car and mingled monotonously with the stench of straw and manure.

Jiro sat silently in the dark corner, waiting for the train to slow down some more. He listened patiently.

The steady clicking gradually subsided in pitch and rapidity till one could almost count them as they dully picked their way over the rails.

Jiro got up, feeling the soreness in his bones. Funny, how he could never get used to sleeping in box cars without getting sore all over. After all, he had been riding them for three years.

He picked up his old suitcase and felt the straps to see that they were secure. He hadn't much to lose but, still, it was all he had.

He walked over to the center of the car and slid the door open a little ways, shivering as the first gust of cold air struck him in the face.

He slowly eased his head out and glanced up and down the yard. No one was in sight. Suitcase in one hand, he leaped clear of the train to the ground, landing on his good right leg, then falling back on the bad one.

He limped across the yard, taking his time and trying to feel a little warmth in the weak rays of the dying autumn sun. He marvelled at his sensitivity to the cold when he thought how much like winter it really was.

He labored over the steep bank at the edge of the yard and stepped out on the broad dirt street which was the main drag from the looks of the town, if one could call it such. He certainly would have rode on to a larger place if he wasn't hungry.

The street was empty except for a car or two and a group of kids shooting marbles across the street from the drug store. They seemed to be having a good time in spite of the cold and the dirt in which they crawled on all fours.

Jiro walked towards the marble players thinking he might watch them for a while and maybe ask a few questions. They might know a place where a guy could get something to eat.

He approached them slowly, sensing the way his leg dragged, then changed his mind and cut diagonally across the street. He quickened his pace as best he could, hoping that the kids wouldn't see him. He kept his eyes straight ahead, pushing his bad leg along like it was something he couldn't decide whether to keep or throw away.

The marbles stopped, the yelling ceased. Jiro felt the anger rush wildly to his face. The kids were watching him, they always did. He wheeled around and caught their inquisitive stares.

"What the hell are you looking at?"

"Nuthin', mister. We're only shootin' megs."

"You lying devils. I ought to kill every damn one of you."

Jiro stumbled along awkwardly, as if in a fog, knowing that the anger would pass. He would not be regretful. He never was. He'd only feel the cold slab of stone that filled his chest constantly.

He reached the door of the small cafe which boasted home-cooked meals in sloppy white letters across the glass window. A neon sign overhanging the board sidewalk simply stated, "Jim's Cafe."

Jiro opened the squeaking door and walked to the farthest stool at the counter, hardly noticing that the place was empty.

The kitchen door swung open and a burly individual in a white apron came out.

"Evenin', mister," he said with practiced cheerfulness, "what'll you have?"

"I won't. I'm broke."

"Then, what the hell are you doin' in here?"

"I want to talk to Jim."

"Jim who?"

"The guy who runs this place. This is Jim's Cafe, isn't?"

"What are you? A wise guy?"

"No, I'm hungry."

"We don't give handouts to bums like you."

Jiro remained silent, as if pondering over some weighty problem, but his face revealed no shame or anger. Finally, he spoke.

"Couldn't you let me work it out?"

"What can you do?"

"Most anything around a restaurant. My dad used to run one."

"Maybe I could use you. What's your name?"

"Jiro. Jiro Nakamura."

"Where you from?"

"Nowhere and everywhere."

"Pretty smart, aren't you?"

"I can work. What else matters?"

"How come you're on the bum? Why ain'tcha working?"

"I've got a bad leg. Nobody wants a guy with a bad leg."

He said this with a tone of reluctance and finality.

"How bad is it?"

"I get around on it, if that's what you mean."

"You are kinda fresh, but I can use a dishwasher right now. My regular man's been on a binge. You couldn't be any worse'n that drunken heel."

"What'll you give me for my working?"

"Let's see. It's six o'clock now. Stick around till midnight and I'll decide."

"I guess that'll be all right."

"The crew down at the roundhouse knocks off at seven. You won't have anything to do till then, but when they come in here, it'll be busy as hell."

"O.K."

"There's some stew back in the kitchen. The bread's under the counter. You'd better eat before the crowd gets here."

The man slapped a few slices of bread on a plate and put it in front of Jiro.

"Go ahead and eat. If there's something you can't find, holler."

He walked along behind the counter to the far end where the cash register was and stared out of the window.

Jiro watched him for a minute then slid off his stool and moved into the kitchen. He threw his hat and suitcase in the corner. He found the stew in a chipped enamel pot on the stove and dipped himself a large plateful of it. He walked out to the counter again and seated himself on the same stool. The man was watching him.

He said, "You limp pretty bad."

Jiro ate without answering.

"You limp pretty bad, don'tcha?"

Jiro crushed the bread between his fingers brutally and let it fall into the steaming stew.

"How'dya get it banged up?"

"I don't talk about it," he replied, forcing the words out.

"You're touchy about it, ain't you?" the man said, as if having made a wonderful discovery.

"What if I am? Now, shut up." The last was hollered in almost a pleading tone.

"Sure," the man said, and turned around to look through the window once more.

Jiro ate slowly, crossing his right leg over the bad left as if trying to hide it. He didn't look up, afraid that the man might be watching him again. Finishing the last slice of bread, he wanted more. He started to get off the stool, but he didn't. He dipped his spoon into the stew and ate it mechanically for several minutes.

Suddenly, he quietly slid off the stool and, keeping his head down, rounded the end of the counter and got some more bread. He climbed back on the stool and resumed his meal, grateful that the man said nothing. He hoped that the man was still staring out the window.

"How long you been on the bum?"

Jiro started, but was relieved that the subject had been removed from his leg.

"About three years."

"How do you like it?"

"Not too bad when there's nothing else to do."

"Ever plan on settlin' down?"

"Who knows?"

"I'd say it's one helluva way to live."

"Maybe there's no other way for a guy like me," Jiro answered, immediately hating himself.

"Whattaya mean, a guy like you? What's wrong with you?"

"Nothing. Forget it.

"Oh, I get it. Your bad pin?"

The voice sounded cruel, as if it was delivered laughing.

"I said forget it."

"Sure I never seen a guy as touchy as you. So what if you got a bum leg. Maybe I'll break mine some day too."

"Shut up, I said."

The man laughed out loud, but as soon as he stopped, anger washed across his face. He yelled menacingly.

"How long does it take you to eat? Get back in the kitchen and scrub the floor."

He lit a cigarette and turned to the window once again.

Jiro burned inside, wondering as he often did how it would feel to kill a man.

He picked up his plate and went back into the kitchen. Filling the pail with hot water, Jiro set to the task of brushing the greasy, filth-ridden floor. He bore down heavily on the wiry brush, finding comfort in the cruel, scraping sounds the wood emitted.

The noise of heavy footsteps approached the kitchen door. It swung open.

"Come out and watch the counter a while. I've gotta run down to the drugstore."

Jiro answered "sure" and continued to brush the floor.

"Get up damn you. Do as I say."

Jiro rose and followed the man out to the counter.

"I'll be right back. Them fellows at the roundhouse'll be comin' in pretty soon. If I'm not here, tell 'em to wait."

The man walked out the door and Jiro watched him through the window as he moved along the sidewalk towards the drugstore.

He sat down on the end stool for the third time, stretching his legs comfortably on both sides of it. He contemplated the nicks in the counter for a moment, then looked up and saw the cash register.

He walked slowly along the back of the counter until he was directly in front of the register. He wondered how much money it concealed. Not enough to be worth the trouble, probably. Been a long time since I saw anything larger than a buck. If I had a thousand cash registers full of money, maybe people would look at my car and clothes instead of at my leg. I wonder how it feels to be rich, so rich that, when people saw you, they only saw how rich you were. How I wish I was filthy rich.

He stood before the register, an almost reverently thoughtful look on his face.

The door opened, but he didn't notice it soon enough.

"What the hell are you doing there?"

"Nothing."

"Nothin' hell, you lousy . . ."

"But, I . . ."

"I've got a damned good notion to have you run in."

"You've got me wrong."

"Wrong, my eye. You were going to steal my money. I knew you were all the time. Thought I went to the drugstore, didn'cha? Well, I didn't. You bums are all alike."

"But I wasn't . . ."

"The hell you weren't. You nuthin' but a cheap crook. Now, get out of my place."

"I tell you, I wouldn't . . ."

"Get out, before I throw you out."

Jiro walked swiftly to the door and a powerful shove from the angry man sent him sprawling to the sidewalk.

"If I ever catch you around this town, I'll kill you."

Jiro picked himself up and limped quickly along the sidewalk.

He stopped suddenly, realizing that he had left his hat and suitcase in the kitchen. It would be useless to go after them now.

He cut across the street in front of the drugstore, not becoming aware of the voices on the other side till he was too close to them. The kids were sitting around, talking and laughing in the dark.

Jiro walked away from the voices. He looked straight ahead, knowing how clearly they must be able to see him against the light of the shop windows.

The youthful voices stopped. A busy hum of unmuffled whispers pierced the silence. They were watching him again. They were talking about him.

Jiro hurried on as fast as he could, felt his way unsteadily down the embankment and limped heavily across the yard towards the trains.

Without Solace

Even Though He Hid Behind a Mask of Insanity, It Didn't End Grief

JOHN OKADA

Influenced perhaps by classic American fiction by Washington
Irving and Charles Brockden Brown that Okada may have encountered in his literature classes at the University of Washington, "Without Solace" focuses on a farmer named Benson, his wife, Emma, and
their sick daughter, Jan. In this macabre tale, Benson denies his daughter's death and carries her corpse out into the countryside, as though
Jan were simply in need of fresh air. Eventually he tires, settles down
beneath an oak tree, and, like Irving's Rip Van Winkle, falls asleep
only to awaken to a new reality. In this alternate reality, he argues
with a disembodied voice—"a strange voice, soft, yet full of power,
and quiet, yet steady and all-penetrating"—reminiscent of those
heard in gothic fiction like *Wieland* by Brown. In Okada's story, Benson engages in a debate with the eerie voice about the injustice of Jan's
death.

Published on April 4, 1947, in the *Northwest Times*.

THE BRIGHT NOON SUN SHONE DIMLY THROUGH THE HEAVILY curtained window of the farmhouse and accentuated the peaceful solemnity of the bedroom. A small girl lay in the large frame bed, the shape of her thin body barely perceptible beneath the covers. She was dying and her pale face, calm and still, seemed to await the end without thought of resisting further. After four days of a violent struggle against the unrelenting disease that gripped her body, she no longer had the strength to open her eyes or the faintest desire to prolong life.

Softly, the door was pushed open and a huge figure stepped into the room. It was Old Benson. He stood by the door for a long time before he crossed over to the bed and slumped slowly to his knees. Steadily, helplessly, the tired father looked upon his daughter's face. "Jan," he whispered almost as if in supplication, "Jan . . . Jan."

The girl remained motionless, giving not the faintest sign that she heard her father's voice.

He continued to look at her, tenderly, painfully. Tears washed freely down the leathery, weather-scarred skin of his cheeks and soaked into his heavy white beard. A giant sob rose in his throat but suddenly lowering his head into his folded arms, he muffled it. The resulting sound was like an empty cry swiftly vanishing into the blackest night. It was a cry of despair, a note of bottomless agony which nothing could soothe.

As he kneeled beside the bed, Old Benson appeared in the dimness of the room like a man bending over while standing. His enormous head was buried in the folds of his long, heavy arms, his great shoulders were drawn upwards alongside his short, muscular neck, and his broad back rose and fell with laboring regularity as he sobbed noiselessly.

Presently, the slow convulsions stopped and Old Benson began to pray. He prayed in a low, mumbling murmur that filtered into the bed covers. He had done a great deal of praying since the seriousness of Jan's illness had become obvious. Jan was all he had, all he lived for.

From the kitchen below, the dim sounds of wood being thrown into an iron stove drifted up. Mama, worried and exhausted as she was, managed still to go about her household tasks. Old Benson thought of his wife, of his deep gratitude for her courage and understanding. She, too, loved and adored Jan as much as he did; but, deep as her grief was, she hadn't permitted herself to collapse as completely as he had. She saw that the cows were milked, the fields plowed and the chickens fed. She managed the farm and cooked the meals and comforted him when his grief became too great to bear alone.

As for him, all he had done the past week was sit beside Jan. When the doctor had ordered him out of the room, he stood in the hallway by the door. From the moment Jan took sick, he thought of nothing else. He had stopped working entirely, not caring whether the cows were milked or the chickens fed. He did not even bother to give directions to the hired hands as he has done each morning for the past thirty years. Jan was his only concern and if she were to die, he could not care to live longer.

A quick tremor ran through the bed and caused Old Benson to lift his head. He saw that Jan was struggling to remove the covers.

"Jan! You mustn't." He reached out swiftly and, murmuring softly to her, grasped her tiny arm. She continued to fight and he felt the small strength of her dying body straining in his hands.

"Please, Jan, please. You must rest quietly."

Her breath came faster and harder through her open lips.

"Jan, you'll tire yourself. Please, lie still."

She pulled at his hands, twisting her body slowly and staring through unrecognizing eyes at his stricken face.

"No, Jan, don't fight. Don't fight. You need to rest . . . rest."

Little dots of perspiration broke out on her forehead, her breathing became heavier and still faster and the force with which she fought him steadily increased.

"Jan . . . Jan."

Suddenly, the struggle ended. Jan lay still on the bed, her eyes closed, her face calm, lifeless.

Old Benson, still holding her arms, looked long into the face of his dead daughter. Following a quick surge of horror and bursting grief upon grasping the implication of Jan's strange conduct, he felt nothing. A blankness pervaded his mind, his eyes remained open but were blind to the immediate surroundings. In truth, he was like a senseless rock plunging downward thru endless fathoms of the deepest ocean.

Gradually, his senses trickled back. His eyes, still fastened on Jan's lovely face, began again to see it. Then came slowly the realization once more of the terrible occurrence. He felt a sharp, fleeting pain stabbing into his heart. Again came a brief period of inexplicable calm followed by an overpowering sense of sorrow and compassion. Suddenly and completely, a new and strange feeling flooded his breast. It was a kind of relief that took hold of his mind and body and freed them of their worries and exhaustion.

"Jan, dear," he whispered tenderly, "you'll take sick if you sleep too much. Look! Look! See what a nice, bright day it is."

Rushing to the window, he hurled aside the curtains. Sunlight streamed into the room.

"Come, Jan. Look out the window. You've never seen the fields as beautiful as they look now."

Old Benson walked back to the bed with eager steps, flung the covers off the still form of his daughter and, carefully taking her into his arms, returned to the window.

Holding her so that she was facing out through the window, he sat in the old rocker and weaved slowly back and forth. Softly, he spoke to her. "See how clear and sharp everything looks. There's Sarah in the lower pasture. She's a real fine cow. The trees look so nice too, and the grass and crops, they're nice. Everything's nice, everything. Calm and lazy and peaceful too. Everything is calm and lazy and peaceful. Green grass . . . green trees, clean fields . . . calm . . . lazy . . . peaceful . . . nice . . . sun so bright . . . should be out . . . should be out."

With his strong fingers, Old Benson brushed back Jan's thick, dark hair. "Yes, Jan dear, we shouldn't be inside on a fine day like this. The warm sun'll do us both a lot of good."

He adjusted her in his arms so that her head was comfortably nested under his chin. The white of his beard crushed softly into her hair. He rose from the rocker and, leaving the bedroom, started down the stairs. His steps were easy and steady and his shoulders squared as if they had never been burdened with emotion.

The kitchen door swung open and a tall, gaunt woman rushed into the lower hallway. Upon seeing her husband and child, the look of intense worry on her tired, handsome face turned quickly into one of uncontrollable horror. "Ben! You'll kill her!"

He stopped halfway down the stairs and gazed with a faintly amused smile at his wife. "No, Emma. We're just going outside for a little while. It's such a nice day."

"No, Ben, no! You don't know what you're doing! Jan mustn't be moved! The strain will kill her! Oh, . . . my poor child. She . . . " Emma stopped, her great concern vanishing suddenly and her face becoming distorted with grief. With lips moving feebly, she trod hesitantly up the stairs. She stared fixedly at the tiny girl in Old Benson's arms. "Jan . . . Jan . . . "

Weakly, Emma reached for her child, but Old Benson would not release her. Emma pleaded hysterically. "Ben. It's happened. It's happened. Jan has left us."

Old Benson regarded his wife with a look of perplexity mingled with humor. "Jan leave us? Emma, how could you say such a thing. She's just going with me for a short walk in the fields. We'll be right back." Giving his wife an assuring pat on the shoulder, he started down once more.

Emma reached protestingly for her child again, but her fingers were no match for the powerful arms of her husband. Overcome by a fit of anguished sobbing, she slumped helplessly onto the stairs.

Old Benson paused for a moment at the doorway and hollered cheerfully to his wife, "We'll be back before supper, Emma." Then he was gone from the house with the child in his arms.

A whole hour had passed before he came to the lower pasture. He spoke continually to Jan, stopping time after time to admire some plant or flower and occasionally resting in the shade of a tree. Now he pulled a handful of alfalfa from the ground and thoughtfully held it out to Sarah who munched it lazily. "Look how gentle she is, Jan. Best cow on the farm."

He slapped the cow affectionately with the palm of his tough hand and walked over to a clump of trees at the far end of the pasture. Feeling somewhat weary, he selected a solidly shaded area beneath a tall oak for a rest. Brushing the small branches away and clearing a little spot in the cool grass, he tenderly laid Jan on the ground and urged her to take a nap. Lying beside her, he slipped an arm under her head and stretched out comfortably. Before long, he was fast asleep.

Old Benson slept for many hours. When he finally woke up, the sun had almost completely disappeared behind the western hills. The pasture was calm, not even the wind stirred the air.

Upon attempting to stretch his arms, he felt the soft weight on his extended arm. Immediately, he remembered Jan and vaguely recollected the pleasant stroll with her that afternoon. He noticed how dark it was and realized that they had slept past time for supper. "Jan," he called quickly, "wake up! Wake up! Our supper will be getting cold. We must hurry."

The girl's dead form remained motionless.

"Hurry, Jan. We've slept too long. Your mother will be getting worried."

He reached for her, intending to shake her to her senses. His hand stiffened abruptly upon touching her cold, rigid body. Terrified, he jerked himself into a sitting position. "Jan! Jan!" Fright, surprise, disbelief, all were contained in his frantic cry.

He grasped her arm. It, too, was hard and cold. Gradually, horrifyingly, the events of the past week drove sharply into his mind and led up to their final, disastrous outcome. For a brief moment, Old Benson was in the bedroom during those last terrible minutes. Now, for the first time, he realized fully the calamitous thing that had befallen him. Filled with grief and anger, sorrow and hatred, he buried his face into his child's breast. Sobbing and swearing he pounded the soft earth with his clenched fists and wildly cursed the God that took away his only happiness.

A voice broke through the darkness. "Old Benson." It wasn't a loud voice and it was difficult to distinguish whether it was that of a woman. It was a strange voice, soft, yet full of power, and quiet, yet steady and all-penetrating.

Ceasing his wild pounding and crying, Old Benson listened.

Once more the voice called. "Old Benson."

"Yes. Yes. Who's calling?

"I who have taken your little girl."

Old Benson jumped to his feet, feeling only the desire to harm the one who had brought such misfortune to him. "Where are you?"

"Here . . . here . . . here."

The voice seemed to originate from everywhere, filling the night with its solemnity and irritating calmness. Old Benson ran through the clump of trees, searching behind the trunks and gazing frantically about him.

"It's no use, Old Benson. Come back here by your little girl and listen to me."

Upon being reminded of Jan, he ceased his wild search and returned to the spot where Jan lay in the grass. Full of grief once more, he raised her off the ground and pressed her lovingly to his breast.

"Old Benson."

"Yes. I'm listening."

"Why do you permit yourself to endure so much suffering."

"Why? You see me here like this and you ask me why?"

"Perhaps, I've stated it wrongly. What I meant to say is that death need not be as terrible a thing as you make it."

"Who are you to speak like this?" Once more Old Benson's voice was angry and deeply bitter. He clutched Jan more fiercely to his body.

"You miss her, don't you?"

"Yes, yes, I miss her enough to feel that life is no longer worth living."

"Why do you feel like this?"

Old Benson gazed out across the dark picture. He could barely see the outline of the hills against the moonless sky. After a long, thoughtful silence, he spoke, almost as if to himself.

"Emma and I, we always wanted children, many children. We both love them very much."

"We were madly in love and extremely hopeful when we got married. That was a long time ago. Emma wanted five children. I didn't care as long as we had many. But the years went by and we were still without children. I didn't give up hope for a great while but nothing happened. Later, I prayed that we might have just one child, at least one, and that, too, seemed too much to ask. I lost hope, became unhappy. The love between Emma and me, that vanished too. I worked hard on the farm, not knowing or caring about anything else. Then, Jan came, eleven years ago. She was the sweetest girl you ever saw. Everything changed after that. Emma and I, we fell in love all over again. I worked harder, minded it less. Life was really good, really worthwhile. Then, last week, Jan took sick. I've always been a good man and I prayed for her every minute but it wasn't any use. She died, and it's wrong. There's no fairness at all, only injustice. I've lost my girl and my faith in God. Why should I want to live any longer?"

"I'm sorry you are so bitter, Old Benson."

"Sorry? Why should you be sorry for me?"

"Because you're wrong, and I want to help you."

"The only thing that can help me now is the return of my little girl."

"Perhaps, I can do that too."

"How? Old Benson sat up erectly on the ground. He gazed absorbed towards the direction from which the voice last seemed to come. "How?" he repeated, "tell me!"

"I shall, but you must do something for me first."

"Yes, anything."

"It won't be easy."

"I don't care. Tell me what it is."

"Find for me just one person who in his lifetime has not suffered from the loss of a friend or relative through death."

Old Benson looked up towards the sky for a long while and said nothing. Thoughtfully, he tugged at his long, white beard. When he spoke, it was almost a shout that escaped from his triumphant lips. "The Jensens! They've always been alone, as long as I can remember. They have no friends, no relations. They certainly never had children."

"The Jensens?"

"Yes, yes."

"Are you sure?"

"Yes, they have the farm next to mine but they keep to themselves. Nobody ever visits them. Jensen and his wife, they've always been alone."

"Do you remember when they came here?"

"Twenty-three years ago and there were just the two of them."

"The Jensens had three boys. The plague killed all of them the year before you knew them.

"That's a lie! They never had any children!"

"The plague killed three, then the Jensens were alone in a way, but not before."

"You lie! You lie!"

"The Jensens are alone now, but they aren't really alone."

"They are! They always have been!"

"No, they've always had their children. They still do."

"What children? They never had any!"

"They still have three. The plague took three but they still have three."

"No! No! No!"

"They still have three." The voice was softer, more distant.

"Three? Three? Stop your lying!"

"They still have three."

The voice was barely audible now and Old Benson realized with terror that it was leaving him. "Wait! You mustn't go. You promised."

"Three . . . three . . . three." With the final word, the night seemed suddenly to plunge deeper into darkness. The voice was gone.

"Come back. My girl. You said you'd give her life once more. You tricked me. Where are you? Where are you?" His voice crying out in wretched agony, Old Benson raved wildly to the heavens.

Presently, exhaustion overcame him and, nodding his head with grief and futility, he lapsed into silence. His hands still clutching Jan's tiny body possessively and his chin resting wearily on her head, Old Benson sat in the grove by the lower pasture and cried over the loss of his little child.

Skipping Millions

JOHN OKADA

Of the short stories published by John Okada in the *Northwest Times,* "Skipping Millions" is the only one narrated in the first person. This relatively mundane tale is told from the point of view of an unnamed store clerk who is more concerned with reading a novel than with serving potential customers. This bookish character is clearly based on Okada himself, who worked at an army surplus store in Seattle. In the story, one customer, a "strange gentleman" enamored with a particular brand of straight-edge razor, eventually commands the clerk's attention. We learn that he is its inventor, a millionaire who moves as if he were skipping. The mildly comic tone and first-person narration of "Skipping Millions" remind one of stories that Japanese American writer Toshio Mori was writing at the same time, like "The Woman Who Makes Swell Doughnuts." Mori had in turn been influenced by Sherwood Anderson's *Winesburg, Ohio,* a volume of connected stories written in a simple style and with first-person narration. Anderson's collection was frequently taught in fiction writing classes of the 1940s and hence may have influenced Okada as well.

Published on April 8, 1947, in the *Northwest Times.*

MR. ABIE K. MUELLERHOFFER WAS SERIOUSLY ENGROSSED OVER some article in the window, but I was unaware that the man outside was Mr. Muellerhoffer or that anyone was outside at all. To be entirely truthful, I was, at the time, so thoroughly negligent of my duties at the store—having been engaged all morning in a fascinating novel about a fascinating woman—that I had long ago lost track of the number of customers who had walked out on account of my unwillingness to rush out and wait upon them with an eager smile as the red-lettered sign on the wall had led them to believe. Even Mr. Muellerhoffer, or rather, the man outside, for he had not as yet entered and introduced himself, would have gone unnoticed had not an overwhelming sense of being watched crept over me as I perused the printed pages of the aforementioned fascinating book.

Attempting to ignore the strange feeling, I mustered forth my maximum powers of concentration, pushed my nose closer to the book and read on. I wasn't very successful, however, for the clawing sensation persisted and became irritatingly worse. By the time it got to the point where I felt as if giant augers were boring holes into my head, I didn't much care whether or not the fellow in the book won four dollars on the pinball machine so that he could court his gal to the plumber's ball. I closed the book indifferently, shoved it aside and, still leaning on the counter, looked up.

A little man was peering in the doorway, directly at me. As soon as I glanced up, however, he hurriedly back-skipped out and busied himself with the inspection of something in the window. Ordinarily, I would have immediately let such an occurrence pass, but the old gentleman, somehow, seemed to demand further study. I skirted around the counter and ventured closer to the window.

The little man had his wrinkled, dark face so close to the huge plate glass that I was fearful lest he should soil it with the blunt tip of his nose. With precision undoubtedly developed through long practice, however, he withheld his nostrils from contacting the glass, but he breathed freely on it. The result was rather humorous. The inevitable blot of fog formed quickly on the pane and, soon, I found myself regarding a stiff, black homburg supported, apparently, by no other means than by a pair of silver-rimmed glasses through which gazed solemn, studious eyes. His ears were partially visible and also suspended in air, and below the blank space was clearly visible his frail body encased in a tight suit of black which contrasted sharply with the large, firm collar of his shirt and a heavily knotted pink tie.

I laughed, and, owing to my coarse nature, rather more loudly than the occasion warranted.

The little man heard me for I saw his eyes dart glaringly at me for just a second. Instantly, however, he had fixed his gaze again on the object in the window and continued his inspection of it unmindful of my presence or of the fact that the greatest portion of his kindly face was obstructed to my view.

Soon, the humor of the spectacle confronting me trickled into a more serious vein as I became more attracted by his intent study of the object in the window. Just as I was about to hazard going closer in order to satiate my curiosity as to what was of such binding interest to the strange gentleman, he skipped—he really didn't skip, but the manner in which he walked rapidly with short, jerky steps made it appear as if he were skipping—over to the doorway and, jutting his face forward with a swift movement of his neck, stared at me. I stared back, too dumbfounded to greet him heartily as my employer had instructed me to do whenever a customer entered the premises. Tiring, obviously, of the stupid grin which I had forced onto my countenance, the little man seemingly decided to speak, for he opened his mouth. It remained open for what seemed a considerable length of time without emitting the faintest sound. A look of doubt crept into his eyes, and slowly continued to spread until his whole face reflected the tremendous gravity of whatever problem his mind was grappling with at the moment. He clamped his mouth shut, skipped out backwards and resumed his former study at the window. This time, he allowed his nose to crush against the glass quite firmly.

I roared happily, but, suddenly fearful of the consequences of my discourteous outburst, drowned it frantically with extreme difficulty.

The little man's gaze did not waver for a moment from the thing in the window. Unable to imprison my curiosity any longer, I started stealthily towards the window display, but, before I got there, he skipped over to the doorway once more. Clasping his thin arms behind him, he leaned forward so that the upper half of his body was inside the store and the remainder of him, still outside. His face glowed with decision. He spoke quickly and I answered accordingly.

"Good morning, young man."

"Good morning, sir." I smiled instinctively.

"Nice day."

"Yes, nice day." I continued to smile.

"Nice store you got."

"Yes, isn't it?"

"You got lots of stuff."

"Yes, haven't we?"

"Business good?"

"Yes, wonderful." My smile was turning sour.

"That's fine. Fine."

"Yes, it is."

An awkward silence wedged itself into the brilliant conversation and, for once, I found myself unable to think of something to say. The little gentleman came to the rescue. He pursed his lips thoughtfully for a minute before he uttered, "Ahhhh . . ."

"Yes?"

"Ahh, I, ahh"

"Yes. What is it??"

"Ahhhh . . ." The affair was rapidly becoming uncomfortable as well as monotonous.

"Yes, yes," I muttered hurriedly, "what do you wish?"

"Ah, that is . . . " Suddenly he flung his left arm forward and pointed suggestively to the window.

"Oh!" I exclaimed with complete understanding, "you wish something in the window."

He nodded his head with excitement. He grinned a huge, happy grin and nodded some more.

I hastened to the shelves by the window and almost had my hands out before I realized that I still didn't know what the little man desired. I looked around at him and smiled foolishly. He merely nodded more vigorously and continued to indicate the shelf with his skinny finger. I inquired patently, "In the window?"

"Yes, yes, right there." His rotating finger indicated all three shelves.

In desperation, I grabbed the mirror from the center shelf to find him shaking his head with disapprobation. I replaced the mirror and repeated the disgusting process with a brush, a comb, hair tonic, soap, cream, powder, three kinds of lotion and two of blades before it dawned on me to ask him what he wanted.

First, however, I closed my eyes and counted up to ten in Greek in order to sufficiently suppress my disfavor towards the difficult customer and, second, I mentally booted myself a dozen times till I almost screamed with pain. I looked at him once more and spoke with cheeriness that had been strained so often that it assumed the nature of a malevolent sneer. I enunciated each word with brutal clarity. "What in the window do you want, sir?"

The neat, little gentleman, slightly flustered by my inability to fathom his thoughts, almost shouted. "That!" Again his frantic finger enveloped all three shelves with his thrusting, circular movements.

I motioned him with extreme kindness to tread inside before he toppled over and to pick out the item which was causing so much disruption before we had become intimately acquainted.

He pointed to himself inquiringly and, when I nodded affirmatively, skipped over to the shelf. He placed his finger swiftly and daintily on the straight-edge razor and indicatively made sweeping motions with his right hand across his face as if to impart to me the information concerning the article's purpose.

My mind, at the moment, was struggling to chase off vague recollections of a bloody murder that had once been performed with a similar object; but, still remembering my station, I graciously removed the article from the shelf and transferred it gently to the little customer's eager, outstretched hands.

He took it tenderly and permitted his eyes to play over the beauty of the article in his hands. Slowly, he opened the gleaming blade and held it up to the afternoon sun which caused the steel to sparkle like the jewel of

Noohimoor. "Nice," he commented ecstatically, then, looking at me, repeated questioningly, "Nice?"

I was ready for him with everything my employer had imparted to me of the secrets of salesmanship and, moreover, with a tremendous sense of urgency regarding the successful completion of the particular sale in progress. "Wonderful, absolutely wonderful!" I shouted at him. "Best razor on the market today. I doubt if you could find another like it in town." I paused for effect and plunged onward. "The blade is constructed of the finest steel, the handle of the finest ivory and the whole thing comes complete with a genuine artificial alligator case of the finest grade. There isn't a finer razor to be had."

The old gentleman was beaming, swallowing every word I uttered as if it were the eternal truth. I mentally calculated the profits from the sale and dealt what I considered the finishing blow. "This," I whispered secretively, "is a pre-war Muellerhoffer."

At this the little man snapped to attention. His eyes sparkled gloriously, his face crinkled up into a thousand ridges with an enormous smile and he proffered his hand with a gallant flourish. "I'm Muellerhoffer," he said happily.

I grabbed his hand, shaking it vigorously, started to inquire, "Shall I wrap it up," but the name Muellerhoffer blazed across my mind as it had for many years across the country and anchored my tongue so that I could only weakly gasp, "You?"

Mr. Muellerhoffer nodded with an impish grin of modesty. "Yes, yes, I'm him. Muellerhoffer, Abie K., Mr."

You mean Muellerhoffer of Muellerhoffer Notions and Lotion Co.?"

"Uhhunh."

"The one that makes these razors?"

"Uhhunh."

"And the knives?"

"Uhhunh."

"And all the notions and lotions you find in all the stores?"

"Uhhunh."

"You're Mr. Muellerhoffer?"

"Uhhunh."

I was flabbergasted. Beyond a doubt, I was conversing with Mr. Muellerhoffer. I fleetingly visualized the old man perched atop a pile of gold as high as the highest mountain and the vision colored my next remark. "But you've got three billion three hundred and thirty three thousand dollars."

"Uhhunh."

" . . . and thirty-three cents."

"Uhhunh."

"You're rich?"

"Uhhunh."

I reeled unsteadily and stared at him. Mr. Muellerhoffer dug busily into his pocket and produced a satchel, but it really wasn't a satchel. It was only a coin purse seven inches long. He flicked the latch open with a swift movement of his thumb, inserted his hand and produced two dollar bills which he placed gently into my hands. "I'll take the razor."

I blurted eagerly, "I'll . . . I'll wrap it for you."

"No, no." He waved a rejecting palm at me and, smiling, tucked the razor into his breast pocket. Gazing timidly but with approval around the store once, he affected a quick curtsy with a nod of his head, skipped a few steps backward and said, "Well, thank you kindly, I must be going now."

Mr. Muellerhoffer backed out of the door and skipped lightly down the street. I watched his little figure till it disappeared around the corner and it wasn't till considerably later in the afternoon that I suddenly remembered not having thanked him for the purchase.

The Silver Lunchbox

JOHN OKADA

"The Silver Lunchbox" has much in common with the classic American short story "Rip Van Winkle" by Washington Irving, as well as anticipating Rod Serling's dreamlike style in *The Twilight Zone*. Irving's story follows Rip and his dog into the countryside, where they meet a strange man who introduces Rip to a drink that makes him sleep for twenty years, after which Rip finds himself in a new reality. Okada's allegorical tale follows Kippy Smith and his dog on the road to school, where they are waylaid by a stranger and end up in another world. The story gets its name from the silver lunchbox that Kippy can win as a prize from his community if he faithfully goes to school for two more weeks and thus attains a total of eight years of perfect attendance. While sauntering to school one morning, however, Kippy and his dog encounter a professorial figure who leads him across the countryside and into the College of Forever. Like Rip, Kippy finds himself out of place, but unlike Rip, he returns to his normal life with new insights about education and life.

Published on April 11, 1947, in the *Northwest Times*.

◆ — ◆ — ◆ — ◆

MISS ZENOBIA QUIGLEY, TEACHER OF READING, WRITING, arithmetic, history, geography, science, drama, handicraft and physical education from the first through the eighth grades inclusive and the unquestioned authority on pedagogical methods in Dream County, adjusted her spectacles with a flourish of her skinny arm and confronted the school board of the Dream County Institution of General Education. Her deep-set eyes twinkled like baby diamonds in her glowing face, her bony fingers played constantly with the polished agate which hung from her neck by means of an enormous gold chain, and she stuttered haggishly when she finally attempted to speak. Zenobia Quigley was in a high state of excited agitation.

The dignified members of the school board of the Dream County Institution of General Education waited patiently. Jim Jones, president of the bank and also of the school board, chewed on his enormous cigar and thought about the new office which he was going to build as soon as the government would release the necessary materials. Elias Brown, the leading farmer of the county, rolled the wad of tobacco expertly within his supple cheeks and eyed the brass spittoon in the corner of the one-room schoolhouse with the calculating eyes of an expert marksman. Fat Horatio White, who lived handsomely on no visible means of income and who had acquired a seat on the board by equally inexplicable methods, had propped his foot on his knee and begun laboriously sharpening his knife on the sole of his shoe. No one spoke a word, not so much out of respect for Miss Quigley who was frantically attempting to compose herself sufficiently to say what she obviously could not or did not wish to conceal, but simply because he had nothing to say. The education of the children of Dream County had been in the capable hands of Miss Quigley for forty-five years and she was the only one who ever found reason to call the board together for the infrequent meetings, but when she whistled, the members came and listened to whatever she found necessary to tell them.

The three continued to wait, the only sound audible in the still room being the "puff puff" of the cigar, the "squish squish" of the tobacco and the "zip zip" of steel whipping across leather. "Puff-squish-zip-puff,

puff-squish-zip-puff, puff-squish-zip-CLANG." Elias Brown had struck the target. He looked at the others for approval, but no one moved.

"Gentlemen," said Miss Quigley at long last, "I have called this meeting today to make an announcement of the utmost importance."

"Puff-squish-zip-puff."

"Gentlemen, I trust that all of you are listening to what I have to say, because it is of the greatest concern to you."

"Puff-squish-zip-puff."

"Gentlemen," began Miss Quigley for the third time, "the silver lunchbox is about to be presented to one of our students."

Jones bit his cigar in half, Brown swallowed his tobacco, and White sliced a hunk of leather from his shoe. In unison they exclaimed unbelieving, "The silver lunchbox?"

"Yes, in two more weeks, Kippy Smith will have maintained a perfect attendance for eight years."

"But, he might have an accident," said Jones.

"He might play hooky," said Brown.

"He might get sick," said White.

"True enough," replied Miss Quigley, "and that is exactly why I asked you gentlemen to meet today. Ever since Paul Green established a near perfect record of seven lunchboxes out of a possible eight some thirty years ago, no student has come close to it until now, and I feel that with success so startlingly near, it would not be unfair if the school board were to see that special precautions were taken to assure the attendance of Kippy Smith during the remaining two weeks."

"By all means," said Jones.

"I agree," said Brown.

"Ditto," said White.

"Now, here's what I propose," began Miss Quigley.

Jones, Brown and White pulled their chairs close around the table.

Miss Quigley continued, "Beginning tomorrow morning, each of us will take turns escorting Kippy Smith to school."

Everyone nodded approvingly.

"Kippy leaves for school each morning at seven-thirty at which time one of us will be present at his home to see that he gets to school. I will take the first morning, Mr. Brown the second, Mr. White, the third, Mr. Jones, the fourth and so on till the two weeks are completed. Is that satisfactory, gentlemen?"

"Splendid," said Jones.

"Excellent," said Brown.

"Ditto," said White.

The school board of the Dream County Institution of General Education adjourned and gathered by the glass case in the back of the schoolroom to admire the sterling silver lunch box with the gold nameplate which had defied possession by any of the two thousand and twenty-one students who attended the school since its establishment seventy-nine years before.

Kippy sat up in bed, his eyes were open. The morning sun was streaming through the window, casting crazy shadows on the yellow bedspread through the frilly curtains. The roosters perched on the white-washed fences in the yard below were crowing. Pap, the collie, was trying to carry bass as usual, succeeding only in emitting weird howls which combined with the dissonant choral efforts of the barnyard group to produce a clamor which was anything but musical except, perhaps, to those occasional city-folks who spent a week or two each year vacationing on the farms and managed to find even the smell of dung an inspiratory item.

Kippy, being a farmer's son and having lived on the farm his entire thirteen years, was not so easily inspired nor was he partial to the symphony conducted by Pap each morning. He simply did not hear it. To him, it was just another morning but since it was just another morning he didn't think about it being that, and if he wanted to think about it he wouldn't have been able to do so for, although he had risen to a sitting position, he was not yet fully awake.

Kippy stared straight ahead through empty eyes, waiting for the curtain of sleep to lift the heavy drowsiness that clouded his mind. The fog lifted and Kippy was suddenly awake, only he found himself confronting the alcoholic gaze of Grandpa Schlitz whose enormous portrait (it had been done by a traveling artist for fifty cents and a loaf of bread in one afternoon) monopolized the opposite wall.

Kippy shuddered, burped sentimentally as he would not have done in front of his parents for fear of the results and laughed until he noticed the clock. It was still forty-five minutes before seven which meant that the alarm had not yet rung. He proceeded to slide under the covers, but suddenly stopped thinking how strange it was that he should have woken up before the sounding of the alarm. It had never happened before. Certainly, such an occurrence was not out of the ordinary and, above all, no worrying matter; but still he felt the necessity of giving the incident further consideration. He could not help but feel that this day would be different. The more he thought of it the more certain he became of the possibility. A torrent of exciting thought pushed through his mind and he could not bear to lie in bed when so many things were waiting to happen to him.

He started to get out of bed and realized that he was following the habitual pattern. If this day was to be different, he would most certainly have to cooperate. He pulled his feet back in, climbed over to the other side of the bed and slid to the floor pleased with his own alertness. He dressed himself quickly, making certain that he reversed the usual process by starting with his shirt, following with the trousers and slipping the shoes on last.

He rushed through the bathroom, gulped down his breakfast in the kitchen, managing, somehow, at the same time to quell his mother's curiosity over his unexpected presence at such an early hour by interjecting unintelligible grunts and nods at proper intervals and stopped to catch his breath only when he was safely outside looking for all the world as he did any other morning when he was starting out to school.

His books, tablets, pencils, crayons, sandwiches, an orange and three raisin cookies were all packed away neatly in the battered green lunchbox which the school board had presented him for a year's perfect attendance. That was seven years ago and, since that time, Kippy had received six more identical lunchboxes, one for each additional year of perfect attendance. This year, if he completed the remaining two weeks of school without an absence, and nothing short of an unforeseen bolt of lightning could possibly interfere, he would gain possession of the sterling silver lunchbox with the shining gold nameplate.

The prospect of being the first student in the history of Dream County to rise to such an unprecedented height of scholastic recognition aroused no enthusiasm in Kippy. He was, on the contrary, rather disturbed over the thought. Kippy was a scholar, a disciple of knowledge and not a collector of lunchboxes, even those made out of sterling silver. He had long disapproved of the system of teaching which had been ingrained into Miss Quigley. Kippy wanted to learn out of archaic textbooks in an academic institution where knowledge flowed through vast halls of learning, a school where white-headed professors spouted words of wisdom the day long and where diligent students rendered their minds and souls completely to the task of gaining worldly knowledge out of massive volumes instead of concerning themselves over attendance and lunchboxes. He felt that the eight years spent in the Dream County Institution of General Education had been totally wasted except, perhaps, in the respect that it had given him a thirst for knowledge which he felt sure that Miss Quigley could never begin to satisfy.

Kippy sighed, realizing the futility of hoping for something which neither Dream County nor his parents could provide. He whistled through his teeth and bounded down the porch stairs and out to the road. He was no longer even hopeful that the day would be different. Life was indeed dull, especially for a kid who had to endure Miss Quigley five days a week. Pap came running out of the yard and the two of them started down the road at a leisurely pace.

The air was clean and still, the grass, the trees and the bushes were dampened to a deep, pleasant green by the morning dew, and the dirt road offered only faint puffs of dust, which settled quickly behind their kicking heels. Kippy loved this time of the day the best and he always made the most of it by adjusting his pace so that he'd get to school not a minute too early. Frequently, he would toss a twig into the fields and Pap would retrieve it in his unfailing manner. They proceeded along the road in their lazy fashion until Pap suddenly dashed forward barking loudly and angrily. Kippy looked ahead and sighted the reason for Pap's strange behavior sitting on the boulder at the curve in the road. It was a man.

Kippy ran after Pap hollering, "Here boy, here boy." Pap was already by the man and growling not unmenacingly, but the stranger did not seem to mind the disturbance. He simply continued to study the huge volume which was resting on his knees. Kippy caught Pap by the collar and reprimanded him into silence. "I'm sorry my dog barked at you," he said, "but he won't bite. He just likes to act mean sometimes."

The stranger, clad in cap and gown, peered through his thick glasses and said in a soft, resonant voice, "He doesn't bother me, son. Let him bark all he wants to." And without another word turned back to his book.

Kippy inspected the old man with natural curiosity. "You're new around here, aren't you?"

The stranger closed his book carefully and chuckled with amusement. "New? I should say not. I've been coming here every morning for years and years."

"I've never seen you."

"You haven't? That's funny. I've watched you and Pap going to school every day for, let's see now, almost eight years isn't it?"

"Yes, but how did you know Pap's name?"

"The same way I know you're Kippy and your teacher, Miss Quigley."

"Gee, but you're smart. You must be a professor."

"I am, professor emeritus of sundry knowledges at the College of Forever."

"Is that around here?"

"Right over the hill behind those bushes."

"Is it a real college, I mean, a big one with lots of students and professors."

"The biggest in the world, son, with so many students and professors that we have never bothered to count them."

"Boy, I bet a fellow could learn a lot there."

"Everything, that is, everything that's ever been written in books."

"Gosh, that's just the kind of a place I've always wanted to go to. Take me there, won't you please?"

"No, son, besides if you don't hurry along to school you're apt to miss out on that grand silver lunchbox."

"It's too early for school yet, and anyway, I don't care about that. It's silly all the fuss they make about that lunchbox."

"Silly? Now, you don't mean that. Why, if I had your chance, I'd be the happiest man in the world. It's things like that lunchbox that make life wonderful."

"I thought you were different, but you look just like old Miss Quigley when you talk about the lunchbox."

"And what's so wrong about that?"

"It's, well, it's just silly."

"You said that before, son."

"I don't care. You've just got to take me to the College of Forever."

"All right," said the old professor, "follow me."

The professor stood up and started through the bushes with practiced ease. Pap, however, made no effort to move and Kippy could not make him budge despite his frantic coaxing. Finally, he gave up and took after the professor who was already starting to ascend the first hill. After what seemed only a few minutes, they came to a vast, green valley crowded with magnificent buildings the size of which Kippy had never imagined possible. Even the words colossal and stupendous seemed grossly inadequate. Kippy would have liked to pause for a moment to view the splendor of the scene which lay before him but he had to hasten to keep up with the professor who hurried ahead.

Presently, they reached the gate of the huge institution, and the professor took his leave saying that Kippy could fare very well for himself if he was certain that he knew what he desired. Kippy thanked him and ventured within the gate.

The campus was swarming with men and women, scholarly looking people who bore heavy briefcases or trudged doggedly along pulling carts loaded with thick volumes. Most of them were old with serious faces and were it not for the caps and gowns, one would have been unable to distinguish between the students and the professors. There was no visiting among the students. No one was talking or laughing or even resting. Those who were stretched out on the green lawns were pondering soberly over their books and the others were hurrying to or from classes. Kippy wandered aimlessly among the buildings, not knowing where to begin.

At length he approached a bespectacled scholar who was sitting on the steps of one of the buildings, deeply absorbed in the pages which he was regarding. Kippy stood nervously for a few moments before he mustered up the courage to speak. "Please, sir, can you tell me where to register?"

"Register?" The man's unfriendly, irritated voice was filled with disbelief.

"Yes, I wish to enroll."

"Stupid," the man hollered, "who ever heard of such a thing."

"But, I'm new here."

"So am I. I've only been here sixty years, and already you're asking questions."

Kippy gulped. "I'm here to study.

"What else would you be here for?"

"But where do I start?"

"Where? Does it matter? Start where you wish."

"But, how?"

"Who cares? That's up to you."

"Please, sir, don't be angry with me."

"Then stop asking me foolish questions. I've only three more years left before I have to take my examination on the ninety-seven basic languages of the universe and I've already wasted too much time with you. Now, be off."

The man turned back to his book and Kippy realized hopelessly that it would be of little use to attempt to extract further information from this curt individual. He continued his wandering until he came upon a kindly, maternal-looking lady who lay on the grass with her eyes closed, appearing quite dead except for the incessant movement of her lips. Kippy thought she looked a little like his mother.

"Please, ma'am," he said politely, "will you help me?"

The lady said nothing. Only her lips kept moving silently.

"Ma'am," said Kippy more loudly, "I want to talk with you."

"Go away," spit out the lady so quickly that Kippy almost did not hear it.

He entreated the lady several times more, but she seemed not to hear him although her face was beginning to show signs of displeasure. In desperation, Kippy finally grabbed the woman by the shoulder and shook her quite violently. She struggled against him for a moment before she leaped up, her eyes wide and sparkling with so much fury that Kippy felt his spine tingle. She mumbled incoherently, leaned forward menacingly and suddenly broke down with hysterical sobs. He was so overcome with fright and astonishment that he could not find the power to speak or move.

"How could you," she cried, then, with a note of pitiful anguish, "I'll have to start all over and I had only two books left."

"Two books?"

"Yes, for my memory course."

"What's that?"

"The recitation by memory without hesitation the three hundred and fifty-two leading novels of the universe."

"What for?"

"What foolish questions you ask. In order to receive my degree in eternal knowledge, of course."

"But why?"

"Does it make any difference why?" Her voice roared. "Now, go on with you and leave me to my occupation else I lose my temper."

Kippy hurried away and when he looked back from a safe distance, the lady had already assumed her original position and was no doubt well into the first book. He walked around taking special care to avoid bumping into anyone and searched without much hope for some kindly soul who might answer a few of his questions in a civil manner. After what seemed hours, he observed a gentleman apparently doing no more than just resting on the lawn and chewing on a blade of grass. Kippy approached him with caution and spoke timidly. "May I ask you a few questions, sir?"

"Certainly, lad," replied the man with surprising friendliness. "I've nothing better to do at the moment and if I can do a good turn for someone before I kill myself, why, splendid."

"Did you say kill yourself?"

"Yes, I haven't decided on the method yet, but I'm sure it won't be too difficult."

"Are you in poor health, sir?"

"I should say not. On the contrary, I'm in the best of health."

"Then why are you going to kill yourself?"

"Simply because I've finally come to the realization that I shall never be able to qualify for a degree in eternal knowledge."

"Why?"

"Ha, ha, ha. You are inquisitive, aren't you, but so was I once. That's why I came to the College of Forever, to satisfy my thirst for universal knowledge, and I've had the most brilliant success in all my studies except one, the simplest of all the courses."

"May I ask what that is?"

"You certainly may. It's the course in Einstein's Theory of Relativity. I've waded blindfolded through the most difficult courses in eternal logic, the universal science, and the heavenly philosophies, and, yet, time after time have I failed to conceive the explanation of Einstein's hilariously simple theory."

"Is that so bad?"

"I should say it is. I can get a degree in random knowledge without Einstein's theory, but I've always had my heart set on getting a degree in eternal knowledge and for that Einstein is an absolute requirement. In other words, I shall never be able to get the degree I want and thus I find it impossible to face myself any longer."

"Oh."

"You said you had some questions, didn't you?"

"No, thank you. I've forgotten."

"Well, if you've got time to spare you might as well help me think up a good way of putting an end to my useless life."

"Some other time," blurted Kippy without thinking and dashed into the nearest doorway in great terror. Some time elapsed before his quaking nerves quieted down and permitted him sufficient composure to survey the building into which he had blindly stumbled.

His first impression was that he was in a lobby of a great theatre. The walls, floor, and ceiling were completely covered with colorful murals depicting the progress of knowledge since the time of primitive savages. Giant chandeliers of the finest workmanship stretched in an impressive line across the room, and the doors were ornamented with intricate celestial carvings the like of which Kippy had never seen in movies. He simply stood in the center of all that wonderful beauty and might have well remained transfixed in just such a position for hours had not his attention been attracted by a blinking object far in the corner. He moved towards it and discovered that it was an ordinary neon sign reading "CLASSROOM" with a huge red arrow underneath it and pointing in the direction of a small door. Kippy pushed the door open gently and peered inside. His mouth dropped open even more.

He saw people, tens of thousands of them packed into a Gargantuan amphitheatre. Not a sound could be heard except for a steady whispering like that of a well-controlled human voice. Kippy tiptoed into the room and searched for a seat. He was unable to find a vacant chair in the first hundred rows, nor did the second hundred provide an end to his search. He kept climbing farther and farther up till he came to the last row. Every seat was occupied. Kippy heaved a disgusted sigh and sat down exhausted on the step. The height to which he had ascended was frightening. He could barely make out the platform at the bottom far below and the lecturing professor was but a tiny, stationary black dot. There were no loud speakers but Kippy could hear the steady whispering as clearly as he heard it at the entrance, though he could still not distinguish any of the words. And, yet, he seemed to be the only one who derived no meaning from the incessant droning, for all the students were industriously working their pencils over large notebooks.

Kippy leaned forward once more as far as his neck would stretch. The whispering became no more intelligible than before, but, suddenly a loud crashing disturbance filled the air. Kippy looked around in horror and was even more horrified when he saw that the awful disturbance was being created by his lunchbox bouncing with increasing momentum down the stepped aisle which he had ascended. "Catch it! Catch it!" he screamed and went bounding down the steps in frantic pursuit. He pursued it all the way to the bottom where the box had finally come to a halt. Kippy retrieved it hastily and proceeded to dust it off when he heard approaching the sound of running feet.

A quick glance was sufficient to assure him of his worst fears. The white-haired professor with the gentle voice was not only shouting but swearing; and with threatening gesticulations was covering amazing ground in spite of his cumbersome dress and apparent old age. A number of the student body with equally unfriendly intentions displayed in their angry faces were also heading swiftly in his direction.

Kippy fled. He ran outside and hastened down one of the innumerable paths which led off from the building, not knowing where it led nor caring about it. He felt urgently only the necessity to keep well ahead of his pursuers who seemed to be increasing in number with each succeeding second. When, finally, he feared that he must soon fall from exhaustion, he emerged onto the open campus and sighted the gateway from which he had entered. With a surge of hope, Kippy dashed for the gate and when he had passed it, he looked back for the first time. It was just a fleeting glance thrown backwards on the run, but the sight of the raving professor leading what must have been the entire student body of the College of Forever doubled the fear in Kippy's heart and also gave him greater strength. He pushed straight for the hills and collapsed only when he had ascended to the top of the highest. He lay panting on the ground with his head buried deep in the grass, knowing that the horrible end was shockingly near; but not a sound could be heard besides his own laboring breath. Slowly, he raised himself and looked down the valley. The professor, the students, and the beautiful buildings had vanished completely. The expansive floor of the valley displayed only its huge, green carpet of grass.

"He must be around here," said Jones.

"He just can't disappear like this," said Brown.

"No, he can't," said White.

Miss Zenobia Quigley was sitting on the stairs of the Dream County Institution of General Learning and crying for the first time in forty-five years. "He wasn't home," she'd mutter between gulping sobs, "he'd already left for school when I got there." She would then add, "But he isn't here," in a tone full of suffering despair and break down completely again.

"Well, we might as well go," said Jones.

"Guess we won't be giving away the silver lunchbox after all," said Brown.

"No, I guess n . . . wait, look!" exclaimed White and pointed his stubby finger down the road.

It was Kippy and Pap and the two of them were racing towards the schoolhouse. Miss Quigley and the three members of the school board hurried out into the yard to meet their prize pupil. They patted him on the back, hugged him and praised him; and they asked a lot of questions. Kippy just shrugged his shoulders and said that he was sorry.

"Kippy, my dear boy," said Miss Quigley through tears of joy, "we thought you were certainly going to be absent."

"Oh, but I couldn't," cried Kippy with alarm. "I've just got to get the silver lunchbox."

"Excellent," said Jones.

"Fine," said Brown.

"Ditto," said White and beamed at the happy group.

Here's Proof!

JOHN OKADA

Perhaps influenced by films like *You Can't Get Away with Murder* (1939) and novels by Dashiell Hammett and Raymond Chandler, as well as the ironic denouements of O. Henry stories, "Here's Proof!" utilizes the conventions of noir. Okada's short story focuses on a group of coworkers who seem to be idly talking about whether it is possible to commit murder, leave no evidence, and avoid all suspicion. One coworker named Stanley, who had secretly killed a man in the past and gotten away with it, now plans to do it again to convince his friends that the perfect murder is indeed possible. "Here's Proof!" provides some insight into Stanley's psychology, an account of this other murder, and a conclusion with a conventional comeuppance. The hard-boiled language of this story anticipates Ichiro's opening internal dialogue in *No-No Boy:* "Christ, he thought to himself, just a goddamn kid is all I was. Didn't know enough to wipe my own nose. What the hell have I done? What am I doing back here? Best thing I can do would be to kill some son of a bitch and head back to prison."

Published on April 15 and 18, 1947, in the *Northwest Times*.

"A PERFECT MURDER? IMPOSSIBLE!" JIM SNEERED OMNISCIENTLY at his friend and emptied the beer glass. "More beer," he hollered without removing his eyes nor his sneer from the three others who occupied the booth in the tavern.

"You're too dogmatic, Jim, and as usual, you're wrong in saying impossible." Hal was a bit flustered from the beer, but his words were clearly spoken and he glanced hurriedly at Mac and Stanley to see how they would consider the problem.

Mac shook his big head in silent affirmation and smiled faintly at Hal as if to tell him that he too felt similarly. Stanley was staring.

"I'm not wrong, and nothing you say is going to make me change my mind." Jim leaned against the back of the booth and added defiance to his still lingering sneer.

Hal thought for a moment. "Look here, Jim, you've got to admit that plenty of murders have been committed and the murderers never found. All you have to do is look in any detective magazine. You find accounts of murders that took place twenty, thirty years ago and the police have almost given up hope of ever finding the guy that did it."

"Sure, but the cops are still looking and as long as the cops are on the job, there's a chance that the guy's going to be found. Justice is a wonderful thing and it doesn't allow perfect murders."

Mac wagged his head again and this time smiled affably at Jim.

"Damn you, Mac," said Hal in disgust, "whose side of this argument are you taking anyway?"

"Neither, or I mean both," spluttered Mac defensively. "I don't feel like talking about killing people."

"Well, what do you want to talk about?"

"About dames, like we always do," retorted Mac very innocently.

"Good idea," said Jim and removed the sneer which he assumed only for the purpose of these frequent arguments.

"Dames it is," said Hal approvingly and raised his glass with a mockingly gracious flourish, and added with unconvincing sarcasm, "A toast to womanhood. If it weren't for them, God knows we wouldn't have anything to talk about."

Jim, Hal and Mac burst into laughter, loud, careless, unrestrained laughter which indicated that they had all consumed enough beer to have been lifted into a state of good-natured insobriety. They might have continued to laugh for some time had they not noticed Stanley. Stanley wasn't laughing. He wasn't even smiling. He was still looking into the foam of his untouched beer with a look of grim thoughtfulness which heavily contrasted the prevailing mood of the happy group.

"Boo!" said Mac fondly, but securing no response, looked at the others somewhat bewildered.

Hal shrugged his shoulders with equal incertitude and reaching over the table shook Stanley as he would have done a sleeping man. "Wake up, fella. Your beer's getting warm."

Stanley ignored Hal also, but he lifted his face and turned to Jim with a gravity of expression that compelled the others to be even more perplexed. "Jim, you're wrong," said Stanley.

"Wrong?"

"A perfect murder is very possible."

"Oh," replied Jim, "I thought we didn't want to talk about it anymore."

"We don't," cried Mac. "We're going to discuss dames."

"That's what I thought," added Hal.

"Shut up you two. This is between Jim and me." Stanley's face showed definitive anger. The others were completely astonished, for Stanley seldom lost his temper and this talk about murder certainly hadn't offended anyone. They listened without saying a word, being totally incapable of conceiving what incited this sudden, unexpected fury in their mild companion.

Stanley continued to look at Jim. "You say that a perfect murder is impossible, but that's because bodies aren't found when really perfect murders are committed."

"Then, I'm still right. If a murder is that perfect, you can't prove that it was done."

"Oh, but that's where you're wrong. I can prove it."

"How?"

Stanley smiled and a queer chuckle gurgled within his throat. "I killed a man two years ago."

"You're crazy."

"No. I'm not crazy and I killed the old fellow to prove to myself that one could murder without ever being discovered."

"You don't expect me to believe that, do you?"

"I do. You've got to believe me."

"Jesus, I didn't think I'd drunk so much beer," said Mac. "I'm hearing things."

"I tell you I'm not lying. I did kill him. I swear I did."

"Sure you did," said Hal grinning, "but you needn't get hysterical about it. We believe you." He winked openly at the others who were laughing softly.

"Go ahead and laugh, you fools!"

"Take it easy," said Jim harshly, "no need to get nasty."

"If you don't like my attitude, you'd better leave." Stanley was not joking.

"Guess I will."

"Getting pretty late," mumbled Hal, "think I'll be going too."

"Me too," spoke Mac. "I'd say we all need some sleep. See you at work, Stanley."

The three of them got out of the booth, and headed for the door after bidding Stanley goodnight. Their parting remarks were unheeded, but as they reached the entrance, Stanley's voice screamed at them. "I'll show you. If it's proof you want, you'll get it."

Going down to the bus stop, the three men said very little, partly because Stanley who always had left the tavern with them was not along this evening, but, moreso, because of the unbelievably stupid reason which had caused them to walk out on him for the first time. Each of them had been affected by the unaccountable behavior of their friend in the bar and he couldn't decide whether to laugh the matter off or to give it more serious consideration. At any rate, a strain of discomfort pervaded their minds. They avoided looking at one another and shuffled down the street in a manner characterized by more instability than was owing to the little beer which they had drunk. At length, Hal found it necessary to speak. "Stanley certainly acted funny, didn't he?"

"Yeah, he sure did," said Mac, "he sure did."

Jim stopped abruptly and turned to the others as if to speak, but as suddenly, changed his mind and started walking once more.

"He always was a little different anyway," said Hal and quickly added with a tone of weak uncertainty, "wasn't he?"

"Yeah," answered Mac, "a little maybe, but it's the first time I've seen him blow up and over a little thing like that too."

"I know, that's what's been bothering me too. Gosh, for a moment I almost believed what he said about having killed a guy."

"Me too, but Christ, I could kick myself for thinking that about Stanley. He wouldn't do a thing like that. He just wouldn't."

"God, no. It's surprising that he'd even joke about it."

"It is. It is."

"We've known him for a couple of months now, haven't we?"

"Yeah, just about that long."

"Never had any trouble with him, have we?"

"Nope, not once."

"He's always been kinda quiet but there's nothing wrong with him as far as I can see."

"Not a thing. Not a thing."

"I can't understand it. It just isn't like him to lose his temper like he did tonight."

Mac didn't answer. Instead, he suddenly burst out with uncontrollable laughter. Hal dropped his look of deep concern and stared dumbfoundedly at Mac. "What's so damn funny?"

"Us," said Mac grinning broadly and in further answer to Hal's questioning gaze repeated. "Yes, us. The way we've been talking you'd think Stanley really killed somebody. What are we so worried about anyway. Maybe he just wasn't feeling good tonight and all that beer he drank made him kinda mean, that's all."

Hal took a deep breath and let it out with a whistle. Then he chuckled and said happily, "Guess you're right. We've just been making a lot out of nothing. Everybody's bound to have an off night, even Stanley. We'd better watch him and make sure he doesn't swallow too much beer next time or he might really kill somebody."

Mac burst into laughter again and Hal joined him.

"How about a song?" said Mac. "I feel like singing."

"Wait." It was Jim who spoke for the first time since the trio had left the tavern. Mac and Hal turned to him, surprised to see that Jim still looked worried.

"What is it?" asked Hal.

"It's about Stanley," replied Jim slowly, "he, well, didn't touch his beer all night long."

The tavern was empty except for a solitary figure who sat in the corner booth hunched over a glass which had long been warm. Upon glancing at the man one might have concluded that he had merely drunk himself into a state of physical insensibility, but such was not the case, for the silent individual grasped with his hands the only glass which he had ordered all night and it was still full. The man was Stanley.

From the small closet in the back of the room, the disturbing sounds of mop-handles, pails and running water could be heard. Finally, the sounds ceased and the janitor emerged from the closet with a bucket full of water and a dirty mop. He set them down and walked over to the booth. "O.K., mister. You said you'd leave when I got ready to work. I'm ready."

Stanley remained motionless.

"Look here!" shouted the janitor, "do you want to be thrown out?"

"That won't be necessary. I'll go," answered Stanley quietly without looking at the man. He got up slowly, almost with effort and permitted himself to be let out of the door which was locked behind him. He remained standing in continued deep thought for some time before he started down the sidewalk with a weariness of pace which seemed to show that he was just walking with no concern as to where he was going and, obviously, not caring. He knew that he had sat many hours in the booth and that it was early morning: he knew that Jim, Hal, and Mac were laughing at him even now because he had confessed the truth; and with the intensity of hate that can only result from long mental self-persecution, he knew that he must plan another murder, a perfect murder.

Since early the previous evening when his three friends had clumsily excused themselves owing to his inimical behavior, Stanley had been forming a hatred towards them and now that the bitterness had swollen to the farthest possible limits of its massive proportions and concreteness, he found that his mind was struggling to conceive a method to make it felt on the fools who had sneered at his assertions.

He recalled clearly the night two years before when he had taken a man's life to satisfy his own irritating doubts as to whether or not murder could be committed without discovery. He had thought about it for a long time though he was certain that it had never been an obsession. He would say that it was more of a curiosity, like that of a child who invades the pantry during the mother's absence and pilfers a cookie. The child may be hungry, or he might simply be naturally a thief. Then again, he might steal because he enjoys the satisfaction which comes from executing a successful act of wrong, but exactly what the motive is, one cannot say in so many words. At any rate, he had murdered a man and felt pleasantly justified when it had proved successful. The killing had been as easy to forget as the child forgets the cookie after he has eaten it, the self-gratification complete in spite of its elusiveness, and the enactment of the crime absurdly simple when viewed in retrospection. It had indeed been as simple as the manner in which it came about.

He had started out for a movie that evening having nothing better to do. He wasn't even thinking about violence—if one could call it that—as he walked easily down the avenue. The night was one of those exceptionally dark evenings when one feels the presence of a solid blanket of cloud pressing close to earth and threatening thunder and rain. The air was cool and damp, the streets more deserted than usual, and the lights within the buildings offered little illumination. He had hardly noticed all this until a blob of flame, a tiny, viscid globule of light which danced hazily in the ethereal darkness. He accelerated his steps, keeping his eye on the luminous blot which gradually increased in size and brightness. Presently, a few of the letters became distinguishable, brilliant letters which flashed on and off. He walked faster, then stopped abruptly. He stared at the marquee only a short distance ahead. It said "Murder! Murder! Murder! Thrilling Triple Bill!"

He watched it for a little while, then turned around and looked down the street along which he had just come. The contrasting darkness was overwhelming, but he still saw the word repeated thrice on the marquee. It was then that he thought how suitable a night it was for a murder and instantly felt compelled to activate the innocent ideas he had entertained concerning a perfect killing. He wasn't a bit excited as he turned off the main avenue and headed for the waterfront, nor was he confused. On the contrary, he was thoroughly composed and even a bit amused at the prospect of fulfilling a crazy desire.

The actual murder was hardly worth considering. He had walked out to the end of one of the innumerable docks and found several persons fishing for bass. He struck up a conversation with one of them, an old man who was sitting off to one side of the dock by himself. He asked the usual questions concerning the appetite of the bass, how many he had caught, how big they were and so on. The old man was of an extremely friendly nature and he spoke at great length of his fishing prowess. After an hour or possibly a little longer, he had looked around the dock and noticed that he and the old man were completely alone. The other fishermen had drifted home. The rest was easy. He struck the old man on the head with a two-by-four, stuffed the body with some effort into a section of concrete water pipe taken from a pile of pipes on the dock and rolled it over the side.

Not a word had ever been mentioned in the papers about it. No one had known what had happened. Not one single soul except himself. That was the trouble. He could never prove it. He had never felt the urge to have others know what he had accomplished. He had been satisfied in keeping the knowledge to himself. He had even glorified in it at times; but, now he had to prove that it could be done, not to the world nor to even a dozen people, but to Hal and Mac and Jim. He would have to commit a second murder, but it would obviously not be as simple as the first. It had to be someone whom the three men would know and miss. It would take time and patience and careful planning.

Stanley felt the cruel agony of scattered thoughts fighting restlessly in his mind to form a plan—a perfect plan for a perfect murder. He had walked miles since leaving the tavern, but he was unaware of it. There had to be a way and he could seek no rest or sleep till his mind stumbled upon it. He repeatedly kept thinking of Hal, Jim and Mac, hating them more with each succeeding thought and feeling more strongly the irresistible compulsion to show them that he would live up to the threat which he had flung at them just before they left him. He wanted to kill all of them, but he couldn't. They would have to be alive if they were to observe the proof which he would provide. His mind was in a mad whirl of hate and cunning, bitterness and persistent inquiry—searching frantically into the obscure recesses of his tangled knowledge for a victim, a situation and a method. Suddenly, out of the maze of haphazard thoughts and grotesque ideas, the plan formed almost as if by itself. It flashed into his mind in such a state of completeness that not a single doubt arose for even a fleeting second. He reviewed it quickly, his breath coming fast. He checked and rechecked and accepted it immediately. The exhilaration and relief of the initial victory was so great that he was unable to contain it. He broke out with sobs of hysterical laughter that echoed rapidly down the dark, silent street. The loud laughter swiftly diminished into a low chuckle and then became a fit of empty coughing as he fell exhausted against a lamp post. After resting a while, he inspected the surrounding buildings but failed to recognize them. Then he realized that he was leaning on a lamp post and looked up to read the street sign. He knew the street but it merely told him that he would have to walk to the other side of town to get to the boarding house where he stayed. He dreaded the walk but as he started back down the street, he was smiling.

The employees of the Wright Construction Company's main office were preparing to go home after another day's work. The girls were straightening out the top of their desks by throwing everything carelessly into the drawers and covering the typewriters. The men, unmindful of the chaotic state of their equipment, had simply ceased working and were regarding the seconds on the wall clock as it labored past the black numbers and finally indicated five o'clock.

Hal got his hat and waited for Jim and Mac to show up. He mumbled "Goodnight" to the men and girls who were leaving, even to Kathy, the bashful, plain blond who worked at the corner desk in the office. After a few minutes, Stanley came out of the doorway. Hal started to turn away unconsciously, but seeing how foolish it was, maintained his position and regarded Stanley who had also seen him and was deliberately avoiding his glance. As he passed with hurried steps, Hal spoke affably, "Goodnight, Stanley."

Stanley made no reply nor did he even look at Hal. He quickened his steps and disappeared around the corner. Hal wasn't surprised anymore; but, still, he couldn't help wondering over the complete unfriendliness of one who had always been amicable enough.

"Well, here we are. Let's be on our way." Mac's loud voice disturbed Hal's brief thoughts and he turned around to face his two friends.

"What's wrong?" asked Jim. "You look worried."

"Oh, it's nothing," said Hal with a trace of concern still lingering on his face. "I just got snubbed by Stanley again. Should be immune to it by now, but I can't help thinking how funny it is."

"Forget it, pal, forget it," said Mac sharply. "He isn't worth thinking about. Way he's been treating us, you'd think we stole his best girl."

"I've quit trying to get a word out of him," said Jim. "After all these weeks I'd expected him to have forgotten our little argument in the tavern, but, no, he won't even look at me."

"Who cares if he doesn't," roared Mac. "Who cares? I sure as hell don't. We don't owe him an apology anymore. Look what happened every time we tried to make up to him. If he wants to be friends with us again, it's up to him. Now, forget him."

"Guess you're right," replied Hal managing to look less concerned. "Let's get going."

The three men started down the corridor, towards the elevator.

Stanley paused for a minute inside the entrance of the building to light a cigarette before he stepped out into the sidewalk and joined the five o'clock crowd. He carried his light topcoat carefully slung over his arm so that the solid weight in the pocket was well-balanced and guarded against dropping or knocking against his body. He had planned carefully and patiently, and now that he saw no reason for stalling any longer, he had decided that the courtship could come to its fruitful termination. He couldn't resist the temptation to smile to himself when he recounted this cleverness in laying the groundwork for the final date.

Meeting Kathy "accidently" and unobtrusively had been too easy. Getting her to go out with him was even easier. She was such a dumb blond, a homely, bashful, scared little kid who believed every silly word he threw at her and whom no one would really miss, though her absence would eventually be noticed. That was the main thing, that in time the proper people would miss her presence in the office unobscured as she ordinarily was at that corner desk of hers. He had been afraid at first that she might be suspicious of his demand, that she would want to tell everybody that the nice-looking Stanley Briggs was dating her, but he managed in his capable way to keep her quiet. He was supposed to be in love with her though he could never think of it were it not for her great usefulness in his plans. He had convinced her with his adroitness of speech and manner that their romance should be kept to themselves, that it was a thing he prized most highly and coveted so jealously that he could not bear to have the fellows at the office teasing him about it. He said that he was extremely sensitive, that he couldn't stand to have people kidding him and that he might lose his affection for her if she were in any way responsible for such an occurrence. Kathy's reaction had been perfect. The thought of losing him had so alarmed her that she clung to him and promised with tears in her eyes that she would never whisper a word.

And so they had been meeting several blocks away in the evening. During the day, he would avoid her as much as possible, talking to her only in the course of business and assuring her with inconspicuous smiles from time to time. No one at the office could ever suspect that he was courting the queer little Kathy whom even the girls seemed not to notice. At night, however, he made love to her, passionate love in small obscure places where they could never be seen by people who knew them. He had hated every minute with her, but that didn't matter now. He would be rid of her forever in a few hours.

Stanley pressed the topcoat tight against his body and quickened his walk as he approached the familiar doorway under which Kathy would be waiting. He wanted to look especially eager tonight, and he felt assured when Kathy came running out and fell in beside him with a big smile on her thin face. Neither of them said a word. Stanley walked and Kathy followed beside him like a faithful puppy. Finally, Kathy spoke. "Where are we going tonight?"

Stanley forced himself to look at her and with as pleasant a grin as he could assume, replied secretively, "Someplace very special, darling."

"Where? Please tell me."

"We're going to have dinner at a cozy little roadhouse about five miles outside of town and, afterwards, we'll go for a nice long drive." He added tenderly, "It might be a bit cold, but we could stay in the car and the moon'll be out."

"That sounds wonderful, but you don't have a car."

"Oh yes I have. I phoned this afternoon and rented one, a nice little coupe just for you and me."

"Darling," she said excitedly, "we do have fun, don't we?" She slipped her arm through his and laughed softly with happiness.

They walked to the garage and Kathy waited outside till Stanley drove out and picked her up. They said very little on the way out to the roadhouse, but Kathy snuggled close to Stanley who put his arm around her possessively when the traffic decreased to a sprinkling of cars out on the highway.

The crowd in the roadhouse was fairly large, but most of them were couples who sat in the booths and seemed not to notice the other people. Stanley and Kathy found a comfortable place in the back room where the lights were dim and the music soft. They ate slowly, keeping the conversation to a minimum and gazing constantly at each other as lovers are inclined to do. They had a couple of drinks apiece and they stepped out on the small floor to dance several times. Stanley was exceedingly tender and amorous and Kathy was hopelessly enamoured. When they finally left the roadhouse, the moon was full and bright.

Stanley drove at a moderate speed deriving extreme pleasure from the cool, steady manner in which he handled the car. One would never have thought that anything was wrong. Kathy sat close to him and mumbled dreamily about the night, the full moon, and their love for each other. The air outside was cold and sharp and the brightness of the moon so great that one could almost see the color of the leaves in the clearly outlined tree tops against the cloudless sky.

An hour later, Stanley turned the car off the narrow dirt road and stopped on a little clearing overlooking the ocean. Even within the car the loud roar of the turbulent waters dashing against the rocks below was steadily audible. Stanley moved his hand slowly to the shelf behind the seat and inserted it in the pocket of his topcoat. He leaned over and kissed Kathy full on the mouth.

"I'm stiff all over from the long drive," he said softly. "Let's get out and stretch a bit."

"All right," replied Kathy somewhat reluctantly. She opened the door and started to climb out.

Swiftly, he pulled the gun from the pocket and fired it twice into the back of her head. She toppled forward to the ground, her legs propped awkwardly on the running board. Stanley kicked her from the car, stepped out into the windy night and flung the pistol into the roaring water. He studied the lifeless body with a look of triumph in his eyes, lifted it and a moment later sent it hurtling over the lonely cliff.

That was easy, he thought. They wouldn't find her for a long time, and when they did, it wouldn't matter anyway. They could never connect her death with him. He was too clever, and he had proved it not once but twice. He climbed into the car and started off feeling a slight regret in having had to go to the expense of renting a car.

The office of the Wright Construction Company was empty except for several people who brought their lunches to work instead of hazarding the almost impossible task of attempting to get lunch for a reasonable price at crowded cafes and drugstore counters in the space of an hour's time. They sat about idly eating sandwiches and washing them down with gulps of coffee or milk brought in thermos bottles. Jim sauntered through the doorway and walked over to the desk were Hal and Mac were comfortably slouched in their chairs. "What a struggle," he said, "it's a crime what a guy has to go through nowadays to get a hamburger and a cup of coffee."

"That'll teach you to forget your lunch," said Hal with a smile.

"Hey, you know what?" shouted Mac. "Do you know what just happened?"

"No, I haven't the faintest idea," replied Mac feigning interest. "Tell me before I bust."

"The cops were here with suits on."

"They sure were, they sure were."

"Well, go on. What did they want?"

"O.K. O.K."

"Well, tell me."

"Don't rush me. They asked a lot of questions, lots of questions."

"About what?"

"That blowsy blond that sits in the corner. She hasn't been here for over a week, you know?"

"What about her?"

"The dicks think she's a missing person."

"You mean somebody's actually missing her?"

"Yeah, yeah, seems she didn't show up at her boarding house for about a week and the landlady got kinda worried it seems."

"She doesn't know when she's well off."

"I know, I know, but it's kinda funny though, I mean a gal like her disappearing like that."

"Maybe she found a man that looked at her twice."

"Could be, could be."

"Look," said Hal interrupting the conversation, "here comes our buddy." They all turned around and saw Stanley coming towards them with a newspaper under his arm.

"Whattaya know?" said Mac with surprise. "Looks like he's coming here."

"Maybe he's finally decided to make up," said Hal.

Stanley came up to the three men and regarded them soberly for a moment before his mouth curved almost imperceptibly into a tight smirk. "Here's proof," he muttered quietly and, throwing the newspaper on the desk, walked away.

The paper had been folded carefully so that the item with the picture over it and the heavy pencil mark around it was readily detectable.

"It's the blond," cried Hal grabbing the paper and swiftly read the brief article. He stared at the other two and with a look of puzzled disbelief and horror on his face exclaimed, "I'll be damned!"

Mac snatched the paper out of Hal's suspended hand. Jim leaned over Mac's shoulder to read the article. Their faces became grim as they read.

Missing for a week from the boarding house where she lives, Miss Kathy Reynolds has been sought unsuccessfully by police throughout the state, it was disclosed this morning.

Mrs. James Arnold, her landlady of the boarding house at 21 Crane St., became worried when Miss Reynolds failed to return for several days and notified the police.

The girl is believed to have been wearing a light brown suit, a pair of low-heeled brown shoes, and a dark overcoat. She is of slight build, has blond hair, blue eyes and a small scar on her left arm. Mrs. Arnold stated that Miss Reynolds was a retiring girl who seemed to have very few friends. The missing girl was employed as a typist at the Wright Construction Co.

Anyone having word of the whereabouts of Miss Reynolds is requested to get in touch with the police immediately.

"Why the dirty skunk," muttered Jim through his teeth, "I'll make him talk." He leaped out of his chair furiously.

Hal grabbed him and forced him to sit down again. "Take it easy, Jim. You won't get him to talk by getting rough. He's too smart. We've got to think this out."

"Yeah," said Mac, "we've got to plan it carefully."

"Guess you're right," said Jim quieting down a little, "the way I feel now, I might kill him."

"No need to," said Hal, "I think I know a way to make him talk."

"How?" asked Mac skeptically. "How?"

"The same way we drove him to it, though we didn't realize it at the time," said Hal.

Stanley didn't accomplish much work that afternoon. He felt too pleased with himself, and most strange of all, now that he'd completed what he had set out to do, he seemed to have lost his intense hate for all three men. He felt only the all-enveloping surge of pleasant satisfaction. He kept glancing over to where Mac, Jim and Hal were going about their work. It puzzled him at first that the three men acted quite naturally, but readily concluded that they must have realized that he had done the job too well to be seriously suspected by the police. Not a single doubt clung to his mind as to the thoroughness of the murder and the security which was his. For a while, he struggled against the almost insuperable urge to yell out the thoughts in his mind, to tell everyone what he had done and to laugh in their stupid, unbelieving faces; but a dangling wisp of reason still prevailed. He played with his pencil, writing his name over and over on a sheet of paper and the words "Stanley Briggs" seemed the most wonderful name that one could desire. In the two words, he saw balance, cleverness, power and unquestionable superiority.

When quitting time came, he didn't get up right away. He sat back in his seat and observed the others drifting out. He watched the girls and the men, dull, slaving people who lived without really living. How common their lives must be, he thought, how dreadfully common. His life was full, exciting, superior, yes, far superior; and yet, he was alone, compelled by necessity of force and number to be like them.

Somewhere, perhaps, lay another world of worthy, capable people where he could pit his qualities and strength against equals; but how utterly impossible it all appeared. He could merely stand in the center of this weary, useless world and watch it revolving aimlessly around him. Life was lonely for one who stood above the common level. When, finally, he got up to leave, the office was bare. He took the elevator to the ground floor and headed for the doorway.

"Stanley," hollered a voice.

He looked towards the wall from where the voice came and saw Hal and Mac. A quick surge of complete terror seized him for a second and he started quickly for the door when Hal called once more. The fright passed and he thought how needless it was to run from them. He stopped in his tracks and Hal and Mac walked over to his side.

"Hello, Stanley," they said cheerfully.

Stanley remained silent and Hal said hurriedly, "Come on, Stanley," and noticing the awkward break, spoke, "there's no need for us to be unfriendly any longer. I think we're all ready to admit that we've been childish about the whole thing."

"We sure have," said Mac. "We sure have."

"I've got to go," said Stanley in a confused tone.

"Please," interrupted Hal, "it really is time we made up. We're willing to forget."

"Yeah," said Mac generously, "let's go over to the beer joint like we used to. It ain't been the same without you. No kidding, I mean it."

Stanley hardly knew what to say. Neither of them had even mentioned Kathy nor the argument which they had had. He wanted to get away from them, to think by himself, but they kept pleading and urging him as if nothing had ever taken place. Finally, he blurted out, "Where's Jim?"

"He'll meet us at the tavern," replied Hal, "he's expecting to see you."

"All right," said Stanley, "but only for a little while."

"Good. Good," said Mac eagerly, "just like old times, the four of us."

When Jim joined them at the tavern, the three had finished their first glass of beer. Jim greeted all of them affably, without paying Stanley special notice, except to remark that he was glad to see him. He gave Hal and Mac a quick meaningful glance and settled down into the booth after ordering another round of beer.

The conversation was of light and incidental things, humorous, witty, even coarse chatter that put them all in a pleasant mood. Stanley was uncomfortable at first, continually watching the faces of others and regarding them with care and suspicion; but he was soon chuckling to himself. The situation was an impossible one and yet, he was there, proving beyond a doubt the inimitable supremacy of his own self. The inward chuckle grew and he broke forth with audible laughter. The others looked astonished for a fleeting second; but they quickly caught up the laughter and turned it into a good-natured roar. They really are fools, he thought. How easy it is to laugh at them when they are so cooperative. The suspicion and discomfort drained away, and he found himself contributing freely to the conversation. He offered to buy the fourth round of beer. Mac seemed especially delighted. "Say, Stanley, you're really O.K.," he said, "you're really O.K."

"Sure," said Hal, "we were fools to argue the way we did anyway."

"Forget it," said Jim, "that argument didn't mean a thing."

Stanley broke in sharply, "What do you mean by that?"

"Nothing," said Jim, "only we almost thought you were serious that night. We thought you really meant what you said."

"Yeah," said Mac through a grin, "we sure did. And that newspaper gag you tried to pull on us this afternoon. We were actually worried for a while. We thought you did kill the blond. No kidding, we did. Why, Jim even saw red for a while."

"I'll say I was fooled," laughed Jim, "but you've got to admit it was a pretty smooth trick."

"A trick?" Stanley's voice was harsh.

"Certainly," said Hal, "you needn't look so surprised. We're wise to you now."

"You're a good actor," said Mac, "a swell actor. I'll bet you got a good laugh at us."

"Why not," chuckled Jim, "it was a damn good joke. Makes me laugh every time I think about it."

"Me too," agreed Hal and burst into laughter.

Stanley grabbed Hal fiercely by the collar. "Shut up!" Then in a low, rapid panting voice he continued. "You stupid fools. I did kill her, do you hear. I killed her, and threw her body over Grey's Cliff but nobody'll ever find it."

"You don't know what you're saying," interrupted Jim.

"Oh yes I do. I promised you proof and you got it. Kathy's dead and I killed her, but you'll never be able to prove it."

"You dirty rat," cried Mac.

Jim reached swiftly across table and sent a crushing blow into his face. Stanley's head snapped back, thudded against the back of the booth and his limp body slid slowly into the seat.

"I hope you heard it," said Jim quietly to the two men who jumped out of the adjoining booth.

"We sure did," said the taller man, pulling out a pair of handcuffs, "but you didn't have to try to kill him."

"He had to," said Mac, "he had to."

The High Cost of Proposals and Presentations

JOHN OKADA

While employed at Hughes Aircraft Company as a technical
writer, John Okada observed defense contractors wasting money
on making and packaging marketing materials for the US military-
industrial complex (to use the term coined earlier that year by President Dwight D. Eisenhower). "The High Cost of Proposals and
Presentations" argues against this practice. Interestingly, Okada
could not resist drawing upon his skills as a playwright and fiction
writer to open his article with a satirical scene. Mr. Blunt, the perpe-
trator of bad taste and excessive spending in this scene, is a version
of the captain in Okada's one-act play, "When in Japan." Both characters are blustery men whose sense of self-importance guides them to
make choices that audiences are meant to ridicule and reject. "The
High Cost" also parodies the defense industry's penchant for con-
cocting unintentionally telling acronyms; Okada's fictional examples
include "Missile Advanced Defense (MAD)" and "Joint Equatorial
Radar Kluge (JERK)." According to Okada's son, this article did lead
to some government reforms in contractor spending.

Published in December 1961 in *Armed Forces Management*.

◆ — ◆ — ◆ — ◆

MR. BLUNT IS THE MILITARY LIAISON MANAGER OF A LARGE midwest electronics company. We find him checking final details in preparation for a visit to the company by a General who is inspecting the company's facilities in order to appraise their adequacy for projected programs. Among other things, Mr. Blunt is making certain that once the General steps down from the plane, he will suffer none of the inconveniences of the average air traveler. The checklist he is presently examining reads as follows:

1. *Contact Joe at airline office. Have him make sure General's baggage is placed in special compartment at that end so it will be first off at this end and waiting at the baggage pickup station when the General gets there.*
2. *Joe at airline again. This time to arrange for Harry to greet General the minute he steps on ground.*
3. *Someone to pick up and carry General's baggage to car.*
4. *Someone to open door leading out to street.*
5. *Car to be waiting directly in front of entrance to airport building. Could be a hot day. Make sure air conditioner isn't malfunctioning like last time.*
6. *Nothing to block parking space in front of main company building. Lawns and walks to be given special attention that morning.*
7. *Someone to open front door of company building.*
8. *Appropriate parties to greet General in the lobby.*

As Mr. Blunt reassures himself that everything has been attended to, his secretary informs him that their man in New York is calling. The New York man has a useful bit of intelligence—at least three of the five other firms conducting study programs on the Missile Advanced Defense (MAD) System are making films, one for certain a 20-minute job in sound and color, as part of the final presentation to the requesting military agency.

Mr. Blunt is aware that a couple of films are in the works, but he doesn't know if one is for MAD. He checks, hopefully, with the Technical Communications Manager and learns the worst. No film has been requested for MAD.

"Well, then, we've just got to have one," he shouts into the phone. "Make it 20, no, we'd better have one 30 minutes long. And with sound and color." He listens to the anguished protests of the Technical Communications Manager and interrupts impatiently: "Don't tell me your problems. My 10-year-old son could do it in two weeks and you've got at least five. Send the authorization up for my signature but, in the meantime, get going on it."

As he hangs up the phone, his assistant Larry walks in with what appears to be a bonus item from the Everlasting Classics of World Literature Club. Two cloth-bound volumes are neatly contained in a cloth-bound case. Larry sets it proudly on Mr. Blunt's desk saying: "Here it is."

"Looks fine," says Mr. Blunt picking it up. "What is it?"

"The technical proposal for the Joint Equatorial Radar Kluge (JERK). Just came in from the bookbinder and not a moment too soon. Ted's flying it back to Washington on the jet tonight to make the 8 A.M. deadline for submittal."

Mr. Blunt's eyes light up a little. "Oh, sure. It threw me for a minute because I thought it was going to be done up in white."

"It was at first, you remember. But we had them redone in maroon when it turned out the manager of the radar division has a phobia against white covers. Gets too dirty. Pretty good point, I think."

"Sure," exclaims Mr. Blunt, "now I remember." He leafs through the expensive, commercially typeset pages and notes the rampant use of colors, illustrated divider pages, multiple acetate overlays, foldouts, and screened block diagrams and schematics. He replaces the two volumes into the case, noting that the fit is very comfortable, and stands it up on his desk. He comments, with admiration: "Looks great, just great. Make sure I get a copy."

"Certainly," says Larry, "but you'll have to keep it locked up. It's secret, you know."

"Yeah, I know," Mr. Blunt utters with a hint of disappointment in his manner. Suddenly, a thought strikes him: "I've got an idea."

"What's that?"

"I was walking through Myron's Leather Shop last week and saw these real fine attaché cases. Real fine ones, I mean."

"Go on."

"How would it be if we got a couple of them—one for the colonel in charge and one for the chief technical evaluator—and put their copies of the books in the cases? No initials on the cases, mind you. Make it look like our man simply forgot to pick up the cases."

"Great," exclaims Larry, "how can we miss? And we sure could use the business what with our big programs running out."

"Don't remind me," moans Mr. Blunt.

As Larry rushes out to take care of the attaché cases, Mr. Blunt reaches into his pocket for a cigarette and comes up, instead, with a business card for the Audio-Visual Equipment Renters Company. He thinks back to his visit to that company and recalls most vividly all the new equipment they had for "wide screen" slides. And portable gold draperies that could be used theater-fashion with the wide screen. As he continues to search for his cigarettes, Mr. Blunt wonders if, perhaps, they couldn't work in the wide screen slide angle for the MAD presentation.

To the uninitiated, the foregoing will probably seem humorous. To those in the Defense industry who have spent sleepless, pressure-filled nights, weekends, and holidays preparing ever bigger and fancier, but not necessarily better, proposal documents and presentations under impossible schedules, each word will probably irritate the ulcer further. To the taxpayer, if he ever finds out, all this will become yet another example of the torrential waste being committed in the name of Defense research and development.

Everyone in the Defense industry and in the commercial printing and publications concerns who has been associated with the "proposal" and "presentationing" end of the business knows that he is grappling with a monster of gradually increasing complexity and proportions. Proposal documents, which several years ago were done simply, austerely, and adequately in the manner of technical papers produced by societies for members and by companies for internal use, have been upgraded to the point where they now frequently outclass in appearance and cost the finer volumes issued by the large book publishers. The entirely adequate, economic approach is now used only when company intelligence reports that a key individual on the requesting agency's proposal evaluation board is known to favor documents that are "sensibly," "reasonably," and "conservatively" prepared. Presentations have also undergone a similar transformation. Where simple flip charts and black-and-white slides were once the rule, the time, planning, equipment, skills, and money put into many current presentations far outstrip those made by advertising agencies to their big clients.

As to how much money is being spent unnecessarily for proposals and presentations cannot be determined without a careful survey. It would appear to be astronomical when viewed in terms of what an intelligent individual would consider adequate. What is spent on a single proposal or presentation, of course, is related to the dollar size of the anticipated contracts. Up to fifty or sixty thousand dollars appears not to be an unusual amount for a company to put into a bidding account for a single proposal and/or presentation.

A SMALL SEGMENT

When the competition is for a large, multimillion dollar program, the figure could and does quickly rise to over a hundred thousand dollars. On an even larger program involving the participation of several large companies as a team, a quarter of a million dollars might be spent by one team. If a dozen teams are bidding, the amount spent by all would be around three million dollars. This represents the expenditure of only a small segment of the defense industry at a given time in response to a single request for proposal by a lone government or military agency.

One large company desperately seeking new business in view of in-house programs nearing termination can, during the course of a year, participate in fifty to a hundred proposal efforts and presentations without difficulty.

A computer would be required to estimate the surely staggering amount spent each year by industry in the pursuit of new and follow-on defense business. A quarter to half of this amount would appear to be a not unreasonable estimate of what could probably be saved if the otherwise painfully explicit government and military agencies would, as explicitly, define in their requests for proposals sensible standards.

SUGAR COATED

Cloth-bound *classified* proposal volumes ($4.25 to bind each of Mr. Blunt's possibly 100 volumes plus $8 for each cloth covered box), unnecessary use of color and screens on art and slides, attractive magazine-type artist's conceptions, wide-screen slides with drapes, outright gift items like attaché cases, and a thousand other cost-adding gimmicks for dressing up a technical document or presentation would be immediately banned.

Why, after all, should a classified document, one of as many as thirty or forty representing different approaches to the same problem and all but the successful one destined to be destroyed within a year's time, have to be an item that looks like a collector's prize? Why, for another, and granting their utility, must slide presentations and films be in wide screen or in full color? Why, to sum up the situation, should a technical document or presentation, ostensibly prepared to further the very serious cause of national defense, contain any embellishment designed solely to impress or to appeal to the aesthete when their only purpose should be to offer to the technical-military group a straightforward, concise picture of the company's technical concepts?

Standards aimed at eliminating these frills—*and eliminating bidding companies who do not abide by the standards to the letter*—can do much to reduce the unnecessary money and effort being frantically poured into "proposaling" and "presentationing."

The Technocrats of Industry

or The Trials and Tribulations of Mr. S.V. and How He Finally Became a Real Engineer. . . .

JOHN OKADA

Okada wrote this satirical essay under the pseudonym John Hillfield (the name Okada roughly translates as "field of hills" in Japanese). It focuses on another fictional character, an electrical engineer named Mr. S.V. (*s.v.* could refer to *sub verbo,* meaning "under the word," or to *side valve*), through whom the essay critiques the defense industry's practice of placing engineers in charge of units outside their expertise, such as sales, public relations, and marketing. An echo perhaps of Jonathan Swift's *Gulliver's Travels,* Mr. S.V.'s "trials and tribulations" include his shock upon moving from a military to an industrial work environment, his stint as a technical writer (Okada's actual job), and his ultimate redemption as a chief staff engineer for perfecting "linearly-programmed, asynchronously-balanced alphabet blocks." By following Mr. S.V.'s misadventures, the essay wryly comments on the industry's wastefulness, inefficiency, and hubris.

Published in March 1962 under the name "John Hillfield" in *Armed Forces Management.*

AN EXAMINATION OF THE QUALIFICATIONS OF THE TOP MAN-
agement of the defense engineering companies, promiscuously spawned
as a result of the missile-electronics-space industrial explosion, reveals
an interesting trait—the engineer in our society is an individual of surprisingly varied talents. He not only invariably occupies the top several
slots of chairman, president, and first through fifth vice presidents, but he
frequently is the chief of such areas as contracts, sales, advertising, public
relations, industrial relations, publications, library services, procurement,
marketing, programming and planning, personnel recruitment and training, management development, and employee recreation. The two areas
where his encroachment appears to be the least successful are the legal
and the financial. This is surprising because purely defense industries
have no financial problems other than how to get more money for a program on which they have already spent four times over the original estimate under which they received the contract from the government and
no legal problems that couldn't be solved with a notary's stamp. At any
rate, probably because of the traditional fear of the NAACP and the IRB,
lawyers and accountants appear to have retained a recognizable niche in
the defense business.

Other than for lawyers and accountants, then, the engineer, at least in
that fenced-in arena of defense (and space) research and development
engineering, has pretty much succeeded in subjugating professionals
without a slide rule. Under the protective umbrella of classified work and
with the doting generosity of rich Uncle Sam, the engineer has constructed for himself an industrial giant designed solely to further his own
comfort and aggrandizement. The result within that monstrously over-
grown, unwieldy industry has been to create a society ruled by narrow,
blinder-equipped engineering minds to the dismay of all other professionals who, for the most part, flutter around the periphery of the industry
without much hope of real advancement or even much attention from the
inner core of engineers. The engineer, no matter how low he is, is something; the non-engineer, no matter how high he is, is nothing to not much
of anything. The distinction between engineer and non-engineer is not as

obvious a dichotomization as it may appear on the surface. The primary bifurcation is, of course, based on the academic degree. In the strong camp sit the ones with the science, mathematics, and engineering degrees. Since human comfort, physical and mental, is a laudable American aim, even for the rugged pioneers who will soon zoom off into the far reaches of space, psychologists and medical types are, except by the conservative band of engineering purists, accepted in this ruling group under the doubtful label of human factors engineers. A single relaxation of this kind would appear to create more than a little hope for those who might attempt to cross over under the guise of syntactical construction engineers (technical writers), or contractual schematic engineers (contract managers), and documentation-information-biblioanalysis engineers (file clerks, typists, librarians, etc.), but attempts to date have been largely futile. Occasionally, however, one finds "passing" as a member of the select group a fleet-footed, high I.Q. English type who has had the unusually good fortune of having his B.A. in Eng. interpreted too hopefully by a desperate recruiter.

A RABBIT-LIKE FACILITY

In the other camp sit the grumbling non-science-degree and non-degree-but-college-caliber types. Granted that a large number of them couldn't cut the mustard in the normal business world and eagerly jumped into a well paying spot in the haphazardly mushrooming save-the-country-from-the-evil-Russians industry, they are nevertheless American human beings entitled to fair treatment under the American concept of human dignity and opportunity. Besides, within the defense industry where, at any given moment, fully half of the participants, engineers and non-engineers, neither know what they are about nor even to whom they are reporting, and the remaining half is busy doing makework or busy making makework, the ability to cut the mustard is of minor significance. More important to personal success is a rabbit-like facility for jumping on the right sandpile at the moment it is about to be injected with a half a billion dollars worth of the taxpayer's money. Overnight, as the sandpile erupts into a mountain of close-mouthed activity, the rabbit finds success and keeps gobbling it up as long as he can keep his balance. Of course, if he wants to prolong his moment of success, he will have to rely on his agility to hop to another promising sandpile before the heady transfusion of dollars into his mountain suddenly runs out and he finds himself disconsolately perching atop a has-been, milked-out, dying pimple of sand.

There are, then, the engineers and the non-engineers as distinguished by degree. Excluding the very top positions in a company, and sometimes not even these, there is also the division by occupation that separates the haves from the have-nots, the leaders from the led, the privileged from the non-privileged, and the thought-molders from the parrots. One is either doing engineering work or he is not. Such is the simple nature of this classification and, as illustrated by the tribulations of S.V., even real engineers are not exempt.

S.V., an electrical engineering graduate of the U.S. Naval Academy had served twelve years as an electronics officer in the service of his country when the injustice of greater responsibility for less than half the pay of his defense industry counterparts socked him in the breadbasket with telling impact. With admirable foresight, he accepted a spot with a company commonly known in the trade as "the country club for engineers."

He spent the first three months getting the feel of the place. Despite his rigid military background, he learned how to come in a little late, take an extra hour for lunch, and phase out a little early at the end of the day. His fellow engineers taught him the intricacies of three-dimensional tick tack toe, blind bridge, and double-reverse chess. Occasionally, he sat in on a "what's-the-competition-doing-that-we-aren't" meeting or "how-can-we-dress-up-our-dog-of-a-radar-and-peddle-it-to-the-army" session. For a while, too, he spent hours each day figuring out how he could spend all of his newfound wealth but, after he moved his family into the custom contemporary on a ½ acre view lot and installed His and Hers convertibles in the oversized double garage, he began to brood about how to go about getting a raise.

His associates were quick to inform him that he could immediately get 21 percent more by going to another company (". . . you see you add 10 percent to what you are already making and they give you 10 percent more to lure you away . . .") or he could stay where he was and settle for a little less by making sounds as if he were planning to leave. Having developed a sense of loyalty to the country club and because of his wife's endearment with the new house and matching Hers convertible, he decided to make sounds. When his boss heard them, the reaction was immediate. ("Why, I've got you scheduled for big things and, besides, if you left so soon, personnel might start investigating me to see why I can't keep my engineers happy.") At the completion of his 90-day probationary period, S.V. received a 12 percent merit increase. Even more providentially his department was placed on a 58-hour work week because, down in the factory, some project manager had driven his station wagon into the plant without proper authorization and, inadvertently throwing it into reverse, backed it into 3 million dollars worth of missile that, in turn, crunched into 3 million more dollars worth of missile and an all-out effort was naturally required to doctor up the two missiles that happened to be the two more than the Russians that we were supposed to have. S.V. wondered why the radar department was going on the long week when the flap was in the missile area, but the weight of his first check with overtime taught him to be prudently quiet. Besides, this gave him that much more time to bone up on double-reverse chess, his ineptitude for which could keep him from becoming a senior staff scientist.

DOUBLE-REVERSE CHESS

At the end of his first year, despite two additional merit raises, a bang-out Christmas thanks to the overtime boodle, and acquisition of a good proficiency in double-reverse chess, S.V., essentially a good guy, and we all know that good guys never really change, began to feel a twinge of guilt at what he, at least, suspected was not an occupation in which he was returning a dollar's worth of engineering know-how for a dollar's worth of pay. He even hoped subconsciously that the department would revert to a 40-hour week. He could understand doing nothing for regular pay, but doing more of nothing for overtime pay did seem a bit unsportsmanlike. Unfortunately, the requirement for a long work week was not reduced even after the two missiles were repaired because, in the meantime, the Russians had orbited a four-room house with a peasant family and pets in residence, and the space race had become that much more intensified. The talk was that everybody right down to the sixteenth-tier subcontractor (except for that electrician fellow at Cape Canaveral who got ruined by publicity) was putting out a special effort.

A good guy's conscience being what it is, though, S.V. eventually found himself actually looking for something to do. In the beginning, it didn't seem like much when he, while leafing through a man-type magazine, came across a hilarious-incidents-at-work column where a number of people had sent in stuff that wasn't too funny and picked up an easy hundred dollars. He recalled something that had happened the last time he had ventured out into the factory area in search of discarded black boxes and stuff that he might use to make his office look a bit more engineering-ish and figured there was something that was really worth a hundred dollars. With this end in mind, he requisitioned a typewriter and, upon receiving it six weeks later, spent several days composing the bit to the magazine.

NOTES TO MILKMAN

There were some skeptical comments made when the word got around that he had requested a typewriter. When, however, the laborious click, click of the keys actually commenced to punctuate the studious quiet of the area and to disturb the eyes-closed, feet-up-on-the-desk thought sessions of rather a large number of his associates, they took notice. More than that, they gradually began bringing to him their correspondence, reports, articles, log books, diaries, notes to the milkman and anything else that required stringing together two or more words into reasonably sensible form. He became immensely popular and very much in demand as attested to by the backlog of work that piled up on his desk. At the same time, he noticed that he wasn't being invited as frequently as before to participate in the various gaming sessions and business conferences, but he didn't pay too much attention to that because he was beginning to feel productive and useful again. In order to keep up with the work, he started to do things like reporting to work on time, working through the lunch hour, taking work home, and sneaking into the plant after hours and on Sundays and holidays. His office now looked more like an editor's den than an engineer's haven. Even the carefully appointed engineering-ish fixtures like the battered waveguides and printed circuit boards were buried under pounds of manuscripts and proofs.

He didn't realize what he was doing to himself, even when they passed over him and promoted several less deserving types to senior staff scientists. Soon, they took away his overtime privileges ("You're not really contributing to the engineering effort any more, S.V."), but he kept right on working day and night and weekends and holidays. Finally, they transferred him and the typewriter into the services area and reclassified him as a technical writer. After all, his proficiency with the machine had gotten to the point where the clatter was fairly incessant.

And this is how S.V. became first a non-engineering engineer and then not any kind of an engineer at all. It should be added that S.V. eventually came to his senses, destroyed his typewriter, and, not only managed to plead his way back into engineering, but was recently upped to chief staff engineer when he perfected the idea for linearly-programmed, asynchronously-balanced alphabet blocks. As chief staff engineer, he reportedly will be making several trips to Europe and the Orient this coming year to investigate a variety of projects so highly classified that they haven't been given names. Needless to say, Mrs. S.V. is deliriously happy at the prospect.

In the interim, S.V., now accepted as an engineer with a knowledge of engineering communications, is discussing with his colleagues the possibility of giving all company documents and correspondence a more engineering-ish appearance by circulating a procedure to the effect that a comma will be placed after every fifth word, a colon after every tenth word, and an asterisk at the beginning and end of every paragraph. ("Those bright English types in the publications department will scream but if they want to keep on eating. . . .")

The latest talk is that a group of non-engineering-degree types led by a couple of non-engineering type engineers is going to ride a bus into the midst of the engineers and demand equal rights. Let's hope that this will be the beginning of the end to professional segregation in our vitally important defense industry.

ESSAYS ON
JOHN OKADA AND
HIS WRITINGS

John Okada's
Rediscovered Writings

Experiments in Form and Approaches to the Absurd

FLOYD CHEUNG

SINCE THE 1976 REPUBLICATION OF JOHN OKADA'S 1957 NOVEL, *No-No Boy,* readers and scholars have assumed it to be his only surviving work. Frank Abe and Greg Robinson's rediscovery of earlier writings—a poem, a play, and five short stories, as well as two later satirical essays— shatters that assumption. Okada scholars already knew that he majored in English and took writing classes at the University of Washington, and that he wrote a second novel-in-progress that his wife burned, but these rediscovered works provide source materials for the study of his development as a literary craftsman. Taken together, they demonstrate beyond a doubt that Okada made conscious literary choices in the writing of his novel, because he clearly tested out different forms of expression in these earlier works. In spite of reviews that critiqued his novel's "poor" or "bad English," we see in antecedent writings that he commanded a range of tonalities from the elevated and proper to the popular and noir.[1] His later essays evince his penchant for humor and satire.

In addition to surveying Okada's experiments with language and genre, we can trace also his use of literature to consider the absurd. Typically, we understand absurdism as "a literary and philosophical movement that flourished after the Second World War" and that maintained that "in a world without God, human life and human suffering have no intrinsic meaning. This sense of a fundamental incongruity between human beings and the conditions of their existence is a recognition of the absurd."[2] Other postwar authors wrote about loss of faith in governmental and religious institutions. Why did the League of Nations fail to control Hitler? How was the Holocaust allowed to happen? What is the role of God in a world that people can destroy in a flash with atomic weapons? Okada, among other Japanese Americans, must have grappled specifically with a loss of faith in the American way. How absurd was it for longtime US residents and citizens to be ripped from their homes, incarcerated without trial, and then asked to fight for the country that persecuted them?[3] Others have noted that *No-No Boy* "spotlights the absurdity of rounding up every American-Japanese citizen and locking them in internment camps or jail."[4] To varying degrees, Okada's earlier works consider the absurdities of a world unhinged not literally by incarceration but in other ways. Hence, these works give us a sense of both Okada's philosophical preoccupations and his capabilities as a writer in the years before he authored *No-No Boy*.

Of course, it is not altogether fair to read these works primarily as stepping stones to his masterpiece. Ideally, each piece would be considered on its own merits, and future scholars surely will do so. For heuristic reasons, however, this initial sounding of Okada's early writings will concentrate on explaining what they can tell us about his experiments in form and approaches to the absurd that anticipate his signal accomplishments in *No-No Boy*.

A POEM DRAFTED THE NIGHT OF PEARL HARBOR

John Okada authored the poem "I Must Be Strong" as an eighteen-year-old student at the University of Washington right after learning of the Japanese bombing of Pearl Harbor on December 7, 1941. This earliest recovered piece—published anonymously in the *University of Washington Daily* on December 11, and reprinted in the *Seattle Star*—shows little evidence of formal experimentation or consideration of the absurd. The eviction has not been announced yet. Instead, in this poem Okada earnestly considers the societal tension that he knows will arise from the fact that he is both "fully American" and a "descendant from Japanese parents."[5] In "I Must Be Strong," Okada participates in a tradition of writers shaken by war who turn to poetry. For instance, upon the outbreak of World War II, W. H. Auden wrote his celebrated poem "September 1, 1939." And after the attack on the World Trade Center in New York, many Americans wrote poems now collected in volumes like *An Eye for an Eye Makes the Whole World Blind: Poets on 9/11*. In the preface to his poem, Okada explains his reasons for responding to the attack on Pearl Harbor in verse: "My mind was in such a state of confusion and entanglement that I was unable to produce an organized and well-unified paper. As a consequence I tried the same thing with poetry." With modesty he admits that the poem is "still unorganized and disunified," but he trusts that "in poetry the reader can read a great deal between the lines."

"I Must Be Strong" lacks meter and traditional rhyme but gathers force from its use of repetition and internal near-rhyme. Of course the repetition of the final two lines of each stanza gives the poem unity. The repetition of "I know" in lines 1, 7, and 14 links Okada's two main realizations: he knows that most Euro-Americans will judge him with suspicion, and he knows that he must find a way to respond with strength. With prescience, Okada's very first line considers the many wars to be fought both on battlefields and in society. "I know now for what war I was born," he begins. In December 1941, we might leap immediately to the US entry into World War II, but Okada surprises us by turning to the mental and social wars that Japanese Americans will have to fight in order to maintain their dignity in the face of racism. This pivot toward the self from the social is not that strange when we consider that Auden, too, wrote of "obsessing our private lives." Okada starts with the general but then moves to the personal: "Every child is born to see some struggle, / But this conflict is yet the worst, / For my dark features are those of the enemy." The word *conflict* stands in here for the interpersonal strife that all Japanese Americans will have to endure in a post–Pearl Harbor world.

The internal near-rhyme in lines 4 and 5 anchors the main theme of the poem. The word *dark* nearly rhymes with the word *heart,* linking the images of "my dark features" and "my heart. . . . buried deep in occidental soil." The tension here between surface and depth, facial features and essential identity, governs the entire poem. Okada knows his own identity deep down but knows also that others will judge him based on his appearance. He develops this theme of surface and depth in the second stanza as he considers these others' outward appearances and possible internal prejudices: "Everyone will smile, but what of their thoughts." Okada, like Auden, stews in his personal feelings of unease, but whereas Auden can afford to take comfort in others knowing his allegiance, Okada cannot. In "September 1, 1939," Auden famously intoned, "We must love one another or die." Okada knew that to do so would require strength on his own part as well as that of his fellow Americans: I must be strong *and* all of us must love one another.

Okada's poem is a remarkably perceptive meditation on race and American society of the time. He was right: "People will say things, and people will do things, / I know they will." President Franklin D. Roosevelt did do something in February 1942 when he signed Executive Order 9066, which enabled the mass incarceration of all Japanese "alien and non-alien"—i.e., both noncitizens and citizens—living on the west coast of the United States. While spending five months behind barbed wire, receiving leave clearance for Nebraska, and then joining the army, Okada discovered ways to "be strong" in the face of incarceration and war. The poem serves as evidence, moreover, of Okada's awareness that "conflict" would persist beyond the closing of the camps and the official end of World War II. After being discharged, Okada would return not only to college but also to writing as a way to contemplate varieties of strength (think of Kenji and Mrs. Yamada in *No-No Boy*) and the costs of internalizing conflict (think of Ichiro and his father). Before writing his remarkable novel, however, Okada learned from thoughtful professors and practiced with shorter forms.

CREATIVE WRITING AT THE UNIVERSITY OF WASHINGTON

John Okada's earliest publications probably grew out of assignments he completed at the University of Washington from 1946 to 1947, where he worked extensively under Grant H. Redford and to a lesser degree with George Milton Savage. While Okada started on his BA in English with a freshman composition class in 1941, the eviction and incarceration in 1942 interrupted his education. When he returned to the university after his military service, Okada worked diligently on requirements for the English major, but he also threw himself into creative writing courses. In his first term back, he took not only an introduction to fiction class but also electives in both dramatic composition and narrative writing. During that spring term of 1946, Okada wrote a one-act play for Savage's class. Afterward, he concentrated on developing his skills as a writer of prose fiction. From the summer term of 1946 until the spring term of 1947, Okada enrolled in two more courses in narrative writing and three in advanced short-story writing, all taught by Grant H. Redford.

In Redford, Okada must have found not only good instruction but also inspiration. As an author, Redford had published short stories in magazines and journals like *Cosmopolitan* and the *Pacific Spectator*, but his greatest influence may have been as a professor.[6] Redford required his students to keep a notebook to record their thoughts and observations. He talked with his students individually and encouraged them to create meaningful narratives from the "stuff of their lives."[7] In 1946, Redford wrote that "there is a crying need in these sick times for someone to discover the meaning of our time, to translate that meaning into a program of action which will lead us to a greater sense of unity and cooperation for a decent and healthy world. What more can a . . . student ask than that he be charged to examine his life and world, discover its meaning, translate it into words which will move us to laughter, to tears, and then to deeds of reconstruction where not only he, but all men, can live in creatively cooperative peace?"[8] This was the high bar that Redford set for his students, including Okada. What Redford called "these sick times," Okada might have called these absurd times following Executive Order 9066.

"WHEN IN JAPAN": A ONE-ACT PLAY

During the spring term of 1946, Okada began his formal training in creative writing with the energetic and popular George Milton Savage. A strong believer in his students and in the importance of staged production as part of their learning process, Savage produced Okada's one-act play, "When in Japan," that summer at the Tryout Theatre.[9] A notice in the June 9, 1946, issue of the *Seattle Times* reported that Okada's work was one of four new works "receiving bouquets from first-night audiences." The script for "When in Japan" was published in two parts in an all-English-language Japanese American newspaper, the *Northwest Times*, on January 2 and 10, 1947, with the subtitle "The Captain Wasn't Too Sharp on Diplomacy." In an accompanying note, the *Northwest Times*'s editor, Budd Fukei, described Okada as "an English major at the University of Washington."

Fukei had been a journalist before the war, and he established this newspaper to help rebuild the Japanese American community in and around Seattle.[10] Of course, the *Northwest Times* featured news of interest to the community, including news of Japan. The paper also maintained a "Nisei Calendar" to promote community events. A section titled "Social Whirl" announced births, weddings, and other milestones. Sports coverage in "The Sporting Thing" was written by "bf" himself.[11] Clearly interested in a broad definition of culture, Fukei's paper also printed the occasional poem, play, or short story. For instance, "Good Bye, Poston!" by Bob Okazaki appeared on January 24, 1947. In addition, the paper maintained a regular section called "The Book Corner," which told of books not only by but also about Japanese and Japanese Americans.[12] Hence, publishing Okada's short works in this forum served to help rebuild the Seattle-area Japanese American community generally and a once vibrant Japanese American literary community specifically.[13]

Fukei described the play in his editor's note as a "one-act comedy belittling an American captain's efforts to democratize the Japanese in Japan." In this work, Okada tested out his comic voice as he considered the absurdity of an occupying force trying to teach democratic ideals. This resonates in some ways with the absurdity of a democracy that would suspend *habeas corpus* and incarcerate its own citizens without trial. In the play, the blustery captain talks about the importance of democracy but treats his staff and his Japanese interlocutors as if he were a beneficent dictator. He tells others that he is helping them to realize their own goals, but in fact he pursues only what he thinks is in their—and ultimately his own—best interest. This rhetoric echoes the euphemistic vocabulary of "evacuation," which suggested that the US military "relocated" Japanese Americans for their own safety. The play emphasizes questions of rhetoric and representation via its setting in an office of the Educational Movies Section of the Civilian Information and Educational Division. Hence, the captain leads a propagandistic communications office in postwar Japan that functions not unlike the US Office of War Information's Bureau of Motion Pictures during the war. In 1943, for instance, the Bureau of Motion Pictures deployed shockingly euphemistic language in the newsreel *Japanese Relocation.* This account told how the US government supposedly helped Japanese American "pioneers" settle land that was "raw, untamed, and full of opportunity"— though the reality, of course, was that the US military forced incarcerees to live in windy, desert prisons.

The captain's office in the play had its real counterpart in Japan, which Okada may have seen during his five-month stint as an interpreter for the US occupying forces. The Civilian Information and Educational Division (CIE) distributed film projectors and documentaries all over the country. "The Americans' aim," according to historian Markus Nornes, "was to spread democracy to the hinterlands, where the realities of the Occupation and the driving forces behind the transformations in the nation were only weakly felt."[14] Just as in the play, the CIE attempted to work with Japanese film crews to create linguistically and culturally accessible materials. And just as in the play, these crews, feeling that they were being bullied, responded by executing a tactic that they had learned from their democratic training: they went on strike. The captain attempts to force the Japanese film crew to produce a documentary on reforming agricultural methods in order to address his top priority: the postwar food shortage. The leader of the crew, however, wants to focus attention on improving the nation's transportation system: "My mother is ninety-one years old. For five long years she has been waiting to see her long absent son. She has not long to live and were it not for the people who run the trains in so inefficient a manner. . . ." Having been disobeyed, the captain loses his temper and yells, "I forbid you to strike! You don't know what you're doing!" This dramatic situation echoes actual events, including General MacArthur's prioritization of agricultural reform and his directive against general strikes, and it anticipates an actual filmmaker strike in 1948.[15] Clearly, Okada paid attention to the American occupation of Japan, and his play offers a satirical critique of its leadership's insensitivity and contradictions.

This critique comes across lightly because the play focuses on the incompetence of the captain. Okada chooses to make him a comic figure. In the *dramatis personae*, Okada describes the captain as "past fifty, grey-haired, mustached, full around the waist but not fat, likes to hear himself talk." He "mooches" cigarettes from his staff and flirts inappropriately with a female officer. He cannot speak Japanese and yet pretends to understand a Japanese script when handed one. Hence, the captain behaves in a way that invites disgust and ridicule. The play is much kinder to the members of the Japanese film crew, even though their limited understanding of English and relatively formal mannerisms contribute to the comedy. A repeated gag involves the Japanese film crew's writer misunderstanding the captain, as when the captain asks, "So you wrote this, did you?" and the writer, who only understands Japanese, "as if frightened, nods negatively furiously," until a bilingual colleague "whispers in his ear, and [he] smiles and nods affirmatively." Directly after witnessing this faulty communication, the audience is made to understand that all of this is lost on the captain, who is "still talking only" to the monolingual writer. At this relatively early moment in the play, we pity the captain even as we titter at his density. Eventually, however, we learn that his lack of "diplomacy," among other skills, dooms his efforts at both self-promotion and assisting in the democratization of Japan.

Very little of this kind of comedy can be found in *No-No Boy*. If anything, readers might find Ichiro's father to be a pitiable but laughable character, but for the most part Okada's novel works in a much darker register. It seems, too, that Okada did not return to writing plays after completing his assignment for Professor Savage's class. Perhaps the genre did not suit his talents or sensibility, even though "When in Japan" was a fairly successful effort, especially for a student work. Additionally, staging plays may have seemed an impractical avenue for an author interested in somehow representing the absurdity of incarceration—at least explicitly during the immediate postwar years when most Japanese Americans did not want to communicate openly about the camps.[16] It took until the 1970s for plays to represent the incarceration on stage.[17] For many, the pain of imprisonment was too raw. Consequently, it is not surprising that Okada would turn away from a mode of literary production that would require finding actors, raising funds, and enticing audiences to attend a public performance about subjects and themes so many wanted to avoid. Okada's one-act comedy demonstrates that he could have pursued a career as a playwright, but his decisive turn toward prose fiction suggests that he found this mode better suited for his purposes and the conditions of his milieu. Although he would not write explicitly about the incarceration until *No-No Boy* in the mid-1950s, during his time at the University of Washington he tested out the possibilities for short stories to represent the absurd.

OKADA'S TURN TO PROSE FICTION

Over the course of two months—March and April of 1947—Okada published five short stories in the *Northwest Times,* all of which gave him the opportunity to showcase various modes of prose storytelling and represent different kinds of absurdity. Practicing the craft of short-story writing surely helped Okada when he sat down to write his novel. For instance, he honed his ability to reveal a character's interior life, establish mood with description and symbolism, and move his readers through a plot efficiently and effectively.

In an unpublished manuscript for a book about reading and writing short stories, Redford stressed the importance of point of view as a way to reveal both a character's interior life and reality itself, explaining: "Point of view is the lens through which all elements of the story must pass before they can be seen by the reader. The placement of the lens will determine what can be seen; the characteristics of it will determine the nature of what is seen. Since the lens is a point-of-view character, his age, intelligence and temperament together with the pressures of time, place and circumstance which may distort him are the factors which will determine the nature of what the reader will see."[18]

Readers familiar with *No-No Boy* know that Okada learned this lesson well: his point-of-view character, Ichiro Yamada, is a masterful construction. Ichiro's parents, his upbringing, his intelligence and temperament, and his choices with regard to the pressures of his time, place, and circumstance, especially the war and incarceration as they impinged on a young Japanese American man—Okada renders all of this with sensitivity and realism. Ultimately, *No-No Boy* succeeds because we "see"— and feel—postwar Seattle through this well-constructed and ingeniously imagined point-of-view character.

Of course, while short stories and novels employ similar techniques, they differ in key ways. Frank O'Connor's theory of the short story, articulated in his book *The Lonely Voice,* continues to be instructive, especially as a way to think about Okada's style and mindset. (It is uncertain whether O'Connor's ideas directly influenced Redford or Okada, but he was certainly a giant of short-story writing and theory in the 1930s through the 1950s and they no doubt knew his work.) Because short stories are much briefer than novels, O'Connor explains, they must distill "a whole lifetime. . . . into a few minutes," and "those minutes must be carefully chosen indeed and lit by an unearthly glow, one that enables us to distinguish present, past, and future as though they were all contemporaneous."[19] Besides this formal difference, O'Connor points us toward what he calls an "ideological" difference: "an attitude of mind that is strongly attracted by submerged population groups, whatever these may be at any given time—tramps, artists, lonely idealists, [and] dreamers. . . . The novel can still adhere to the classical concept of civilized society, of man as an animal who lives in a community, as in Jane Austen and Trollope it obviously does; but the short story remains by its very nature remote from the community—romantic, individualistic, and intransigent."[20] O'Connor's theory also reminds us that many short stories focus on the absurd—or at least the difficult, if not impossible, search for meaning. Their characters often face "defeat inflicted by a society that has no sign posts, a society that offers no goals and no answers."[21] Ultimately, O'Connor's theory describes Okada's approach to short stories well. In addition, we can see the possible influence of this theory on his novel writing, for instance in how he adapts the idea of focusing on a member from a submerged group to develop the character of Ichiro Yamada.[22]

"WHAT CAN I DO?"

Before Okada wrote about Ichiro Yamada's quest, however, he focused on one stop on the journey of a man named Jiro Nakamura in the short story "What Can I Do?" Published on March 25, 1947, this story features a wounded, hungry Japanese American vagrant who jumps off of a moving freight train and attempts to find food and work at a local café. Noticing this character's bad left leg, readers who know Okada's novel will be tempted to see Jiro Nakamura as a precursor not of the no-no boy Ichiro Yamada but of his wounded, veteran friend Kenji Kanno. Jiro, however, may or may not be a veteran; the story leaves the cause of his wound vague. Instead, "What Can I Do?" focuses on the emotional turmoil and hopelessness of Jiro's life in the aftermath of his wound, no matter how he received it. The story is not told in the first person, but the title invites the reader to identify with Jiro's plight and ask, in his place, what could I do? The owner of the café, Jim, who has given him food in exchange for labor, comments on Jiro's transient lifestyle: "one helluva way to live." Jiro responds, "Maybe there's no other way for a guy like me," to which Jim follows up with "Whattaya mean, a guy like you?" Jiro provides no answer, however. The source of his trouble may be his leg injury, but the wound actually seems to symbolize something else.[23] Perhaps "a guy like me" is marked by race? Critic James Kyung-Jin Lee theorizes "woundedness as intrinsic to Asian American identity," and Viet Thanh Nguyen explains that to "be a minority is to be defined, to some extent, by the wounding or damage done to one on the basis of being a minority."[24] Or perhaps "a guy like me" has committed some crime or mistake from which he must run? This possibility, of course, leads us to think of Ichiro, who, at the beginning of No-No Boy, thinks that he has erred by resisting the draft.[25] Alternatively, he may have committed some other deed—perhaps even an admirable one, the consequence of which is his wound, which leads us to think about Kenji. Yet the very vagueness of Jiro's source of trouble suggests that this story is concerned not with causes but with consequences.

Jiro suffers, and readers are asked to empathize with his suffering regardless of its cause. We learn that he feels physical pain in his leg, that he is sensitive to the cold weather, and that he is hungry. Like Ichiro, Jiro is hungry, and he does not know how to satisfy his hunger—figuratively at least.[26] Also like Ichiro, Jiro does not know where he is going. "Jiro stumbled along awkwardly, as if in a fog," the narrator tells us and then adds information about his emotional state: "the anger would pass. He would not be regretful. He never was. He'd only feel the cold slab of stone that filled his chest constantly." We are meant to feel this passing anger, persistent cold, and irresistible burden. In this story, Okada hones his ability to depict suffering in a psychologically realistic way with clipped sentences, sensory terms, and concrete images such as these. As Redford explains in his manuscript on short stories, "We perceive the world only through our senses. Only what can be seen, heard, tasted, smelled or touched is 'real.' . . . The artist—and to a degree the artist that exists in every man—is distinguished primarily by his power to translate what he senses into sensible shapes."[27] In this regard, Okada distinguished himself quickly and well.

His success derives also from his subtle ability to slip from third-person narration into first-person interior monologue, a stylistic technique that he may have learned from studying short-story writers like Katherine Mansfield under Redford's tutelage. Redford admired, for instance, Mansfield's "Bliss," passages of which "shift" from third-person narration to present tense, which "aligns us with the character's immediate present," according to narratologist Violeta Sotirova.[28] Readers of Okada's novel will recall such moments as when Ichiro first considers his mother's advice: "Think more deeply and your doubts will disappear. You are my son." As critic Frank Chin points out, this statement "triggers a spinning, running internal monologue that is one of the most powerfully moving passages in Asian American writing," one that begins in the third person but then shifts into the first: "No, *he* said to *himself* as *he* watched her part the curtains and start into the store. There was a time when *I* was your son. There was a time that *I* no longer remember when you used to smile a mother's smile and tell me stories . . . about the old woman who found a peach in the stream, and, when her husband split it in half, a husky little boy tumbled out to fill their hearts with boundless joy. *I was that lad in the peach*" (emphasis added).[29] In Okada's earlier work, we see a similar shift from third-person narration to Jiro's mind: "*He* walked slowly along the back of the counter until *he* was directly in front of the register. . . . Been a long time since *I* saw anything larger than a buck. If *I* had a thousand cash registers full of money, maybe people would look at my car and clothes instead of at my leg" (emphasis added). Some reviewers critique Okada's narrative perspective in his novel as "inconsistent," but we can see that he practiced it in this short story and drew upon established models by modernist writers like Mansfield.[30]

In "What Can I Do?" Okada demonstrates his early mastery of a psychologically realistic style. The story climaxes by putting readers inside Jiro's mind as he briefly considers the idea of stealing money from Jim's cash register.[31] What *can* he do? Jiro could steal but decides against doing so. In any case, he suffers, since Jim gets the wrong impression and chases him out of the café and back onto the street. As Frank O'Connor might put it, society offers no signposts for where Jiro should head next or what he should do. In addition, he is a member of a submerged group, but we are not exactly sure which group. In answer to the question "Where are you from?" Jiro responds, "Nowhere and everywhere." While Jiro is the only explicitly Japanese American character to appear in Okada's five short stories, his racialized identity is not clearly the source of his troubles. He is an Everyman figure who happens to have a Japanese name. In *No-No Boy,* Okada would pointedly explore quandaries precipitating from the friction between individual and community, but in this short story, he concentrates on a tightly bounded incident to reveal the bleakness of a submerged character's past, present, and future. "What Can I Do?" focuses not on a cause of absurdity like wartime incarceration or postwar occupation but on how the psychological and social consequences of previous damage, whether self- or other-inflicted, at once torment a character's state of mind and foreclose his life chances in an absurd world without signposts. In Jiro we have a character that anticipates both Ichiro and Kenji. More importantly, we have in him an example not of what haunted Okada but of how he could depict a mind and life so haunted.

Certainly interested in loss, grief, and psychological suffering, Okada continued with such subject matter in "Without Solace," published on April 4, 1947. This short story focuses on an old farmer named Benson who lived with his wife Emma for twenty years before they conceived a daughter, Jan. At the opening of the story, we learn that Jan "took sick" a few days ago, and then over the course of the story, we witness her death and Benson's emotionally charged and gothically inflected reaction. If we assume that Okada wrote this while taking short-story courses, we might think that he had been influenced by Washington Irving and Edgar Allan Poe, two masters of the genre.[32] In Okada's story, Benson denies his daughter's death, carries her out into the country as if on a stroll, takes a nap with her corpse, and then engages in a conversation with a disembodied voice.

Before this climactic conversation, however, we witness Okada's skill at depicting psychological realism. With language that will resonate with readers who know his novel, this story's narrator tells us that Benson "looked into the face of his dead daughter. Following a quick surge of horror and bursting grief upon grasping the implication of Jan's strange conduct, he felt nothing. A blankness pervaded his mind, his eyes remained open but were blind to the immediate surroundings. In truth, he was like a senseless rock plunging downward thru endless fathoms of the deepest ocean." This representation of denial may remind us of Ichiro's mother's belief that Japan has won the war. The novel picks up on the story's simile as well: "Ma is the rock that's always hammering, pounding, pounding, pounding in her unobtrusive, determined, fanatical way until there's nothing left to call one's self."[33] The rock imagery here suggests that the idea of *gaman,* or endurance, can be taken too far. Hardness that leads to denial can send one down into the depths of depression and towards potential destruction of self and others. Making Ma the hard character and Pa the relatively soft, "spineless nobody" in the novel aligns with the fact that during the incarceration the patriarchal authority of Issei men was degraded as some, including Okada's own father, were imprisoned apart by the Justice Department, and many lost their primary means of livelihood and identity.[34] Some first-generation women in this context had to take over as heads of households. Ma, of course, is an extreme, fictional case. In "Without Solace," however, traditional gender norms prevail. Benson is the rock, and Emma is relatively soft, even as she tries to stop him from carrying their lifeless daughter outside: "Her fingers were no match for the powerful arms of her husband. Overcome by a fit of anguished sobbing, she slumped helplessly onto the stairs."

Once outside, Benson carries Jan's corpse across the farmland and eventually tires. Like Washington Irving's Rip Van Winkle, he falls asleep and then awakens to a new reality. Even the language echoes that of Irving's fantastical sketch: "Old Benson slept for many hours. When he finally woke up, the sun had almost completely disappeared behind the western hills. The pasture was calm, not even the wind stirred the air." This eerie stillness suggests the stoppage of time. In this alternate reality, which may be simply Benson's perspective distorted by unbearable grief, a disembodied voice engages him in conversation. Benson explains to the voice, "Life was really good, really worthwhile. Then, last week, Jan took sick. I've always been a good man and I prayed for her every minute but it wasn't any use. She died, and it's wrong. There's no fairness at all, only injustice. I've lost my girl and my faith in God." In Jan's death, Benson faces the absurd. What is one to do in the face of such loss? Where are the signposts that might lead to solace? After the death of a child, after your country imprisons you without trial, is there "no fairness at all, only injustice"? Benson talks out the first version of this question with the disembodied voice, which of course may be his own conscience à la Edgar Allan Poe.[35] This technique anticipates the many introspective moments we spend with Ichiro in *No-No Boy*, albeit without the supernatural aura. Recall, for instance, when Ichiro dreams about one day buying a home only to be interrupted by his conscience: "As his heart mercifully stacked the blocks of hope into the pattern of an America which would someday hold an unquestioned place for him, his mind said no, it is not to be."[36] At the conclusion of "Without Solace," the voice reminds Benson that everyone suffers and that everyone grieves for someone. *Shikataganai*, one might say—some things cannot be helped. But does this realization provide solace? Although the story ends with a sense of closure and perhaps even catharsis, the title suggests that solace may be impossible to achieve in this absurd world.

"SKIPPING MILLIONS"

Published a few days later, on April 8, 1947, Okada's short story "Skipping Millions" tells the relatively mundane tale of an inattentive, unnamed store clerk who is more concerned with reading a novel than serving potential customers. He admits, "I had long ago lost track of the number of customers who had walked out on account of my unwillingness to rush out and wait upon them." According to Frank Abe, this clerk is based on Okada's own postwar experience managing an army surplus store owned by a friend in Seattle; and of course, Okada liked to read. Perhaps not coincidentally, this story is the only one told in the first person.[37]

Eventually one customer gets the clerk's attention, a "strange gentleman" enamored with a particular brand of straight-edge razor, "a pre-war Muellerhoffer," displayed in the store window. It turns out that the customer is Abie K. Muellerhoffer himself, the inventor of the razor. "Skipping Millions" gets its title from the fact that this character is a millionaire whose "manner" of walking "rapidly with short, jerky steps made it appear as if he were skipping." This skipping motion, as well as Muellerhoffer's other mannerisms, including pressing his nose against the window and gesturing without speaking, lead the clerk to be somewhat dismissive of, if not downright disrespectful toward, his customer. He even laughs at him several times. Not until the revelation of his identity near the end of the story does the clerk straighten up. In fact, he is "flabbergasted."

Certainly not as absurd as his other stories, "Skipping Millions" seems to critique most severely, though still lightly, the clerk. The customer may be odd, but he deserves attention. The narration itself encourages readers to prioritize him, since Muellerhoffer is both named and introduced at the outset of the story. The clerk, whom we meet next, barely rouses himself from his book to serve him in the first place, and then does not take him seriously until he learns of his high position. Without much ado, the story asks us to reflect on how we come to know one another and how we ought to treat one another. What do we mean to one another? Are we sometimes so absorbed in our own preoccupations that we barely notice others? Are others important only insofar as they impinge on our immediate interests? What makes a person worthy of respect? Perhaps Okada wondered what bystanders to the incarceration—at least the less vicious ones—thought about their Japanese American neighbors. Perhaps Okada, inspired by Professor Redford to "discover the meaning of our time," resolved to notice and care. Just as this clerk eventually turns his attention to Muellerhoffer, Okada eventually would write from the perspective of a draft resister, even though he himself was a veteran.

"THE SILVER LUNCHBOX"

Like "Without Solace," Okada's next short story, "The Silver Lunchbox," published on April 11, 1947, experiments with Rip Van Winkle–esque plot elements. This much more allegorical tale follows Kippy Smith, a boy on track to earn a silver lunchbox as a prize from his community if he faithfully goes to school for two more weeks, making a total of eight years of perfect attendance.[38] At the beginning of the story, however, Kippy seems not to care, motivated only by the pursuit of knowledge, not by signs of recognition. The narrator explains in a relatively elevated tone: "The prospect of being the first student in the history of Dream County to rise to such an unprecedented height of scholastic recognition aroused no enthusiasm in Kippy. He was, on the contrary, rather disturbed over the thought. Kippy was a scholar, a disciple of knowledge and not a collector of lunchboxes, even those made out of sterling silver." Kippy performs his nonchalance by taking a detour from his path to school one morning. Like Rip Van Winkle, Kippy is traveling with his dog when he encounters a strange, professorial figure who leads him across the countryside and into an alternate universe. In Kippy's case, the dog is too wary to follow his master to the College of Forever.

At first, Kippy is excited at the prospect of truly becoming a disciple of knowledge at the College of Forever, especially since he does not think highly of the education he was getting in Dream County, but he soon discovers that the kind of learning pursued in this alternate universe seems absurd. For example, he meets a student who says, "I've only three years left before I have to take my examination on the ninety-seven basic languages of the universe"; another who is silently working on the "recitation by memory without hesitation the three hundred and fifty-two leading novels of the universe"; and yet another who is contemplating suicide because he doesn't understand Einstein's theory of relativity, which would enable him to get a "degree in eternal knowledge" (his accomplishments so far qualify him only for a "degree in random knowledge"). All of these students work monomaniacally on their scholarly projects that seem to be ends in themselves. In the climax of the story, Kippy angers an immense classroomful of students by noisily dropping his green lunchbox. He runs back to the road, where he meets members of the Dream County school-board, and since no time passed in this reality, he is now ready to earn that silver lunchbox.

The thematic point of connection between "The Silver Lunchbox" and *No-No Boy* emanates from their protagonists' ideas about education. Like Kippy, Ichiro once upheld a noble sense of the scholarly life. Before incarceration, Ichiro derived deep satisfaction from "the weighty volumes which he had carried against his side so that the cloth of his pants became thin and frayed. . . . and the slide rule with the leather case which hung from his belt like the sword of learning which it was."[39] With a certain dreaminess reinforced by repetitive phrasing, he recalls thinking, "To be a student in America was a wonderful thing. To be a student in America studying engineering was a beautiful life." Ichiro's education, of course, was "interrupted" by the incarceration.[40] Kippy's elevated sense of the scholarly life is shattered, in contrast, by his encounters with students and professors who seem to be so absorbed in their own projects that they do not have time or attention for anything else. Perhaps this serves as a subtle commentary on academicians' lack of response during the incarceration? Perhaps this story invites us to ask what the purpose of higher learning is, if it does not motivate moral action? When Ichiro talks with his old engineering professor, the latter says, "Tough about the evacuation. I really hated to see it happen. . . . Families uprooted, businesses smashed, educations interrupted. You've got a right to be sore." The professor "hated to see it happen," but like most Americans, he did nothing at the time. He had the academic freedom that almost all professors of American universities have, but he did not use his position and power to speak or act against what he knew was wrong.[41] This, then, may be the absurdity pointed at in this short story: education might provide sign-posts but has no meaning unless those signposts lead to action.

"here's proof"

Published in two parts on April 15 and April 18, 1947, Okada's next story, "Here's Proof," exhibits an entirely different tone but still deals with the absurdity of an unjust world. While "The Silver Lunchbox" featured a fan-tastical setting and proper English, "Here's Proof" returns to the kind of gritty environment and vernacular speech that appears also in "What Can I Do?" and that critic Joseph Entin identifies as noir in *No-No Boy*.[42] Entin rightly points out that Ichiro sometimes expresses his introspectiveness in the hard-boiled language of noir: "Christ, he thought to himself, just a goddamn kid is all I was. Didn't know enough to wipe my own nose. What the hell have I done? What am I doing back here? Best thing I can do would be to kill some son of a bitch and head back to prison."[43] Although there is violence and death in the novel, there is no first-degree murder. The same cannot be said for "Here's Proof," which focuses on a group of coworkers at a bar who seem to be idly talking about whether it is possible to commit murder, leave no evidence, and avoid all suspicion. Jim declares, "Justice is a wonderful thing and it doesn't allow perfect murders." Hal disagrees, and Mac remains silent on the topic, but even when the friends change the subject to "dames," Stanley broods over Jim's declaration. In fact, Stanley had murdered an old fisherman two years before for no reason except that he could.[44] Now, he feels the necessity to commit another murder, to prove to his coworkers that a "perfect murder" is possible.

Like Jiro in "What Can I Do?," Benson in "Without Solace," and Ichiro in *No-No Boy,* Stanley in this story experiences psychological torment, which we readers get a sense of via Okada's narration: "With the intensity of hate that can only result from long mental self-persecution, he knew that he must plan another murder, a perfect murder." With cold efficiency,

Stanley goes on to seduce a female office-mate, kill her, and go back to work for weeks without raising anyone's suspicion. Meanwhile, one day Jim complains about lunchtime traffic, with an irony perceptible to the reader, if not to Jim, Hal, or Mac: "What a struggle. . . . it's a crime what a guy has to go through nowadays to get a hamburger and a cup of coffee." Of course, Stanley finally cannot stand that his three friends do not know of his accomplishment, so he boasts about it to them. Closure does not arrive, however, until Jim gets him to tell the details of his crime in the hearing of plainclothes police officers at the bar where the story began. Jim punching out Stanley fulfills another noir convention.

Interestingly, Stanley's motive for committing murder departs from usual expectations. He has nothing against his victims, nothing material to gain from their deaths, and nothing to fear from them. Stanley commits what he deems to be "perfect" murders only to demonstrate— to himself initially and to his coworkers eventually—that he can do it. Of course, one absurdity here is that anyone would devalue human life so thoroughly. Just because you can kill someone does not mean that you should. Similarly, just because FDR could ignore the Bill of Rights and order the War Relocation Authority to round up people and incarcerate them in horse stalls does not mean that he should have done so.[45] The federal government treated Japanese Americans as if they had committed a crime. The real crime, however, was the incarceration itself.[46]

Would Professor Grant Redford have been proud of his student John Okada? The registrar of the University of Washington was kind enough to share a list of the courses he took, but rules prevented her from telling me his grades. Fortunately, we can discern from Okada's texts themselves that he learned from models like Katherine Mansfield, Sherwood Anderson, Washington Irving, and Edgar Allan Poe how to craft stories with various styles of narration, degrees of allegorical meaning, and kinds of closure. We can see, too, that Okada must have learned also from writers of noir like Dashiell Hammett. In short, we can safely say that Okada began to master the craft of prose-fiction writing by the end of his undergraduate career. Furthermore, Okada was able to publish his writing not long after he wrote it, if what he was submitting to the *Northwest Times* was indeed his classwork. Redford did not put much stock in publication, however, as an indicator of worth.[47]

For a truer evaluation, let us return to Redford's idea that a writer ought to "examine his life and world, discover its meaning, translate it into words which will move us to laughter, to tears, and then to deeds of reconstruction where not only he, but all men, can live in creatively cooperative peace."[48] Based on his early writings and his novel, we can claim confidently that Okada examined not only his own life but also the lives of others. His ability as a veteran to imagine and represent what it might have been like for a no-no boy to return to his community remains the most awesome recommendation of his power as an author. In his early writings too, we can see Okada developing his ability to represent the kind of inner turmoil that he would later plumb in the depths of Ichiro Yamada's psychology. And certainly Okada answered his professor's call to examine his world. Redford decried "these sick times." For his part, Okada observed and considered absurdity—in the depravities of some fellow humans, the lack of signposts provided by society, and the unwillingness of some to act even when the writing is on the wall.

Did Okada discover the meaning of life or the world and translate it for his readers? Mainstream writers of the absurd tradition would say that there is no meaning to be discovered. Consider, for instance, the relative absence of "meaning" in Samuel Beckett's *Waiting for Godot* or Albert Camus's *Myth of Sisyphus*. Okada, however, more in a humanistic existential vein, leaves open the possibility that people create meaning, that they believe in and stand for something beyond themselves. Acknowledging that "despair was part of the nature of the human condition," humanistic existential philosopher Hazel Barnes "emphasized that men and women, through their actions, defined themselves and acted upon the world, making it, bit by bit, a better place."[49] In Okada's earlier work, we might recall that the members of the Japanese film crew hold fast to their priorities over those of the inept captain; Jim initially offers a job to Jiro, even though their relationship eventually sours; Benson begins to mourn his daughter; Kippy escapes the College of Forever; and Jim punches out Stanley. In spite of all that he has gone through by the end of his journey in *No-No Boy*, Ichiro holds onto "a glimmer of hope."[50]

Did Okada, however, answer Redford's charge to move readers to construct conditions in which all people could live in "creatively cooperative peace"? To answer this question, let us turn to another source from Okada's education: Joseph Barlow Harrison. In 1946, besides teaching Okada modern American literature, Professor Harrison also published *If Men Want Peace: The Mandates of World Order,* which collects ideas from several University of Washington faculty members about how to reconstruct the world. As Harrison puts it in his contribution, "We are in the midst of one of the greatest crises in human history. We can resolve it or we can be destroyed by it."[51] He was especially concerned that people from different racialized origins recognize their common humanity. A realist and keen observer, Harrison knew that while some dominant attitudes regarding race had changed, others had not. For instance, referring to the heroics of the 442nd Regimental Combat Team, he acknowledged that "we . . . recognize that a Japanese American can be as loyal as any other American in a foxhole," but he also could imagine "the return of a wounded Japanese-American veteran to a community which had not yet taken down its hoarding [signs reading], 'No Japs wanted here!'"[52] Harrison believed that if people wanted peace, the world would need not only good ideas for practical reform but also "arts and letters" that would help us perceive one another's "vision" and "consciousness," that is, imagine beyond our own limited points of view. "Each of us lives largely in a very private house, the house of the separate personality," Harrison explains. "The noisiest of us tell each other little about its inner appointments. The least noisy artist tells most. He tells most because he is able to create the symbols which are the only language that can shape and communicate these hidden half-realizations."[53] John Okada, even in his earliest writings, reveals the "inner appointments" of submerged personalities living in an absurd world and begins to communicate "hidden half-realizations" that culminate later in "that faint and elusive insinuation of promise" we witness Ichiro chasing at the end of *No-No Boy.*[54]

SATIRICAL ESSAYS AFTER *NO-NO BOY*

After the novel's publication, Okada secured a job as a technical writer at Hughes Aircraft Company in Fullerton, California, where he worked from 1958 until 1961. There he became familiar with defense industry trade magazines like *Aviation Week* and *Armed Forces Management.* The two selections reprinted in this volume—"The High Cost of Proposals and Presentations" and "The Technocrats of Industry"—were written right after he left his job at Hughes to take another in the advertising industry. Both pieces reconfirm Okada's authorial powers, this time in the genre of the satirical essay. Compared with the subtlety of his short stories, these essays offer more direct critique, taking as their target absurdities of the "military-industrial complex," as Dwight D. Eisenhower termed it. Okada was concerned here with the tendency of the military-industrial complex to serve as an end in itself, rather than for a genuine purpose, like national defense. He populates these essays with characters and institutions driven by myopic self-interest and mismanagement, although they might represent themselves as having loftier aims.

In "The High Cost of Proposals and Presentations," Okada opens with a scenario that satirizes a blowhard manager, Mr. Blunt, who wastes taxpayer money by producing overly elaborate contract-bid packaging. A version of the captain in "When in Japan" who makes films to teach democracy to the Japanese, Mr. Blunt plans to rent special wide-screen projection equipment and portable gold draperies for a film to promote the Missile Advanced Defense System. Everyone in the scenario calls this system—without irony—MAD. Okada was obviously having fun with the industry's affected acronyms. The Hughes Aircraft Company at the time was in fact developing a new missile defense system to replace one called Semi-Automatic Ground Environment, or SAGE.

In "The Technocrats of Industry," Okada offers an extended critique perhaps all the more brazen because he does so behind the safety of a pseudonym, John Hillfield (the name Okada roughly translates as "field of hills" in English). Instead of only a scenario, the entire essay satirizes a military-industrial complex that employs engineers to oversee everything from sales and public relations to library services and recreation. Taking a cue perhaps from Jonathan Swift's satire *Gulliver's Travels,* Okada's piece follows the "trials and tribulations of Mr. S.V.," an electrical engineer who finds himself at first shocked by and then inured to problematic defense industry workplace customs.

Most of the essay pokes fun at the wastefulness and self-absorption of the military-industrial complex, but it also includes several self-referential moments. For instance, the essay jokes that recruiters desperate for engineers sometimes mistake those with a "B.A. in Eng." as qualified. Of course, Okada himself studied English in college. Also, the main character of the satire, Mr. S.V., reaches a low point when he is demoted from engineer to technical writer, which was Okada's actual job. Hence Okada, like this character, found his calling in writing. When writing, Mr. S.V. feels "productive and useful." Years earlier, Professor Grant Redford charged his student John Okada with the task of making himself productive and useful as a creative writer.

These two articles appeared in the straightforward trade publication *Armed Forces Management,* but they sparkle with humor and irony. The former even led to changes in the way that defense contractors do business, according to Okada's son, Matthew. We remember John Okada for his signal contribution in *No-No Boy,* but even as a technical writer he found ways to answer Redford's charge to examine "these sick times" and move the world toward "deeds of reconstruction." Just as he had considered various forms of absurdity in his early writings and novel, his satirical essays questioned the absurdity of the war machine itself.

A Seed in a Devastated Landscape

John Okada and Midcentury Japanese American Literature

GREG ROBINSON

JOHN OKADA'S 1957 NOVEL *NO-NO BOY* IS NOTABLE FOR ITS EXPLO-ration of the crippling legacy of wartime confinement on postwar Japanese communities, as seen through the painful readjustment of the draft resister Ichiro Yamada following his release from prison. Critics have claimed the book as an *urtext* of contemporary Asian American literature, for in setting the work within postwar ethnic Japanese communities and exploring the durable impact of racism on their members, in a manner very different from that of the white liberal or African American writers of the postwar era, Okada anticipated the work of later generations of ethnic writers.

In a real sense, *No-No Boy* bears double witness to the collective wartime trauma of West Coast Japanese Americans. Beyond the novel's contents, the damaged state of the community revealed itself in the overall absence of response to its initial publication. Latter-day fans of Okada, shocked by the paucity of contemporary reviews, have often assumed that this silence was a product of intervention by conservative Nisei (American-born Japanese) opposed to the author's message. As writer Frank Chin stated, "The JACL [Japanese American Citizens League] drove *No-No Boy* off the shelves when it first came out."[1]

However, not only does Chin confessedly lack direct evidence for this assertion, but the claim also obscures larger structural realities. First, by the time Okada began publishing his work, in 1946–47, the rich literary culture that had grown up in West Coast Japanese communities during the prewar years had been destroyed, and there were no longer circles of *littérateurs* to engage authors in any collective forum. Because the institutional framework that enabled authors to develop their art in conversation with the community was absent, Okada's was inevitably a solitary voice. Secondly, by the time *No-No Boy* came out, a decade-long period of silence regarding the wartime events had set in. Amid the climate of mass amnesia, mainstream presses ceased to bring out new books of any kind on the subject, whether by Nisei or others, and any discussion of the legacy of the camps was consequently stifled. Thus, to properly situate Okada's writings—his short stories as well as his novel—and his achievement in publishing them, it is necessary to examine the larger historical context surrounding literature by Nisei.

THE "GREAT NISEI NOVEL"

In the years preceding World War II, there was an explosion of creative writing by West Coast Nisei, which in a sense marked the community as unique: with the possible exception of Jewish Americans, no other second-generation ethnic group of the early twentieth century fostered such an intense flowering of literary activity. During the 1930s, Nisei authors published hundreds of stories and essays in English, as well as book reviews, poems, and translations of Japanese works.

The literary culture of the Nisei developed in response to a number of factors. First, there was the cultural baggage they had absorbed from their Issei (immigrant) parents. As a result of policies of universal primary education in Meiji-era Japan, virtually all Japanese of both sexes were literate in their native language. From the dawn of Japanese settlement in the United States, the Issei continued to produce vernacular newspapers and magazines, and individuals—especially women—remained active in producing poetry as well as diaries and letters. Even if the largest part of Issei output was in Japanese and thus little read by the Nisei, who generally lacked Japanese reading skills (not to mention sufficient interest), the existence of a literate community among their parents nevertheless provided the young generation an immediate and clear model.[2]

A related element of importance in the outpouring of literature was the existence of high-quality free public education in West Coast states such as California and Washington that had sizable Nisei populations. As part of their high school coursework, students took English and journalism classes and were thereby exposed to Western literature. High school and university newspapers and literary volumes in turn provided outlets for stories and poems by Nisei writers. Indeed, a significant fraction of the contributors to the prewar Nisei press (and of Nisei generally) were college-educated.

As importantly, community leaders provided Nisei writers with resources and encouragement. By the end of the 1920s, as the Nisei generation began to emerge, the main ethnic Japanese newspapers on the West Coast, beginning with Los Angeles's *Rafu Shimpo* and San Francisco's *Nichi Bei Shimbun* and *Shin Sekai,* gradually instituted English-language pages under the direction of Nisei editors. In 1931 Henry Shimanouchi and Goro Murata, editors of the fledgling English section of *Rafu Shimpo,* began to devote a page to Nisei writing on a regular basis and instituted monthly literature prizes. Shortly thereafter, local Issei editor Sei Fujii founded the upstart daily *Kashu Mainichi.* Fujii hired Wally Shibata as English-page editor, and soon after recruited the teenage Larry Tajiri, first as Shibata's assistant, then as his replacement. Shibata and Tajiri established a permanent Sunday art and literature page that drew fiction, translations, essays, and poetry from a host of Nisei authors. Soon other newspapers adopted the practice. In 1934 Tajiri moved to San Francisco to become English editor of *Nichi Bei Shimbun.* The literature section he edited there was generally conceded to be the best at the time on the West Coast.

Meanwhile, a few young Nisei writers started literary clubs to foster mutual support and discussion. Out of these clubs came a series of small literary reviews: In Salt Lake City, poet Yasuo Sasaki founded *Reimei,* which published four issues from 1931 to 1933. After Sasaki moved to Los Angeles, he and journalist/poet Mary Oyama Mittwer (his future sister-in-law) created the Nisei Writers Group (later the Nisei League of Writers and Artists) and produced a few issues of a magazine, *Leaves* (1934–35). Seattle-born journalist Eddie Shimano, while a student at Cornell College in Iowa, persuaded the college English department to sponsor a magazine of Nisei writing. Joining forces with the Nisei Writers Group and others, in 1936 Shimano produced a single issue of the journal, titled *Gyo-Sho*. Both the volume's title and its handsome design expressed the level of ambition of its contributors. As Shimano explained in the editor's preface: "GYO-SHO, literally Dawn-Bell, means 'the peal of the gong at the break of day.' . . . And so we think of this magazine as the bell which we strike to announce to the world a new day, symbolizing the awakening of the Nisei." Editor James Omura published literature by Toshio Mori and other Nisei in his San Francisco–based monthly review, *Current Life*, during 1941–42.

The presence of an ethnic readership did not mean that Nisei writers remained inward looking: indeed, they were intensely interested in mainstream literary developments, especially on the West Coast. Nisei newspapers published reviews of popular novelists such as John Steinbeck. Mary Oyama Mittwer and other Nisei invited such stalwarts as William Saroyan and John Fante to lecture to their clubs. However, the West Coast Nisei had little access to outside commercial outlets for their own writing. George Furiya, acclaimed by Tajiri and other *littérateurs* as the finest of the younger generation, wrote a pair of novels with Japanese American characters, *Bread* and *Act of God,* but was unable to find a publisher for either. The sole breakthrough artist on the West Coast was Toshio Mori, whose short stories appeared in small journals such as *Writer's Forum* and *New Directions.* In 1941, with the endorsement of William Saroyan, Mori received a contract for his short-story collection *Yokohama, California* from Caxton Printers in Caldwell, Idaho. In the wake of Pearl Harbor, however, the publisher shelved the project and did not bring it out until 1949.

A few novels by Nisei did appear during the prewar years. Karl S. Nakagawa (a.k.a. Kay Karl Endow), a native of Sacramento, produced two books: the mystery story *The Rendezvous of Mysteries* (1928) and the adventure tale *Transpacific Wings* (1935). Both were published by vanity presses, and the second was marketed as part of a scheme to raise money for a bogus transpacific flight by the author, who was also an aviator. Meanwhile, Hawaiian Nisei journalist James T. Hamada came out with *Don't Give Up the Ship* (1933). These works shared several elements. First, it would be generous to describe them as poorly written—they were superficial, meandering, and melodramatic. Further, nothing directly marked them as Japanese American writing: centered on white protagonists, they did not feature any Japanese American characters or settings. Lastly, they were published by small presses with limited or nonexistent advertising budgets.[3]

Yet the overall quality of prewar community writing, which in any case varied widely, is beside the point here. Rather, what is noteworthy is its essentially autonomous and collective nature: the Nisei wrote primarily among and for themselves. One product of this consciousness was that a large portion of their output centered on Japanese American characters, or somehow addressed the condition of Japanese Americans. Even when such pieces were not strictly autobiographical in nature—as many were— their creators could take for granted that they were part of a community of writers expressing the point of view of the group. Indeed, Larry Tajiri speculated constantly in his columns about which young artist would be the one to write "the great Nisei novel" that would effectively dramatize and explain the particular experience of the group.

Still, their group identity, and the ethnic readership they gained, came at a price. As Nobutaka Ike commented early in 1941 in an eerily prescient essay, Nisei had little chance of succeeding as novelists unless they were willing to buck general opinion, as many community elders actually looked down on intellectual activity. Worse, he asserted, even if a Nisei writer did manage to overcome this conditioning and set out to create a mainstream novel, what would he write about? The Issei had rich material for a novel—"There is something epic about people being torn from their root to be transplanted in another soil"—but the American-born had no such material in their experience as a racial minority. "It is extremely doubtful that a great novel could be written about race prejudice. And even if a great novel could be written, it would arouse little interest. Why should the millions of Americans who compose the reading public be interested in the problems of a few tens of thousands of second generation

Japanese when millions and millions [of Southern blacks] suffer even greater handicaps as John Dollard's 'Caste and Class in a Southern Town' has shown us?"[4]

The wartime confinement of Japanese Americans had a paradoxical impact on Nikkei writing. On the one hand, the issue of mass confinement opened the doors of mainstream media for the first time to Nisei authors, at least for nonfiction. Nisei writers and critics such as Larry Tajiri, Mary Oyama Mittwer, Ted Nakashima, Ina Sugihara, and Eddie Shimano produced articles about the plight of Japanese Americans for mass market periodicals such as *Liberty*, the *New Republic*, and *Saturday Review*; liberal journals such as *Common Ground*, the *New Leader*, the *New Republic*, and *Commonweal*; and even the African American press. Yet the total amount of literature published by Japanese Americans during the war was greatly reduced. Executive Order 9066 led to the closing of the West Coast Nikkei-run newspapers and the dispersal of writing groups. While officially sponsored (and censored) inmate-run newspapers were created at each of the ten government camps inland where Nisei were confined, they featured little fiction or poetry. Larry Tajiri and his wife, Guyo, transformed the JACL bulletin, *Pacific Citizen*, into a full-fledged weekly newspaper, which began publishing in June 1942 but ran almost no literature in its pages.

There were a few outlets for creative writing by inmates. A circle of writers at Topaz formed the literary review *Trek*, which published three issues. Newspapers at other camps ran one-off supplements with stories, such as the *Tule Lake Dispatch* at the Tule Lake camp and *Pulse* at the Granada camp. The *Poston News-Courier* featured Hisaye Yamamoto's serial potboiler, "Death Rides the Rails to Poston," and Kenny [Kenji] Murase's camp sketches featuring a Mexican-Indian boy, "Little Esteban." There were comic strips such as Chris Ishii's "Lil Neebo" at Santa Anita and Amache, and George Akimoto's "Lil Dan'l" at Rohwer.

No doubt understandably, wartime writing by Japanese Americans focused on the lived experience of confinement. Larry Tajiri's sole literary work of the period, commissioned by *Trek*, was a fictionalized narrative of Nisei leaving camp and resettling outside, while two of Toyo Suyemoto's camp poems appeared in *Yale Review* in 1945. Hiroshi Nakamura wrote a full-length "documentary novel," *Treadmill* (eventually published in 1996). Larry Tajiri predicted that the camp experience would lead ultimately to a flowering of literature. "Perhaps from now till the end of the Nisei generation every Nisei will want to write that book as 'the' Nisei novel, just as four years ago every newspaperman wanted some day to write 'the great American novel.'"[5]

THE POSTWAR DECLINE

In the early postwar years, the majority of mainland Nikkei returned to the West Coast and restarted their lives. The prewar ethnic Japanese dailies resumed operation, and new journals such as San Francisco's *Hokubei Mainichi* appeared. Outside the West Coast there were new weekly papers such as the *Chicago Shimpo* and New York's *Hokubei Shimpo*. A number of new all-English weeklies were founded as well, including *Crossroads* in Los Angeles, the *Progressive News* in San Francisco, and the *Northwest Times* in Seattle. There were also the Chicago-based glossy magazines *Nisei Vue* and *Scene*, plus *Bandwagon*, the magazine of the Nisei Progressives in New York.

Much of this flowering of journalism proved ephemeral. By the end of the 1950s the English-only weeklies and magazines had died out, and the bilingual papers focused primarily on Japanese-language news. In any case, even at the height of this publishing activity, there was no real revival of prewar Nisei literary life. Hisaye Yamamoto, one of the few Nisei to continue publishing, noted sadly in 1968 (at a time when she described her own chief occupation as "housewife"): "I don't know of any Nisei devoted to serious writing as a life work; neither do I know of any Nisei gathering together these days to discuss literature."[6]

Such a void can best be explained as an interlocking mix of lack of supply and lack of demand. On the one hand, the former outlets for creative work disappeared. Although the Tajiris reviewed books in the *Pacific Citizen* during the early postwar years, and published a series of literary sketches on resettlement by Toshio Mori and Jobu Nakamura, they did not include a regular fiction page. The West Coast vernaculars ceased to feature weekly literary sections and reduced their space for fiction to the odd holiday issue, and the new Nisei press failed to take up the slack. There was little in the way of group literary activity. In the late 1940s, with encouragement from Mary Oyama Mittwer (who had become a crusading newspaper columnist for *Rafu Shimpo*), a set of young Nisei in Los Angeles, including the brothers Albert and Gompers Saijo and Hiroshi Kashiwagi, formed a playwriting group, which helped to launch Albert Saijo and Kashiwagi on their careers. The group did not survive, however, and seemingly had no real counterparts elsewhere.

The failure of Nisei writers to produce literature was not simply a result of the decline of community publishing venues; it was also a cause. Put simply, the generation of West Coast writers who published in the literary pages of the prewar vernacular press all but vanished. Some took up careers and families, leaving them too busy to concentrate on literature. As Larry Tajiri lamented in 1954, "I've never gotten around to even trying to write that Great American Novel. Now that I've gotten older, I'm not sure I can any more."[7] Major figures such as Togo Tanaka, Vince Tajiri, Joe Oyama, Yasuo Sasaki, Toyo Suyemoto, and Kenji Murase resettled in the East or Midwest and lost their connection with the West Coast press. (A few Nisei moved even farther afield: John Fujii and Tamotsu Murayama settled in Japan, George Furiya in Brazil, and Chiye Mori in the Philippines!) Others, such as Roku Sugahara, George Watanabe, Sam Hohri, and Carl Kondo, suffered poor health and an early demise. Finally, the traumatic impact of the wartime experience left its mark. Formerly productive authors such as Eddie Shimano and Shuji Fujii ceased to publish fiction, apparently because of writer's block.

What literature there was by the postwar generation of mainland Nisei authors, most of whom lived outside the West Coast, focused mainly on non-Japanese subjects. The most mass-market productions, such as Robert Kuwahara's syndicated comic strip *Miki* (1945–50) and Mitsu Yamamoto's magazine story "The Good News," published in the *New Yorker* in 1957, had no identifiably Asian characters. Chicago-based pulp writer Milton Ozaki wrote multiple mystery novels, beginning with *The Cuckoo*

Clock (1946), before eventually introducing a Nisei detective protagonist, Ken Koda, in *The Case of the Deadly Kiss* (1957). Clifford Uyeda's *The Deer Mountain* (1959), a tale of Alaska cannery life, while avowedly based on the author's own prewar experience, included only white characters.

Interestingly, a recurring element in postwar Japanese American writing was life in Japan. This was an odd change of perspective, in that few prewar Nisei wrote about Japan, and also given the emphatic nature of most Nisei's wartime self-identification with the United States against the Japanese enemy.[8] Nonetheless, throughout the postwar era, Nisei invented or adapted various Japan-based stories. Okada's one-act Occupation play, "When in Japan," was arguably the earliest example. Sanae Kawaguchi wrote and illustrated two children's books set in traditional Japan, *Taro's Festival Day* (1957) and *The Insect Concert* (1958). Yoshiko Uchida began her children's publishing career with *The Dancing Kettle and Other Japanese Folk Tales* (1949). Kenneth Yasuda produced a volume of translations of Japanese haiku poetry.[9]

POSTWAR WRITING ON CAMP

Nisei authors during the postwar era remained all but silent regarding the community's wartime experiences.[10] True, a few works were set in camp, such as Hiroshi Kashiwagi's short play "Laughter and False Teeth," which received a set of amateur performances in 1954; Hisaye Yamamoto's short story "The Legend of Miss Sasagawara" (1950); and Iwao Kawakami's 1947 poem "The Paper," on the shooting of inmate James Wakasa. Guyo Tajiri's 1948 lyric "JACL Hymn" referenced confinement, as did a few Nisei published memoirs, most notably Miné Okubo's graphic narrative *Citizen 13660* (1946), Monica Sone's 1953 *Nisei Daughter*, and Koji Ariyoshi's *From Kona to Yenan*, which appeared serially in 1952.[11] Shelley Nishimura Ota, a Hawaii-born Nisei living in Wisconsin, published a novel about Japanese Americans, *Upon Their Shoulders* (1951). While it took place primarily in wartime Hawaii, the narrative included one Issei interned in a Department of Justice camp on the mainland. Another Nisei from Hawaii, Lawrence Sakamoto, published a novel in Japanese translation, *Nisei Butai* (Nisei Troops), about wartime Japanese communities in Hawaii and the

442nd Regimental Combat Team. An older Nisei, Kazuo Miyamoto, began work in these years on a novel that discussed Japanese Americans shipped to camps on the mainland, but the final product, *Hawaii: The End of the Rainbow*, was not published until 1964. Jon Shirota began work in 1963 on his Pearl Harbor–themed novel *Lucky Come Hawaii* (1965).

Still, the fact that there was no great outpouring of literature by postwar Nisei on their wartime experience and postwar resettlement is striking, the more so in that such community silence persisted during a time when these became popular subjects for books by non-Japanese, including Florence Crannell Means's *The Moved-Outers* (1945), Anne Emery's *Tradition* (1946), and Karon Kehoe's *City in the Sun* (1946). Most notably, James Edmiston, a former WRA resettlement officer turned screenwriter, produced the novel *Home Again* (1955). This Micheneresque saga focuses on a Japanese American family's experience at the Heart Mountain camp and its members' return to the West Coast, where they struggle to confront West Coast bigots with the help of a sympathetic WRA officer. One interesting element of *Home Again* that foreshadows Okada's novel is that one of the members of the family, Kazue Mio, is a wartime draft resister—making it the first-ever literary representation of the Fair Play Committee. Although Edmiston portrays Kazue's mentor (a fictional counterpart of Kiyoshi Okamoto) as motivated by pro-Tokyo sentiment and hypocritical in claiming his constitutional rights as an American, Kazue's refusal to enlist and his acceptance of punishment for his actions are portrayed in an overall sympathetic light as idealistic, if misguided.[12]

JOHN OKADA'S STRUGGLE

Whatever the salience of the various factors involved in the large-scale shutdown of Nisei literature after World War II, it seems fair to assert that its demise shadowed the career of John Okada. For by the time he began publishing his first stories, in the months after the end of World War II, Okada was not continuing an established West Coast Nisei literary tradition; rather, he was planting a seed in a devastated landscape that once was rich farmland.

It is true that Okada, as a college student, was able to place his first stories with a community newspaper and to secure publication (as well as performances) of his short play. Although the process by which *Northwest Times* editor Budd Fukei learned of Okada's work and agreed to put it out has been lost to history, Okada's war record may have helped impress Fukei, a staunch supporter of the Nisei soldiers of the 442nd and later the editor of the Nisei Veterans Committee newsletter. The fact that Okada's stories ran in the journal's opening issues suggests that Fukei was looking to build a diverse readership. Just two years later Fukei invited the Supreme Court litigant and former draft resister Gordon Hirabayashi to contribute a regular column.

Still, after he ran Okada's initial set of stories (plus writings by Bob Okazaki), Fukei ceased to feature literature in *Northwest Times*. Aside from the matter of financial support, in intellectual terms such a cutoff meant Okada lacked the resources that had guided his predecessors—regular contact with a ready-made, knowledgeable audience to shape his ideas, and support from other local writers with similar goals to help him develop his craft. The lack of community support may explain why a full decade elapsed between Okada's initial publications and the appearance of *No-No Boy*.

What is more, by the time John Okada completed his novel in the mid-1950s, a marked leveling-off in public discourse about wartime confinement had taken place. The causes of this silence are not altogether clear, and no doubt result from a confluence of factors, including the end of de jure discrimination against Japanese Americans, mass prosperity, and a conservative McCarthy-era political climate. In any case, there was no further camp literature. While the Hollywood film *Hell to Eternity* (1960) contained one scene set in the Manzanar camp, James Edmiston was unable to sell a film adaptation of *Home Again*. There were even signs of willed forgetting. Vanya Oakes's children's book *Roy Sato, New Neighbor* (1955), set among a multigenerational West Coast family, deliberately effaced the camp experience, as later did Leo Politi's *Mieko* (1969).

This climate of silence surely weighed in the fate of Okada's work. While we do not know the names of the mainstream presses that Okada approached with his manuscript, we do know that they were unwelcoming. In the circumstances, Okada was both logical and creative in contacting the Charles E. Tuttle Co. as a potential outlet for his work. Founded in 1948 by Tuttle, a former staff officer in the US Occupation of Japan, with branches in Tokyo and in Tuttle's hometown of Rutland, Vermont, the firm specialized in books about Japan.

No-No Boy appeared in May 1957 in the Far East, and the last week of June in the US. The book received a diversity of reviews in publications from around the globe—including Japan, Hong Kong, and Canada—as well as various mentions in the American press, most notably Earl Miner's brief critique in the *Saturday Review,* as well as a positive notice in Bill Hosokawa's *Pacific Citizen* column.[13] Initial commentaries on the book reflected the prevailing climate of opinion, with critics starkly divided over both Okada's literary abilities and his larger portrait of the racial prejudice and internal conflict to which Japanese American communities were exposed.

Sales of the book were disappointing, and it soon dropped from sight. Tuttle's sales staff may bear some responsibility for this failure, as they were unaccustomed to both the genre and the subject matter. While Tuttle featured nonfiction works by a handful of Japanese Americans, including Jack Matsuoka and John M. Yumoto, plus Kenneth Yasuda's translations of Japanese poetry, Okada's was one of the few fictional works Tuttle put out during the 1950s, and the only one with a Japanese American protagonist. Charles Tuttle later claimed that his firm had made an extra effort to publicize the book in terms of outreach and review copies, though they lacked any real budget for advertising.[14] No doubt in keeping with their usual system, they underlined the work's essentially Japanese character and sent review copies to journals such as the *Journal of Asian Studies.*[15] Japanese Americans alienated from Japanese life could not have been expected to welcome such a book. Still, even if Okada's book had been better marketed, it would probably have had difficulty attracting large-scale attention or sales among Nisei. As Tuttle himself remarked: "At the time that we published it, the very people whom [*sic*] we thought would be enthusiastic about it, mainly the Japanese-American community in the United States, were not only disinterested but actually rejected the book."[16]

That said, it is plausible to argue that any work touching on the war-time events would have faced difficulties finding a Nisei audience in 1957, when no community newspapers ran book reviews or featured literature sections: the problems that Okada's novel encountered were not primarily a function of its specific content about "No-No Boys." As noted above, Okada was not the first novelist to take as his subject the wartime incarceration, or even the Nisei draft resisters—Edmiston's *Home Again* had already done so. Still less was it rejected because of any radical or oppositional political messages. Rather, to the extent that Okada's text was referenced at all by early commentators, it was as a conservative work. William Peterson, whose 1966 *New York Times* article on Japanese Americans has frequently been cited as a founding text for the "model minority" image of Asian Americans, summarized the book as an anti-protest novel: "In John Okada's novel *No-No Boy*, written by a veteran of the Pacific war about a nisei who refused to accept the draft, the issue is sharply drawn.... The hero struggles to find his way to the America that rejected him and that he had rejected. A nisei friend who has returned from the war with a wound that eventually kills him is pictured as relatively well-off.... In contrast to the works of James Baldwin, this is a novel of revolt against revolt."[17] JACL columnist Bill Hosokawa described Okada's work in positive terms as "a gutty novel about an evacuee who was moved to reply negatively to the War Relocation Authority's so-called loyalty questionnaire [that] still makes good reading."[18]

CONCLUSION

However much the demise of literature among postwar Japanese Americans posed an obstacle to the initial publication and success of John Okada's *No-No Boy*, in the long run it may have proved invaluable. The cutoff of Nisei literature left him free to cast his net large, as he was single-handedly responsible for dramatizing central aspects of Japanese American life. Such isolation served him well. Already before World War II, Nobutaka Ike had warned of trouble for Nisei novelists: "Because he must necessarily draw from his own experiences, the Nisei novelist will most likely write about the community—and woe be unto him if he does.

Practically everyone whom he might have known will assume that the villain was patterned after him and take it for a personal insult. And if he should neglect to speak of the community in the most glowing terms, he will most likely find himself a social outcast."[19] Okada's marginal status as a writer meant that he was able to center his work on community breakdown and interpersonal conflict without experiencing pressure to censor his views. In sum, the same larger forces that condemned Okada to obscurity in the short term also made possible his ultimate triumph.

Questioning *No-No Boy*

Text, Contexts, and Subtexts

STEPHEN H. SUMIDA

JOHN OKADA'S *NO-NO BOY* IS MORE DIFFICULT A NOVEL TO COM-
prehend than most readers give it credit for.[1] The narrative point of view
of the novel is predominantly that of its protagonist, Ichiro Yamada, most
often in a limited third-person narration but sometimes in first-person
monologues and soliloquies that reinforce the impression that Ichiro's
point of view is transparently expressed and is obliquely the author's own.
In my reading, Okada establishes the character's point of view as *unreliable* at the beginning of the novel, in the rather long chapter 1; only to the
extent that the protagonist grows in his understanding of himself and his
problems does Ichiro's point of view become more reliable by the novel's
end.[2] This growth or development of the protagonist's character, however,
is itself in question, as if Okada were writing his fiction to determine
whether and how Japanese America would survive or die in the aftermath
of the people's imprisonment in American concentration camps in World
War II.

Questioning the reliability of the narrative point of view does not come
easily. Okada's third-person narration seems to imply its reliability rather
than its limitations. In third-person narration, Okada plots the novel as
a sequence of *actions* in the "present" that delineate the material, "real"

conditions of the story. These actions occur in factual settings mainly in Seattle, Washington, and Portland, Oregon, from the fall of 1946 to the spring of 1947. The novel begins with such a factual set of assertions: "Two weeks after his twenty-fifth birthday, Ichiro got off a bus at Second and Main in Seattle. He had been gone four years, two in camp and two in prison."[3] Within the documentary facts of plot and setting, however, runs a continual interior monologue on the part of the protagonist, who exists in a turmoil of self-doubt, self-loathing, memories, forgettings, rage, depression, and blame, though in one moment he experiences a "glimmer of hope," "that faint and elusive insinuation of promise" that the Japanese American people might still survive, their history continue (221). Immediately implying the interiority of Ichiro's thinking and feeling, the second paragraph of chapter 1 follows from the first quoted above: "Walking down the street that autumn morning with a small, black suitcase, he felt like an intruder in a world to which he had no claim. It was just enough that he should feel this way, for, of his own free will, he had stood before the judge and said that he would not go in the army. At that time there was no other choice for him" (3).

It would appear that we, reading these first five sentences of *No-No Boy*, have no choice but to accept Ichiro's memory of standing before the judge, even though the novel's beginning implies a question: Why is it that a man of twenty-five is called a "boy"?

Questioning Ichiro's point of view runs counter not only to the way Okada documents plot and setting but also to the way characters who are opponents in the novel agree with one another, making it appear that there are no opposing, synthesizable sets of assumptions underlying their arguments against one another. For example, in Ichiro's first encounter after stepping off the bus, Eto Minato, wearing army fatigues to show that he is a Nisei veteran (4–6), remembers that Ichiro did not serve in the US military in the war, affirming what a page earlier Ichiro admits, that he had refused to "go in the army" (3). Eto Minato spits on Ichiro with a contempt that Ichiro is already heaping upon his own self.

Another instance of this agreement between opponents' views is how, while condemning his mother for being a "Jap," Ichiro, like his mother, implicitly defines "Japanese" and "American" in the assimilationist, binary, and problematically simplistic and stereotyping way the US government and society used in order to "justify" the incarceration of both Issei parent and Nisei child in concentration camps. If all three—the US government, the Japanese Issei mother, and Ichiro the Nisei son—agree that being "Japanese American" is a matter of sorting out assumed "Jap" characteristics from presumed "American" ones, resulting in the unavoidable and permanent alienation of Nisei from America by "reason" of immutable "race," then must not this way of defining the Japanese American self be unquestionable? Add Eto and Ichiro's brother Taro to the conflict between the supposedly "loyal" and "disloyal" in America, and it would seem that Okada is in effect expounding the assimilationist way of defining "Japanese American" as being "partly Japanese" and "partly American." But the paradigm pitting "Japanese" characteristics against "American" values and identity in order to separate the "loyal" from the "disloyal" itself begs the question of what these terms mean. A glimmer of hope is that Kenji and Emi and their families have discerned or are learning a "pattern" other than assimilation, by the questions their experiences are raising.

The irony that opposing characters share similar underlying assumptions pales in the shadow of an even graver irony: the assumptions underlying Ichiro's contempt for himself and for his mother, the characterizing of Mother as a "Jap," as well as Mother's enmity against America in her insistence that she is "Japanese," repeat the grounds that America both assumed and stated for putting Japanese Americans into concentration camps. Ichiro's mother, too, has assimilated the ideology that dominates her and her sons, and tragically, after the war the mother and son are, in their thoughts and actions, as if psychically back in the concentration camps.

The way opponents in the novel unknowingly agree in their assumptions with one another and with American society at large creates an appearance of certainty about what wrong Ichiro has committed. In his hindsight, Ichiro assumes that his refusal to serve in the military was based on his having declared himself a "Jap," "disloyal" to America, under his mother's influence. Other assumptions naturally follow: about why his mother and her "Japanese" parental authority over her son are to blame for his being punished for being a "Jap"; why Mother believes Japan has won the war and will soon liberate her and her son from America; and how impossible it is, as Ichiro believes, for him to be fully an "American." This appearance of certainty would prevail in *No-No Boy* if not for Okada's calling it into question in ironical, sometimes all but unspoken ways. Yet a realization that Okada creates in Ichiro an *unreliable point of view* depends first of all on his creating the appearance of reliability.

HISTORICAL CONTEXTS AND THE TEST OF RELIABILITY: THE HOUSES OF KUMASAKA AND EMI

A point in chapter 1 where this certainty is implicitly yet sharply questioned by the novel's historical context occurs when his mother takes Ichiro to the house of the Kumasaka family to show him the misery Mrs. Kumasaka endures for having foolishly allowed her son to fight and be killed in the war in Europe. On this visit Ichiro learns that his friend Bobbie, one of the Kumasaka sons, was shot by a German sniper. Mother's judgment against the Kumasakas presents her at her meanest, as when she tersely levels a charge against Mrs. Kumasaka: "To raise the child into a man one can be proud of is not play. Some of us succeed. Some, of course, must fail. It is too bad, but that is the way of life" (26). In turn, Ichiro ratchets up his hate for his mother.

The visit to the Kumasakas also functions in another way in Okada's novel. The incident both implies and demonstrates that Ichiro's point of view is unreliable. Ichiro's interpretation of how the Kumasaka family lived before the war begins with an account, told from his point of view, of why they have recently bought a house in Seattle:

> The Kumasakas had run a dry-cleaning shop before the war. Business
> was good and people spoke of their having money, but they lived in
> cramped quarters above the shop because, like most of the other Japa-
> nese, they planned some day to return to Japan and still felt like tran-
> sients even after thirty or forty years in America and the quarters
> above the shop seemed adequate and sensible since the arrangement
> was merely temporary. That, [Ichiro] thought to himself, was the reason

why the Japanese were still Japanese.. . . . [They] continued to maintain their dreams [of returning to Japan]. . . . by living only among their own kind and by zealously avoiding long-term commitments such as the purchase of a house. (24–25)

These comments about the Kumasakas and their purchase of a house, even as he takes his first look at it, are based on Ichiro's ignorance of history and of the American laws that govern Issei, an ignorance he shares with the general American public. He knows with certainty that the Kumasakas did not buy a house before the war, when they seemed to have money. But he does not know or remember that the anti-alien land law in the state of Washington and other states in the American West prohibited the Issei from buying any real property, whether it be land, a building, or a house.[4] Then who bought the house, and why now? It must be that the Nisei, American-born children of the Kumasaka immigrant parents bought the house, now that the war is over. It may be that to afford it they used the death benefit from the loss of brother Bobbie. But why didn't the Nisei Kumasakas, American citizens by virtue of their birth on American soil, buy the house before the war, when the family already seemed to have earned and saved enough money? One answer is that they were not yet of legal age to enter into a real estate contract, twenty-one. They reached legality during their three-year imprisonment in concentration camps, 1942–1945.[5]

Presuming to know the Kumasakas, Ichiro is condescending; his interpretation of how they lived without buying a house before the war is facile, and it supports the prejudiced belief that Issei and other Asian immigrants demonstrated their lack of commitment to the United States by their supposed choice not to invest in real estate or to become US citizens—which they were forbidden to do by US law.[6] This is an aspect of a "sojourner theory," an excuse to deny immigrants certain rights because they are characterized as merely passing through America to make money and return with it to their homelands, and it is something that Ichiro assumes and repeats throughout the novel.

If the purchase of the house is a fulfillment of the immigrants' ambitions, and not an unexpected change of plans, then we may better feel the depth of Mrs. Kumasaka's grief when she hears again from Bobbie's war buddy Jun about how Bobbie was killed. She weeps "without shame and alone in her grief that knew no end" (29). In his thoughts about the Kumasakas and their purchase of a house, Ichiro knows that they have accomplished something that he fears he himself will never manage to do. The Kumasakas have at last bought a house in spite of the laws that have obstructed them. Who knows, then, what part of Mrs. Kumasaka's weeping flows rather from triumph and joy?

Return now to the first page of chapter 1 with its emphasis on Ichiro's age. In the fall of 1946 he has just turned twenty-five. Two years earlier, in 1944 when he was twenty-three, he was sent to prison. Two years before that, in the spring of 1942, the mass incarceration of the Nikkei of Seattle commenced. This was before his twenty-first birthday (which occurred in the autumn of 1942, according to the emphatically stated facts about his age). Even if he had the money and if he understood the legalities and real estate protocols of buying a house himself, he could not: he was not of legal age. During his time in a concentration camp, followed by time in a federal penitentiary—presumably McNeil Island, just west of Tacoma, Washington—Ichiro came of legal age, but he was retarded from maturing in a society that otherwise would expect a young adult to carry on with getting married, buying a house, and having children, the conventional, heterosexual American Dream that Ichiro fetishizes yet believes he will never achieve because he is a no-no boy. Ichiro represents the generation of Nisei who came of age inside the camps and were delayed from becoming socially contributing adults. In this sense, though he is now "more of a man" than when he "would not go into the army" (3), Ichiro is as naive as a child in his assumptions about the Kumasakas and other Issei.

A third instance of Okada's placing a character within a carefully wrought historical and legal context of date and age, this time again involving alien land laws, occurs in the fourteen pages (77–91) he devotes to introducing Emi, the woman whose ability to love, as well as to lose love yet still go on to embrace love again, counteracts Ichiro's initial revulsion on seeing his family's shared bedroom, which makes him feel like "puking" and wonder "if his folks still pounded flesh" (8). On a crisp, early spring morning after the wounded war veteran Kenji Kanno has brought

Ichiro and Emi together, Ichiro looks across the farmland outside Emi's back porch and sees a man in the distance, "a tiny, dark shape stooped over in earnest industry" (86). "That's Mr. Maeno," Emi remarks. "He leases my land." Ichiro does not ask what she means by "my land" or how she is able to lease it to Mr. Maeno, presumably an Issei farmer. Three pages later, Ichiro is again appreciating how "quiet and peaceful and clean and fresh and nice" Emi's place is—"nice house, nice yard, nice you," he says to her. Emi asks, "How old are you?" Twenty-five, he answers, as Okada once again reminds us of his age. "I'm twenty-seven," Emi says (89). The age difference is significant not only in that Okada characterizes Emi as being more mature than Ichiro but also because her age means she was twenty-two in 1941, old enough to buy the house and land before the attack on Pearl Harbor.

It is likely that Okada knew the law; as a child of the manager of three residential hotels in Seattle—like Monica Sone in *Nisei Daughter*—he grew up understanding that his parents could not own either the building or the land underneath it. They could lease the hotel under a business name, an entity that is not a person with a race, but they could not own the real estate.

While questioning the reliability of Ichiro's point of view, I am also presenting possible "answers" to the question of why and how the Kumasakas managed to buy their house now, in 1946, a story based on historical facts about Washington's alien land laws and Nikkei responses to them. But historical facts alone do not establish a "reliable" subtext for Okada's words. Now let us see how characters' personal, subjective contexts are loaded with contradictions rather than certainty.

Having questioned the reliability of Ichiro's assessment of the Kumasakas and their house, we can now return to the earlier pages of chapter 1 and reread what has been told from his point of view. Take, for instance, Ichiro's contempt when he first arrives at his parents' mom-and-pop grocery store. Ichiro's initial talk with Pa stokes the son's criticism of his mother. When Ichiro hears from his father that Mother goes thirteen and a half blocks to the Wonder Bread factory to buy bread to sell at her tiny grocery store, Ichiro is incensed. He calculates that after paying the bus fare, Ma makes only ten cents on the Wonder Bread loaves she sells. But,

Pa says, she pays no bus fare: "Mama walks." Ichiro's contempt for his mother now erupts in sarcasm: "His father had said, 'Mama walks' and that made things right with the world. The overwhelming simplicity of the explanation threatened to evoke silly giggles which, if permitted to escape, might lead to hysterics. He clenched his fists and subdued them" (10). Soon Ichiro sees before him "the woman who was his mother and still a stranger because, in truth, he could not know what it was to be a Japanese who breathed the air of America and yet had never lifted a foot from the land that was Japan" (12).

If we accept Ichiro's view that his mother never lifted a foot from Japan, how is it that she knows how to buy bread at the Wonder Bread factory outlet to sell in her store? How is it that she and Pa even managed to open their store when in 1945, a year before Ichiro's return, they were released from a concentration camp with twenty-five dollars apiece and a bus ticket and told simply to go away? Even if his parents speak little English, they have survived thirty-five years in America. Rather than condemning her, it is easy to imagine Ma as a hero in a different novel of immigration, where her walking to Wonder Bread to buy discounted goods and saving the bus fare for a profit of thirty-five cents would be a demonstration of her devotion to her family and of her support of them, penny by penny, under harsh conditions. Not a "factual," historical context, but a moral one—a matter, that is, of relations between and among persons— that puts Ichiro's judgment of his mother in doubt. His judgment echoes the government's pegging her as a "Jap."

HISTORICAL CONTEXTS AND ANOTHER
TEST OF RELIABILITY: MR. KANNO'S MEMORY
OF THE NISEI SOCIOLOGIST

At dead center of the narrative pages of John Okada's *No-No Boy* is a memory of a lecture by a young Nisei sociologist addressing Issei parents in the camp. The visiting speaker, "struggling for the words painstakingly and not always correctly selected from his meager knowledge of the Japanese language . . . managed to impart a message of great truth . . . that the old Japanese, the fathers and mothers, who sat courteously attentive, did not know their own sons and daughters." The sociologist scolds the Issei for failing to be "American" parents to their Nisei children. He scornfully asks, "How many of you are able to sit down with your own sons and own daughters and enjoy the companionship of conversation? How many, I ask? If I were to say none of you, I would not be far from the truth." The sociologist goes on to expound upon how supercilious his own parents have been to him and how American parents are by contrast so close, affectionate, and communicative with their American children (112–13).

Here at the center of the novel Okada in effect presents a crucial test, like a midterm exam, of how we are reading his book.

Some readers readily agree with the "truth" of what the sociologist says. He expresses a dominant, American assimilationist and Orientalist idea of cultural conflict between the two generations and assumes that "American" culture is innately superior, which justifies a Western domination of the East as if for Orientals' own good.[7]

A radically different way of reading the speech of the sociologist is to question his premises. Is it true that Issei failed to be close and companionable with their Nisei children? Isn't it the *closeness* of Issei to their children that condemned the Nisei to the American concentration camps in the first place?[8]

In a striking way, the memory of the sociologist's visit to the American concentration camp is uncharacteristic of the novel: for it is Mr. Kanno's memory—Kenji's father's—not Ichiro's. Here in Mr. Kanno's memory we have a dramatic shift from the confines of Ichiro's tortured thinking. Even while we read the sociologist's rant, we should be mindful of how it occurs in the context of a longer passage that is about Mr. Kanno, of all Issei characters the most companionable with his six children.[9] Kanno's memory of the incident drifts off with a reflection on an Issei couple, after the sociologist's lecture, walking to where their daughter is enjoying a dance with her Nisei friends; from outside the social hall, he recalls, "they watched longer than usual and searched longingly to recognize their own daughter" (113). Mr. Kanno is a widower. It is not his wife and himself that he is imagining sympathetically as the Issei couple. With Mr. Kanno as an epitome of the loving Issei parent and friend, we may glimpse the capacities other Issei parents have of love for their children under the unjust and punitive conditions imposed on them with an aim of breaking up Japanese American communities and families. The Nisei sociologist too, unwitting fellow, is being used by the government as an instrument to effect that breakup with his terrible and earnest message.

WHO OR WHAT IS A "NO-NO BOY"?

The most monstrous, unresolved historical *un*certainty in *No-No Boy* concerns its very title. Who or what is a "no-no boy"? Why did they exist? We return again to page 3, where Ichiro asks, "What the hell have I done?" The question is basic to a reading of this novel. And it leads to another: Can a no-no boy be drafted? If so, how? It appears that Okada's knowledge of no-no boys and the various and even contradictory ways in which they were punished was incomplete, in part because he was already at war overseas when no-no boys and draft resisters took their stands. Yet his novel raises profound questions about historical contexts that otherwise seem certain.

As mentioned in the introduction to this volume, the term *no-no boy* specifically refers to the twelve thousand who were sent to the Tule Lake Segregation Center for answering "no" to two of the questions in the March 1943 questionnaire alternately titled "Application for Leave Clearance" or "Statement of United States Citizen of Japanese Ancestry," nicknamed the "Loyalty Questionnaire" or "Loyalty Oath." As a group, they were distinct from the 315 young men convicted of resisting the draft from camp.

My definition of "no-no boy" is somewhat different, and the difference leads us in different directions when reading Okada's novel. I define "no-no boy" to include those who answered "no" to either or both questions 27 and 28 of the questionnaire but were *not* segregated at Tule Lake.

In my reading of the novel, the question arises as to how a no-no boy could be served a draft notice in June 1944 after his answers to the 1943 questionnaire presumably showed he was "disloyal" to America.

Okada, as a storyteller refraining from lecturing on the historical contexts surrounding his narrative, withholds his own explications of his novel's title and the questionnaire from which it derives. This lack of explication compels me to question Ichiro's certainty that he must have done something wrong. I presume that Ichiro answered "no" in the questionnaire, and when he subsequently answered "no" to his draft orders and to the judge, he thought that he was doing the right thing, questioning the government's violation of citizens' rights. For Ichiro Yamada, this right thing has turned into a wrong. What turns Ichiro's resistance against injustice into a conclusion that he was wrong to resist is his imprisonment for draft evasion. Somehow federal imprisonment from 1944 to 1946 has made him forget his reasons for both stands I infer he took: as a no-no boy in 1943 and as a draft resister in 1944. Remembering the reasons given by other resisters, Ichiro thinks them "flimsy and unreal," and he alludes to his own change of mind and heart when he asserts that time in prison would get resisters to "see the truth" (32). Ichiro's false causality that *because he was punished he must have done something wrong* begs the question of what he did that was wrong—and *was* it wrong? This is emblematic of how many Nikkei felt after the war. In the judgment of society, they were punished with incarceration because they must have done wrong: *they were wrong for being born Japanese.*

THE STORY OF HAJIME JIM AKUTSU AND ICHIRO'S UNRELIABLE MEMORY

The case I am making, that Ichiro could be thought of as both a no-no boy and a draft resister, is paralleled by the experience of the actual person who was John Okada's model for the fictional Ichiro. This person was Hajime Jim Akutsu. As documented in the biography of Okada in this volume, Akutsu answered "yes-no" on the questionnaire but was not segregated. In 1944, a year after he answered "no," he resisted the draft and, like the fictional Ichiro, served two years at the McNeil Island Federal Penitentiary in Washington. Akutsu was probably among Okada's prime sources of information about no-no boys, at a time when most of the Nikkei community considered the topic unspeakable. As a veteran of the Military Intelligence Service, Okada himself was under a gag order regarding his wartime experience. So about their experiences, Okada asked, Akutsu talked, and Okada listened.

By his own account, Akutsu was a no-no boy. By his own account, too, even before the 1943 questionnaire, he was an active protester in Minidoka. He would tell of catching a mess hall cook stealing food to sell on the black market. Jim and his brother Gene ambushed this cook one night, "banging him up," as Akutsu would put it. The next morning a camp official took the battered cook to the Akutsu family's barrack to show the mother what her sons had done. Instead of ordering Jim and Gene to atone for their deed, the official ordered Mrs. Akutsu to kneel at the cook's feet and beg forgiveness for them. This utter, abject humiliation of Mrs. Nao Akutsu crushed whatever hopes had carried her from Japan to America at the turn of the twentieth century. According to Akutsu, she and her husband were hereditary Christians born of families who for nearly three centuries had secretly practiced their faith, punishable by death if exposed, in Tokugawa Japan. Jim's parents came to America buoyed by their prospects for living in a country where being Christian was not a crime. In America, however, they found discrimination by race, ethnicity, and nationality.

Jim Akutsu tried to tend to his mother after the catastrophe that drove her to curl up on her cot and refuse any food from the mess hall. Jim sought help from the camp hospital, but with inadequate medical capabilities in the camp, the hospital was of little use. In the context of this experience, when the questionnaire was issued in 1943 Akutsu angrily answered "no," and he continued to protest, agitate, and be a "troublemaker" in Minidoka. He was served his draft notice in June 1944, and he protested it, accusing the camp officials of tampering with it.

Jim Akutsu's documents throw his conviction for "draft evasion" into serious doubt.[10] The photocopy of his "Order to Report for Induction" states that it was postmarked June 10, 1944. He was ordered to report to the hospital at Hunt, Idaho (the location of the post office for the Minidoka concentration camp), for a pre-induction medical examination, and he was to do so at 1:00 P.M. on "the 21 day of May, 1944." The impossibility of following the order stunned him. How could he report for induction more than two weeks *before* the order was even mailed?

Akutsu was arrested and charged with draft evasion because he did not report as ordered.[11] In the Federal Court in Boise, Idaho, when he attempted to explain the impossibility of following the draft order because of the contradiction in dates, he was silenced; the only question before the court was whether he had reported as ordered, and he was convicted. By this time Akutsu regarded the impossible order he was given, together with its consequences, as his punishment for having answered "no" a year earlier in the Loyalty Questionnaire. Despite the bald miscarriage of justice, Akutsu would nevertheless smile about how when the Minidoka draft resisters arrived on McNeil Island and counted up their number for the first time, there were forty-seven of them. They took courage from this number because it is the number of the Forty-Seven Loyal Rōnin in the heroic tale *Chūshingura*.[12]

Thus when the fictional Ichiro, still suffering from the trauma of his imprisonment, thinks of his punishment as "just," this too is a revision, distortion, rationalization, or forgetting of what happened to Akutsu, Okada's source, because Akutsu never had a chance either to obey or to evade the draft. He was "framed up," as he put it. Did Okada deliberately change Akutsu's story into Ichiro's forgetting why he disobeyed his draft order? Close scrutiny of Ichiro's status as both a no-no boy and a draft resister, an ostensible contradiction in terms, raises the possibility that Okada deployed an unreliable point of view to expose the problematic racism and blind nationalism that underlie the treatment not only of no-no boys and draft resisters but of all Nikkei—and, by extension, the treatment of all "loyal citizens" of the United States.[13]

Moved by the strange story of Jim Akutsu, one of my students asked, if Ichiro is based on Akutsu, which character is based on Akutsu's friend John Okada? We noticed a resemblance between Okada and Kenji. If so, the student continued, what was Okada's disability, as Kenji is disabled by the loss of his right leg in combat. They cut out his tongue, I said to the student, who immediately remembered that Okada was ordered not to speak of his service in World War II.[14]

"TELL ME, MOTHER, WHO ARE YOU?"

Insofar as Ichiro is unreliable even in his certitude that he had made the wrong choice in refusing military service, can we rely on his judgment regarding the character who vexes him the most, his mother? She may be the most tragic character in Asian American literature up to the 1970s; until then most works followed a paradigm of immigration that was upward bound, with the second generation better off than the first.[15] Ichiro's mother is like all the Nikkei characters in *No-No Boy*, including the veterans: they are all victims of the eviction and incarceration aiming to scatter and destroy them. As I have remarked above, for Ichiro to blame his mother for his incarcerations is to blame the victim.[16]

While his blaming often points outward, at his mother, the most introspective of Ichiro's attempts to blame her occurs in a monologue in which he questions himself. Ma reads her son a letter from Brazil confirming, she says, that Japan has won the war and is sending an imperial ship to repatriate the loyal Japanese of Seattle. Ichiro calls the letter and his mother "crazy." She replies, "It is not I who tell you that the ship is coming. It is in the letter. If you have come to doubt your mother—and I'm sure you do not mean it even if you speak in weakness . . . Think more deeply and your doubts will disappear. You are my son, Ichiro" (15). Here Ichiro's monologue commences, breaking through the third-person voice of the narrative:

> No, he said to himself as he watched her part the curtains and start into the store. There was a time when I was your son. There was a time that I no longer remember when you used to smile a mother's smile and tell me stories about gallant and fierce warriors who protected their lords with blades of shining steel and about the old woman who found a peach in the stream and took it home and, when her husband split it in half, a husky little boy tumbled out to fill their hearts with boundless joy. I was that boy in the peach and you were the old woman and we were Japanese with Japanese feelings and Japanese pride and Japanese thoughts because it was all right then to be Japanese and feel and think all the things that Japanese do even if we lived in America. (16)

Ichiro goes on to regret that "I was not strong enough to fight you" and that as a result he "did not love [America] enough." He was "still half Japanese," which meant he was only half American. The twirling, dizzy monologue spirals on to where Ichiro wishes desperately that he were either one or the other, whole, and blames his mother and himself and "the world which is made up of many countries which fight with each other and kill and hate and destroy but not enough, so that they must kill and hate and destroy again and again and again" (17), passing momentarily through one of those instances where Ichiro's self-absorption parts like eyelids and he glimpses that his problem involves larger problems of nationalist hostilities in the world. The monologue is Ichiro's declaration of his "dual identity," exactly the formulation of Japanese-versus-American identity that the 1943 questionnaire in the concentration camps was based upon. Whereas here he blames both himself and his mother for his responses to the questionnaire, he also expresses a kind of gratitude to "the government" for teaching him the "wise," "strong" lesson that he was wrong. By blaming Mother and himself, he is unable to acknowledge that it was not she, powerless, nor he, also powerless, but the government that wronged them in incarcerating the Japanese American people.

The monologue begins with a curious equivocation that merges into the duality Ichiro goes on to ascribe to his identity. He no longer remembers the stories his mother once told him; yet he does remember: the "gallant and fierce warriors who protected their lords with blades of shining steel" is an allusion to *Chūshingura*, the heroic story that Jim Akutsu and his cohort of draft resisters from Minidoka remembered.

Then there is the story of the boy who tumbled out of the peach and blessed the old, childless couple: "Momotaro," among the best-known folk tales in Japan.[17] Ichiro's half-memory of how the boy arrived "to fill their hearts with boundless joy" itself contains Ichiro's own feelings, his joy over being loved when he was born. Yet he no longer remembers; he has lost his history, having been forced to forget. And this forgetting is central to the lesson the Momotaro story is supposed to teach. When the demons in the story periodically steal the people's treasures, they steal the symbols of the people's history and in so doing erase vestiges of that history, that culture, and that identity. In Okada's experience, the theft of a people's history would be called "assimilation."[18]

Not until the beginning of chapter 5 does Ichiro soften his confused hatred enough to ask, but to himself, "Tell me, Mother, who are you?" At his mother's death by drowning, he still has not asked her about "a time when you were a little girl" or about "my grandparents, whom I have never seen or known because I do not remember your ever speaking of them except to say that they died a long time ago." It is he who neither speaks to her nor asks her, yet he is in effect pleading for an historical, intergenerational continuity that the Momotaro story signifies: "Tell me everything and just a little bit and a little bit more until [my grandparents'] lives and yours and mine are fitted together, for they surely must be" (95–96).

Okada gives us ways of answering Ichiro's question, "Tell me, Mother, who are you?" Pa explains to Ichiro that the letters he and Ma have been receiving from Japan, begging for food after Japan's defeat, are "from my brothers and cousins and nephews and people I hardly knew in Japan thirty-five years ago, and they are from your mama's brother and two sisters" (35).[19]

Now, in 1946, Ichiro is twenty-five. He was born in the fall of 1921. Ma and Pa arrived "thirty-five years ago," in 1911. Ma and Pa were childless for ten years in Seattle, before Ichiro "tumbled out to fill their hearts with boundless joy" and Ma at last had the opportunity to "smile a mother's smile" and tell her son "stories about gallant and fierce warriors. . . . and the boy in the peach" (16). Ichiro himself says, "I was that boy in the peach." What has happened to Ichiro to make him forget or ignore the fragmented parts of his and his parents' histories: what Japan was like when they left, what his parents may have wanted during their childless first decade in America, why they stayed here, how both Japan and America have changed between 1911 and 1941, how imprisonment during the war changed Japanese Americans and America. And why and how does Mother love Ichiro still?

Okada's way of answering his implicit question, "Is Mother Japanese, or is she Japanese American?" is by giving us one of the main "shadow characters" in the novel (that is, one who does not appear in person), Ma's sister in Japan. Ma insists the letters are American propaganda meant to demoralize her. But the *Japanese* sister has never left Japan. Her experience of Japanese history since Kin Yamada's emigration in 1911 enables, even forces, her to understand that in the recent three decades militarism grew so dominant that Japan dared attack the United States in 1941, after invading Manchuria and China in 1931 and 1937. In Japan, Ma's sister knows that Hiroshima and Nagasaki have been obliterated by atomic bombs. Okada's own parents came from Hiroshima, and if he imagined Ma's sister as a survivor of the devastation there, he would surely feel the connection with his own family.

The Japanese sister in her final letter pleads for "a few pieces of candy" for her children: "It has been so long since they have had any. I am begging and feel no shame, for that is the way things are" (99). In Seattle, by contrast, Kin Yamada has candy: she sells it in her store. This is America, the land of the victorious. How different Kin-chan is from the Japanese woman who is her sister. Ichiro's mother has experienced a lifetime, longer than the years she lived in Japan, in Seattle and in a concentration camp in Idaho. Until she at last has to believe her sister's letter, Kin Yamada has no doubt that she is "Japanese." Nor does Ichiro doubt this. The Japanese sister's letter is Okada's device for enacting, without having to explicate, how the Japanese sister is Japanese while Ma, both a subject and an agent of American history, is *Japanese American*. So is Ichiro. They are two generations of a shared culture, and their conflict with each other is intergenerational but not intercultural; the conflict is not between being "Japanese" and being "American," as was assumed in the camps.[20]

In his attempt to disavow his mother, Ichiro repudiates Japanese culture he assumes is embodied in her. Yet when a person in power, Mr. Carrick, a Caucasian, asks him in Japanese, "*Nihongo wakarimasu ka?*" Ichiro directly replies, "Not too well" (133–34); likewise, when Mr. Morrison asks the same question in Japanese, Ichiro answers, "A little bit" (193). In each of these instances the speaker of Japanese being white may seem to Ichiro to validate the language while at the same time allowing him to play the role of judging the speaker's correctness. These two sentences in Japanese are the only two in the entire novel; except for these sentences and the word *Nisei*, every Japanese term is paraphrased in English— for example, "the boy in the peach" rather than "Momotaro." At one point Pa prepares dinner by "chopping up a head of cabbage for pickling" (96).

The cabbage and the pickling have names in Japanese that are commonly known to Japanese Americans. Pa is making *tsukemono* from *hakusai*, and the word *pickling* gives it a different taste altogether—but Okada clearly avoids using the Japanese words. Why?[21]

EMI

Emi, both reliable and complicated, is one of Ichiro's foils. Her story (77–91, fourteen consecutive pages) epitomizes many of the issues that torment Ichiro, yet at the same time her story gives us a different way from Ichiro's of understanding Japanese American experience—through story and as history. Emi and her family are central to Okada's performance of conflicting ideologies in *No-No Boy*.

The disclosure of Emi's story begins with a conversation that Kenji and Emi share when Kenji drives Ichiro for the first time to Emi's house south of Seattle. Ichiro is passed out in Kenji's car after drinking at the Club Oriental and brawling with Taro's friends. We hear Kenji ask about Emi's dad, and she replies that he is "[s]ick of Japan and Japanese and rotten food and sicker still of having to stay there." Kenji then asks about "Ralph" and whether Emi still loves him. Not knowing how or what to answer, Emi squirms. Kenji says, "If I were you and my husband signed up for another hitch in Germany without even coming home or asking me to go over and be with him, I'd stop loving him. I'd divorce him" (78). Ichiro now enters the house and meets Emi for the first time. He sits at the piano and plays. Seeing his "big and husky back," she has the impression that Ichiro is Ralph, and Kenji agrees (79–80).

As their attraction for each other grows, Ichiro asks Emi about her parents. Emi's mother died in 1939. "It was just as well," she says. "The war would have made her suffer" (83). "Dad is in Japan," she goes on. "He asked to be repatriated and he's been there five months." Her father, like Ichiro's mother, believed that Japan had won the war, but now, suffering in Japan, "he doesn't any more. He wants to come back" (84). Ichiro asks Emi what made his mother and her father so "sick" and "crazy"—wonders why he, too, was sick when he answered "no" to the questionnaire—and Emi replies by voicing thoughts and words that echo Ichiro's: "It's because we're American and because we're Japanese and sometimes the two don't mix. It's all right to be German and American or Italian and American or Russian and American but, as things turned out, it wasn't all right to be Japanese and American. You had to be one or the other." She knows she is giving Ichiro a stock answer. "I don't know . . . I don't know," Emi continues. Ichiro, pleading that "I've got to know," begins to sob, "[l]ost and bewildered like a child frightened," with Emi drawing his face "against her naked breast" (84). It is the first time in the novel that Ichiro cries.

Except for Ralph, Emi's family both by blood and by marriage is a family of resisters.[22] Emi may be as unable as Ichiro to answer his questions about the problems and meaning of being Japanese American, but she knows and understands her family's histories of resistance. They all are "shadow characters," and she their storyteller.

The next morning Emi tells Ichiro her story. Her husband, Ralph, has reenlisted in the US Army in Germany, refusing to return home because of his shame over his much older brother Mike, an American veteran of World War I, who "burst into a fury of anger and bitterness and swore that if they treated him like a Japanese, he would act like one." Mike "ended up at the Tule Lake Center," presumably because he answered "no" in the Loyalty Questionnaire. At Tule Lake, Mike "became a leader in the troublemaking, the strikes and the riots." Mike went so far as to elect expatriation to Japan, "a country he didn't know or love," Emi goes on, "and I'm sure he's extremely unhappy." Oblivious to the parallels between Mike and himself, Ichiro remarks, "I can't say I blame him. . . . He's got more right than I have" (90–91).

Mike, Emi's father, probably her mother had she lived to experience the mass incarceration, and Emi herself with her capacity to remember, tell, and understand their stories are all resisters against the unjust acts of the government led by President Franklin Delano Roosevelt. And Emi is patriotic in her way, saying, "I can remember. . . . when we sang 'The Star-Spangled Banner' and pledged allegiance to the flag at school assemblies, and that's the feeling you have to have . . . that feeling flooding into your chest and making you want to shout with glory" (88–89).

Emi implicitly answers Ichiro's opening question about her family not by naming their "Japanese" and "American" traits (as Ichiro does in labeling his mother), not by checking boxes befitting their "identities," but by telling their stories.[23]

Silences, too, are meaningful in Okada's storytelling. Two pop-cultural allusions that are unnamed beneath the narrative are worth presenting because Okada, with his knowledge of Japanese language and culture, surely had them in mind as he told the story of Ichiro Yamada.

One occurs in the scene where Taro directs two of his friends to ambush Ichiro outside the Club Oriental, where Ichiro and Kenji are drinking. Taro appears, saying he wants to talk with Ichiro outside. Ichiro doesn't notice Taro's friends entering the doorway or Taro's signal to them to wait outside. Kenji notices. Drunk, Ichiro quarrels, then agrees to go outside with Taro to talk. Told to stay behind, Kenji gives Ichiro a sideward look and cautions, "Watch yourself" (72). Outside, Ichiro follows his brother down Maynard Alley and into a vacant lot,[24] where Taro's boys jump on him and kick him to the ground. One of them snaps open a knife and slides it under Ichiro's belt. Suddenly Kenji, who has silently limped onto the scene, raps his cane, hard, against the wrist of the youth holding the knife, who drops the weapon.[25] The surprised boys try to rattle Kenji with taunts. Kenji slashes his cane across the back of the second attacker. The thugs back off and run. Taro seems already to have fled the scene.

Okada's telling of the scene resembles not just any Hollywood fight, but a *chambara*, a flowery, cheap (and in truth, outrageously entertaining) "samurai movie." Okada and his Nisei friends would have spent many hours each week watching samurai movies at neighborhood theaters such as the Atlas on Maynard Avenue S.[26] And what samurai movie wouldn't be made even better by featuring not a conventionally handsome hero but a one-eyed, one-armed swordsman, a blind swordswoman, or a sightless wanderer who passes as an itinerant masseur and gambler—or Kenji Kanno, the one-legged hero with a cane for a sword? This scene in particular, as a silent allusion to that beloved and popular genre, suggests how much fun John Okada must have had on most nights he spent writing.

The other silent allusion is to the Japanese folk tale "Urashima Taro." The story of "Momotaro," the Peach Boy, endures among Japanese American generations owing to its theme of the heroic restoration of the people's treasures, the symbols of their history to be passed on to posterity. "Urashima Taro" is a different story altogether, one that teaches by means of its somber outcome. The haunting motifs and themes of the story may be why the Urashima story appears more often as an explicit and imaginative allusion in works of Asian American literature than does the more widely known story of the Peach Boy with its happy ending.[27]

In a contemporary telling of the story, Urashima is a boy of fourteen who cares for his mother and grandmother in a fishing village. He also cares for the creatures of the sea, the shore, and the sky when they are in distress. He is a good boy (think Eagle Scout). One day Urashima comes upon a group of bad boys beating with sticks on the belly of a sea turtle they have overturned on the beach. Urashima chases the boys away, rights the turtle, and sends the turtle back into the sea. Later the turtle reappears and invites Urashima to climb onto its back for a ride down into the undersea world. The turtle takes the youth to the palace of the king and queen of the undersea. There Urashima is welcomed by the Princess, who for three days treats Urashima to luxurious entertainment. Being a good boy, Urashima tells the Princess that he must return to the surface world, where his mother and grandmother need his care. The Princess reluctantly agrees and gives Urashima a memento of his visit: a jeweled box containing his memories of the Princess, her court, and their time together; however, she cautions, if he ever opens the box, the memories will all be lost. Then she takes Urashima into an atrium where four doors open, one at a time, allowing Urashima and the Princess to experience the seasons, each in turn—spring, summer, autumn, and winter.

After showing her guest this miraculous passage of time, the Princess releases Urashima to the care of the turtle, who carries him with his jeweled box up through the sea and onto the shore. There Urashima dimly recognizes the contours of mountains, but there are massive trees that he cannot remember on the edge of the village. He cannot find his house.

When he asks, the people don't know Urashima, his mother, or his grand-mother. Children summon the oldest man in the village, and when Urashima cries to the elder that he has been gone for only three days but his village seems so changed, the old man says, "*Mukashi mukashi*—long, long ago—there was a boy named Urashima who deserted his mother and grandmother. He was born three hundred years ago—three hundred and fourteen, to be exact!" In shock and despair, Urashima slumps under a large tree, and in the realization of his loss of everything else he lifts the jeweled box and opens it. The memories of his visit to the undersea world rise out of it like smoke. Urashima instantly turns into an old man, very old, a pile of dust.

What a story for our Issei grandmothers to tell us Sansei kids when we were small! Its evocativeness to our Issei forebears, though, might well have been astonishingly simple: if they themselves were to return to Japan after thirty-five years or more in America, all would have changed. Japan would have changed, and, profoundly, the Issei themselves had changed by their experiences, their histories, and their memories. In the 1940s on the West Coast of the United States, the reenactment of the story of Urashima Taro had even more awful and tragic an application than the Issei could have imagined before the war. In 1942 the Nikkei were taken from their homes to the netherworld of the concentration camps, and when they tried to return to places like Seattle, history had already changed their homes into places alien to them.

I have returned periodically to the first page of chapter 1 of *No-No Boy*. Now I return once more. After the repeated details about his age and the passage of time in the previous four years, Ichiro wishes in effect that he could turn time backwards, to retreat to prison and away from the Seattle of today where he feels he doesn't deserve to be. Then he observes his surroundings: "He walked toward the railroad depot where the tower with the clocks on all four sides was. It was a dirty looking tower of ancient brick. It was a dirty city. Dirtier, certainly, than it had a right to be after only four years" (3). Ichiro, now a stranger in his own town, is like Urashima come home—the difference being that when Urashima realizes that all, including himself, have changed in the passage of time, he per-ishes, but Ichiro, from the first narrative page on, must live.

STEPHEN H. SUMIDA

CONCLUSION: CULTURE AND IDENTITY
AS A NARRATIVE "PATTERN"

Subtleties of Okada's way of portraying Mother, an Issei, as Japanese American urge us to ask what, then, "identity" and "culture" mean. Moreover, we may assume that Okada was trying to work out a theory of culture and identity that would *not* lead back, as the "half Japanese, half American" formulation does, into a justification for imprisonment in concentration camps of any group of people in America for being racially "alien." To understand Mother as a *Japanese American*, in contrast to her *Japanese* sister, is to define her (as well as her sister's) identity by her history—the plot and ever-accumulating sum of her decisions, the influences around her to make those decisions, her actions, and her influences on others—rather than by what she or anyone else calls her culturally and racially determined attributes of "Japanese" custom, unchanging "tradition," or "values."

The 1943 Statement of United States Citizen of Japanese Ancestry, with its underlying assumptions and contradictions, is an excellent representation of an assimilationist paradigm.[28] As such, the opposition of cultures in that paradigm is uneven, a comparison of unequals. What the questionnaire assumes is "Japanese"—such as adherence to Shinto or Buddhist philosophies or the practice of judo, kendo, or kyudo—stamps a Japanese American as to some degree unchanging, "traditional," and powerless to escape being "Japanese, whereas what is assumed to be "American" is "modern," even "progressive," and always changing—a living culture.[29]

What alternatives to assimilation, Orientalism, and racism does Okada offer?

Twice in the novel Kenji thinks of how the course of life follows a "pattern," and that any change of conditions in that pattern would mean a turn into a different story, a different course of life. Kenji and his father have been talking about the father's blaming himself for Kenji's loss of a leg in the war. Pop, as Kenji calls him, intuits that his son will soon die from the festering wound. Kenji reassures his father that if he had stopped the son from going to war for America, things would have changed: "Every time I think about it that way, I also have to think that . . . you and I would probably not be sitting down and having a drink together and talking or not talking as we wished" (111). Stretched out on his bed, Kenji reflects on what he has just said to his father. "It made a lot of sense," his soliloquy begins. "If, in the course of things, the pattern called for a stump of a leg that wouldn't stay healed, he wasn't going to deny the fact, for that would mean another pattern with attendant changes.. . . ."

By the "pattern," Kenji does not simply resign himself to a fatalism that determines every event in the course of a life. The next time he thinks of the pattern is after he has witnessed a nasty racist incident in the Club Oriental when a Nisei named Floyd tries to bring two black friends into the bar and all three are ejected.[30] Repelled by this Asian American intolerance of African Americans, Kenji "thought about these things and tried to organize them in his mind so that the pattern could be seen and studied and the answers deduced therefrom. And there was no answer because there was no pattern and all he could feel was that the world was full of hatred" (123).[31] The changes in Kenji's idea of a life "pattern" include random, not fated, acts of hatred, and the pattern is thereby ever changing.

In Okada's *No-No Boy*, what emerges as a different paradigm from assimilation is an underlying theory, or a glimpse of one that may be what Kenji sees as a "pattern," where culture and identity are not already determined, monological, and dictated from an already scripted decree but are always under historical—that is, social, collectively human— construction. The historical construction of culture proceeds *dialogically*, by the interaction of different, contending voices.[32] By this theory or "pattern," history itself is made from the actions of human beings, and history is an open-ended hard drive of records of continual change. Thus, "continuity" means not what is "preserved," but rather the *course of change*, as indicated at the end of an episode in a TV serial: "to be continued." By "to be continued" we understand that the *story* will continue to develop and change, through textual and subtextual *dialogue* that is still to come.

In the theory of culture and identity underlying *No-No Boy*, the opposite of continuity is not "change" but *discontinuity*, which was the ultimate aim of the incarceration and attempted diaspora of Japanese Americans in World War II. Okada shows how the diaspora failed. Even Eto Minato in the novel can see that Nikkei have returned home, rather than being totally scattered in the winds.

Okada's novel stands more as a structure rather than as a description of a "real person," as evidenced by its ending. Slumped against a wall outside the Club Oriental after having seen Freddie's obscenely violent death, Bull bellows a cry that seems to be that of a man who has been to war and was able to kill only by shutting off his emotions, and who now at last can cry. Ichiro stands witness in the alley. He "put a hand on Bull's shoulder, sharing the empty sorrow in the hulking body, feeling the terrible loneliness of the distressed wails, and saying nothing." Ichiro turns away and walks down the alley, chasing "that faint and elusive insinuation of promise as it continued to take shape in mind and in heart" (221). The novel began with Eto, posing as a war veteran, spitting on Ichiro the no-no boy. The novel ends with Ichiro comforting the distraught war veteran Bull. This trajectory, I believe, is the arc of the story and a measure of the inches or miles Ichiro has traveled on Japanese America's and America's road of "Rehabilitation."

By structuring the novel to end this way, Okada shows Ichiro not merely as "unreliable," full of hatred for his pitiable mother, but as a character who serves Okada's purposes of creating a larger vision of Japanese American culture, identity, and history that eludes the dual-identity, assimilationist paradigm. It is a vision of "Americans" defined not simplistically by race but by their stories.

Why did Okada choose to write about a no-no boy and draft resister, the lowest member of his society and not a war hero? Take the draft resister Gary, an artist, who works at the Christian Rehabilitation Center in Seattle (190). Gary feels "like a guy that's come back from the dead," and, he says to Ichiro, "there's a peace about it" (200). This statement intimates that John Okada, too, came to terms with death, but in warfare. Unable to write his story of his own military service, and choosing not to focus on an exceptional "model" of a veteran like Bull as a protagonist, Okada instead decided to write about the dissident. Not the highest, most admired member of society—but if the *lowest* member of society can survive, then all the rest of us have a chance. Okada made a brilliant choice of a protagonist.

By teaching us to look toward a continuing history, *No-No Boy* implies that history will always repeat itself in new forms, with new lessons to apply. Like a prophecy, Okada's novel is applicable for all times, including today. The novel travels some distance away from sympathetic questions about the conflict that Ichiro Yamada experiences and how he feels about it. *No-No Boy* is a novel that withholds satisfaction, and my aim in this essay has been to carry my thoughts about the novel not to conclusions but perhaps to a fresh reading, something that the book continually invites.[33]

False Constructions of Loyalty

The Real Resistance against Incarceration

MARTHA NAKAGAWA

GIVEN THE FEW PORTRAYALS OF JAPANESE AMERICAN WORLD War II protesters in works of fiction, readers can be forgiven for assuming that the protagonist of John Okada's *No-No Boy*, Ichiro Yamada, is representative of all Nisei resisters. He is not, and this presents a problem in reading the book within the context of a history that is far more nuanced. This chapter examines the differences between several different types of protest against the wartime concentration camps, and shows how one book regrettably reinforced several persistent myths about Japanese American resistance to incarceration: that those who protested were disloyal to the United States; that those who protested made the wrong decision for themselves and their families; or that those who protested were motivated by self-hatred.[1]

"NO-NOS" VS. DRAFT RESISTERS

Ichiro in the novel is pejoratively called a "no-no boy," and the author gave this epithet to the title of his book. By doing so, however, he knowingly or unknowingly confused two distinct types of Nisei resistance.

As shown in the introduction to this volume, the first emerged in 1943 when twelve thousand men and women answered "no" to two contentious questions on a mismanaged registration administered jointly by the army and the War Relocation Authority.[2] The questions were designed to assure the public that only those men whom the government certified as loyal to the United States would be allowed into the army as volunteers; for women, the question was adapted for service in the Women's Army Auxiliary Corps. The questionnaire was also used to clear those in the general camp population for release from camp if they had outside sponsors at a college or job.

Anxieties arose over whether answering "yes" to question 27, asking about willingness to serve in the armed forces of the United States, meant a person was automatically volunteering for the army. Also problematic was question 28, asking a compound question of swearing allegiance to the United States and forswearing allegiance to the Japanese emperor, since a "yes" answer implied that the respondent had once sworn an allegiance to the emperor of Japan that they never had. For those who answered "no" to these poorly written questions, the unintended consequence was to create, on paper, a class of so-called *disloyals* who could then be easily segregated from the rest. They were shipped off to the Tule Lake Segregation Center, which the government designated for "disloyals." The Japanese American community itself bought into the notion that these men and women were "disloyal" and came to refer disdainfully to segregees as "no-nos."

The second form of mass protest emerged a year later, in January 1944, when the army reinstituted the draft for the Nisei in camps. These were the draft resisters. These young men had answered "yes-yes" to the loyalty questionnaire (those who qualified their answers received individual hearings) and were therefore deemed "loyal"; however, they refused to report for induction while imprisoned in an American-style concentration camp until their rights were first restored and their families released from camp. In all, 315 were convicted of violating the Selective Training and Service Act of 1940 and sentenced to an average of three years in a federal penitentiary, alongside hardened criminals. They were pardoned by President Truman on December 23, 1947.[3]

These two types of protesters—draft resisters and "no-nos"—were not one and the same. As depicted in Okada's novel, Ichiro is clearly a draft resister who served two years in a federal penitentiary, yet throughout the story he is called the eponymous "no-no boy" of the book's title.

ICHIRO'S INABILITY TO ARTICULATE
THE PATRIOTISM OF THE REAL RESISTERS

Further blurring these distinctions is the absence in Okada's novel of any sense of the motives driving the real-life resisters. Frank Emi was a leader of the organized draft resistance by the Fair Play Committee at the camp at Heart Mountain. Jim Akutsu and Frank Yamasaki were friends of Okada's from Seattle who resisted the draft at Minidoka. What troubled all three on reading *No-No Boy*, in addition to the title, was Ichiro's inability to articulate the American patriotism that lay at the heart of the real resistance. Emi was unable to relate to the character of Ichiro and suspected the author of a promilitary bias, as Okada had volunteered for the Military Intelligence Service.

> He's a good writer, pretty verbose, but he writes about Ichiro from his standpoint as a veteran. And he must have a very anti-resister feeling to portray Ichiro as a whining, self-pitying, weak-kneed person. The resisters that I know are very firm in their belief that they did what was right and they don't take any guff that he had to take. Especially that portion where his so-called friend at first got to the point where he starts spitting on him. I think any of our resisters would have probably hauled off and smacked him.[4]

While Akutsu welcomed the opportunity that renewed interest in the novel provided for him to tell his own story, he resented the suggestion that he was the source for Okada's Ichiro, complaining that he "writes of me not as a strong person but as a weakling."[5] Yamasaki also rejected the portrayal of Ichiro; he saw the character's lack of self-esteem as a reflection of Okada's own.[6] Bill Nishimura, a "no-no" who was a former prisoner of the Colorado River WRA camp (commonly referred to as Poston), the Tule

Lake Segregation Center, and the Santa Fe and Crystal City Department of Justice camps, never wanted to read the book. Heart Mountain resister Yosh Kuromiya at first had the same reaction, but changed his mind.

> I was puzzled to discover that Frank Chin, Lawson Inada, et al. regarded John Okada as an outstanding Nisei writer, so I read and re-read *No-No Boy* several times in the hope of discovering what I had missed. I still haven't grasped the real message of the book. Nonetheless, I now regard John Okada as an extraordinary pioneer of Asian American literature.[7]

REJECTING THE MYTH THAT ALL WHO PROTESTED WERE PRO-JAPAN

Ichiro's life was entwined with that of his immigrant mother, who clung to the *kachigumi* (winning group) belief that demanded continued loyalty to the emperor, despite word of Japan's surrender.[8] It is only natural for an immigrant to retain love of one's native country, especially if the new host country bars them from naturalized citizenship. It was easy for the government to frame Japanese American protest against its actions as a pro-Japan element disloyal to the United States. This marginalizing of protest was endorsed and encouraged by the Japanese American Citizens League (JACL), the only national leadership for the Nisei, which waived the Nisei right to protest the eviction, collaborated with the government during the incarceration, and urged the segregation of what it called "troublemakers."

The reality was very different. The loyalty advocated by the Heart Mountain Fair Play Committee (FPC) was loyalty toward the US Constitution, not to the government or to white acceptance. The protest of the FPC was in the best American tradition of civil disobedience going back to the Boston Tea Party, a point explicitly stated in the FPC's manifestos:

> Without any hearings, without due process of law as guaranteed by the Constitution and Bill of Rights, without any charges filed against us, without any evidence of wrongdoing on our part, one hundred and ten

thousand innocent people were kicked out of their homes, literally uprooted from where they have lived for the greater part of their life, and herded like dangerous criminals into concentration camps with barbed wire fences and military police guarding it, AND WHEN WITHOUT RECTIFICATION OF THE INJUSTICES COM-MITTED AGAINST US NOR WITHOUT RESTORATION OF OUR RIGHTS AS GUARANTEED BY THE CONSTITUTION, WE ARE ORDERED TO JOIN THE ARMY THRU <u>DISCRIMINA-TORY PROCEDURES</u> INTO A <u>SEGREGATED COMBAT UNIT!</u> Is that the American way? <u>NO!</u>[9]

By contrast, the valor of the Nisei soldiers inducted from the camps addressed none of the constitutional issues raised by the mass incarceration. What their record accomplished was to restore the public's faith in the loyalty of Japanese Americans, and serve the public relations campaign by the government and JACL to win racial acceptance for the Nisei after the war. JACL national secretary Mike Masaoka exhorted the Nisei to prove their loyalty by being "ready and willing to die" in a "baptism of blood," a self-sacrifice that had less in common with constitutional principles than with the fervor of samurai in Japan who carried out the orders of their lord without question, even unto death.[10]

THE "RECIPROCAL OBLIGATION OF ALLEGIANCE" AND THE DECISION TO RENOUNCE US CITIZENSHIP

The author touches upon a third form of mass protest in the story of Mike, a character who angrily renounced his US citizenship and applied for expatriation to Japan. The government conveniently enabled this action in 1944 by passing the Denaturalization Act, allowing citizens to renounce their birthright in time of war, followed by Proclamation 2655, enabling the government to deport such renunciants as enemy aliens. Between December 1944 and April 1946, the US attorney general approved 5,589 requests for renunciation, nearly all of them from segregees at Tule Lake.[11]

However, when interrogated by the government during the war or interviewed by historians and journalists afterward, most of those who renounced indicated they did so not out of loyalty to Japan, but under the duress of an unjust incarceration. This was their protest against a government that had evicted them from their homes, placed them in concentration camps, then demanded that they or their sons or brothers or husbands potentially sacrifice their lives fighting in a segregated army unit. The demoralized renunciants resented the fact that their allegiance to the government had not been returned. This idea of the "reciprocal obligation of allegiance" was raised in a class-action lawsuit, *McGrath v. Abo*, in which appellate judge William Denman wrote, "Absent protection, allegiance is no longer obligatory. Absent protection, allegiance becomes, again, a matter of choice."[12] Absent protection, the Tuleans exercised their freedom to choose whether or not to remain citizens of the United States. Abo's attorney, Wayne Collins, told his client that despite the scorn from others, he needn't feel ashamed of renouncing his citizenship: "You did so because the government took advantage of you while it held you in duress and deprived you of practically all the rights of citizenship."[13] As Patrick Gudridge puts it, "In renouncing citizenship, they proclaimed themselves constitutionally quintessentially 'American,'"[14] in sharp contrast to their perception by the public and by Okada.

ICHIRO'S SELF-HATRED: A FALSE PICTURE

Okada peppers Ichiro's dialogue with such phrases as "we made a mistake" or "there is no retribution for one who is guilty of treason." Freddie, another draft resister, says, "You and me, we picked the wrong side."[15] From this, readers may erroneously conclude it was a mistake for Japanese Americans to protest during the war. Of course, if these readers understood the case made by Stephen Sumida earlier in this volume of the author providing an unreliable narrative, perhaps they would reconsider.

Other than the mother, who is shown to have grown insane, all of Okada's characters seem to struggle with being of Japanese descent, a message summed up by Kenji, the veteran: "Go someplace where there isn't another Jap within a thousand miles. Marry a white girl or a Negro or an Italian or even a Chinese. Anything but a Japanese."[16] This is, again, in line with the message of the wartime government and the JACL's Masaoka: Japanese Americans were told to forget the Japanese language and culture, adopt Anglicized names, and avoid creating Japantowns after the war. By 1979, Japanese American women had the highest rate of out-marriage of any Asian Pacific American group on the US mainland.[17]

But not all Japanese Americans lost their sense of ethnic pride. After the war, many protesters took occupations in farming or gardening that enabled them to be their own boss. The Gardena Valley Gardeners Association, which counted many former Tuleans among its eight hundred members, promoted Japanese language and culture through an annual show, beautification programs to create traditional Japanese gardens throughout Southern California, and regular maintenance landscaping at Buddhist temples, Japanese language schools, community centers, and elder care facilities.[18] Others used their bilingual fluency to act as bridges with then-fledgling Japanese companies such as Honda, Toyota, and Sony that wanted to do business in the United States. Unlike the self-hating characters in Okada's fictional world, these people did not suppress their "Japaneseness"; they embraced it.

CONCLUSION

John Okada deserves credit for framing his book around the character of a resister, but he missed the opportunity to portray the depth and breadth of the principled protest in camp. By reinforcing the false constructions of loyalty continually created by the government through waves of eviction, segregation, Selective Service, and the push to expatriate the prisoners, the novel contributed to popular misconceptions about Japanese American resistance inside the camps, thus inadvertently doing the real resisters a great disservice.

Contesting Japanese American Identity

A Literature Review of *No-No Boy*

JEFFREY T. YAMASHITA

JOHN OKADA'S *NO-NO BOY* IS CELEBRATED AS A PRIME EXAMPLE of Japanese American literature for its detailing of the psychological, material, and political consequences of the incarceration and their impact on the lived experience of the book's protagonist, Ichiro Yamada. Scholarly discussion and critical interest in the novel continues to grow, more than sixty years since its initial publication. This review of the critical literature charts the history of that discussion and synthesizes the main discussions, debates, and contestations. Not surprisingly, the critical literature has mirrored larger trends in the field of Asian American literature, focusing in particular on the complexity of Asian American subject formation and the novel's challenge to the discourse of the "model minority myth."[1]

This essay focuses on two major periods of literary criticism of Okada's novel: (1) the mid-1970s through the early 1990s and (2) the early 1990s through 2015.[2] The first period parallels what Asian American literary scholar Colleen Lye has described as "first-wave Asian American literary history,"[3] when literary scholars were especially interested in the relationships between literary and historical evidence. This first period of *No-No Boy*'s literary history can be best described as (1) an exploration of the internal dilemma of claiming a privileged American or subordinated Asian identity and (2) a celebration of marginality and the power of "otherness" to demonstrate the uniqueness and complexity of minority discourses.[4] By the early 1990s, Asian American literary studies were witnessing a "second wave," in which the epistemological concerns revolved around concepts of anti-imperialism, antinationalism, and the material specificity of literature.[5] During this period literary criticisms of Okada's novel mirrored the larger trends in Asian American literary studies, analyzing issues of US empire and nationalism during the Cold War and the intersectional racial and gendered identities of Ichiro's subject formation.

Two points are especially important for understanding *No-No Boy*'s literary historical trajectory. First, the discussions and debates on Okada's novel are situated within two interrelated epistemic positions—"Japanese American studies" and the larger, panethnic "Asian American studies." Although both positions speak to similar themes, topics, and experiences, they have distinct priorities in terms of analysis of Okada's novel. Throughout this essay, I will note the differences between the academic criticisms from Japanese American studies and Asian American studies in order to clarify the claims, perspectives, and arguments from both fields.

Second, the predominant topic that has occupied the interests of academic scholars, as evidenced by over twenty peer-reviewed articles and anthology chapters spanning forty years, is the contested subject formation of Okada's main protagonist, Ichiro Yamada. In *No-No Boy,* Ichiro, who returns to Seattle in the aftermath of World War II, negotiates a conflicted identity as "Japanese American"—a conflict rooted in his refusal to be drafted from an incarceration camp during the war. As a result of his refusal he was imprisoned for two years, and he has been shamed by some in the Japanese American community, including its veterans. Ichiro has a tenuous relationship with his strong-willed mother, has trouble constructing and claiming his Japanese American identity in relation to Japanese Americans and other racial groups, and is disillusioned by the racist treatment he receives in US society. The novel fascinates many literary scholars because it rejects the "model minority myth," with its stereotypes of the hardworking, docile Japanese American subject, and offers a gripping account of the harsh realities of Japanese American survival and identity formation in the postwar era. Ultimately, due to the deep admiration for *No-No Boy* and its value to the field of both Japanese American studies and Asian American studies, much literary criticism has aimed at creating generative discussions around Ichiro's subject formation.

FIRST-WAVE ASIAN AMERICAN LITERARY HISTORY: THE "COMPLETION" OF ICHIRO YAMADA

No-No Boy's literary history from 1974 to 1990 illustrates how literary scholars of that time dealt with Ichiro's individual subjectivity—through ideas of whiteness, assimilation, and gender. John Okada's novel was reintroduced into the minds and interests of Asian American writers and scholars with the publication of the fifth chapter of the book in the seminal 1974 collection *Aiiieeeee! An Anthology of Asian American Writers*, edited by Frank Chin, Jeffery Paul Chan, Lawson Fusao Inada, and Shawn Hsu Wong. The four then helped pay for republication of the novel, establishing it as a foundational work that the University of Washington Press has since kept in print.

Literary scholar Jinqi Ling points out that during this time, literary thought on the novel emphasizes Ichiro's "'completion' of his quest for a sense of 'wholeness' as a Japanese American or his ultimate overcoming of self-hatred through an 'accretion of positive experiences.'"[6] Indeed, the *Aiiieeeee!* editors counter the stereotype of Asian American docility and subordination with an alternative vision of Asian American empowerment while championing both Okada and his protagonist Ichiro as prime examples.[7] To these editors, Ichiro stands as a figure of resistance in creating a distinctly celebratory Japanese American identity. Writing a few years later, in 1979, Dorothy Ritsuko McDonald validates Ichiro's racial identity by claiming that he becomes "whole" through his relationship with whiteness and specifically Christianity.[8]

The *Aiiieeeee!* anthology proved important in providing a platform for Asian American literary scholars and showcased both Okada and Ichiro.

However, the anthology's approach to liberation falls along the lines of a masculinist position that has been critiqued by Asian American feminists such as Shirley Geok-lin Lim.[9] Discussion surrounding the masculinist approach to Asian American empowerment and the reclamation of Asian American women's experiences and voices has also informed the contentious relationship between academics and writers within Asian American studies.[10] Colleen Lye speaks about this internal fighting within Asian America: "The growth of academic criticism and of commercial literary publishing since the 1970s has tended to witness a tension between academics and writers" because of differing perspectives on authenticity, representation, and discursive power.[11] In this era, the question of *who* is able to discursively create authentic Asian American characters and *what* that authenticity looks like became important themes that challenged the notion that Ichiro "completes" his identity through his individual subjectivity.

SECOND-WAVE ASIAN AMERICAN LITERARY HISTORY: DECONSTRUCTION OF *NO-NO BOY* AND OKADA

By the early 1990s, many literary scholars within Asian American studies began to analyze texts by taking into account imperialism, nationalism, ambivalence, and the material to understand power relations. These scholars adopted a critical discourse analysis approach that focused on social problems and political issues rather than on discourse structures removed from their social and political contexts; interdisciplinary forms of knowledge; explanations framed in terms of properties of social interaction and social structure rather than descriptions of discourse structures; and the ways discourse structures enact, confirm, reproduce, or challenge relations of power and dominance in society.[12]

Jinqi Ling's 1995 essay "Race, Power, and Cultural Politics in John Okada's *No-No Boy*" exemplifies this trend, standing as a distinct break between the first and second waves of both Asian American and Japanese American literary studies. Ling's work shifts the critical framework from an affirmation of Ichiro's "completion" as a "whole" Japanese American to placing Okada's literary creation in its context of the 1950s, which "implicitly calls for a breakdown of the discourse that governed the relations of Japanese Americans to the mainstream." Rather than perpetuating a "completed" model minority narrative of the docile Japanese American, Ling's provocation challenges other scholars to critically engage the context and content of *No-No Boy*.[13] Scholars adopting a similar critical discourse analysis approach to understand Ichiro's subject formation discuss issues of (1) dual identity, (2) race and gender identities, (3) comparative racialization, and (4) discursive structures. These four issues form the backbone of the second-wave analyses of *No-No Boy*.

The scholarly discussion around Ichiro's "dual identity" resurfaced in the 1990s. Writing in *Amerasia Journal*, a leading Asian American studies journal, in 1993, William Yeh examines both John Okada and Ichiro Yamada and argues that "the history of [*No-No Boy*] is as significant as the story within it; both its context and content represent a state of liminality."[14] Although Yeh does not explicitly reference Lawson Inada, his discussion of liminality—a state of in-betweenness—builds on Inada's earlier rumination on Ichiro that, "for the American born, being American was no longer taken for granted. In the 'double war,' they were all 'aliens.' It was if the term 'Japanese-American' no longer signified a viable whole but denoted an either/or situation, a double bind."[15] Rather than an "either/or" binary, Yeh is interested in the middle position that is neither Japanese nor American but Japanese American, a liminal position occupied by both author and protagonist.[16]

In 1996, Stan Yogi published an article on the concept of "dual identity" within the novel in *MELUS: Multi-Ethnic Literature of the US*. Yogi's article addresses similar points to those in William Yeh's article and uses similar examples from the text. Yogi contends that "through Ichiro's journey to re-establish himself as an American, Okada explores the gray area between the oppositions that develop around polarized definitions of 'Japanese' and 'American.'"[17] This "gray area" could be interpreted as a liminal position, but in contrast to Yeh's focus on the liminal positions shared by Okada and Ichiro, Yogi considers only the oppositions within Ichiro's individual subjectivity. Specifically, Yogi examines the identities of "Japanese," "Japanese-American," and "American" and discusses the various oppositions and inner turmoil of a "split" or multiple identities in a society that can only understand *one* identity. Yogi goes on to trace the reconciliation that occurs within these oppositions and within certain scenes in the novel to illustrate the fluidity between opposition and reconciliation within *No-No Boy*.

Ethnic studies scholar Stephen H. Sumida has also reflected on the changing contours of Asian American studies with regard to the concept of dual identity. In his article "The More Things Change: Paradigm Shifts in Asian American Studies," published in 2000, Sumida briefly details the tensions between the two dominant intellectual camps about the meaning of "dual identity"—on the one hand, an identity based on a glorification of an assimilationist US identity, and on the other hand, an identity resistant to assimilation. Sumida says that Okada's novel stands in counterpoint to assimilationist Asian American literary texts, writing that even while Ichiro believes in an Asian American dual identity, Okada challenges "the reductive essentialism of how Japanese Americans and others have been defined by genetic and inherited attachment to cultures thought inimical to the US."[18] To Sumida, Ichiro's ambivalent, liminal identity serves as the basis of a distinctly Japanese American identity that moves beyond a duality of either Japanese or American.

The second major debate in this phase of *No-No Boy* criticism centers on the intersectional understandings of the interplay between race and gender identities, specifically racialized masculinities, within both the text and the period of publication. Asian American literary scholars Viet Thanh Nguyen and Suzanne Arakawa both use a comparative method in interrogating Okada's novel. In *Race and Resistance: Literature and Politics in Asian America* (2002), Nguyen devotes a chapter to exploring Ichiro's racialized manhood in relation to Filipino American writer Carlos Bulosan's 1946 memoir *America Is in the Heart*. Thinking through his own experiences as a Vietnamese American writer, Nguyen argues that while both Okada and Bulosan use legible tropes of freedom and materialism to speak to mainstream US society, "the recuperated manhood presented at the books' conclusions is compromised or limited by the authors' flexible strategies, their decision to accommodate, even marginally and ironically, to the demands of the dominant society."[19] For Nguyen, Bulosan's and Okada's protagonists seek to reclaim the ability to be free men, but they are ultimately denied due to the exclusionary restrictions applied to Asian American men.[20]

Working within the context of Japanese American literary studies, Suzanne Arakawa also interrogates Ichiro's racial masculinity, this time through a comparison with writer Toshio Mori's incarceration camp stories from the 1940s and 1950s. Arakawa juxtaposes Ichiro's representation of his male body with those of the male characters in Mori's stories in order to highlight dissent, male culture, and American identity within the negotiations of a Japanese American male identity. Arakawa suggests that both Okada and Mori present "a clearinghouse of male anxieties stemming from enforced stasis as well as rootlessness; both writers use the Japanese American male body . . . to undermine larger assumptions about established discourse, especially the discourse of war."[21] The romantic, patriotic discourse of war is incongruent with Ichiro's experiences of self-hatred and inner turmoil. To Arakawa, Ichiro is a discursive tool allowing Okada to reflect on the Japanese American male subject and an empowering form of resistance to the totalizing discourse of US patriotic military participation.

Literary scholars Bryn Gribben and Daniel Y. Kim introduce psychoanalytical approaches to this discussion of racialized masculinities and also focus on the novel's Cold War context. Bryn Gribben's 2003 article "The Mother That Won't Reflect Back: Situating Psychoanalysis and the Japanese American Mother in *No-No Boy*" discusses ways in which the use of the psychoanalytic discourse of "momism" "serves an exclusionary function and prohibits uncomplicated access to Western identity for the Japanese American male." Gribben views psychoanalysis as ultimately inclusionary only to white America, and he shows how Ichiro's subject formation reveals these limitations. Gribben specifically psychoanalyzes the relationship between Ichiro and his mother and ultimately contends that the "novel seems to present itself as a psychological bildungsroman in which the protagonist, Ichiro, struggles to separate himself from uncertainty and continue progress toward a unified identity."[22]

Ethnic studies scholar Daniel Y. Kim follows the same approach but emphasizes the context of the Cold War to situate Ichiro's racialized masculinity. His 2005 article "Once More, with Feeling: Cold War Masculinity and the Sentiment of Patriotism in John Okada's *No-No Boy*" also addresses Ichiro's racialized masculinity through the term *momism*, which Kim defines as individuals or groups "purported to identify those subjects who were vulnerable to subversion and suggested how their loyalty could be shored up." Rather than citing Gribben's article, Kim grounds his analysis in the work of Jinqi Ling and Viet Nguyen, who argued for a more concerted effort to analyze both the text and the period of publication. By treating the novel's Cold War context as fundamental to comprehending Ichiro's subject formation, Kim particularly centers the nonnormative nature of Ichiro's masculinity, demonstrating "how it both echoes and reworks dominant psychological narratives of the early Cold War period."[23] Instead of presenting Ichiro as an exemplary case of a romanticized racial masculinity (echoing past attempts like the *Aiiieeeee!* anthology), Kim allows for a reading that legitimates Ichiro's nonnormative masculinity in the face of both US imperial aspirations and Cold War gender anxieties. Although Kim explores Ichiro's racialized masculinity through his relationship with his mother, that racialized masculinity operates primarily along the racial lines of white–Japanese American.

Moving beyond a binary racial lens, in the third major theme of second-wave *No-No Boy* criticism scholars in the 2010s have reexamined Okada's novel to reveal Ichiro's relational racialization with other non-white characters, especially African Americans, exposing the potential for coalitional politics that transcend the mere recognition of relational and differential racialization. These scholars, such as James Kyung-Jin Lee and Helen Jun, have extended sociologists Michael Omi and Howard Winant's seminal work on racial formation to think beyond the scholarship on *No-No Boy* that only examined the race relations between Japanese Americans and white America,[24] or between Japanese Americans and other Asian ethnic groups.[25] By incorporating an analytic that includes other racial groups, Lee and Jun offer new insights into Ichiro's racial formation.

Helen Jun's chapter "Blackness, Manhood, and the Aftermath of Internment in John Okada's *No-No Boy* (1957)" in her *Race for Citizenship* (2011) explores the intersectional processes of black racialization and the formation of Japanese American masculinities as represented in Ichiro's interactions with different characters. Her work examines how the black social spaces of Ichiro's home in Seattle enable Okada to explore the contradictions of Ichiro's Japanese American and Asian American national identity. Jun argues that "*No-No Boy* is told from the space of the multiracial ghetto and negotiates Orientalist exclusion and national displacement through gendered discourses of black urban pathology." Ichiro, along with his Japanese American community, is deemed an outcast, placed outside the cultural boundaries of the US nation. Jun argues that through the conception of black social spaces, which she describes as "being in the cultural boundaries of the US nation," Ichiro is able to renegotiate his claims for inclusion.[26]

Like Jun, Lee also explores Ichiro's racial identity by taking cues from the study of black racialization. In the 2012 anthology *Racial Formation in the Twenty-First Century*, Lee's chapter "The Transitivity of Race and the Challenge of the Imagination" articulates a need for a literary archive that can "displace the narrative of a future that is already a past, sad prophecy fulfilled." Lee specifically names Okada's novel as a prime example that complicates Omi and Winant's notion by articulating "that the racial imagination, like power, is not something that is seized, but an act, many acts in fact, of creativity." Within Asian American literary studies, Lee points out, contemporary Asian American literary scholars assert "subjectlessness or melancholy as our theoretical starting point." The tension within this relationship is that for sociologists, the process of racialization is dependent upon creating and recreating constructions of racial meaning through imagining new futures. However, Lee contends that Asian American subjects are "already a past, sad prophecy fulfilled," which denies them recognition as active agents and positions them as passive subordinates with no futures. Lee points to scenes such as Ichiro's interaction with Rabbit, the black shoeshine man "who, unlike everyone else in the story, says to Ichiro of his decision to refuse the draft, 'Good boy. If they'd a come for me, I would have told them where to shove their stinking uniform.'" Such scenes, Lee hopes, provide a way to create an "ineluctably differentiated humanity." By thinking about how blackness has been relegated to nonhumanity, Lee proposes, we are able to think about how the case of Ichiro opens up new humanities that are unintelligible to positivist futurities of race.[27]

The fourth and final major theme within the literary history of the second-wave scholarship on *No-No Boy* centers on interpreting the novel's protagonist and its structure from the fields of postcolonial studies, psychology, and noir. Pulling from theories within postcolonial studies, Benzi Zhang employs Mikhail Bakhtin's theory of literary carnival, which is an attempt to locate discourses that are in opposition to canonization and totalization, to stake a claim that *No-No Boy* offers a narrative of a "democratic vision of culture and literature as non-hierarchical plural systems." Zhang attempts to show that *No-No Boy*, if understood through such carnivalistic discourse, can offer a counter text to the "hegemonic power of totalization—'the capability of certain formations to position everything else in a negative relationship to it.'" In this act of resistance to totalization lies what Zhang believes is the essence of Okada's novel and Japanese American literature writ large: "The 'renegotiation' between the hegemonic culture and various cultural differences."[28]

Asian American literary scholars Floyd Cheung and Bill E. Peterson draw on the field of psychology to interpret *No-No Boy*. Writing in 2006, they use Dan McAdam's 1988 life-story model of identity to help readers "conceptualize human identity in terms of a story" when unpacking the novel.[29] As described by Cheung and Peterson, the life-story model incorporates three mutually constitutive aspects of individual identity: "the somatic order (one's body as it is understood to have qualities such as race, gender, or age), the social order (the social forces associated with a time and place that delineate ideologies of race, gender, and age, for example), and the personal order (one's idiosyncratic way of understanding and relating to the world and oneself)."[30] Through these three-layered "orders," Cheung and Peterson contend, McAdam's theory provides a coherent approach for understanding Ichiro's subjectivity within the spatial and temporal context in the novel. More importantly, they believe that the application of the life-story model of identity clarifies the past literary concerns around Ichiro's identity, making sense of both macro and internal issues that Ichiro faces in *No-No Boy*.[31]

Applying a critical theory approach to Asian American literature, Joseph Entin proposes an alternative way of thinking about the psychic torment Ichiro endures as a result of his refusal to serve in the US military: noir. Noir, according to Entin, emphasizes the "hidden secrets, dark deeds, and social estrangement," and provides a useful lens for analyzing the relationships between negative and affirmative sentiments in Okada's novel. If we were to specifically locate the noir, which represents a discourse of negative feelings, this approach would reveal that, "the novel is suspended between a discourse of affirmative, patriotic sentiment and a rhetoric of negative feelings."[32]

Since the early 1990s, the literary criticism on *No-No Boy* has followed the path of a more critical engagement with Ichiro's individual subjectivity by taking into account the context of the publication, the intersectional identities of race and masculinities, comparative racialization, and structural perspectives. Although *No-No Boy* has been highly analyzed by scholars of Asian American studies, Japanese American studies, English, postcolonial studies, psychology, and comparative literature, there is still more engagement with Okada's novel for future scholars. Certainly, the new biography and rediscovered texts by Okada in this volume will add fresh resources for their consideration.

Republishing and Teaching
No-No Boy

SHAWN WONG

NO-NO BOY IS AT THE VERY FOUNDATION OF WHAT I KNOW about Asian American literature. It's a big part of my reason for becoming a writer and a teacher. To understand how important it was, requires a look at the state of Asian America in the 1960s.

There was no Asian American studies. I was the only Asian American writer that I knew in the entire world, but it dawned on me, in 1969 at age twenty, that there must be others out there. I started looking, and I found a lot of bad books: Charlie Chan books, Fu Manchu books, tour guides, restaurant guides, cookbooks filled with stereotypes, from non-Chinese writers, or non-Asian writers posing as Asian writers. My teacher, Kay Boyle, mentioned that one of her creative writing graduate students was Jeffery Chan at San Francisco State. He was also an unpublished writer. I got in touch, and Jeff said, "Oh, you live in Berkeley, there's this guy named Frank Chin who lives right down the street from you." I called Frank up and said, "I understand you are a writer and you've actually published something. I'd like to meet you." And so between the three of us, we started a quest to find other books. We trolled the used bookstores

---

This essay is based on a 2006 interview of Shawn Wong by Frank Abe.

on Telegraph Avenue and found an anthology of Fresno poets; on the cover was a group photo of twenty poets, one of whom looked Asian. It turned out to be Lawson Inada. And so the four of us, we figured we couldn't be the only Asian American writers in the world. There must have been someone who came before.

We bought all the books we could find—they were only twenty-five or fifty cents—and *No-No Boy* was one of them. Being writers, we judge a book by its cover, so we'd look at the cover and go, oh, what's this book about? Here's this guy covering his face, in the barbed wire, and the title is "no-no." And I'm thinking this book is about denying somebody is Asian. But as you start reading it, you realize very quickly it's a book about Japanese America, and it wasn't about Japan, and it was such a relief to start reading a book that was expressing a sensibility we were still trying to define as fellow writers. It was one of those books that you don't believe you're actually reading it when you're reading it.

No-No Boy resonated so much with the things I was trying to figure out as a young undergraduate at Berkeley. I was of draft age during the Vietnam War. The book was about making those decisions: should I go into the army and potentially fight a war I thought was unjust, or should I go to prison?

We wrote to Charles Tuttle, who had published it in Japan. We soon discovered it was published in 1957 in a hardcover edition of 1,500 copies, and fifteen years later it was still in print. That meant less than one hundred copies had sold per year. It was $3 in hardcover, so we started buying copies, just to give to people: "Read this book, it's a really great book."

We wanted to meet the author. We called Dorothy Okada, John Okada's widow, and that's when she told us, "You're too late. John Okada is dead." He had died only a few months before—we just missed meeting him—but the four of us wanted to find out more about the person behind the book. The letters Tuttle sent to us revealed that Okada had written a second novel about the Issei. We went down to Los Angeles to meet Dorothy. We asked of course about the novel. She informed us that she had offered the papers to UCLA—all of John Okada's papers—but UCLA had never heard of him and turned the offer down, so she burned all of his papers. As writers, we were sitting there looking at her, stunned that anybody would burn somebody's creative work. I don't think we even knew what to say next.

REPUBLISHING THE NOVEL

The four of us thought this book should be republished when it finally went out of print. And we thought, well, the book takes place in Seattle: let's see if we can get the University of Washington Press to reprint it. We got a letter campaign going in 1975, congressmen and senators, people from the Japanese American community, writing to the University of Washington Press saying this was Japanese America's only known novel. The Press turned us down, but then made us a curious offer, saying, if you give us $5,000, we'll publish it for you. The four of us were not MBA geniuses, but we realized that we could give ourselves $5,000 and publish the book ourselves. We had our own organization called CARP, the Combined Asian-American Resources Project, which we'd just invented. We got the book typeset. We asked our friend Robert Onodera to design the cover, and went to press. We had raised only about half of the money needed to print the book, but we went to press anyway, knowing that when the book came off the press we'd have to pay the balance. It was going to take a couple of thousand dollars, so we contacted the *Pacific Citizen* newspaper, the national newspaper read by all Japanese Americans at the time, and told them we were publishing this book whose time had come, and we would offer $2 off to anyone who would order it in advance. The *Pacific Citizen* ran basically a free ad for us, and the orders started pouring in.

The first orders came from only Japanese American people. It was a book that Japanese America had always heard of, but nobody had read it. The community decided that it was time to read it. There were baby-boomers like me who were trying to rediscover our personal histories. The first printing was three thousand copies, and they were all sold before the book came off the press, so we were able to pay the bill and even go into a second printing thanks to the money we had raised. It was one of the first books to become a staple in the early Asian American studies classes.

The *Seattle Times*'s Mayumi Tsutakawa interviewed me and published a story about how we got turned down by the University of Washington

Press. The next day I get a phone call from the Press saying, "Mr. Wong, we read the article, and we'd like to meet with you." I walk into the conference room, and there's the entire staff sitting around the table, about twenty people, and Don Ellegood, the executive director, gets up and says, "The first thing I'd like to do is apologize on behalf of the Press. This is a book that we should have published. Your story of publishing it and selling it by mail is a stroke of genius, and we want to publish it now." I was so mad! I had to personally package and mail out every one of those books myself, not to mention haul up the second printing from the Bay Area. So I go on this little lecture about how there were other books in Asian American literature that needed to be reprinted, and why don't you reprint some of those? And the interesting thing is, they ask, "What are the titles?" So I start mentioning *Yokohama, California* by Toshio Mori, *Eat a Bowl of Tea* by Louis Chu, and so on. And the UW Press started publishing them, faithfully, one after the other. Years later I finally said to them, "Okay, you can have *No-No Boy*. We're out of the publishing business." And the final episode of the story is that the book has sold its 150,000th copy at the University of Washington Press. Its time had definitely come.

TEACHING THE NOVEL

John Okada worked in isolation, as a lot of Asian American writers did. Louis Chu sort of invented language, whole cloth. John Okada invented what he believed was Japanese American English on the page. When you read *No-No Boy*, it has that 1950s tone. It's partly a voice from the Japanese American community, but it's also very much written from that voice of 1950s radio shows.

No-No Boy is very melodramatic. If you read the preface out loud, about Pearl Harbor and its aftermath, it sounds like Walter Cronkite, in the way of its phrasing and the melodrama. We asked Dorothy Okada, "If John didn't know any other writers, where did he learn this from?" And she said that he listened to the radio. And that made sense to us. When you read the book out loud, you hear that radio voice in his narrative. Those long monologues in *No-No Boy* sound just like an old radio show, where the hero is thinking to himself, like a detective show, or film noir.

No-No Boy would make for a good movie, but it definitely would be a great radio drama.

So if you ask students to watch old WWII newsreels, and listen to the narrator speaking, then have them read *No-No Boy* out loud, it's the exact same voice. By asking the students to read it out loud, you can hear that melodrama, that dramatic narrative voice.

Okada does some unusual things with the language. In places there are silences, and of course the book is about silence and absence. It's in some ways a metaphor for all that's missing in the Japanese American community in that time. Unnaturally long silences, where Ichiro is watching his mother move about the store. There's that incredible scene where Ichiro has returned to Seattle after taking Kenji to Oregon; he's come back to Emi's house and he's in the distance, and Emi thinks it's Kenji, and she's happy at first. Then she realizes it's Ichiro. He thinks she's happy to see him, but he realizes she thinks he's Kenji, there's this huge disappointment on her face. And there's this huge sadness on the part of Ichiro that she wasn't waiting for him. This void and silence is a huge part of the novel, and if you think of it as a radio play, one of the things that's more noticeable on a radio play is the dead silence, radio silence, where there's nothing but silence in the air. It seems to last longer than on film. You can almost hear Okada saying, "I'm going to write the most painful scene I can, and I'm going to make people feel that pain."

On a very high level, I ask students to examine the characters and the context in which they are set. If you can imagine Okada sitting in a room writing this book—Japanese America has already lived out that dramatic plot, so he's writing historical fiction of something that's already happened. But it's the 1950s, Japanese America's experience in WWII was just ten years old. He's wasn't out there to retell history, to dump a lot of facts in his book, to even editorialize. He certainly was well read and literate, but to be able to hear that narrative voice in his ear was an amazing feat, since he had no models. He had no Japanese American literary tradition to call upon or to inform his work. The man wrote in complete isolation.

If you read *No-No Boy* and knew nothing about Japanese America, you would wonder, "What do you mean he spent two years in camp and two years in prison, what does that mean? What happened just before? And what does 'no-no boy' mean as a phrase?" I would ask students to go back to the historical record and see what happened, to look at how Japanese Americans were evicted, and how that vacuum was filled by other people. They return not as the same people who left America: they have to learn how to read again, learn how to take the bus again, because they've lost some ability to function. They say they never returned; the person who left, never came back. Certainly Kenji wasn't the same person physically, and Ichiro wasn't the same person mentally, nor was his family. I see this return even more clearly now with soldiers and veterans transitioning to civilian life after being deployed in Iraq and Afghanistan. I teach story-telling workshops in the Red Badge Project (*theredbadgeproject.org*) to veterans, many of whom struggle with PTSD, and I see Okada's character, Ichiro, in all of them. It's more than a Japanese American story—it's an American story.

What's interesting is how long it took Japanese America to write about the camps. The defining experience of Japanese America is the camps, and when you look at *No-No Boy*, it's really about the camps. It's not set in camp, but it is camp. It's the same with *Yokohama, California*. When I teach both of these books, I ask, "Here is the defining moment of the Japanese American experience, the concentration camps—now, if you were a writer, wouldn't you write about that first?" But Japanese American writers didn't. Then I ask, "What if everything they wrote was about camps, it just wasn't *set* in camp." The short stories of Hisaye Yamamoto were all written and published after camp, they're about prewar Japanese America, but when you read them you realize: this is what America destroyed. This organic wholeness, the world of the Japanese American rural farmer in her stories, doesn't exist anymore, it's gone. *No-No Boy* is about the aftermath of camp, but it's also about camp. It's about the great divide in camp, when the loyalty oath was imposed on Japanese America and divided families, divided husbands and wives, divided everyone in camp, and this is the result.

From a writer's point of view, what's important about *No-No Boy* is that an author felt that he had to tell a story about his community, and there was no model there for him, so he felt it was up to him to tell that story. It's a remarkable decision for somebody to say, "I think I'll write a novel about Japanese America, and I don't know another Japanese American work out there, but I'm going to write this novel." And then to also assume responsibility—to say, "Now that I've written that novel, I'm going to write a novel about the Issei generation." It wasn't about celebrity or making lots of money, but that he felt that the story should be told and it should get out there.

Nightsong in Asian America

LAWSON FUSAO INADA

After helping to rediscover *No-No Boy* and interview Dorothy Okada, Lawson Inada wrote this poem in 1972 as the preface to a special Asian American literature edition of *Yardbird Reader,* a literary annual of African American work. *Yardbird's* editorial directors were writers Ishmael Reed and Al Young, and the guest editors for volume 3 were Shawn Wong and Frank Chin.

♦ — ♦ — ♦ — ♦

For the living memory of John Okada, pioneer, novelist: No-No Boy, *1957*

The sky fits perfectly on all matter.
Nothing is jagged enough: volcanic
mass of the Cascades; structures of Seattle.

To come upon disaster at Cottage Grove—
the smashed front end of a Chevrolet,
occupants and lights strewn in order. . . .

Which is why the moon hides
half of itself over Roseburg, or beacons
seek and find in the cracks of cliffs.

Nappa tsukemono in the back seat
spreads its lovely, abundant musk.

Everything we eat needs rice.
These supplies must reach the people.

Afterword

JOHN OKADA FELT THE URGENCY TO WRITE A NOVEL THAT might define his generation—perhaps even the great Nisei novel that so many hoped would emerge. James Omura, Larry Tajiri, and Bill Hosokawa all envisioned an epic that spanned the immigration of their Issei parents, the second world war, and the hysteria that swept up both Issei and Nisei. Hosokawa even speculated that Okada might be the one to write it.

Fast-forward to the present, and in the final accounting John Okada's *No-No Boy* is the Nisei novel that has stood the test of time. His story of one man who said no to injustice, at a time when unconditional submission to authority was the only accepted response, speaks more clearly to us now than it did then. When it was first published, in the devastated landscape of postwar Japanese America, all the author and his community could imagine for their collective future was a faint and elusive "glimmer of hope." That all changed with two later events: a congressional finding that the root causes of the eviction and incarceration were race prejudice, war hysteria, and a failure of political leadership; and Japanese America's belated embrace of the principled resistance in camp to the wartime violations of their civil and constitutional rights.

At the present moment, what Okada called "the indignation, the hatred, the patriotism of the American people" that targeted innocent Americans following the attack on Pearl Harbor is rising once again. The normalizing of racism and nativism at the highest levels of government has legitimized hostility toward and legalized punitive measures against others based on their differences—whether it be their religion, their race, or their immigration status. *#Resistance* is now part of the national discourse, a hashtag in social media. From "the darkness of the alley of the community that was a tiny bit of America," the historical memory of Japanese American resistance in the American twentieth century lives inside John Okada's *No-No Boy*. In the twenty-first century, it is a history that is no longer remote or academic—and with knowledge of that history comes the responsibility to stand in defense of others threatened by the same prejudice, hysteria, and failed political leadership.

FRANK ABE
DECEMBER 7, 2017
SEATTLE

ACKNOWLEDGMENTS

The editors wish to acknowledge the support of the Smith College Office of the Provost, Department of English Language and Literature, and American Studies Program for making portions of this book possible.

Frank Abe is grateful to Frank Chin, Shawn Wong, Lawson Inada, and Jeff Chan for restoring John Okada to American literature; Frank Chin for his essay inspiring this search; Thomas Girst, Kazuo Ito, and Larry Tart for their research and interviews with people long gone; and research associates David Cho, Ian D. Houghton, Isabella Jaravata, Camille Naga-sawa, Bethany Narita, and Thien-Kim Vo. Thanks to Tom Ikeda, Brian Niiya, Caitlin Oiye and everyone at Densho; and Feliks Banel, Gerardo A. Colmenar, Roger Daniels, Steven Doi, Art Hansen, David Ishii Bookseller, Ryusuke Kawai, Rob Ketcherside, Dr. Sumi Lavin, Marjorie Lee, James McIlwain, James McNaughton, Eric Muller, Ishmael Reed, Vickie Saku-rada Schaepler, Jean Sherrard, Barbara Takei, and Dr. Benjamin Tong for their invaluable contributions. For video interviews with Okada family and friends, Frank is indebted to the production team of Shannon Gee, Carol Hasegawa, and Stevan Smith, and the grant support of the Indepen-dent Television Service (ITVS) Diversity Development Fund, the Wash-ington Civil Liberties Public Education Program, and the Seattle CityArtist Projects program. Thank you Laureen Mar, wise soul.

Greg Robinson wishes to thank Thanapat Porjit for research and other support, Maxime Minne for this book's index, and Christopher Bram, Jean-Francis Clermont-Legros, Elena Tajima Creef, Brian Niiya, Christian

Roy, Vince Schleitwiler, Jeannie Shinozuka, Chris Suh, Heng Wee Tan, Duncan Ryuken Willlams, and Paul Yamada for their kind assistance.

Floyd Cheung wishes to thank University of Washington registrar Virjean Edwards and archivist Diana Shenk for their assistance with identifying Okada's classes and professors; Sheri Cheung and Bill Peterson for their comments on early drafts; and Miriam Mosher and Rachel Foster for research assistance.

At the University of Washington Press we are indebted to many, especially editor in chief Larin McLaughlin, production editor Margaret Sullivan, the close eye of copyeditor Anne Canright, and Mellon Diversity Fellow Mike Baccam.

Finally, this book would not have been possible without the patience and grace of John Okada's family: Dorothy, Dorothea and Matthew, Roy and Mary, Connie and Arlene, and Beverly, Pam, Robert, Sally, and Emiko.

NOTES

1   The Japanese in America name their generations: Issei for the immigrants denied naturalized U.S. citizenship by racial exclusionary law until 1952; Nisei for their second-generation children, American citizens by birthright; and the third-generation Sansei, mostly born after the camps.

2   Anonymous, "I Must Be Strong," *University of Washington Daily*, December 11, 1941, 1.

3   Ibid.

4   John Okada, *No-No Boy* (Seattle: University of Washington Press, 2014), xxiii. All citations in the notes refer to this edition.

5   See my PBS film *Conscience and the Constitution* (2000) for the story of JACL collaboration with the government and its suppression of camp resistance.

6   Eric Muller, Email to the author, August 9, 2017.

7   On page 57, Ichiro tells Kenji, "I wasn't in the army, Ken. I was in jail. I'm a no-no boy." Draft resisters went to jail; no-nos went to Tule Lake. On page 69, a voice in the crowd at the Club Oriental jeers, "No-no boys don't look so good without the striped uniform." The striped uniform of course meant a prison jumpsuit.

8   As shown in the Okada biography, another factor may be that soldiers upon discharge from the Military Intelligence Service were told not to talk about their classified exploits. See also the chapter by Stephen Sumida for a discussion of Akutsu's dual status as draft resister and self-proclaimed "no-no boy" who was never segregated to Tule Lake.

9 Floyd Cheung and Bill E. Peterson, "Psychology and Asian American Literature: Application of the Life-Story Model of Identity to *No-No Boy*," *CR: The New Centennial Review* 6, no. 2 (Fall 2006): 191–214.

10 These break down as the first Tuttle edition of 1,500 hardcover and 1,500 softcover, two CARP printings of 3,000 each, and eighteen printings by UW Press to date, with gross sales of more than 194,000 books and ebooks.

"AN URGENCY TO WRITE"

1 John Okada resume, Bancroft Library, University of California, Berkeley, BANC FILM 3101, at tail end of microfilm of Dorothy Okada transcript [hereafter cited as John Okada 1957 resume]. While undated, internal references place this annotated work history as written in April or May 1957.

2 Death certificate, Washington State Board of Health.

3 Birth certificate, Seattle–King County Dept. of Public Health. The middle name is alternately spelled as Koso. The midwife was Sumi Tajiri. The document records his birthdate as September 22, and that is the date he gave throughout his life on all his school, camp, military, and job records. His widow evidently believed his birthdate to be September 23, perhaps confusing it with his birth year of 1923, and that is the date recorded on his death certificate and on his grave.

4 Yoshito Okada, Alien Enemy Control Unit, Case file 146-13-2-82-637, Records of the Department of Justice, Record Group 60. Enemy Alien Litigation Case Files, Box 608, National Archives, College Park, MD [hereafter cited Okada Alien Enemy file]. With postwar changes in naming conventions, this address is now known as Hiroshima-ken, Hiroshima-shi, Asakita-ku, Kabeminami, according to journalist Ryusuke Kawai, who retranslated *No-No Boy* into Japanese in 2016.

5 Family tree by Beverly Okada, daughter of Roy and Mary Okada and John's niece.

6 Paul Spickard, *Japanese Americans: The Formation and Transformations of an Ethnic Group*, rev. ed. (New Brunswick, NJ: Rutgers University Press, 2009), 15.

7 Yoshito Okada, quoted in Kazuo Ito, *Issei: A History of Japanese Immigrants in North America*, translated by Shinichiro Nakamura and Jean S. Gerard (Seattle: Japanese Community Service, 1973), 321–22.

8 Okada Alien Enemy file.

9 Gary Iwamoto, "Rise and Fall of an Empire: Furuya," *International Examiner*, August 17–September 6, 2005, 16.

10 Photograph dated 1915, in possession of Beverly Okada.

11 Okada Alien Enemy file. Montana did not enact an alien land law until 1923. In the one hundred years since their purchase, the lots have remained vacant even as homes were built around them, and the land remains in the family today.

12 1920 US Census record.

13 The kanji for Kozo is 幸三, according to Kawai.

14 Okada Alien Enemy file.

15 Murray Morgan, *Skid Road: An Informal Portrait of Seattle* (Seattle: University of Washington Press, 1982), 8; Jim Yoshida and Bill Hosokawa, *The Two Worlds of Jim Yoshida* (New York: William Morrow, 1972), 15. Jim Yoshida grew up at the Grand Central Hotel at 212 First Avenue S. and was friends with Robert Okada.

16 "Haunting in the Media," MerchantsCafeandSaloon.com

17 The building still stands today at 109½ Yesler Way, with a historical marker billing the Merchants Cafe and Saloon as "Seattle's Oldest Restaurant."

18 Roy Okada, Interview with the author, September 23, 2006, Seattle, WA (video recording) [hereafter cited as Roy Okada interview, Sept. 23, 2006]. Minor edits have been made in some interview excerpts for clarity and sense.

19 Paul Dorpat, *Seattle Now & Then*, vol. 3, 2nd ed. (Seattle: Tartu Publications, 1994), 228.

20 Ito, *Issei,* 522–24.

21 Roy Okada, "My Story," undated notes c. 2005 for classroom presentations.

22 Monica Sone, *Nisei Daughter* (Seattle: University of Washington Press, 2014), 15–18.

23 Ito, *Issei,* 529. The site is now occupied by the Salvation Army's William Booth Center.

24 Roy Okada, "My Story."

25 Roy Okada interview, Sept. 23, 2006.

26 Robert and Roy Okada, Interview with Frank Chin, Lawson Inada, and Stephen Sumida, June 27, 1976 (audio recording), in Robert Okada papers, University of Washington Special Collections, Manuscript Collection No. 3064, Accession No. 3064-001 [hereafter cited as Robert and Roy Okada interview].

27 John Okada, *No-No Boy* (Seattle: University of Washington Press, 2014), xxiii.

28 Robert and Roy Okada interview.

29 "The Trojan Times," *Seattle Daily Times*, December 3, 1931.

30 John Okada 1957 resume.

31 Robert and Roy Okada interview.

32 Nile Thompson and Carolyn J. Marr, *Building for Learning: Seattle Public School Histories, 1862–2000* (Seattle: School Histories Committee, Seattle School District, 2002), 109. The Gatzert school building was demolished in 1987, but the stone entry arch was preserved as part of a new building for the Seattle Indian Health Board. A new Gatzert School was built nearby at 13th and Yesler.

33 From *Grade Club Magazine*, June 1930, 33–34, as cited in Doris Hinson Pieroth, *Seattle's Women Teachers of the Interwar Years: Shapers of a Livable City* (Seattle: University of Washington Press, 2004), 146. In *No-No Boy* (89), singing "The Star-Spangled Banner" in school would make Emi want to "shout with glory."

34   Dolores Sibonga, Personal communication with the author, September 23, 2017. As president of the "GACC," the future Seattle city councilmember and candidate for mayor got to crank up the record player near the school exit.

35   Roy Kumasaka, Interview with the author, October 23, 2013, San Jose, CA [hereafter cited as Kumasaka interview 2013].

36   Frank Ashida, Interview with the author, August 14, 2006, Issaquah, WA (video recording) [hereafter cited as Ashida interview].

37   Roy Kumasaka, Interview with the author, September 16, 2006, Seattle, WA [hereafter cited as Kumasaka interview 2006].

38   Kumasaka interview 2013.

39   Okada Alien Enemy file.

40   Sone, *Nisei Daughter*, 22–23.

41   Beverly Okada, "Yoshito and Takayo Ota Okada," Remembrance Project, www.remembrance-project.org/tributes/form-uploads/yoshito-takayo-ota-okada.html.

42   Roy Okada, Interview with the author, August 16, 2006, Kent, WA (video recording) [hereafter cited as Roy Okada interview, Aug. 16, 2006].

43   "Woman Tries to Leap over Bridge: John Okada Dreams of Being Sir Galahad," *Great Northern Daily Press*, November 2, 1936, 1.

44   "Record Crowd Sees Akiyama Win," *Seattle Sunday Times*, May 2, 1937, 5. The notion of a prize made of silver would recur in "The Silver Lunchbox."

45   "Thursday's Winners!", *Seattle Daily Times*, November 29, 1937, 23. As one of four runners-up, Okada's entry was unfortunately not printed.

46   Thompson and Marr, *Building for Learning*, 36–39. The school was demolished in 1974 and is now the site of Seattle Central College.

47   Larry Rumley, "Nisei Dilemma Is Basis of Novel," *Seattle Times Sunday Magazine*, March 6, 1977, 13.

48   Broadway High School yearbooks from the collection of Steven Doi.

49   Unsigned memo, December 21, 1942, War Relocation Authority Evacuee Case File, National Archives, Washington, DC [hereafter cited as John Okada WRA file].

50   Roy Okada interview, Aug. 16, 2006; Okada, *No-No Boy*, 9. The giant red-neon Wonder Bread sign atop the factory was a local landmark until the building was demolished in 2007. Preservationists saved the sign, and it now sits atop the Legacy at Pratt Park apartment complex on the same site.

51   Ibid.; Robert and Roy Okada interview.

52   "Here's Hoop Player's Lists," *Japanese-American Courier*, December 2, 1939, 3.

53   The Nipponkan is now occupied by a messenger service.

54   Ashida interview.

55 WRA Form 26, John Okada WRA file; Toby Sullivan, Kodiak Maritime Museum, Email to the author, November 1, 2017, Kodiak, AK.

56 Yoshida and Hosokawa, *Two Worlds*, 28.

57 Bebe Horiuchi, "Detroit: Unassuming Writer Hailing from Seattle Holder of Two M.A.s.," *Pacific Citizen*, October 11, 1957, 5.

58 Matthew Okada, Interview with the author, August 12, 2006, Pasadena, CA (video recording) [hereafter cited as Matthew Okada interview].

59 Francis Mas Fukuhara, *Uncommon American Patriots* (Seattle: Nisei Veterans Committee, 1991).

60 Roy Okada interview, Aug. 16, 2006.

61 "Japanese American Trainees, Company A, 33rd Battalion," http://bit.ly/2k23w01. The entry for Haita states "brother in Japanese army." Thanks to James McIlwain for locating this document.

62 Okada Alien Enemy file.

63 "Seattle's 1941 High School Graduates," *Seattle Times*, June 8, 1941, 16.

64 This is the journey taken by Ichiro on pp. 48–49 of the novel. Thanks to Rob Ketcherside for the history of Seattle Transit bus routes.

65 University of Washington transcripts courtesy of registrar Virjean Edwards and archivist Diana Shenk; Robert and Roy Okada interview.

66 Phillip Akutsu, Email to the author, June 9, 2006. Phillip is Jim's son. His father also gave his name at various times as Jim Hajime Akutsu.

67 Jim Akutsu, Interview with the author and Frank Chin, January 31–February 1, 1997, Seattle, WA [hereafter cited as Jim Akutsu interview 1997].

68 Ibid.

69 "Seattle Assumes Wartime Pace; 51 Japs Held," *Seattle Star*, December 8, 1941, 6.

70 "We Are Loyal to U.S.," *Seattle Star*, December 8, 1941, 4.

71 "Signs Wrecked by Irate Mob of 300," *Seattle Star*, December 9, 1941, 1.

72 "Student Tells Dilemma of U.S.–Loyal Japanese," *Seattle Star*, December 16, 1941, 16.

73 "Murder Mystery in Chinatown: Fear Tutor Victim of 'Execution,'" *Seattle Star*, December 12, 1941, 1.

74 "No Clues in 'Headsman' Killing Here," *Seattle Star*, December 13, 1941, 4.

75 Bill Hosokawa, *Out of the Frying Pan: Reflections of a Japanese American* (Niwot, CO: University Press of Colorado, 1998), 27.

76 "1,300 Seattle Japanese Pledge Loyalty," *Seattle Daily Times*, December 23, 1941, 8; "Community Renews Loyal Pledge at Rousing Americanism Rally," *Japanese-American Courier*, December 26, 1941.

77 Eric Muller, *Free to Die for Their Country: The Story of the Japanese American Draft Resisters in World War II* (Chicago: University of Chicago Press, 2001), 41.

78   Kumasaka interview 2006.

79   Okada Alien Enemy file. Both Robert and Roy recalled the arrest occurring the day after Pearl Harbor, but the FBI report establishes the date and time.

80   Roy Okada, "My Story."

81   Okada Alien Enemy file.

82   Jim Akutsu interview 1997. Akutsu recalled the arrest occurring on December 7, but the FBI report establishes the date and time.

83   "103 Japs Seized in Seattle; All State Now Defense Zone," *Seattle Times*, February 22, 1942, 1.

84   "FBI Nabs 500 Coast Aliens," *Seattle Post-Intelligencer*, February 22, 1942.

85   Roy Okada, "My Story."

86   "Campus Japanese Face Evacuation," *University of Washington Daily*, March 4, 1942, 1; WRA Form 26, John Okada WRA file.

87   WRA Form 26, John Okada WRA file.

88   "Tears, Staccato Chatter Flow as Jap Menfolk Leave Seattle," *Seattle Times*, March 19, 1942, 12.

89   Louis Fiset, *Imprisoned Apart: The World War II Correspondence of an Issei Couple* (Seattle: University of Washington Press, 1997), 36.

90   Testimony of Masao Takahashi to the US Commission on Wartime Relocation and Internment of Civilians, quoted in Doug Chin, *Seattle's International District: The Making of a Pan-Asian American Community*, 2nd ed. (Seattle: International Examiner Press, 2009), 75.

91   This address now lies under the Interstate 90 overpass.

92   Thompson and Marr, *Building for Learning*, 109.

93   Jim Akutsu interview 1997.

94   Rumley, "Nisei Dilemma."

95   Hosokawa, *Out of the Frying Pan*, 34; Sone, *Nisei Daughter*, 171.

96   Jim Akutsu interview 1997.

97   Ibid.

98   Sone, *Nisei Daughter*, 172–73. Area A is now once again a parking lot, across from the main Blue Gate at the fairgrounds.

99   Jim Akutsu interview 1997.

100 June Mukai McKivor, ed., *Kenjiro Nomura: An Artist's View of the Japanese American Internment* (Seattle: Wing Luke Asian Museum, 1991), 20.

101 Roy Okada, Interview with the author, September 17, 2016, Renton, WA [hereafter cited as Roy Okada interview, Sept. 17, 2016].

102 McKivor, ed., *Kenjiro Nomura*, 22.

103 Louis Fiset, *Camp Harmony: Seattle's Japanese Americans and the Puyallup Assembly Center* (Urbana: University of Illinois Press, 2009), 102.

104 Ashida interview.

105 Shosuke Sasaki, Interview with the author and Stephen Fugita, May 18, 1997, Seattle, WA (video recording for Densho, Densho ID: ddr-densho-1000-78-1).

106 Jim Akutsu, as told to Stephen Sumida. See Sumida's chapter in this volume for a fuller version of this story.

107 Frank Okada, Interview with Barbara Johns, Archives of American Art, Smithsonian Institution, August 16–17, 1990 [hereafter cited as Frank Okada interview].

108 Fiset, *Imprisoned Apart*, 40–41.

109 Tetsuden Kashima, *Judgment without Trial: Japanese American Imprisonment during World War II* (Seattle: University of Washington Press, 2003), 31. The same subscription to *Sokoku* magazine wrongly incriminated the Akutsu's father and kept him interned at Fort Missoula for nearly two years.

110 John Okada, Letter to William Collins, c. June 1942, Okada Alien Enemy file. This letter presages the preface to *No-No Boy,* where an unnamed draft resister pleads with a judge to release his father from "that other camp" to rejoin his mother.

111 The documents cited in this section are found in Okada Alien Enemy file.

112 University of Washington Libraries, "Interrupted Lives: Japanese American Students at the University of Washington, 1941–1942," www.lib.washington .edu/specialcollections/collections/exhibits/harmony/interrupted/index.

113 Ashida interview.

114 Allen W. Austin, *From Concentration Camp to Campus: Japanese American Students and World War II* (Urbana: University of Illinois Press, 2007), 16.

115 Wayne W. Johnson letter to Joseph Conrad, August 17, 1942, John Okada WRA file.

116 Unsigned memo, December 21, 1942, John Okada WRA file.

117 Jim Akutsu interview 1997.

118 Jim Akutsu, Testimony to the Commission on Wartime Relocation and Internment of Civilians, September 9, 1981, Seattle, Jack and Aiko Herzig Papers (Collection 451), Box 63, Folder 1, UCLA Library Special Collections, Charles E. Young Research Library.

119 Jeffery F. Burton, Mary M. Farrell, Florence B. Lord, and Richard W. Lord, *Confinement and Ethnicity: An Overview of World War II Japanese American Relocation Sites* (Tucson: Western Archeological and Conservation Center, 1999), 205.

120 Frank Yamasaki, Interview with Lori Hoshino and Stephen Fugita, August 18, 1997, Seattle, WA (video recording for Densho; Densho ID: ddr-densho-1000-107) [hereafter cited as Yamasaki interview 1997].

121 "Ten Students Relocated," *Minidoka Irrigator* 1, no. 4 (September 25, 1942), 1, in Densho Digital Archive, Densho ID: denshopd-i119-00004.

122 Ashida interview.

123 Vickie Sakurada Schaepler, Telephone interview with the author, January 13,
     2017, Kearney, NB. Vickie is the niece of Shogi Sakurada.

124 Hisanori Kano, *Nikkei Farmer on the Nebraska Plains: A Memoir,* edited by Tai
     Kreidler, translated by Rose Yamamoto (Lubbock: Texas Tech University Press,
     2010), 149.

125 Ashida interview.

126 William M. Tuttle, *"Daddy's Gone to War": The Second World War in the Lives of
     America's Children* (New York: Oxford University Press, 1993), 167.

127 "Firemen Called to Blaze in North Part of Town," *Mitchell Index,* July 29, 1944, 1.

128 Ashida interview.

129 Scottsbluff College transcript, courtesy of registrar Roger Hovey. The school is
     now known as Western Nebraska Community College.

130 Roy Okada interview, Sept. 17, 2016.

131 Scottsbluff College transcript.

132 "Army to Take Nisei Soldiers: Must Speak and Read Japanese," *Tulean Dispatch,*
     August 10, 1942, 2.

133 Ashida interview.

134 "Minnesota's Remarkable Secret School for Language," JACL Twin Cities
     Chapter Curriculum and Resource Guide, www.tcjacl.org/wp/wp-content
     /uploads/2014/04/MISGuide2013.pdf.

135 Joseph D. Harrington, *Yankee Samurai: The Secret Role of Nisei in America's
     Pacific Victory* (Detroit: Pettigrew Enterprises, 1979), 258.

136 Ashida interview.

137 Kumasaka interview 2013.

138 Kumasaka interview 2006. In the novel, the name Eto is given to the Nisei
     soldier who spits on Ichiro.

139 Masaharu Ano, "Loyal Linguists: Nisei of World War II Learned Japanese in
     Minnesota," *Minnesota History* 45, no. 7 (1977): 273–87; James McNaughton,
     *Nisei Linguists: Japanese Americans in the Military Intelligence Service during
     World War II* (Washington, DC: US Army Center of Military History, 2006),
     108–12; Joe Milanoski, "Camp Savage Memories," in *John Aiso and the MIS:
     Japanese-American Soldiers in the Military Intelligence Service, World War II,*
     edited by Tad Ichinokuchi and Daniel Aiso (Los Angeles: MIS Club of Southern
     California, 1988), 54.

140 McNaughton, *Nisei Linguists,* 106.

141 "Charlie" Yoshitaka Robert Okada, "What Price Glory!" in *And Then There Were
     Eight: The Men of I Company, 442nd Regimental Combat Team,* edited by Edward
     Yamasaki (Honolulu: Item Chapter, 442nd Veterans Club, 2003), 253.

142 Arlene Yamada, Email to the author, November 9, 2017; Roy Okada interview, Sept. 17, 2016.

143 "The Ten Thousand," *Minidoka Irrigator* 3, no. 49 (January 29, 1944).

144 Roy Okada interview, Sept. 17, 2016.

145 Lila Middleton, Telephone interview with author, November 9, 2017, Ione, WA. Thanks also to Faith McClenny and the Pend Oreille County Historical Society.

146 US Army Separation Qualification Record, March 15, 1946, in possession of Dorothea Okada.

147 "Army Announces U.S. Soldiers of Japanese Ancestry Assigned to Central California Camp," *Pacific Citizen*, August 26, 1944, 3.

148 "Pinedale (detention facility)," *Densho Encyclopedia,* http://encyclopedia.densho .org/Pinedale_(detention_facility)/

149 James D. Braden, "Japanese Code Intercept Unit WWII: 8th AAF RSM," http:// freepages.military.rootsweb.ancestry.com/~braden.

150 Edward Bradfield, *The Story behind the Flying Eight-Ball* (Unpublished squadron history, mimeographed and saddle-stitched on Guam, October, 1945), 22. Okada brought his copy with him back to the States; it is now in the possession of Dorothea Okada.

151 Braden, "Japanese Code Intercept Unit."

152 Bradfield, *Story behind the Flying Eight-Ball,* 25–28.

153 McNaughton, *Nisei Linguists,* 130.

154 Larry Tart, *Freedom through Vigilance, Vol. IV: History of U.S. Air Force Security Service (USAFSS) Airborne Reconnaissance, Part 1* (West Conshohocken, PA: Infinity Publishing, 2010), 1734–35.

155 Ibid., 1738.

156 Ibid., 1735.

157 McNaughton, *Nisei Linguists,* 371.

158 Tart, *Freedom through Vigilance,* 1739.

159 Bradfield, *Story behind the Flying Eight-Ball,* 39, and "Military Intelligence Service (MIS) Registry Merged (alphabetical)," compiled by Seiki Oshiro, Paul Tani, Mitzie Matsui, and Grant Ichikawa, https://java.wildapricot.org /resources/Documents/WWII MIS Registry (Merged) July 2007.pdf.

160 Okada, *No-No Boy,* xxvi.

161 Tart, *Freedom through Vigilance,* 1741–42.

162 James McNaughton, Email to the author, December 4, 2017.

163 Tart, *Freedom through Vigilance,* 1737, 1740.

164 Bradfield, *Story behind the Flying Eight-Ball,* 39.

165 Roy Okada interview, Aug. 16, 2006.

166 Richard Hugo, *The Real West Marginal Way: A Poet's Autobiography*, edited by Ripley S. Hugo, Lois M. Welch, and James Welch (New York: W. W. Norton, 1986), 95.

167 Undated 1945 photograph, in possession of Roy Okada.

168 McNaughton, *Nisei Linguists*, 372.

169 Ashida interview.

170 Mitzie Matsui, "The Military Intelligence Service Story," in *Unsung Heroes: The Military Intelligence Service, Past—Present—Future* (Seattle: MIS Northwest Association, 1996), xii.

171 Connie Okada, Email to the author, March 6, 2007.

172 Frank Chin, "Whites Can't Relate to John Okada's Book *No-No Boy*," *Pacific Citizen*, Holiday Issue, December 23–30, 1977, 55–56.

173 Thanks to James McIlwain for providing this history.

174 Dr. Robert Okada, Telephone interview with the author, October 30, 2017, Tulsa, OK. Robert is the son of Yoshitaka Robert and Jane Okada, and John's nephew.

175 Jimmy Yamashita, "Po Valley Campaign (Gothic Line)," unpublished company history.

176 Jimmy Yamashita, Telephone interview with author, March 31, 2016, Glendora, CA. In the novel, the fictional Bobbie Kumasaka is hit out of nowhere by a single bullet, just before the German surrender.

177 Beverly Okada, Email to the author, August 22, 2017.

178 Braden, "Japanese Code Intercept Unit."

179 Bradfield, *Story behind the Flying Eight-Ball*, 42.

180 Ibid., 98.

181 "History of the MIS," Military Intelligence Service Association of Northern California, www.njahs.org/misnorcal/essay.htm.

182 US Army Separation Qualification Record, March 15, 1946, in possession of Dorothea Okada; "Reminiscences of Grandison Gardner: Oral History, 1959," Henry H. Arnold project, Columbia University Libraries, Columbia Center for Oral History.

183 McNaughton, *Nisei Linguists*, 451.

184 Orientation talk for interviewers, November 8, 1945, pt. 1, Tokyo, Japan (audio recording), United States Strategic Bombing Survey. Records of the United States Strategic Bombing Survey, Record Group 243. National Archives, College Park, MD. Training at the Meiji Building by a Lt. Nelson for interviewers of air raid survivors.

185 McNaughton, *Nisei Linguists*, 451.

186 Thomas Girst, *Art, Literature, and the Japanese American Internment: On John Okada's "No-No Boy"* (Frankfurt, Ger.: Peter Lang, 2015), 122.

187 United States Strategic Bombing Survey, Summary Report (Pacific War), July 1, 1946, 26. Records of the United States Strategic Bombing Survey, Record Group 243, National Archives, College Park, MD.

188 James McIlwain, Email to the author, March 27, 2017, quoting Seiki Oshiro, keeper of "The MIS Registry"; James McNaughton, Email to the author, November 22, 2017.

189 Elisa Law, curator of the Hunt Hotel exhibit, public comments, April 21, 2017.

190 Barbara Johns, *Signs of Home: The Paintings and Wartime Diary of Kamekichi Tokita* (Seattle: University of Washington Press, 2011), 54. Tokita provided the model for Gary, the sign painter Ichiro visits at the "Christian Rehabilitation Center" at the start of chapter 10.

191 Kiyonosuke Akutsu, Alien Enemy Control Unit, Case file 146-13-2-82-481, Records of the Department of Justice, Record Group 60. Enemy Alien Litigation Case Files, Box 608, National Archives, College Park, MD [hereafter cited as Akutsu Alien Enemy file].

192 Okada Alien Enemy file.

193 Roy Okada interview, Sept. 17, 2016. The hotel site at 604½ Sixth Avenue S. was demolished and rebuilt in 1983 as Ocean City Restaurant. It's now Little Sheep Mongolian Hot Pot, a chain restaurant from China.

194 Dennis Tsuboi, Telephone interview with the author, March 28, 2017, Renton, WA. Tsuboi is the eldest of Keichi and Sueko Takemura's grandchildren.

195 Girst, *Art, Literature*, 119.

196 Roy Okada interview, Sept. 17, 2016.

197 Quintard Taylor, *The Forging of a Black Community: Seattle's Central District from 1870 through the Civil Rights Era* (Seattle: University of Washington Press, 1994), 174. Taylor adds, "Wartime internee John Okada captured much of this feeling among the new African Americans who inhabited his former neighborhood, Jackson Street . . . aptly terming it, 'persecution in the drawl of the persecuted.'"

198 Paul de Barros, *Jackson Street After Hours: The Roots of Jazz in Seattle* (Seattle: Sasquatch Books, 1993), 76.

199 Frank Okada interview.

200 Hugo, *Real West Marginal Way,* 54.

201 Chet Skreen, "Reviewers Stand," *University of Washington Daily*, May 3, 1946, 2.

202 "Carroll's Revue Stinkeroo Compared to All-U Show," *University of Washington Daily*, May 3, 1946, 1.

203 George Milton Savage family papers, University of Washington Special Collections, Manuscript Collection No. 5400, Accession No. 5400-001 [hereafter cited as George Milton Savage papers].

204 This street is now known as NE 42nd Street, after the city added to the directional mapping of streets in 1961. Thanks to Jean Sherrard. An unmarked structure

now occupies the site, between an alleyway and the Cafe on the Ave on University Way.

205 "Four Authors Watch Plays First Night," *University of Washington Daily*, June 11, 1946, 1.

206 Jo Anne Oass, "Campus Memo: Playwright Lab," *Seattle Times*, June 9, 1946, 18. The other three one-acts were "Flame and Ashes" by Blanche Sisley, "Hello, Twelve Bucks" by Carroll Ellerbe, and "Half-Way Home" by Joe Copson.

207 Roy Okada interview, Sept. 17, 2016.

208 "Four Authors Watch Plays First Night." Sadao Jim Ikoma was a fellow UW student and the son of Sadahiko Ikoma, publisher of the *Hokubei Hochi*, or *North American Post*.

209 Oass, "Campus Memo," 18.

210 Roy Okada interview, Aug, 16, 2006.

211 George Milton Savage papers.

212 John Okada 1957 resume. Okada put this experience directly into his story "Skipping Millions."

213 "905 Students on U. Honor Roll," *Seattle Times*, January 26, 1947, 7.

214 Girst, *Art, Literature,* 134. This story has not been found.

215 Robert and Roy Okada interview. This story has also not been found. Interviewer Frank Chin noted the similarity of Roy's description with the later 1968 John Boorman film, *Hell in the Pacific*, starring Toshiro Mifune and Lee Marvin.

216 Frank Yamasaki, Interview with Alice Ito, November 5, 2001, Seattle, WA (video recording for Densho; Densho ID: ddr-densho-1000-131).

217 Ibid.

218 Jim Akutsu interview 1997.

219 Jim Akutsu, Interview with the author and Frank Chin, August 28, 1993, Seattle, WA (video recording for *Conscience and the Constitution*; Densho ID: ddr-densho-122-12).

220 Gene Akutsu interview.

221 Yamasaki interview 1997.

222 Jim Akutsu, Interview with Art Hansen, June 12, 1997, Seattle, WA (video recording for Densho; Densho ID: ddr-densho-1000-2-1) [hereafter cited as Jim Akutsu Densho interview].

223 The name of the club was forever tarnished by the 1983 execution-style murder of thirteen people in a gambling robbery. The Wah Mee Massacre remains the largest mass murder in Washington State history. The building was razed in 2015, two years after fire damaged the top two floors.

224 Roger Shimomura, quoted in "The Wah Mee," in *Ghosts of Seattle Past: An Anthology of Lost Seattle Places,* ed. Jaimee Garbacik (Seattle: Chin Music Press, 2017), 43.

225 Danny Woo, quoted in Frank Chin, "The Wah Mee," *Seattle Weekly*, May 4, 1983, 31.

226 Chin, "The Wah Mee."

227 Akutsu had written to journalist James Omura in Denver, who had urged the draft resisters at Heart Mountain to organize, and to Fair Play Committee leader Frank Emi, but he may not have shared these stories with Okada. *No-No Boy* is devoid of any reference to the kind of principled resistance, founded on the Constitution, that would have provided a context for Ichiro's actions.

228 Kumasaka interview 2006. A notable draft resister hired at Olympic Foundry was Min Tamesa, one of the seven leaders of the Fair Play Committee.

229 Jim Akutsu interview 1997. In the novel this story informs the character of Birdie, the ironworker who defended the sign painter and draft resister Gary from the Nisei veterans and whose car was sabotaged because of it.

230 Chittenden was the son of engineer Hiram M. Chittenden, namesake for the Ballard Locks in Seattle. In the novel, Ichiro studied civil engineering and climbs the stairs to see Professor Baxter Brown in much the same way.

231 Jim Akutsu Densho interview.

232 Kozy K. Amemiya, "Being 'Japanese' in Brazil and Okinawa," Japan Policy Research Institute, Occasional Paper No. 13, May 1988, www.jpri.org/publications /occasionalpapers/op13.html. Thanks to Barbara Takei for this background.

233 Sally Okada Mizuki, Telephone interview with the author, November 13, 2017, Kent, WA. Tetsuo was Yoshito's younger brother who after camp settled in Auburn, south of Seattle, and helped out one day a week at the Pacific Hotel. Sally is one of Tetsuo's daughters, and a cousin of John Okada.

234 Jim Akutsu Densho interview.

235 Gene Akutsu interview.

236 "Woman Kills Self in Hospital," *Northwest Times*, September 30, 1947, 1.

237 Gene Akutsu interview.

238 "Deaths, Funerals," *Seattle Times*, September 28, 1947, 34.

239 Jim Akutsu, as told to Stephen Sumida.

240 Fukuhara, *Uncommon American Patriots*. Haita's memorial photograph hangs in a gallery of fallen servicemen at the entry to Seattle's Nisei Veterans Hall on South King Street, and his name is etched into a brick in the NVC Foundation's Japanese American Memorial Wall, close to bricks naming the four Okada brothers, who all served.

241 "Nisei Killed in Italy to Be Buried in Japan," *Seattle Times*, January 17, 1948, 1.

242 "Purple Heart Awarded Posthumously," US Army Signal Corps photo, March 22, 1948, Army Heritage and Education Center, Henry Utley Milne Collection, Carlisle, PA. Mr. Haita's first name appeared in the photo caption as Bunsaku and in the *Seattle Times* as Dunusaku.

243 "Nisei Killed in Italy to Be Buried in Japan."

244 "Auction of Confiscated Bar Equipment Brings State $391," *Seattle Daily Times*, January 14, 1948, 4; John Okada 1957 resume.

245 See Girst, *Art, Literature,* 123–27, for a detailed discussion of the courses Okada took, based on a study of his transcripts.

246 Will Alpern, handwritten note in margin of a letter to Beverly Okada, undated, in envelope postmarked January 26, 1995.

247 Dorothy Okada, Interview with Frank Chin and Lawson Inada, November 16, 1971, Pasadena, CA, 60. Typed transcript in personal collection of the author; the transcript is archived at the University of California, Berkeley, Bancroft Library, BANC FILM 3101. [Hereafter cited as Dorothy Okada interview 1971.]

248 Arlene Yamada, Telephone interview with the author, September 24, 2016, Seattle.

249 Dorothy Okada interview 1971, 6.

250 Ibid., 10.

251 Girst, *Art, Literature,* 123.

252 Dorothy Okada interview 1971, 60.

253 Ibid., 9.

254 Dorothy Okada, Interview with the author, August 12, 2006, Pasadena, CA [hereafter cited as Dorothy Okada interview 2006].

255 Dorothy Okada, Interview with Frank Chin and Shawn Wong, January 5, 1972, Pasadena, CA, 86. Typed transcript in personal collection of the author; the transcript is archived at the University of California, Berkeley, Bancroft Library, BANC FILM 3101. [Hereafter cited as Dorothy Okada interview 1972.]

256 US Army Separation Qualification Record, in possession of Dorothea Okada.

257 Okada, *No-No Boy,* 171. Rev. Ichikawa's grandson, Prof. Scott Kurashige, says the priest "also had a relatively high-pitched voice just as Okada describes . . . it's definitely him." Kurashige, Email to the author, May 18, 2017.

258 Ito, *Issei,* 529.

259 Horiuchi, "Detroit: Unassuming Writer," 5.

260 Marriage certificate, King County Auditor, June 17, 1950.

261 "Social Whirl: June Wedding," *Northwest Times,* June 28, 1950, 4.

262 Dorothy Okada interview 1971, 7. Keichi Takemura had passed away a few years earlier.

263 Dorothy Okada interview 1972, 70.

264 John Okada 1957 resume.

265 Ibid.

266 Departmental Reports 1951, bound typescript archived in the Seattle Room, Seattle Public Library. Thanks to Debra Cox, Special Collections.

267 Rob Ketcherside, *Lost Seattle* (London: Pavilion Books, 2013), 72.

268 John Okada 1957 resume.

269 Departmental Reports 1952, bound typescript archived in the Seattle Room, Seattle Public Library.

270 "Tours of Library Scheduled," *Seattle Times*, June 5, 1952, 40.

271 *Flash* (newsletter of the Seattle Public Library Staff Association) 12, no. 1 (February 1953): 5.

272 Frank Chin, "In Search of John Okada" (Afterword to *No-No Boy*), 229.

273 Departmental Reports 1953, bound typescript archived in the Seattle Room, Seattle Public Library.

274 Hiromi Nishimura, Interview with the author, November 19, 2016, Seattle, WA [hereafter cited as Nishimura interview]. The Prince of Wales Apartments still stands at the corner of 20th Avenue and Denny Way.

275 John Okada 1957 resume.

276 Dorothy Okada interview 1971, 35.

277 *Detroit Library Commission Proceedings,* Regular Meeting, June 16, 1953, 1232.

278 Mary Klanian, Telephone interview with the author, May 4, 2014, Somers, NY [hereafter cited as Klanian interview].

279 John Okada 1957 resume.

280 Klanian interview.

281 Greg Robinson, *After Camp: Portraits in Midcentury Japanese American Life and Politics* (Berkeley: University of California Press, 2012), 48.

282 Mary Kamidoi, Scott Kurashige, and Toshi Shimoura, eds., *Exiled to Motown: A Community History of Japanese Americans in Detroit* (Detroit: Detroit JACL History Project Committee, 2015). Highland Park was the area where, in 1982, Vincent Chin would be mistaken for Japanese and clubbed to death by two autoworkers.

283 *Flash* 12, no. 5 (October 1953): 4.

284 Chin, Afterword to *No-No Boy*, 230.

285 Dorothea Okada, Telephone interview with the author, October 16, 2016, Pasadena, CA. This incident is fictionalized in *No-No Boy*, pp. 229–30.

286 Betsy Stickels Perry, Telephone interview with the author, April 10, 2016, Adrian, MI [hereafter cited as Perry interview].

287 Frank Okada interview.

288 Rose Morita and Susan Morita-Sakamoto, Personal communication with the author, July 27, 2017, Campbell, CA. The late Seattle redress activist Henry Miyatake first suggested Morita was the source for the character name, and Mrs. Morita confirmed that her husband was known by the nickname, which he never liked. Martha Nakagawa notes that Hajime in Japanese means "beginning" or "first," the same as Ichiro.

289 Okada, *No-No Boy*, 8.

290 Ibid., 123.

291 Ibid., 8.

292 Thanks to Gary Iwamoto for identifying this building, now occupied by House of Hong Restaurant.

293 Dorothy Okada interview 1971, 39; Dorothy Okada interview 1972, 89.

294 Dorothy Okada interview 2006.

295 Dorothy Okada interview 1972, 81.

296 Ibid., 55.

297 John Okada, Letter to Meredith Weatherby, February 14, 1956, Frank Chin papers, Wyles Mss 103, Department of Special Research Collections, UC Santa Barbara Library, University of California, Santa Barbara [hereafter cited as Frank Chin papers]. Thanks to UCSB librarian Gerardo A. Colmenar. Charles Borst was a Tuttle employee. For the name Take, Okada may have intended to write Tak, a common nickname that is short for Takashi and other variants. Okada clearly identifies Ichiro as a draft resister, then confuses his terms when he calls the draft resister Freddie, "another No-No Boy." Of Okada's use of the word *treason*, Stephen Sumida notes, "It was still in an era of McCarthyism. Even in that letter Okada had to be careful not to criticize the US government overtly, so he does it obliquely in terms of a 'great county that's willing to correct its mistakes.'"

298 "About Us," Tuttle Publishing, www.tuttlepublishing.com/about-us.

299 James A. Michener, *The Modern Japanese Print: An Appreciation* (Tokyo: Charles E. Tuttle, 1968).

300 Nicholas Ingleton, "Obituary: Charles E. Tuttle," *Independent,* July 6, 1993, www.independent.co.uk/news/people/obituary-charles-e-tuttle-1483336.html.

301 Michener, *Modern Japanese Print.* Weatherby was known for his work with homoerotic literature and photography, and later founded Weatherhill, another publisher of books on Japanese art and culture.

302 John Okada, Letter to Charles Tuttle, May 1, 1956, Frank Chin papers.

303 Dorothy Okada interview 1972, 60.

304 *News Bulletin* 21, no. 2 (December 1955).

305 John Okada 1957 resume.

306 John Okada resume, Biographical files, UCLA Library Special Collections, University Archives Reference Collection, University Archives Record Series 745 [hereafter cited as John Okada 1966 resume]. Thanks to Marjorie Lee, Julianna Jenkins, and Molly Haigh.

307 Contract, in possession of Dorothea Okada. The contract is the first known reference to the book's title. The exchange rate in 1956 was ¥360 to the dollar. The $150 advance would be worth roughly $1,350 in 2018 dollars, based on the average annual inflation rate of 3.67 percent of the US Consumer Price Index.

308 Shawn Wong secured the book's Class A US copyright in Dorothy's name in 1977. Shawn Wong letter to Dorothy Okada, April 21, 1977, in possession of Shawn Wong.

309 The photo appears with the book review "Seattle-Born Author Writes about Conflicting Loyalties," *Seattle Daily Times*, August 11, 1957.

310 *Flash* 15, no. 3 (March 1957): 7.

311 Chin, Afterword to *No-No Boy*, 230.

312 John Okada 1957 resume.

313 Charles Tuttle letter to Frank Chin, August 16, 1971, Frank Chin papers; and Brandy LaMotte, Tuttle Publishing product manager, Telephone interview with author, October 27, 2017, North Clarendon, VT [hereafter cited as LaMotte interview]. The hardcover sold for $3.00 in the United States and $2.50 in the Far East. Tuttle considered reissuing the paperback in 1971 for sale worldwide, but returned the rights to Dorothy in 1973 (Charles Tuttle, Letter to Reuben Becker, November 13, 1973, Frank Chin papers).

314 "Seattle-Born Author Writes about Conflicting Loyalties;" LaMotte interview.

315 John Okada, Letter to Meredith Weatherby, May 7, 1957, Frank Chin papers.

316 Charles Tuttle, Letter to Frank Chin, December 6, 1972, Frank Chin papers.

317 *Japan Times*, May 24, 1957. A mention in Tuttle's letter of December 6, 1972, leads Greg Robinson to believe that this unsigned review was written by Ken Yasuda, an inmate of Tule Lake who lived in Japan after the war and whose book of translations of Japanese haiku was published by Tuttle in the same year as *No-No Boy*.

318 John Fujii, *Yomiuri Japan News*, May 12, 1957.

319 *Publishers Weekly*, June 17, 1957, 69.

320 Earl Miner, "Modern Tragedy," *Saturday Review*, September 7, 1957, 33.

321 Bill Hosokawa, "From the Frying Pan," *Pacific Citizen*, September 27, 1957, 2.

322 Perry interview.

323 Dorothy Okada interview 2006.

324 Girst, *Art, Literature*, 133.

325 Frank Okada interview.

326 Kumasaka interview 2006.

327 Angie Lead, "A Granddaughter Honors a Soldier Who Sacrificed Much," *Seattle Times*, May 27, 2012.

328 Keith Yamaguchi, Telephone interview with the author, September 26, 2017, Seattle, WA.

329 Jim Akutsu interview 1997.

330 Jim Akutsu Densho interview.

331 Frank Yamasaki, Email to the author, August 4, 2006.

332 Dorothy Okada interview 1972, 68–69.

333 Horiuchi, "Detroit: Unassuming Writer," 5. The reference to two master's degrees may be misleading. Although he earned his degree in Librarianship from a graduate school at the UW, he identifies it on his resume as a bachelor's degree.

334 Bebe Horiuchi Reschke, Interview with the author, July 3, 2016, Klamath Falls, OR.

335 "No-No Boy," *Supervisors Digest* (staff newsletter of Chrysler Missile Operations) 2, no. 3 (September 1957): 1, archived at the University of California, Berkeley, Bancroft Library, BANC FILM 3101.

336 *Flash* 29, no. 8 (April 1971): 8.

337 Charles Tuttle, Letter to Frank Chin, December 6, 1971, Frank Chin papers.

338 Charles Tuttle, Letter to Frank Chin, August 16, 1971, Frank Chin papers.

339 Dorothy Okada interview 1971, 21.

340 Matthew Okada interview.

341 D. Kenneth Richardson, *Hughes after Howard: The Story of Hughes Aircraft Company* (Santa Barbara: Sea Hill Press, 2012), 165.

342 John Okada 1966 resume.

343 Dorothy Okada interview 1971, 25.

344 John Okada 1966 resume.

345 John McDonough and Karen Egolf, *The Advertising Age Encyclopedia of Advertising* (New York: Fitzroy Dearborn, 2003), 366.

346 Kenneth W. Cowans, "Working at Hughes Aircraft Company," unpublished oral history, Local History Room, Fullerton (California) Public Library. Thanks to Larry Iboshi and JoAnn Cowans.

347 Matthew Okada interview.

348 George Tsuda, "My Work-Related Memories at Hughes Aircraft Co.," unpublished oral history, Local History Room, Fullerton (California) Public Library.

349 John Okada, "The High Cost of Proposals and Presentations," *Armed Forces Management*, December 1961, 16.

350 Matthew Okada interview.

351 Matthew Okada, Email to the author, August 11, 2017.

352 Okada identified this article as his own in his 1966 resume.

353 Girst, *Art, Literature*, 134–35. The kanji ideogram for Okada, according to *No-No Boy* translator Ryusuke Kawai, breaks down as 岡 (*oka* = hill) and 田 (*da* = rice paddy), so that Okada more precisely translates as "hill–rice paddy."

354 John Okada 1966 resume; McDonough and Egolf, *Advertising Age Encyclopedia*, 487.

355 Dorothy Okada interview 1972, 77.

356 Ibid., 72.

357 Dorothea Okada, Email to the author, August 22, 2016.

358 Dorothea Okada, Interview with the author, August 12, 2006, Pasadena, CA (video recording) [henceforth cited as Dorothea Okada interview].

359 Ibid.

360 Matthew Okada interview.

361 Ibid.

362 Dorothy Okada interview 1972, 79–80.

363 Girst, *Art, Literature,* 130.

364 Dorothy Okada interview 1972, 90.

365 Matthew Okada, Telephone interview with the author, June 18, 2017, Pasadena, CA.

366 Matthew Okada, Telephone interview with the author, June 5, 2016, Pasadena, CA.

367 Ibid.

368 Dorothea Okada interview.

369 Ibid.

370 Matthew Okada interview.

371 Dorothy Okada interview 1971, 36–37.

372 Frank Okada interview.

373 Nishimura interview.

374 Dorothy Okada interview 1972, 71.

375 Matthew Okada interview. Matthew has no memory of what the outline revealed.

376 Frank Okada interview.

377 Dorothy Okada interview 1972, 63.

378 Girst, *Art, Literature,* 134.

379 Dorothy Okada interview 2006.

380 John Okada 1966 resume.

381 Matthew Okada, Email to the author, August 11, 2017.

382 Dorothy Okada interview 1971, 25, 95, 99.

383 Dorothea Okada interview.

384 James Cox, Letter to Circulation Department staff, October 13, 1967, John Okada biographical files, UCLA Library Special Collections, University Archives Reference Collection, University Archives Record Series 745 [hereafter cited as John Okada UCLA biographical file].

385 Jinqi Ling, "*No-No Boy* by John Okada," in *A Resource Guide to Asian American Literature*, edited by Sau-ling Cynthia Wong and Stephen H. Sumida (New York: Modern Language Association of America, 2001), 142.

386 Matthew Okada interview; and telephone interview with the author, June 18, 2017, Pasadena, CA.

387 John Okada, Letter to Robert Vosper, March 22, 1968, John Okada UCLA biographical file.

388 James Cox, Letter to Circulation Department staff, March 27, 1968, John Okada UCLA biographical file.

389 Bill Hosokawa, *Nisei: The Quiet Americans* (New York: William Morrow, 1969), 257.

390 Conrad S. Josias obituary, *Los Angeles Times*, November 28, 2009.

391 Matthew Okada interview.

392 Milford Davis, Telephone interview with the author, February 25, 2007, Laguna Woods, CA [henceforth cited as Davis interview].

393 Dorothea Okada, Telephone interview with the author, June 5, 2016, Pasadena, CA.

394 Dorothy Okada interview 1971, 40–41.

395 Ibid., 43.

396 Ibid., 41.

397 Ibid., 43.

398 Dorothy Okada interview 2006.

399 Certificate of death, Los Angeles County Health Department, February 24, 1971. This is the first instance of Okada's date of birth being recorded in error as September 23. Birthdays were not much observed in the household, so the discrepancy was never noticed after his death.

400 Davis interview.

401 Dorothea Okada interview.

402 *Flash* 29, no. 8 (April 1971): 8. This tender, unsigned remembrance was likely penned by Doris Mitchell.

403 Dorothy Okada interview 1972, 83. The Okada family plot is located at the east end of the cemetery near Meridian Avenue N.: Resthaven Section 2, Lot 335, Grave 3.

404 Girst, *Art, Literature,* 133.

405 Dorothy Okada interview 1971, 16–17.

406 Dorothy Okada interview 1972, 63–64.

407 In 1971, UCLA had a well-established Department of Oriental Languages, founded in 1947. The Asian American Studies Center at UCLA was created in 1969, not long before Okada's death.

408 Chin, Afterword to *No-No Boy,* 228.

409 Frank Chin, *Born in the USA: A Story of Japanese America, 1889–1947* (Lanham, MD: Rowman & Littlefield, 2002), 472.

410 Frank Okada interview.

411 Dorothea Okada interview.

412 The painting hangs in the tenth-floor Reading Room of the new Seattle Central Library, on the same site where John once worked.

413 James McIlwain, Email to the author, March 27, 2017; James McNaughton, Email to the author, November 22, 2017.

JOHN OKADA'S REDISCOVERED WRITINGS

1   See Gordon Hirabayashi, Review of *No-No Boy* by John Okada, *Pacific Affairs* 53, no. 1 (1980): 176–77; and Eugene Tashima, Review of *No-No Boy* by John Okada, *Humboldt Journal of Social Relations* 6, no. 2 (1979): 196–98.

2   This definition comes from *The Columbia Dictionary of Modern Literary and Cultural Criticism* (New York: Columbia University Press, 1995).

3   Fukei uses the term *persecution* in his book, *The Japanese American Story* (Minneapolis: Dillon Press, 1976), 28.

4   "*No-No Boy,* John Okada," *River Pine Anthology of Civic Discourse,* March 8, 2012, https://riverpineanthologyofcivicdiscourse.wordpress.com/2012/03/08/no-no-boy-john-okada/. Michael Cornelius Harnett mentions Jeanne Wakatsuki Houston's representation of the absurd in *Farewell to Manzanar* in "Humor as an Enhancement of Writing Motivation and Competence" (PhD diss., University of California, Santa Barbara, 2007), 90.

5   Introduction to "I Must Be Strong," *University of Washington Daily,* December 11, 1941, 1.

6   The poet Richard Hugo, for instance, remembered Grant Redford as "a very good short-story writing teacher" in *The Real West Marginal Way: A Poet's Autobiography,* edited by Ripley S. Hugo, Lois M. Welch, and James Welch (New York: W. W. Norton, 1986), 54.

7   Grant Redford, "Of Teachers, Students, and 'Creative Writing,'" *English Journal* 42, no. 9 (December 1953): 496.

8   Grant Redford, "To Speak Right, *Write!*" *Western Speech* 10, no. 2 (March 1946): 9.

9   Savage founded the Tryout Theatre in 1943, and hundreds of plays enjoyed their premiere performances there. The fifty-five-seat venue was located at 1316 E. 42nd Street, just off University Way. See Walden P. Boyle, John R. Cauble, and William W. Melnitz, "George Milton Savage, Theater Arts: Los Angeles," *University of California: In Memoriam, September 1978* (Berkeley: University of California Regents, 1978).

10 Aimed primarily at second-generation readers, the paper featured "News of the Nisei World," as the top left-hand corner of the front page always trumpeted. On the importance of newspapers as a way to rebuild community, see Greg Robinson, ed., *Pacific Citizens: Larry and Guyo Tajiri and Japanese American Journalism in the World War II Era* (Urbana: University of Illinois Press, 2012).

11 Budd Fukei specialized in sports reporting before the war. For more on the importance of sports for the Japanese American community, see Alison Wrynn,

"The Recreation and Leisure Pursuits of Japanese Americans in World War II Internment Camps," in *Ethnicity and Sport in North American History and Culture,* edited by George Eisen and David Wiggins (Westport, CT: Greenwood, 1994), 117–31.

12 Sometimes, the paper mentioned upcoming releases in stand-alone articles like "Mother of Five Wrote Her Novel in 'Snatches,'" *Northwest Times,* January 14, 1947, 2.

13 For a history of "the vibrant literary life of Nisei in the prewar years," see Stan Yogi, "Japanese American Literature," in *An Interethnic Companion to Asian American Literature,* edited by King-Kok Cheung (New York: Cambridge University Press, 1997), 125–55.

14 Markus Nornes, *Forest of Pressure: Ogawa Shinsuke and Postwar Japanese Documentary* (Minneapolis: University of Minnesota Press, 2007), 3.

15 On agricultural reforms in postwar Japan, see Toshihiko Kawagoe, "Deregulation and Protectionism in Japanese Agriculture," in *The Japanese Experience of Economic Reforms,* edited by Juro Teranishi and Yutaka Kosai (New York: St. Martin's, 1993), 366–91. MacArthur had forbidden "strikes that jeopardize occupation aims" as early as 1946, according to Lindesay Parrott, "Political Strikes Face Tokyo Curb," *New York Times,* November 30, 1946, 6. On the 1948 strike at the Toho film studios, see Nornes, *Forest of Pressure,* 5–6.

16 For more on the silence that followed incarceration, see Emiko Omori, *Rabbit in the Moon* (Mill Valley, CA: Wabi-Sabi Productions, 1999).

17 According to Greg Robinson, Soon-Tek Oh's *Tondemonai,* which premiered in 1970, was the "first commercially-produced play to dramatize the Japanese American wartime confinement. . . . though Hiroshi Kashiwagi's poignant play *Laughter and False Teeth* had been given a private staging at the University of California, Berkeley in 1955." See Robinson, "Early Play Took an Unflinching Look at the Trauma of the Wartime Incarceration," *Nichi Bei Weekly,* May 30, 2013. Even earlier, some university productions pointed to the effects of incarceration and World War II, even if they did not represent the events on stage. See Josephine Lee, "Asian Americans in Progress: College Plays 1937–1955," in *Re/collecting Early Asian America: Essays in Cultural History,* edited by Josephine Lee et al. (Philadelphia: Temple University Press, 2002), 307–25.

18 Grant Redford, "A Doorway to the Art of the Short Story," Grant Redford Papers USU_COLL MSS 245, Box 15, Special Collections and Archives, Utah State University Merrill-Cazier Library, Logan, Utah, 7. The manuscript is dated 1962, but we can assume that it captured the main ideas about writing that he likely taught throughout his career. I offer my thanks to Clint Pumphrey, manuscript curator at Utah State University, for providing access to this source.

19 Frank O'Connor, *The Lonely Voice: A Study of the Short Story* (New York: Harper, 1963), 22.

20 Ibid., 20–21.

21 Ibid., 18.

22 For a fuller discussion of O'Connor's short-story writing, see Michael Neary, "The Inside-Out World in Frank O'Connor's Stories," *Studies in Short Fiction* 30 (1993): 327–36.

23 Jiro's wound may have resonance with the character Jake's wound in Ernest Hemingway's *The Sun Also Rises* (1926), especially insofar as the latter's injury symbolizes impotence. My colleague Bill E. Peterson (personal communication) also mentions the legend of the Fisher King, the wounded keeper of the Holy Grail, whose wound symbolizes the suffering of his country. Finally, Jiro's wound anticipates Kenji's missing leg, which also suggests impotence since he has to send in Ichiro as a pinch-hitter to meet Emi's needs.

24 James Kyung-Jin Lee, "Elegies of Social Life: The Wounded Asian American," *Journal of Race, Ethnicity, and Religion* 3 (2012): 15; and Viet Thanh Nguyen, "Speak of the Dead, Speak of Viet Nam: The Ethics and Aesthetics of Minority Discourse," *New Centennial Review* 6, no. 2 (2006): 11.

25 Ichiro in fact blames himself for sacrificing this good life by resisting the draft.

26 For instance, on p. 53 of the novel, Ichiro "felt empty and quietly sad and hungry."

27 Redford, "A Doorway," 2.

28 Redford mentions his use of Mansfield's works in his classes in "Of Teachers," 495. For an analysis of Mansfield's "Bliss," see Violeta Sotirova, *Consciousness in Modernist Fiction: A Stylistic Study* (New York: Palgrave, 2013), n.p.

29 Frank Chin, "In Search of John Okada," (Afterword to *No-No Boy*), 255.

30 Some contemporary readers complain of inconsistency in their online reviews at Goodreads.com and Amazon.com.

31 This moment may remind some readers of Hurstwood in front of a safe full of money in Theodore Dreiser's novel *Sister Carrie* (1900). Unlike Hurstwood, however, Jiro dismisses the temptation, but not before Jim gets the wrong impression.

32 Okada may have encountered Irving's and Poe's works in his American literature classes with Joseph Barlow Harrison and Russell Blankenship as well. It is entirely possible, however, that Okada was influenced also by other genres, especially suspense literature like Dorothy B. Hughes's *Dread Journey* (1945) and films like Frank Capra's *It's a Wonderful Life* (1946).

33 John Okada, *No-No Boy* (Seattle: University of Washington Press, 2014), 13.

34 The "spineless nobody" comes from Ichiro's point of view in *No-No Boy*, p. 13. For sad, powerful examples of this phenomenon, witness the deterioration of the father in Jeanne Wakatsuki Houston's *Farewell to Manzanar*, as well as that of Okada's own father, as described in Frank Abe's biography in this volume.

35 Or perhaps this conversation recalls that between Clarence and George Bailey in *It's a Wonderful Life*.

36 Okada, *No-No Boy*, 48.

37 The narrative voice and mundane setting of this story may have been influenced by Toshio Mori, who in turn was influenced by Sherwood Anderson.

38 See Frank Abe's biography in this volume for stories about Okada's own penchant for entering various kinds of contests.

39 Okada, *No-No Boy*, 49.

40 Ichiro's old professor uses this word (ibid., 51).

41 A few Japanese American students, like Gordon Hirabayashi, did resist by challenging the curfew and exclusion orders that led to incarceration. He was supported by Quakers and the ACLU. See Gordon Hirabayashi, *A Principled Stand: The Story of Hirabayashi v. United States* (Seattle: University of Washington Press, 2013).

42 Joseph Entin, "'A Terribly Incomplete Thing': *No-No Boy* and the Ugly Feelings of Noir," *MELUS* 35, no. 3 (Fall 2010): 85–104.

43 Okada, *No-No Boy*, 3.

44 This story takes its theme from Fyodor Dostoevsky's *Crime and Punishment* (1866), in which the character Raskolnikov seems to have committed a perfect murder. And, like Stanley's friends, "those closest to Raskolnikov can hardly be aware of his real, private darkness" (Richard Freeborn, *Dostoevsky* [London, Haus: 2003], 72). The famous 1924 murder trial of Leopold and Loeb also may have been on Okada's mind. For a history of the shift from detective literature to suspense literature in the 1940s, see David Bordwell, "Murder Culture: Adventures in 1940s Suspense," March 2013, www.davidbordwell.net/essays/murder .php#_ednref22.

45 For much more detail and nuance regarding FDR's role, see Greg Robinson, *By Order of the President: FDR and the Internment of Japanese Americans* (Cambridge, MA: Harvard University Press, 2001).

46 For a discussion of the incarceration as a hate crime, see Barbara Perry, ed., *Hate and Bias Crime: A Reader* (New York: Routledge, 2012), 17–18.

47 Redford critiques, for instance, "the overwhelming facts of mathematical chance" and "the whims and accidents of editorial practice" that writers who seek publication face. See his essay "Publish or Else," *Bulletin of the American Association of University Professors* 38, no. 4 (1952/1953): 616.

48 Redford, "To Speak Right," 9.

49 George Cotkin, "Existentialism," in *Oxford Encyclopedia of American Cultural and Intellectual History* (Oxford: Oxford University Press, 2013). Cotkin explains that this postwar American version of existentialism "was traditional liberalism updated with a dash of existential anxiety." See also Hazel Barnes, *Humanistic*

Existentialism: The Literature of Possibility (Lincoln: University of Nebraska Press, 1959), 368–69.

50 Okada, *No-No Boy*, 221. While some critics have focused on Ichiro's failed identity quest, Bill E. Peterson and I argue that Ichiro is not fully to blame. We make the case that Ichiro does alter his mindset, or *psyche,* such that, unlike Kenji, whose body, or *soma*, is too damaged to continue, Ichiro can entertain hope. Unfortunately, his *ideological setting* did not provide a range of scripts that were viable for Japanese Americans like him at the time. See Floyd Cheung and Bill E. Peterson, "Psychology and Asian American Literature: Application of the Life-Story Model of Identity to *No-No Boy*," *CR: The New Centennial Review* 6, no. 2 (Fall 2006): 191–214.

51 Joseph Barlow Harrison, "Arts and Letters," in *If Men Want Peace: The Mandates of World Order*, edited by Joseph B. Harrison, Linden A. Mander, and Nathanael H. Engle (New York: Macmillan, 1946), 232.

52 Ibid., 235, 236. Harrison's ignorance of resisters and sympathy for veterans were common at the time. It would take until the 1990s for public attitudes to begin changing in this regard.

53 Ibid., 239. For a critique of Okada's "reliance on evoking (presumed) human universals," see Jinqi Ling, *Narrating Nationalisms: Ideology and Form in Asian American Literature* (New York: Oxford University Press, 1998), 49.

54 Okada, *No-No Boy*, 221.

A SEED IN A DEVASTATED LANDSCAPE

1 "Introduction to a Conversation on John Okada's *No-No Boy*, with Frank Chin, Frank Emi, and Yosh Kuromiya; Lawson Inada, Moderator," 2001, www .resisters.com/study/okada_no-no-boy.pdf. See also Chin's odd claim that *Pacific Citizen* columnist Bill Hosokawa denounced the novel: https://chintalks .blogspot.com/2010/04/narasakis-no-no-boy-vs-john-okadas-no.html.

2 There were, in addition, a few English-language works by early Issei writers such as Sadakichi Hartmann (1867–1944), Yone Noguchi (1875–1947), and Etsu Inagaki Sugimoto (1874–1950), which at least some Nisei read.

3 A few other volumes by Nisei were published outside the West Coast: biracial author Kathleen Tamagawa's memoir *Holy Prayers in a Horse's Ear* (1932), Chiyono Sugimoto Kiyooka's travel book *Chiyo's Return* (1935), and verse by poets Kimi Gengo and Kikuko Miyakawa. Hawaii-born Naoto Nakashima published *Tanpenshu Hawaii Monogatori* (1936) in Japan.

4 Nobutaka Ike, "Nisei Novel—Again," *New World Sun,* January 10, 1941, 2.

5 Larry Tajiri, "Experiences of Evacuation Provide Material for Literature," *Pacific Citizen,* January 7, 1943, reprinted in Greg Robinson, ed., *Pacific Citizens: Larry*

and Guyo Tajiri and Japanese American Journalism in the World War II Era (Urbana: University of Illinois Press, 2012), 157.

6   Hisaye Yamamoto, "Writing," *Rafu Shimpo*, December 20, 1968, reprinted in Yamamoto, *Seventeen Syllables*, edited by King-Kok Cheung (New Brunswick, NJ: Rutgers University Press, 1994), 60.

7   Larry Tajiri, letter to Miné Okubo, October 18, 1954, in Robinson, ed., *Pacific Citizens*.

8   Writing on Japan was not restricted to Nisei—Issei such as Taro Yashima [Jun Iwamatsu] and Toro Matsumoto also wrote about Japan. A pair of Kibei authors residing in postwar Japan distinguished themselves: Yoshio Abe published a three-volume Japanese-language novel about the camps, *Niju kokusekisha* [The Man of Dual Nationality] (1971–1973), and Hawaii-born Hanama Tasaki produced a notable English-language war novel, *Long the Imperial Way* (1950).

9   Two books by French Nisei novelist Kikou Yamata, *Lady of Beauty* (1954) and *Three Geishas* (1956), appeared in translation.

10   My literal view of silence as marking trauma through the absolute absence of words overlaps with King-Kok Cheung's argument that the indirection and apparent simplicity of stories by Asian American women writers constitutes a form of "articulate silence" that expresses pain. See King-Kok Cheung, *Articulate Silences: Hisaye Yamamoto, Maxine Hong Kingston, Joy Kogawa* (Ithaca, NY: Cornell University Press, 1993).

11   Latter-day critics tend to study Okubo's and Sone's texts as sites of resistance. In Okubo's case, the constraints of official support and the need to encourage resettlement clearly shaped her writing and her public presentation. See Greg Robinson, "Birth of a Citizen: Miné Okubo and the Politics of Symbolism," in *Miné Okubo: Following Her Own Road*, edited by Greg Robinson and Elena Tajima Creef (Seattle: University of Washington Press, 2008), 149–66.

12   On camp literature, especially by non-Japanese, see Greg Robinson, "Writing and Imaging the Internment," in *Cambridge Companion to Asian American Literature*, edited by Crystal Parikh and Daniel Kim (New York: Cambridge University Press, 2015), 45–58.

13   See Earl Miner, "Modern Tragedy," *Saturday Review*, September 7, 1957, 33; Bill Hosokawa, "From the Frying Pan," *Pacific Citizen*, September 27, 1957, 2.

14   Charles Tuttle, letter to Frank Chin, December 6, 1971, Frank Chin Papers, Wyles MSS. 103, Department of Special Research Collections, UC Santa Barbara Library, University of California, Santa Barbara. Hereafter cited as Frank Chin Papers.

15   "Other Books Received," *Journal of Asian Studies*, 17, no. 3 (May 1, 1958): 505.

16   Charles Tuttle, letter to Frank Chin, August 16, 1971, Frank Chin Papers.

17   William Peterson, "Success Story, Japanese American Style," *New York Times Magazine*, January 9, 1966, 36.

18   Bill Hosokawa, "U.S. Nisei Literature," *The New Canadian*, November 14, 1972, 1.

19   Ike, "Nisei Novel—Again," 2.

QUESTIONING *NO-NO BOY*

1   By "most readers" I mean the up to 195 students annually who studied the novel with me from 1981 to 2016—most of whom at first reading have assumed that the third-person narrative point of view is reliable. It has been a privilege to have read and questioned the novel with so many students, and I thank them for what I have learned from them. My fellow readers also include my colleagues Sherman Alexie and Juan Felipe Herrera and our graduate teaching assistants through the years.

2   By "unreliable narrative point of view" I do not mean that Okada is unreliable. I use the term to distinguish the third-person narrative voice of *No-No Boy* from the voice of an "unreliable narrator," a term that usually refers to a first-person narrator, who by definition is not "omniscient" but has a point of view that is limited to that character's sensibilities and understandings. Okada limits the third-person narration of the novel to the protagonist's point of view as well— except in certain passages told through the points of view of other characters. Departures from Ichiro's limited point of view may be calling for keen attention to these exceptional passages. The narrative devices of unreliable first-person and limited third-person narration depend on us readers to question the limitations they impose on our readings and understandings of the characters. The limited narrative voices lead us to ask what they are *not* saying.

3   John Okada, *No-No Boy* (Seattle: University of Washington Press, 2014), 3. All in-text citations refer to this edition.

4   The first Constitution of the State of Washington, in 1889, prohibited anyone without a sincere intention of becoming a US citizen from owning any real property. Washington passed another alien land law in 1921 and, in an amendment in 1923, closed a loophole that had enabled Issei to buy real estate by putting their assets under the names of Nisei of legal age. This amendment, however, was inconsistently enforced. See Roger Daniels, Sandra C. Taylor, and Harry H. L. Kitano, eds., *Japanese Americans: From Relocation to Redress* (Seattle: University of Washington Press, 2013); and David A. Takami, *Divided Destiny: A History of Japanese Americans in Seattle* (Seattle: University of Washington Press, 1998).

5   In *Nisei Daughter* (1953), Monica Sone writes about an event in the Minidoka concentration camp, the wedding of her brother Henry and his bride, Minnie, that relates to this focus on the Kumasakas' children. Okada's similar attention

to Nisei ownership of houses, symbolic of Niseis' coming of age, may reflect his predecessor's work.

6   Later, in a monologue in chapter 3, Ichiro does acknowledge that he knows that the Issei have been denied US citizenship, but he twists this knowledge into blaming *them* for clinging to their "Japanese" nationality.

7   References to "Orientalism" are so deeply embedded in critiques of colonialism and imperialism that the book of that title by Edward Said (1978) may nowadays go subsumed and uncited. See also Robert G. Lee, *Orientals: Asian Americans in Popular Culture* (Philadelphia: Temple University Press, 1999); and Christina Klein, *Cold War Orientalism: Asia in the Middlebrow Imagination, 1941–1961* (Berkeley: University of California Press, 2003).

8   I thank Daryl Maeda for this insight into the sociologist's self-contradiction.

9   In the novel even Pa has conversations with his son Ichiro—or tries to. Pa often asks Ichiro about his years in prison and how he is feeling. It is Ichiro who cannot or will only barely converse.

10   Akutsu distributed copies of his testimony and a copy of his Order to Report for Induction at the Seattle hearing of the Commission on Wartime Relocation and Internment of Civilians, September 9, 1981. I draw also from a speech Akutsu delivered at Washington State University in 1982.

11   Eric L. Muller, in his *Free to Die for Their Country: The Story of the Japanese American Draft Resisters in World War II* (Chicago: University of Chicago Press, 2001), notes that Akutsu was "charged and arrested when he failed to report in July" (75).

12   See Takeda Izuma, Miyoshi Shōraku, and Namiki Senryū, *Chūshingura (The Treasury of Loyal Retainers): A Puppet Play*, translated by Donald Keene (New York: Columbia University Press, 1971).

13   Akutsu was not alone in being treated in an inconsistent manner once he answered "no" to the 1943 questionnaire. Tsuguo "Ike" Ikeda described in a seminar (December 1, 2002) how he deliberately answered "no" to question 28, went on to consider himself a no-no boy, was neither segregated nor sent to Tule Lake, but was served a draft notice around June of 1944. Ikeda did not resist the draft, though he was perplexed about how he could be drafted when he had earlier answered "no." He served in the US Military Intelligence Service. His widow, Sumiko, says that they knew of other no-no boys who were served draft notices. In an individual case, Gordon Hirabayashi openly refused to fill in the questionnaire and was sentenced to time in the McNeil Island penitentiary for draft evasion.

14   For another analysis and interpretation of the trope of disability in *No-No Boy*, see Cynthia Wu, "'Give Me the Stump Which Gives You the Right to Hold

Your Head High': A Homoerotics of Disability in Asian American Critique," *Amerasia Journal* 39, no. 1 (2013): 3–16.

15   Contrary to Ruth Ozeki's assertion in the 2014 edition of *No-No Boy*, it is not the "very first Japanese American novel." Okada's was preceded by James T. Hamada's *Don't Give Up the Ship* (1933) and Shelley Ayame Nishimura Ota's *Upon Their Shoulders* (1951). Ota's book is like *No-No Boy* in critically questioning themes such as injustice in a continuous narrative about Japanese immigrants and their children—including an Issei character sent to a Department of Justice internment camp and another arrested by the FBI but soon released. For discussions of these novels, see my *And the View from the Shore: Literary Traditions of Hawai'i* (Seattle: University of Washington Press, 1991).

16   *No-No Boy* shares with other works of "minority" American literature a characteristic of having collective protagonists and antagonists. When I state that Ma is a "victim," I mean in part that she is not "the antagonist" opposing the protagonist Ichiro. To identify Ma as his antagonist would deflect (as Ichiro does) responsibility for the incarceration of Nikkei away from the government and society of the United States. In other words, the government and society are the collective antagonist, and if so, then the protagonist is not Ichiro alone but all the Nikkei and by extension all people subjected to injustice. Seeing his mother transformed into a part of a collective protagonist may transform her from being a "victim" to being an agent herself of historical, cultural change.

17   See John Dower, *War without Mercy and Power in the Pacific War* (New York: Pantheon Books, 1986).

18   Frank Chin first pointed out to me and others that "Momotaro" is a story of victory against assimilation and of the restoration of a people's history and identity.

19   See also page 19, where Ichiro ruefully asserts, in a monologue, that his parents have been in America for "thirty-five years without becoming less Japanese."

20   Momoko Iko, in her drama *Gold Watch* (in *Unbroken Thread: An Anthology of Plays by Asian American Women,* edited by Roberta Uno, 105–53 [Amherst: University of Massachusetts Press, 1993]), expresses an idea of how Issei and Nisei are two generations of a shared and continually changing Japanese American culture when the father Masu tells his son Tadao, "We were born, Tadao, to different times, so our lives are different, must be different, if we are to survive" (136). The character does not differentiate his son from himself by "culture," but by the passage of time.

21   Compared with the ambiguities of Ichiro's present experience of Japanese culture, references to American popular culture and the streets and neighborhoods of Seattle and Portland situate Ichiro on solid ground. Beneath its fictional name, the Club Oriental is the historically infamous Wah Mee Club. There young

couples dance to a "Ralph Flanagan tune" on the juke box (66). The presence of African Americans on South Jackson Street is a reminder of how that street was a stage for Seattle's jazz scene before the war. Ichiro remembers the music of Glenn Miller and Tommy Dorsey from his youth (181). On the piano in Emi's house he plays "Sentimental Journey," ironically a favorite of Nikkei in the concentration camps. The clock tower of the train station, the red Wonder Bread sign up the Jackson Street slope, the Safeway store where Mr. Kanno buys a whole chicken to roast, the Burnside Café in Portland: all are material signs that not only Ichiro but all the Nikkei are at home—or trying to be—in America.

22 Okada scatters other statements of resistance throughout the novel. First among them is in Okada's preface, where the "blond giant from Nebraska," having listened to the Nisei soldier's terse account of how his parents are living in an American concentration camp, tells the Nisei comrade that if the American government were to treat his family that way, "They could kiss my ass" (xxvi–xxvii). In another moment, the black man called Rabbit declares, in reference to draft resisters being singled out for special punishment, "If they had come for me, I would of told them where to shove their stinking uniform too" (210).

23 The character type of Emi is resonant in literature. Her apparition recurs in— or by similarities and differences is comparable with—Suzy Song, who tells Victor Joseph stories of his dead father, in Sherman Alexie's screenplay for *Smoke Signals* (1998). Until then, Victor is scornful of stories, storytelling, and the storyteller, his talkative traveling companion and childhood sidekick Thomas Builds-a-Fire. After Suzy, Victor listens to Thomas's stories too. Emi's mix of criticism of and patriotism for America occurs also in other works concerning Asian American citizenship, among them Bulosan's *America Is in the Heart* and Genny Lim's play *Paper Angels* (1991).

24 The vacant lot appears to be at the corner of Maynard Alley and S. Weller Street, at what is now the parking lot of Tai Tung Restaurant.

25 This is sharply reminiscent of the lynching of Joe Christmas in William Faulkner's *Light in August* (1932). Both thematically and stylistically, *No-No Boy* shows influences of Faulkner.

26 The *Northwest Asian Weekly* newspaper now occupies this site.

27 Urashima reappears, for instance, in Toshio Mori, *The Woman from Hiroshima* (San Francisco: Isthmus Press, 1978); Harry H. L. Kitano, *Japanese Americans: The Evolution of a Subculture* (Englewood Cliffs, NJ: Prentice-Hall, 1976); Mei-mei Berssenbrugge, *Mizu* (Victoria, TX: Chax Press, 1990); Juliet S. Kono, "Ojichan" in her *Hilo Rains* (Honolulu: Bamboo Ridge Press, 1988); and, I argue, in *No-No Boy*. See *Urashima Taro*, illustrated by George Suyeoka (Waipahu, HI: Island Heritage,1973), for children.

28 See my "Immigration, Diaspora, Transnationalism, and the Native: The Many-Mouthed Bird of Asian/Pacific American Literature in the Early Twenty-First Century," *EurAmerica* 40, no. 2 (2010): 359–92. My attempt there is to explicate a theory of culture and identity that my students once named "dialogical, diachronic pluralism," and to relate this theory to other current theories and developments in the study of Asian American literature.

29 Researcher Aiko Herzig-Yoshinaga found a copy of the 1943 questionnaire in the National Archives that was unusual for the attachment of a two-page draft typescript of a "Grading System" for determining which "subjects" would be eligible for relocation out of the camps and which would be "rejected." Any answer of "no" to question 27 or 28 would be grounds for "rejection." In question 16, about religion, a Shintoist would be rejected, while a Buddhist would receive "1-minus." Practitioners of Japanese martial arts ("Kyudo, Jyudo, or Kendo," for instance) would be "referred" and interrogated. The questionnaire itself was of an actual no-no boy, in the Heart Mountain, Wyoming, camp, dated March 23, 1943.

30 This is the second major incident in the novel involving African Americans and Asian Americans, the first being the opening confrontation between Ichiro and the "Negroes" outside the pool parlors on Jackson Street. The third concerns Birdie, an older African American man who defended the draft resister Gary at the iron foundry (199). Fourthly, Ichiro has a memory of a church in Idaho where the white congregation welcomed him but left a "white-haired Negro" standing alone in the back of the church without offering him a seat or even speaking to him (204). Because of this witnessing of racism, Ichiro quits going to Christian churches.

31 Studying the novel with me in the spring of 2016, Juan Felipe Herrera called my attention to the word *pattern* on page 123 and asked if I knew what Kenji or Okada meant by it. His sense of intrigue with the word has led me to think about it ever since.

32 By using the term *dialogical* in its various forms here and elsewhere in this essay, I am alluding to the work and theories of M. M. Bakhtin, such as his *The Dialogic Imagination: Four Essays*, edited by Michael Holquist, translated by Caryl Emerson and Michael Holquist (Austin: University of Texas Press, 1981).

33 An earlier version of this chapter is my article, "*No-No Boy* and the Twisted Logic of Internment," *Journal of the Asian American Literature Association*, no. 13 (2007): 33–49.

FALSE CONSTRUCTIONS OF LOYALTY

1 The author's late father was a "no-no" from Topaz in central Utah. Neither he nor his "no-no" or renunciant friends bore any resemblance to the character of Ichiro.

2   United States Department of the Interior, War Relocation Authority, *Impounded People: Japanese Americans in the Relocation Centers* (Washington DC: Government Printing Office, 1946), 97–140.

3   *Federal Register* 12, no. 230 (1947): 8731–44.

4   Frank Emi, Interview with Frank Abe, August 13, 2006, San Gabriel, CA (video recording).

5   Jim Akutsu, Interview with Art Hansen, June 12, 1997, Seattle, WA.

6   Frank Yamasaki, Telephone interview with Frank Abe, November 22, 2008, Seattle, WA.

7   Yosh Kuromiya, Email to the author, April 14, 2017.

8   See the explanation of *kachigumi* in the Okada biography on page 67.

9   Fair Play Committee, Bulletin #3, March 4, 1944. See the full text online at: http://resisters.com/conscience/resistance/we_hereby_refuse/04_fpc_3.html.

10   Mike Masaoka, Minutes of the Special Emergency National JACL Conference, November 17–24, 1942, Salt Lake City, UCLA Library, Department of Special Collections, Collection 2010, Box 296.

11   US Department of the Interior, War Relocation Authority, *Impounded People*, 133.

12   Patrick O. Gudridge, "The Constitution Glimpsed from Tule Lake," *Law and Contemporary Problems* 68 (2005): 103. *McGrath v. Abo* began as one of four class-action lawsuits, *Abo v. Clark*, filed by attorney Wayne Collins on behalf of the renunciants. It placed the burden of renunciation on government duress, but it was undermined by a subsequent case, *Acheson v. Murakami*, which placed the burden of renunciation on the individual, forcing Collins to file thousands of individual affidavits to restore citizenship. The final case concluded in 1963, twenty-three years after Collins filed his initial lawsuit. Wayne Collins Papers, Bancroft Library, University of California, Berkeley.

13   Wayne Collins, Letter to Tadayasu Abo, February 1957, cited in Roger Daniels, *The Japanese American Cases: The Rule of Law in Time of War* (Lawrence: University Press of Kansas, 2013), 123–29.

14   Gudridge, "Constitution Glimpsed from Tule Lake," 107.

15   John Okada, *No-No Boy* (Seattle: University of Washington Press, 2014), 43.

16   Ibid., 147.

17   Harry H. L. Kitano, "The Japanese American Family," in *Ethnic Families in America: Patterns and Variations*, 3rd ed., edited by Charles H. Mindel, Robert W. Habenstein, and Roosevelt Wright, Jr. (New York: Elsevier Science, 1988), 270. Kitano shows that the out-group marriage rates for Japanese in Los Angeles in 1979 was more than 60 percent.

18   Martha Nakagawa, "Gardena Valley Gardeners Association to Disband," *Rafu Shimpo*, December 30, 2015, 1.

1   Although there are many scholarly works on *No-No Boy* by undergraduates, such as honors theses, undergraduate journal articles, and course papers, this essay draws primarily from the literary criticism from peer-reviewed articles and anthology chapters by academics in Asian American literary studies at universities and colleges in the United States.

2   I was unable to locate any peer-reviewed articles or published manuscripts dealing with the literary criticism of *No-No Boy* before 1975.

3   Colleen Lye, "Reading for Asian American Literature," in *A Companion to American Literary Studies*, edited by Caroline F. Levander and Robert S. Levine (Malden, MA: John Wiley, 2011), 484.

4   Kim, "Defining Asian American Realities through Literature," *Cultural Critique* 6 (Spring 1987): 88.

5   Lye, "Reading for Asian American Literature," 484.

6   Jinqi Ling, "Race, Power, and Cultural Politics in John Okada's *No-No Boy*," *American Literature* 67, no. 2 (1995): 362. See also Jinqi Ling, "*No-No Boy* by John Okada," in *A Resource Guide to Asian American Literature*, edited by Sau-ling Cynthia Wong and Stephen H. Sumida (New York: Modern Language Association of America, 2001), 145–46; Lawson F. Inada, "Of Place and Displacement: The Range of Japanese-American Literature," in *Three American Literatures*, edited by Houston A. Baker Jr. (New York: Modern Language Association of America, 1982), 263; Frank Chin et al., eds., *Aiiieeeee! An Anthology of Asian-American Writers* (Washington, DC: Howard University Press, 1974); Elaine H. Kim, *Asian American Literature: An Introduction to the Writings and Their Social Context* (Philadelphia: Temple University Press, 1982), 147–56; Dorothy Ritsuko McDonald, "After Imprisonment: Ichiro's Search for Redemption in *No-No Boy*," *MELUS* 6, no. 3 (Autumn 1979): 19–26; Gayle K. Fujita Sato, "Momotaro's Exile: John Okada's *No-No Boy*," in *Reading the Literatures of Asian America*, edited by Shirley Geok-Lin Lim and Amy Ling (Philadelphia: Temple University Press, 1992), 256.

7   Chin et al., eds., *Aiiieeeee!*

8   McDonald, "After Imprisonment."

9   Shirley Geok-Lin Lim, "Japanese American Women's Life Stories: Maternality in Monica Sone's *Nisei Daughter* and Joy Kogawa's *Obasan*," *Feminist Studies* 16, no. 2 (Summer 1990): 289–90.

10   Stephen H. Sumida, "The More Things Change: Paradigm Shifts in Asian American Studies," *American Studies International* 38, no. 2 (2000): 97–100.

11   Lye, "Reading for Asian American Literature," 486.

12 Teun A. Van Dijk, "Critical Discourse Analysis," in *The Handbook of Discourse Analysis*, edited by Deborah Tannen et al., 2nd ed. (Malden, MA: John Wiley, 2015), 467.

13 Ling, "Race, Power, and Cultural Politics," 362–64.

14 William Yeh, "To Belong or Not to Belong: The Liminality of John Okada's *No-No Boy*," *Amerasia Journal* 19, no. 1 (1993): 121.

15 Inada, "Of Place and Displacement," 260.

16 Yeh, "To Belong or Not to Belong," 124.

17 Stan Yogi, "'You Had to Be One or the Other': Oppositions and Reconciliation in John Okada's *No-No Boy*," *MELUS* 21, no. 2 (Summer 1996): 64.

18 Sumida, "The More Things Change," 101.

19 Viet Thanh Nguyen, *Race and Resistance: Literature and Politics in Asian America* (Oxford: Oxford University Press, 2002), 62–63.

20 Nguyen has mentioned that within Asian American literary circles, literary scholars tend to lionize "bad actors" who do not conform to mainstream, assimilationist paradigms (ibid., 144).

21 Suzanne Arakawa, "Suffering Male Bodies: Representations of Dissent and Displacement in the Internment-Themed Narratives of John Okada and Toshio Mori," in *Recovered Legacies: Authority and Identity in Early Asian American Literature*, edited by Keith Lawrence and Floyd Cheung (Philadelphia: Temple University Press, 2005), 183–206.

22 Bryn Gribben, "The Mother That Won't Reflect Back: Situating Psychoanalysis and the Japanese American Mother in *No-No Boy*," *MELUS* 28, no. 2 (Summer 2003): 33.

23 Ibid.

24 Michael Omi and Howard Winant, *Racial Formation in the US: From the 1960s to the 1990s*, 2nd ed. (New York: Routledge, 1994); Shirley Geok-Lin Lim, "Assaying the Gold: Or, Contesting the Ground of Asian American Literature," *New Literary History* 24, no. 1 (Winter 1993): 153; Yogi, "'You Had to be One or the Other'"; Yeh, "To Belong or Not to Belong"; D. Kim, "Once More, with Feeling."

25 Sumida, "The More Things Change," 97–101; Nguyen, *Race and Resistance*, 61–86.

26 Helen Jun, *Race for Citizenship: Black Orientalism and Asian Uplift from Pre-emancipation to Neoliberal America* (New York: New York University Press, 2011), 53.

27 James Kyung-Jin Lee, "The Transitivity of Race and the Challenges of the Imagination," in *Racial Formation in the Twenty-First Century*, edited by Daniel Martinez HoSang, Oneka LaBennett, and Laura Pulido (Berkeley: University of California Press, 2012), 64–65.

28 Benzi Zhang, "Mapping Carnivalistic Discourse in Japanese-American Writing," *MELUS* 24, no. 4 (Winter 1999): 19, 21.

29   Dan P. McAdam, *Power, Intimacy, and the Life Story: Personological Inquiries into Identity* (New York: Guilford Press, 1985).

30   Floyd Cheung and Bill E. Peterson, "Psychology and Asian American Literature: Application of the Life-Story Model of Identity to *No-No Boy*," *CR: The New Centennial Review* 6, no. 2 (Fall 2006): 192.

31   Ibid., 197.

32   Joseph Entin, "'A Terribly Incomplete Thing': *No-No Boy* and the Ugly Feelings of Noir," *MELUS* 35, no. 3 (Fall 2010): 86–87.

BIBLIOGRAPHY

SECONDARY SOURCES

Abe, Frank. *Conscience and the Constitution*. Seattle: Resisters.com Productions, 2000; 2-disc DVD, 2011.

Amemiya, Kozy K. "Being 'Japanese' in Brazil and Okinawa." Japan Policy Research Institute, Occasional Paper No. 13 (May 1988).

Ano, Masaharu. "Loyal Linguists: Nisei of World War II Learned Japanese in Minnesota." *Minnesota History* 45, no. 7 (1977): 273–87.

Arakawa, Suzanne. "Suffering Male Bodies: Representations of Dissent and Displacement in the Internment-Themed Narratives of John Okada and Toshio Mori." In *Recovered Legacies: Authority and Identity in Early Asian American Literature*, edited by Keith Lawrence and Floyd Cheung, 183–206. Philadelphia: Temple University Press, 2005.

Austin, Allen W. *From Concentration Camp to Campus: Japanese American Students and World War II*. Urbana: University of Illinois Press, 2007.

Bakhtin, M. M. *The Dialogic Imagination: Four Essays*. Edited by Michael Holquist; translated by Caryl Emerson and Michael Holquist. Austin: University of Texas Press, 1981.

Barnes, Hazel. *Humanistic Existentialism: The Literature of Possibility*. Lincoln: University of Nebraska Press, 1959.

Berssenbrugge, Mei-mei. *Mizu*. Victoria, TX: Chax Press, 1990.

Boyle, Walden P., John R. Cauble, and William W. Melnitz. "George Milton Savage, Theater Arts: Los Angeles." In *University of California: In Memoriam, September 1978*. Berkeley: University California Regents, 1978.

Burton, Jeffery F., Mary M. Farrell, Florence B. Lord, and Richard W. Lord. *Confinement and Ethnicity: An Overview of World War II Japanese American Relocation Sites.* Tucson: Western Archeological and Conservation Center, 1999.

Cheung, Floyd, and Bill E. Peterson. "Psychology and Asian American Literature: Application of the Life Story Model of Identity to *No-No Boy.*" *CR: The New Centennial Review* 6, no. 2 (Fall 2006): 191–214.

Cheung, King-Kok. *Articulate Silences: Hisaye Yamamoto, Maxine Hong Kingston, Joy Kogawa.* Ithaca, NY: Cornell University Press, 1993.

Chin, Doug. *Seattle's International District: The Making of a Pan-Asian American Community.* 2nd ed. Seattle: International Examiner Press, 2009.

Chin, Frank. *Born in the USA: A Story of Japanese America, 1889–1947.* Lanham, MD: Rowman & Littlefield, 2002.

———. "In Search of John Okada." Afterword to *No-No Boy*, by John Okada. Seattle and San Francisco: Combined Asian-American Resources Project, Inc., 1976; Seattle: University of Washington Press, 1979 (253–60). New University of Washington Press edition, 2014 (223–32). Originally published in a slightly different form in the *Seattle Weekly* 1, no. 14 (June 30–July 6, 1976): 10–11.

———. "The Wah Mee." *Seattle Weekly*, May 4, 1983.

———. "Whites Can't Relate to John Okada's book *No-No Boy.*" *Pacific Citizen*, Holiday Issue, Dec. 23–30, 1977, 55–56.

Chin, Frank, Jeffrey Paul Chan, Lawson Fusao Inada, and Shawn Wong, eds. *Aiiieeeee! An Anthology of Asian-American Writers.* Washington, DC: Howard University Press, 1974.

Cotkin, George. "Existentialism." In *Oxford Encyclopedia of American Cultural and Intellectual History.* Oxford: Oxford University Press, 2013.

Daniels, Roger. *The Japanese American Cases: The Rule of Law in Time of War.* Lawrence: University Press of Kansas, 2013.

Daniels, Roger, Sandra C. Taylor, and Harry H. L. Kitano, eds. *Japanese Americans: From Relocation to Redress.* Seattle: University of Washington Press, 2013.

de Barros, Paul. *Jackson Street After Hours: The Roots of Jazz in Seattle.* Seattle: Sasquatch Books, 1993.

Dorpat, Paul. *Seattle Now & Then.* 3 vols. 2nd ed. Seattle: Tartu Publications, 1994.

Dower, John. *War without Mercy: Race and Power in the Pacific War.* New York: Pantheon Books, 1986.

Entin, Joseph. "'A Terribly Incomplete Thing': *No-No Boy* and the Ugly Feelings of Noir." *MELUS* 35, no. 3 (Fall 2010): 85–104.

Fiset, Louis. *Camp Harmony: Seattle's Japanese Americans and the Puyallup Assembly Center.* Urbana: University of Illinois Press, 2009.

———. *Imprisoned Apart: The World War II Correspondence of an Issei Couple.* Seattle: University of Washington Press, 1997.

Freeborn, Richard. *Dostoevsky.* London: Haus, 2003.

Fukei, Budd. *The Japanese American Story.* Minneapolis: Dillon Press, 1976.

Fukuhara, Francis Mas. *Uncommon American Patriots.* Seattle: Nisei Veterans Committee, 1991.

Garbacik, Jaimee, ed. *Ghosts of Seattle Past: An Anthology of Lost Seattle Places.* Seattle: Chin Music Press, 2017.

Girst, Thomas. *Art, Literature, and the Japanese American Internment: On John Okada's "No-No Boy."* Frankfurt, Ger.: Peter Lang, 2015.

Gribben, Bryn. "The Mother That Won't Reflect Back: Situating Psychoanalysis and the Japanese American Mother in *No-No Boy.*" *MELUS* 28, no. 2 (Summer 2003): 31–46.

Gudridge, Patrick O. "The Constitution Glimpsed from Tule Lake." *Law and Contemporary Problems* 68, no. 2 (Spring 2005): 81–118.

Hamada, James T. *Don't Give Up the Ship.* Boston: Meador, 1933.

Harnett, Michael Cornelius. "Humor as an Enhancement of Writing Motivation and Competence." PhD diss., University of California, Santa Barbara, 2007.

Harrington, Joseph D. *Yankee Samurai: The Secret Role of Nisei in America's Pacific Victory.* Detroit: Pettigrew Enterprises, 1979.

Harrison, Joseph Barlow, Linden A. Mander, and Nathanael H. Engle, eds. *If Men Want Peace: The Mandates of World Order.* New York: Macmillan, 1946.

Hirabayashi, Gordon. *A Principled Stand: The Story of Hirabayashi v. United States.* Seattle: University of Washington Press, 2013.

———. Review of *No-No Boy* by John Okada. *Pacific Affairs* 53, no. 1 (1980): 176–77.

Horiuchi, Bebe. "Detroit: Unassuming Writer Hailing From Seattle Holder of Two M.A.s." *Pacific Citizen,* October 11, 1957.

Hosokawa, Bill. *Nisei: The Quiet Americans.* New York: William Morrow, 1969.

———. *Out of the Frying Pan: Reflections of a Japanese American.* Niwot: University Press of Colorado, 1998.

———. "U.S. Nisei Literature." *The New Canadian,* November 14, 1972.

Hugo, Richard. *The Real West Marginal Way: A Poet's Autobiography.* Edited by Ripley S. Hugo, Lois M. Welch, and James Welch. New York: W. W. Norton, 1986.

Ichinokuchi, Tad, and Daniel Aiso, eds. *John Aiso and the MIS: Japanese-American Soldiers in the Military Intelligence Service, World War II.* Los Angeles: MIS Club of Southern California, 1988.

Ike, Nobutaka. "Nisei Novel—Again." *New World Sun,* January 10, 1941.

Iko, Momoko. *Gold Watch.* In *Unbroken Thread: An Anthology of Plays by Asian American Women,* edited by Roberta Uno, 105–53. Amherst: University of Massachusetts Press, 1993.

Inada, Lawson F. "Of Place and Displacement: The Range of Japanese-American Literature." In *Three American Literatures,* edited by Houston A. Baker Jr., 254–65. New York: Modern Language Association of America, 1982.

Ito, Kazuo. *Issei: A History of Japanese Immigrants in North America*. Translated by Shinichiro Nakamura and Jean S. Gerard. Seattle: Japanese Community Service, 1973.

Iwamoto, Gary. "Rise and Fall of an Empire: Furuya." *International Examiner*, August 17–September 6, 2005.

Johns, Barbara. *Signs of Home: The Paintings and Wartime Diary of Kamekichi Tokita*. Seattle: University of Washington Press, 2011.

Jun, Helen. *Race for Citizenship: Black Orientalism and Asian Uplift from Pre-emancipation to Neoliberal America*. New York: New York University Press, 2011.

Kamidoi, Mary, Scott Kurashige, and Toshi Shimoura, eds. *Exiled to Motown: A Community History of Japanese Americans in Detroit*. Detroit: Detroit JACL History Project Committee, 2015.

Kano, Hisanori. *Nikkei Farmer on the Nebraska Plains: A Memoir*. Edited by Tai Kreidler; translated by Rose Yamamoto. Lubbock: Texas Tech University Press, 2010.

Kashima, Tetsuden. *Judgment without Trial: Japanese American Imprisonment during World War II*. Seattle: University of Washington Press, 2003.

Ketcherside, Rob. *Lost Seattle*. London: Pavilion Books, 2013.

Kim, Daniel Y. "Once More, with Feeling: Cold War Masculinity and the Sentiment of Patriotism in John Okada's *No-No Boy*." *Criticism* 47, no. 1 (Winter 2005): 65–83.

Kim, Elaine. *Asian American Literature: An Introduction to the Writings and Their Social Context*. Philadelphia: Temple University Press, 1982.

———. "Defining Asian American Realities through Literature." *Cultural Critique* 6 (Spring 1987): 87–111.

Kitano, Harry H. L. "The Japanese American Family." In *Ethnic Families in America: Patterns and Variations,* edited by Charles H. Mindel, Robert W. Habenstein, and Roosevelt Wright Jr., 258–75. 3rd ed. New York: Elsevier Science Publishing, 1988.

———. *Japanese Americans: The Evolution of a Subculture*. Englewood Cliffs, NJ: Prentice-Hall, 1969.

Klein, Christina. *Cold War Orientalism: Asia in the Middlebrow Imagination, 1941–1961*. Berkeley: University of California Press, 2003.

Kono, Juliet S. *Hilo Rains*. Honolulu: Bamboo Ridge Press, 1988.

Lee, James Kyung-Jin. "Elegies of Social Life: The Wounded Asian American." *Journal of Race, Ethnicity, and Religion* 3 (2012): 1–21.

———. "The Transitivity of Race and the Challenges of the Imagination." In *Racial Formation in the Twenty-First Century*, edited by Daniel Martinez HoSang, Oneka LaBennett, and Laura Pulido, 57–65. Berkeley: University of California Press, 2012.

Lee, Josephine. "Asian Americans in Progress: College Plays 1937–1955." In *Re/collecting Early Asian America: Essays in Cultural History*, edited by Josephine Lee et al., 307–25. Philadelphia: Temple University Press, 2002.

Lee, Robert G. *Orientals: Asian Americans in Popular Culture*. Philadelphia: Temple University Press, 1999.

Lim, Genny. *Paper Angels* (1991). In *Unbroken Thread: An Anthology of Plays by Asian American Women*, edited by Roberto Uno, 18–52. Amherst: University of Massachusetts Press, 1993.

Lim, Shirley Geok-Lin. "Assaying the Gold: Or, Contesting the Ground of Asian American Literature." *New Literary History* 24, no. 1 (Winter 1993): 153.

———. "Japanese American Women's Life Stories: Maternality in Monica Sone's *Nisei Daughter* and Joy Kogawa's *Obasan*." *Feminist Studies* 16, no. 2 (Summer 1990): 289–312.

Ling, Jinqi. *Narrating Nationalisms: Ideology and Form in Asian American Literature*. New York: Oxford University Press, 1998.

———. "*No-No Boy*, by John Okada." In *A Resource Guide to Asian American Literature*, edited by Sau-ling Cynthia Wong and Stephen H. Sumida, 140–50. New York: Modern Language Association of America, 2001.

———. "Race, Power, and Cultural Politics in John Okada's *No-No Boy*." *American Literature* 67, no. 2 (1995): 359–81.

Lye, Colleen. "Reading for Asian American Literature." In *A Companion to American Literary Studies*, edited by Caroline F. Levander and Robert S. Levine, 483–499. Malden, MA: John Wiley, 2011.

Matsui, Mitzie. "The Military Intelligence Service Story." In *Unsung Heroes: The Military Intelligence Service, Past—Present—Future*. Seattle: MIS Northwest Association, 1996.

McAdam, Dan P. *Power, Intimacy, and the Life Story: Personological Inquiries into Identity*. New York: Guilford Press, 1985.

McDonald, Dorothy Ritsuko. "After Imprisonment: Ichiro's Search for Redemption in *No-No Boy*." *MELUS* 6, no. 3 (Autumn 1979): 19–26.

McDonough, John, and Karen Egolf. *The Advertising Age Encyclopedia of Advertising*. New York: Fitzroy Dearborn, 2003.

McKivor, June Mukai, ed. *Kenjiro Nomura: An Artist's View of the Japanese American Internment*. Seattle: Wing Luke Asian Museum, 1991.

McNaughton, James C. *Nisei Linguists: Japanese Americans in the Military Intelligence Service during World War II*. Washington, DC: US Army Center of Military History, 2006.

Michener, James A. *The Modern Japanese Print: An Appreciation*. Tokyo: Charles E. Tuttle, 1968.

Morgan, Murray. *Skid Road: An Informal Portrait of Seattle,* First illustrated ed. Seattle: University of Washington Press, 1982.

Mori, Toshio. *The Woman from Hiroshima*. San Francisco: Isthmus Press, 1978.

Muller, Eric. *Free to Die for Their Country: The Story of the Japanese American Draft Resisters in World War II.* Chicago: University of Chicago Press, 2001.

Nguyen, Viet Thanh. *Race and Resistance: Literature and Politics in Asian America.* Oxford: Oxford University Press, 2002.

———. "Speak of the Dead, Speak of Viet Nam: The Ethics and Aesthetics of Minority Discourse." *New Centennial Review* 6, no. 2 (2006): 7–37.

Nornes, Markus. *Forest of Pressure: Ogawa Shinsuke and Postwar Japanese Documentary.* Minneapolis: University of Minnesota Press, 2007.

O'Connor, Frank. *The Lonely Voice: A Study of the Short Story.* New York: Harper, 1963.

Okada, John. "Here's Proof." *Northwest Times,* April 15 and 18, 1947.

———. "The High Cost of Proposals and Presentations." *Armed Forces Management,* December 1961.

———. (as "Anonymous"). "I Must Be Strong." *University of Washington Daily,* December 11, 1941; *Seattle Star,* December 17, 1941.

———. *No-No Boy.* Tokyo and Rutland, VT: Charles E. Tuttle, 1957; Seattle and San Francisco: Combined Asian-American Resources Project, 1976; Seattle: University of Washington Press, 1979 and 2014.

———. "The Silver Lunchbox." *Northwest Times,* April 11, 1947.

———. "Skipping Millions." *Northwest Times,* April 8, 1947.

———. (as John Hillfield). "The Technocrats of Industry." *Armed Forces Management,* March 1962.

———. "What Can I Do?" *Northwest Times,* March 25, 1947.

———. "When in Japan: A Comedy in One Act." *Northwest Times,* January 2 and 10, 1947.

———. "Without Solace." *Northwest Times,* April 4, 1947.Okada, "Charlie" Yoshitaka Robert. "What Price Glory!" In *And Then There Were Eight: The Men of I Company, 442nd Regimental Combat Team,* edited by Edward Yamasaki, 253. Honolulu: Item Chapter, 442nd Veterans Club, 2003.

Okubo, Miné. *Citizen 13660.* New York: Columbia University Press, 1946; Seattle: University of Washington Press, 2014.

Omi, Michael, and Howard Winant. *Racial Formation in the US: From the 1960s to the 1990s.* 2nd ed. New York: Routledge, 1994.

Omori, Emiko. *Rabbit in the Moon.* Mill Valley, CA: Wabi-Sabi Productions, 1999.

Ota, Shelley Ayame Nishimura. *Upon Their Shoulders.* New York: Exposition Press, 1951.

Ozeki, Ruth. Introduction to *No-No Boy,* by John Okada. Seattle: University of Washington Press, 2014.

Perry, Barbara, ed. *Hate and Bias Crime: A Reader.* New York: Routledge, 2012.

Peterson, William. "Success Story, Japanese American Style." *New York Times Magazine,* January 9, 1966.

Pieroth, Doris Hinson. *Seattle's Women Teachers of the Interwar Years: Shapers of a Livable City*. Seattle: University of Washington Press, 2004.

Redford, Grant. "Of Teachers, Students, and 'Creative Writing,'" *English Journal* 42, no. 9 (December 1953): 490–96, 509.

———. "To Speak Right, *Write!*" *Western Speech* 10, no. 2 (March 1946): 7–9.

Richardson, D. Kenneth. *Hughes after Howard: The Story of Hughes Aircraft Company*. Santa Barbara: Sea Hill Press, 2012.

Robinson, Greg. *After Camp: Portraits in Midcentury Japanese American Life and Politics*. Berkeley: University of California Press, 2012.

———. *By Order of the President: FDR and the Internment of Japanese Americans*. Cambridge, MA: Harvard University Press, 2001.

———. "Early Play Took an Unflinching Look at the Trauma of the Wartime Incarceration." *Nichi Bei,* May 30, 2013.

———, ed. *Pacific Citizens: Larry and Guyo Tajiri and Japanese American Journalism in the World War II Era*. Urbana: University of Illinois Press, 2012.

———. "Writing and Imaging the Internment." In *Cambridge Companion to Asian American Literature,* edited by Crystal Parikh and Daniel Kim, 45–58. New York: Cambridge University Press, 2015.

Robinson, Greg, and Elena Tajima Creef, eds. *Miné Okubo: Following Her Own Road*. Seattle: University of Washington Press, 2008.

Rumley, Larry. "Nisei Dilemma Is Basis of Novel." *Seattle Times Sunday Magazine,* March 6, 1977.

Sato, Gayle K. Fujita Sato. "Momotaro's Exile: John Okada's No-No Boy." In *Reading the Literatures of Asian America,* edited by Shirley Geok-Lin Lim and Amy Ling. Philadelphia: Temple University Press, 1992.

Spickard, Paul. *Japanese Americans: The Formation and Transformations of an Ethnic Group*. Rev. ed. New Brunswick, NJ: Rutgers University Press, 2009.

Sone, Monica. *Nisei Daughter*. Boston: Little, Brown and Company,1953; Seattle: University of Washington Press, 2014.

Sotirova, Violeta. *Consciousness in Modernist Fiction: A Stylistic Study*. New York: Palgrave, 2013.

Sumida, Stephen H. *And the View from the Shore: Literary Traditions of Hawai'i*. Seattle: University of Washington Press, 1991.

———. "Immigration, Diaspora, Transnationalism, and the Native: The Many-Mouthed Bird of Asian/Pacific American Literature in the Early Twenty-First Century." *EurAmerica* 40, no. 2 (2010): 359–92.

———. "*No-No Boy* and the Twisted Logic of Internment." *Journal of the Asian American Literature Association,* no. 13 (2007): 33–49.

———. "The More Things Change: Paradigm Shifts in Asian American Studies." *American Studies International* 38, no. 2 (2000): 97–114.

Takami, David A. *Divided Destiny: A History of Japanese Americans in Seattle.* Seattle: University of Washington Press, 1998.

Takeda Izuma, Miyoshi Shōraku, and Namiki Senryū. *Chūshingura (The Treasury of Loyal Retainers): A Puppet Play.* Translated by Donald Keene. New York: Columbia University Press, 1971.

Tart, Larry. *Freedom through Vigilance.* Vol. 4: *History of U.S. Air Force Security Service (USAFSS) Airborne Reconnaissance, Part 1.* West Conshohocken, PA: Infinity Publishing, 2010.

Tashima, Eugene. Review of *No-No Boy* by John Okada. *Humboldt Journal of Social Relations* 6, no. 2 (1979): 196–98.

Taylor, Quintard. *The Forging of a Black Community: Seattle's Central District from 1870 through the Civil Rights Era.* Seattle: University of Washington Press, 1994.

Thompson, Nile, and Carolyn J. Marr. *Building for Learning: Seattle Public School Histories, 1862–2000.* Seattle: Schools History Committee, Seattle School District, 2002.

Tuttle, William M., Jr. *"Daddy's Gone to War": The Second World War in the Lives of America's Children.* New York: Oxford University Press, 1993.

United States Department of the Interior. War Relocation Authority. *Impounded People: Japanese Americans in the Relocation Centers.* Washington DC: Government Printing Office, 1946.

Urashima Taro. Illustrated by George Suyeoka. Waipahu, HI: Island Heritage, 1973.

Van Dijk, Teun A. "Critical Discourse Analysis." In *The Handbook of Discourse Analysis,* edited by Deborah Tannen et al., 2nd ed. Malden, MA: John Wiley, 2015.

Wrynn, Alison. "The Recreation and Leisure Pursuits of Japanese Americans in World War II Internment Camps." In *Ethnicity and Sport in North American History and Culture,* edited by George Eisen and David Wiggins, 117–31. Westport, CT: Greenwood, 1994.

Wu, Cynthia. "'Give Me the Stump Which Gives You the Right to Hold Your Head High': A Homoerotics of Disability in Asian American Critique." *Amerasia Journal* 39, no. 1 (2013): 3–16.

Yamamoto, Hisaye. *Seventeen Syllables.* Edited by King-Kok Cheung. New Brunswick, NJ: Rutgers University Press, 1994.

Yeh, William. "To Belong or Not to Belong: The Liminality of John Okada's *No-No Boy.*" *Amerasia Journal* 19, no. 1 (1993): 121–33.

Yogi, Stan. "Japanese American Literature." In *An Interethnic Companion to Asian American Literature,* edited by King-Kok Cheung, 125–55. New York: Cambridge University Press, 1997.

———. "'You Had to Be One or the Other': Oppositions and Reconciliation in John Okada's *No-No Boy.*" *MELUS* 21, no. 2 (Summer 1996): 63–77.

Yoshida, Jim, and Bill Hosokawa. *The Two Worlds of Jim Yoshida*. New York: William Morrow, 1972.

Zhang, Benzi. "Mapping Carnivalistic Discourse in Japanese-American Writing." *MELUS* 24, no. 4 (Winter 1999): 19–40.

ARCHIVES AND PERSONAL PAPERS

Akutsu, Jim. Testimony to the Commission on Wartime Relocation and Internment of Civilians. September 9, 1981, Seattle. Jack and Aiko Herzig Papers (Collection 451), Box 63, Folder 1. UCLA Library Special Collections, Charles E. Young Research Library, Los Angeles, CA.

Alien Enemy Control Unit. Records of the Department of Justice, Record Group 60, Enemy Alien Litigation Case Files, Box 608. National Archives, College Park, MD.

Bradfield, Edward. *The Story behind the Flying Eight-Ball*. Unpublished squadron history, mimeographed and saddle-stitched on Guam, October, 1945.

Chin, Frank papers. Wyles Mss 103. Department of Special Research Collections, UC Santa Barbara Library, Santa Barbara, CA.

Departmental Reports 1951–53. Bound typescripts archived in the Seattle Room, Seattle Public Library.

Gardner, Grandison. "Reminiscences of Grandison Gardner: Oral History, 1959." Henry H. Arnold project, Columbia University Libraries, Columbia Center for Oral History, New York.

Hughes Aircraft Company employee oral histories. Local History Room, Fullerton Public Library, Fullerton, CA.

Okada, Dorothy. Interviews. Bancroft Library, UC Berkeley, BANC FILM 3101, Berkeley, CA.

Okada, John. Biographical files. UCLA Library Special Collections, University Archives Reference Collection, University Archives Record Series 745, Los Angeles, CA.

———. Evacuee Case File. Records of the War Relocation Authority, Record Group 210. National Archives, Washington, DC.

Okada, Roy. "My Story." Undated notes c. 2005 for classroom presentations.

Savage, George Milton. Family papers. Manuscript Collection No. 5400, Accession No. 5400-001, University of Washington Special Collections, Seattle, WA.

United States Strategic Bombing Survey. Records of the United States Strategic Bombing Survey, Record Group 243. National Archives, College Park, MD.

Yamashita, Jimmy. "Po Valley Campaign (Gothic Line)." Unpublished company history.

"About Us." Tuttle Publishing. www.tuttlepublishing.com/about-us.

Braden, James D. "Japanese Code Intercept Unit WWII: 8th AAF RSM." http://freepages.military.rootsweb.ancestry.com/~braden.

Fair Play Committee. Bulletin #3. March 4, 1944. http://resisters.com/conscience/resistance/we_hereby_refuse/04_fpc_3.html.

Japanese American Trainees, Company A, 33rd Battalion. http://bit.ly/2k23wol.

Military Intelligence Service Association of Northern California. "History of the MIS." www.njahs.org/misnorcal/essay.htm.

Military Intelligence Service (MIS) Registry Merged (alphabetical), compiled by Seiki Oshiro, Paul Tani, Mitzie Matsui, and Grant Ichikawa. https://java.wild apricot.org/resources/Documents/WWII MIS Registry (Merged) July 2007.pdf.

"Minnesota's Remarkable Secret School for Language." JACL Twin Cities Chapter Curriculum and Resource Guide, 2013. www.tcjacl.org/wp/wp- content/uploads/2014/04/MISGuide2013.pdf

Okada, Beverly. "Yoshito and Takayo Ota Okada." Remembrance Project. www.remembrance-project.org/tributes/form-uploads/yoshito-takayo-ota-okada.html.

"Pinedale (detention facility)." *Densho Encyclopedia.* http://encyclopedia.densho.org/Pinedale_(detention_facility)

University of Washington Libraries. "Interrupted Lives: Japanese American Students at the University of Washington, 1941–1942." www.lib.washington.edu/special collections/collections/exhibits/harmony/interrupted.

CONTRIBUTORS

FRANK ABE wrote, produced, and directed the PBS documentary *Conscience and the Constitution*. He is currently collaborating on a graphic novel dramatizing the resistance to wartime incarceration, and blogs at Resisters.com. With Frank Chin, he helped create the first "Day of Remembrance" events, and helped launch Chin's Asian American Theater Workshop in San Francisco. Abe was senior reporter for KIRO Newsradio in Seattle, and served as communications director for two King County executives and the King County Council. He has been published in *Bloomsbury Review*, *Amerasia Journal*, *Frontiers of Asian American Studies*, and many newspapers.

FLOYD CHEUNG is professor of English language and literature and of American studies at Smith College, and founding chair of the Five College Asian/Pacific/American Studies Certificate Program. He has edited H. T. Tsiang's novels *And China Has Hands* (Ironweed Press, 2003) and *The Hanging on Union Square* (Kaya Press, 2013), *Sadakichi Hartmann: Collected Poems, 1886–1944* (Little Island Press, 2016), and helped recover other early Asian American texts. His poems can be found in *Mascara Literary Review*, *qarrtsiluni*, *Rhino*, and in his chapbook, *Jazz at Manzanar*.

LAWSON FUSAO INADA is a poet laureate for the state of Oregon. He coedited the landmark anthologies *Aiiieeeee!* and *The Big Aiiieeeee!*, edited *Only What We Could Carry*, and authored the poetry collections *Before the War*, *Legends from Camp*, and *Drawing the Line*.

MARTHA NAKAGAWA has worked as assistant editor of the *Pacific Citizen* newspaper, a staff reporter for *Asian Week* and *Rafu Shimpo*, and a writer for the *Hawaii Herald, Nichi Bei Times,* and *Hokubei Mainichi.* She helped process the massive Jack and Aiko Herzig Collection at the UCLA Asian American Studies Center, and is assisting the UCLA AASC with the Eji Suyama Endowment Project to preserve the history of Japanese American protest during World War II.

GREG ROBINSON is professor of history at l'Université du Québec à Montréal. A specialist in North American ethnic studies and US political history, he is the author of *By Order of the President: FDR and the Internment of Japanese Americans* (Harvard University Press, 2001), *A Tragedy of Democracy: Japanese Confinement in North America* (Columbia University Press, 2009), *After Camp: Portraits in Midcentury Japanese American Life and Politics* (University of California Press, 2012), and *The Great Unknown: Japanese American Sketches* (University Press of Colorado, 2016).

STEPHEN H. SUMIDA is professor emeritus of American ethnic studies, University of Washington. His teaching career in universities in the United States and Japan spanned forty-eight years, including his presidencies of the Association for Asian American Studies and the American Studies Association, chairmanship of his UW department, a year-long Fulbright grant, and his current roles as a stage actor. Sumida first read *No-No Boy* in 1975, at the beginning of his work in Asian/Pacific American interdisciplinary literary studies.

SHAWN WONG is author of the novels *Homebase* and *American Knees,* and coeditor of the groundbreaking *Aiiieeeee! An Anthology of Asian American Writers* and *The Big Aiiieeeee!* He is a professor of English at the University of Washington, a former chair of the Department of English, and a former director of the University Honors and Creative Writing Programs.

JEFFREY T. YAMASHITA is a fourth-generation Japanese American from Hawai'i. He is a doctoral candidate in ethnic studies at the University of California, Berkeley, under the guidance of Michael Omi, Evelyn Nakano Glenn, and Catherine Ceniza Choy.

INDEX